KEEPING *the* FAITHS

The Freed family's journey from Swiss Mennonites to Pennsylvania Methodists

Sermons and Lectures 1875-1885
of William, Alpheus, and Benson Freed

Edited, with notes and introduction, by
Joyce Wilcox Graff,
further genealogical research by
John C. Freed
and Foreword by
Curtis Grayson Smith

Boston, 2020

Cover art: Sampler by Lydia Freed, age 10, under the tutelage of Martha R. Wilson, 1826. Lancaster Mennonite Historical Society Museum, Lancaster, Pennslvania.

ISBN: 978-0-9907504-5-1 (paperback)
ISBN: 978-0-9907504-6-8 (ebook)

Library of Congress Control Number: 2019949718

Registered trademark

Garnet Star Publishing, Boston, Massachusetts

Printed in the United States of America

Dedicated with love and thanks
to our parents,
our grandparents,
and our ever-growing number of cousins,
and most of all to our sons
Damon Erik Graff
Ryan Justin Freed-McLeod

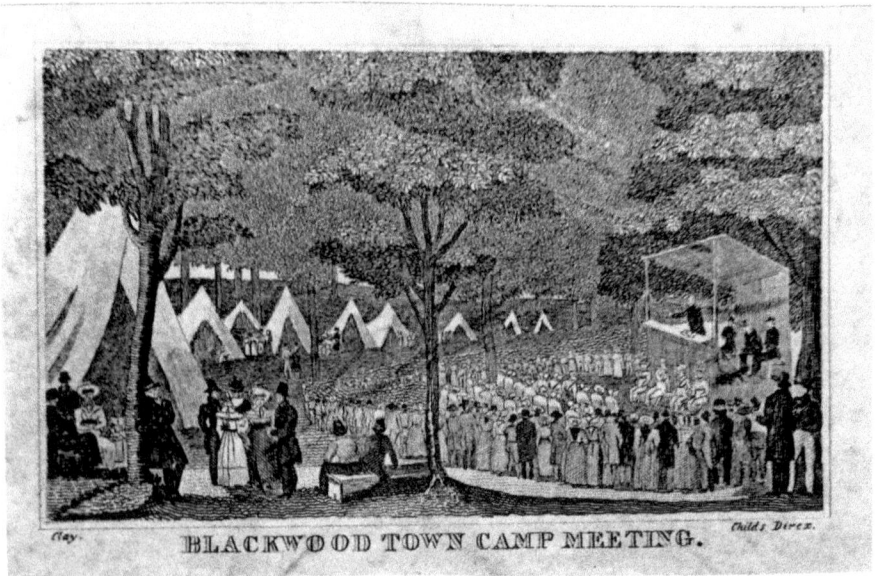

Blackwood Town Camp Meeting
frontispiece, *The Camp Meeting Chorister* (Philadelphia, 1852). Reprinted with the
permission of the Nutter collection, Boston University School of Theology.
Photo by Boston University Photo Service.

CONTENTS

FOREWORD

There is something powerful, almost magical, about family. It is cliché to say there is a connection, but there truly is. I admit, I don't often think about it or feel it my daily life. I can easily go through periods of time without giving much thought to my family heritage and history. Sometimes, the lives of those who came before me seem distant, remote, and disconnected.

Reading through the works of these four men who preached the gospel, the connection comes alive for me. I am not a preacher, but have preached and I am regularly asked to take the pulpit and share a message. Most of my life, I spoke in front of large groups of gathered people and delivered messages of things falling from the sky—not fire and brimstone as my ancestors spoke of—but rain, snow, and ice. For more than 20 years, I was a television meteorologist, a profession the men in this book couldn't have conceived. In my time on TV, I was asked to lead mission trips and broadcast them from overseas to Fort Wayne, Indiana, where I forecasted the weather. Over the course of four years, I broadcast from Israel, Zambia, Haiti, and Guatemala. Those trips changed my life. In real time, they gave me a perspective I couldn't gain through pictures or words. It is transcendent to walk, talk, and eat with people from the other side of the globe. They expanded my horizon and my thinking, and I started to view the world as a smaller place and humanity as a unified body. Those trips also opened the door to a new opportunity to preach the gospel. Churches started to invite me to preach—an unforeseen impact of the trips—one I have been humbled and honored to accept. Over the past several years, I have been a guest preacher on more than twenty occasions, and I've even performed two wedding ceremonies, including my oldest son Brooks' marriage to my daughter-in-law, Stacie. To play a role in their union and the real-time continuation of our families' heritage was emotional and surreal.

As I have had the privilege of sharing the gospel, it has drawn me closer to God. Now, in reading the words of my ancestors, I feel the sharing of the gospel has drawn me closer to my past and given me a more tangible appreciation for the people who brought our family where it is today. I love the words of my Aunt Joyce, in her introduction, as she reminds us of the world in which these sermons were written and delivered. These men lived less than 200 years ago, but it might as well have been a million years ago. Their existence bears almost no resemblance to mine. If they were dropped into the United States today, they wouldn't even begin to comprehend the things we take for granted: cars, computers, and handheld devices which literally connect us to the world and put all the information of history at our fingertips. They wouldn't understand the freedom which comes from assuming illness is a nuisance and not a sign that death is imminent. None of us knows how much time we have on this earth, but in our age, death does not lurk around every corner the way it did for our ancestors.

Despite all of our differences, it is the common bond of faith and the freedom and willingness to share it that unites me with these men. Jesus is the same yesterday, today, and forever. Hebrews 13:8 tells us that, and no matter how much our world changes, no matter how much our perspectives are altered, that fact remains. I understand the world around my ancestors shaped how they felt about different races, different religious viewpoints, and the other differences in life which can divide us. I am sad to say, in this way, I think the men of this book would very much recognize the world today. We still live in a world where the differences of people drive hatred and violence. I choose to look at those differences as a beautiful picture of the diverse landscape that is a humanity created in the image of a loving Father. The Jesus I know from The Bible, does not divide, he unites. He loves all equally and models that for us in the synagogue, at the well, in the streets of Galilee and Jerusalem, in every moment of his life, and ultimately on the cross. He opens the door for all people and promises life eternal. I believe heaven will be full a mosaic of people from all nations, colors, and backgrounds. I look forward to meeting the men of this book there. They are my family and my brothers in Christ.

Curtis Grayson Smith

Fort Wayne, Indiana

PREFACE

This book is a companion piece to *A Freed Family History*, published 1981 by Gateway Press, Baltimore.[1] In Part V of that book there is a substantial discussion of William Walton Freed, including a complete transcription of his account of his voyage in 1878-79 from San Francisco to Dublin.

In order to complete the research which went into that book I studied a number of original handwritten manuscripts. Because of the delicacy of the originals, and because of the spelling and punctuation problems discussed below, I transcribed them for my own use. By the time I finished the basic research for *A Freed Family History* I had much more than I needed on William Freed and, as a bonus, I had a set of transcriptions of sermons in my word processor. I decided to assemble the transcriptions for the family members who had shared the originals with me as ten photocopied notebooks.

The sermons and lectures reproduced in this book are copied from original manuscripts of these four brothers. They were kept in a leather box by William Freed's wife Amelia, who cherished them. She loved to take them out and read them. After her death they passed to her son Walter Freed, and after his death they were distributed among his children. I am grateful to June Freed Wilcox, Marian Freed Hege, Donald Wayne Freed, and Bruce J. S. Freed for sharing their manuscripts with me so that I could transcribe them. In addition, I am grateful to Richard Storck, another grandson of William Freed, for lending me the photographs of the Freed siblings which are included here.

The original manuscripts have been reproduced faithfully. I have taken the liberty of regularizing spelling and punctuation to make them more readable for the modern reader. William Freed's sermons are essentially one huge run-on sentence. There are rare periods, and no paragraph divisions. Periodically there is a symbol which looks like an "X" with a circle around it, which turns out to be a major pause, or essentially a paragraph mark. These were likely added by him as signals for pausing when speaking them aloud.

---

1   Rights are now owned by Garnet Star Publishing, Boston. The book is now available on the internet at archive.org.

I have sometimes had to add a word to complete the sentence. Spelling and routine grammar mistakes I have corrected without comment. Where I have inserted a word, it is enclosed in square brackets. Where the writer has used an obscure or obsolescent word or reference, I have defined it in a footnote or added a synonym in brackets to assist understanding without interrupting the flow of the text.

The hymns which have been added throughout are ones which were mentioned in one of the sermons, or were remembered by my mother, June Freed Wilcox, to be favorites of William and Amelia Freed. References do not always accompany the illustration. See the List of Hymns and Illustrations for the complete list of references.

Thanks are due to the staff of the library at the Boston University School of Theology for their assistance in locating the old hymns and documents which have added so much to this book. And as ever, special thanks to Marian Freed Hege and June Freed Wilcox, my faithful proofreaders.

Joyce Wilcox Graff
Boston, 1981

I would like to thank all those who read and commented on this revised manuscript and helped to shape its published form. In particular, thanks go to Ruth Storck Jacobson of Grand Junction, Colorado, the last living grandchild of William Walton Freed, who left us earlier this year.

Richard Storck had kindly lent me photographs of these gentlemen which I screen-statted for photocopy in 1981. Fortunately, Marilyn Davies Rumley, great-granddaughter of Alpheus, was able to share copies of the same photographs which had been sent out to Kansas, sharing momentos between the two brothers.

Special thanks also to my cousin John C. Freed of Paris, France, for his additional research on the early Freeds; to my nephew Curtis Grayson Smith of Fort Wayne, Indiana, for his Foreword; and most of all to my brother, James Hammond Wilcox of Memphis, Tennessee, for his careful sleuthing through genealogical records to supplement the original research I did forty years ago. He and John are the ones who completed the early Freed genealogy. This has been a team effort.

Joyce Wilcox Graff
Boston, 2020

FINDING OUR ANCESTORS

Peter Fridli	m.	Catharina Wundt
b. 1580		b. 1575
Peter Fridli	m.	Barbara Schaller
b. 1603		
Heinrich Fridli	m.	—
b. 1635		
Heinrich Friedt	m.	—
1655-1710		
Johannes Friedt/Freed	m.	Christianna __
1682-1744		ca. 1688-1746
Heinrich Fried	m.	Anna ___
1712-1786		1718-1803
Heinrich Fried	m.	Veronica Schleiffler
1754-1820		1755-1839
Abraham S. Freed	m.	Catherine Ecker
1785-1840		1775-1854
Rev. Abraham Freed	m.	Mary Singer
1817-1865		1827-1893
William Walton Freed	m.	Amelia Doebler
1850-1928		1850-1939

Our earliest Freed ancestor immigrated from the Palatinate region of Germany to America in the early 1700s. Johannes Friedt took possession of his land April 1, 1723 — 123 acres and an adjacent plot of 100 acres in Skippack Townships. The deed, dated April 8, 1724, was kept among the family's important papers, but never registered with the county. This document eventually fell into the hands of Governor Samuel Pennypacker of Pennsylvania, who made some notes in the margin in 1902.[1]

---

1   This document is now in the collection of the Pennypacker Mills Museum, Schwenksville, Pennsylvania.

In 1981 I was not able to determine which of three Freeds in the area might be the father of Rev. Abraham Freed. His birth record had been lost in a courthouse fire, and all three of the possible candidate Freeds had children with the same first names.

Rather than guess, I left some clues in a footnote. Some clues in the notebooks of Milton Freed, one of the siblings featured in this book, included a visit to "Aunt Mary Shirk, Jan. the 5 on Tuesday 1904, left March 5, Saturday, 1904...Shirk Barn built in 1798. It was one hundred and six year[s old] when we visited Aunt Mary in 1904."[2]

Years later, genealogist Milton S. Haldeman recognized "Aunt Mary Shirk" as his own ancestor and led us to a sampler[3] made by Lydia Freed, the sister of Rev. Abraham Freed, which names all her siblings as well as her parents.

With this evidence in hand, we were able to move reliably backward in time to the point of immigration to these shores. I will share what my brother Jim Wilcox and I learned here, and in the chapter following, my cousin John Freed will share the excellent investigative reporting he has achieved which takes us back into the 16th Century in Europe. See "Our Immigrant Freeds" on page 57.

Johannes Friedt (1682-1744) was born in Aspisheim in the Palatinate, now Germany, near Frankfurt. Mennonites and other Anabaptists (who believed children should be baptized once they had the ability to choose rather than as infants) were being persecuted and killed in Europe for their heretical beliefs.

He came to America between about 1710, bought land in Skippack 1722-24, and is buried in Lower Skippack Mennonite Cemetery, Montgomery County, Pennsylvania. His gravestone reads "John Freit", with wife Christianna.

Henry Freed (1712-1786) was probably born in America. He is buried in Jerusalem Union Cemetery, Bucks County, Pennsylvania, with his wife Anna. Anna's will is recorded in Norriton, Montgomery County, Pennsylvania, July 3, 1895, Henry Freed, administrator.

Abraham S. Freed (1785-1840) broke with the Mennonite Church and joined the growing Methodist movement. As a result he was shunned by the Mennonites and denied burial in the Mennonite cemetery in Lancaster. His friend David Mayer, also a Methodist, made space in his family burial ground for Abraham and his wife to be buried,

---

2   Notebook of Milton Freed, family papers, as quoted in Graff & Wilcox, *A Freed Family History*, 1981.

3   Author of *Descendants of Christopher Haldeman*.

next to the cornfield behind his house. While the house has been sold, the Mayer burial ground has been preserved.[4]

In 1826 under the tutelage of Martha Wilson, Lydia and her sister Mary made samplers, a learning tool for sewing that exercized their ability to embroider designs and letters. Lydia included the names of her parents and siblings: Abraham and Catherine Freed and their children Jacob, Henry, Lydia, Mary, Fanny, and Abraham. Our great-great-grandfather Abraham Freed (1817-1865) was the son of Abraham Freed (1785-1840).[5]

Sampler by Lydia Freed, 1826. Lancaster Mennonite Historical Society Museum, Lancaster, Pennslvania.

Lydia's sister Mary is the Aunt Mary (Freed) Shirk visited by Milton Freed and mentioned in the *Freed Family History*, who lived to be

4   When plans were made for a shopping mall, the Shoppes at Belmont, that would have covered the tombs, local preservationists successfully lobbied to save the graveyard. FindAGrave memorial ID 207186862, 1570 Fruitville Pike, Lancaster PA.

5   This sampler is in the collection of the Lancaster Mennonite Historical Society Museum, Lancaster, Pennsylvania. Her sister Mary's sampler (Mary Freed Shirk) is in the collection of the Muddy Creek Farm Library Museum, Ephrata, Pennsylvania. See "Hint: Look Everywhere!" by James H. Wilcox, *Pennsylvania Mennonite Heritage*, 34:3, pp. 42-44.

100 years old in 1913.[6]

Lydia's brother, Abraham Freed, was born 8 January 1817 in Pottstown, Pennsylvania. He followed his father's example to become an itinerant Methodist preacher, married Mary Singer 9 November 1845.

Abraham Freed was a respected minister of the Methodist Church. The best account of his life is to be found in an elegeic entry in the Minutes of the Philadelphia Conference of the Methodist Church in 1865. The following in quoted in its entirety:

> Rev. Abraham Freed, by the will of God, closed his labors, and his life, on the 28th day of February 1865, at Bridgville, Delaware, aged 48 years.
>
> He was born near Pottstown, Pennsylvania, on the 28th day of January, 1817, and from his earliest youth was remarkable for more than ordinary seriousness and gravity of character, induced, no doubt, by convictions of the exceeding sinfulness of sin, and the necessity of spiritual regeneration; and by his habitually devout deportment, was marked as one that feared God.
>
> Throughout the period of his youth, and of his early manhood, the early inclinations of his heart grew with his growth, and matured with his strength — prompted him to humble prayer for help and grace to work out his own salvation. Contending with his usual doubts and difficulties, it was not until the year 1840 that he obtained from God indubitable evidence that he was born from above. This event occurred during his residence in Marietta, Pennsylvania.
>
> An early life of such sincere seriousness, followed by a new spiritual life of zeal and devotion, combined with his peculiar amiability, commended him to the confidence of the church, and soon brought him successively into the positions of class leader, exhorter, and local preacher.
>
> In 1843 he was admitted on trial to the Philadelphia Annual Conference, as a travelling preacher. He loved the Itinerancy, and was never known to crave any particular appointment, or to complain of any direction the church may have given to his labors.
>
> His first Circuit was Kent, Md.,; 1844 Nottingham; 1845 Cecil; 1846 Denton; 1847 Stoddartsville; 1848 Tremont; 1849 Lehman's Chapel; 1850-51 Attleborough; 1852-53 Springfield; 1854-55 Pottstown; 1856-57 Anamessex; 1858-59 Church Creek;

---

6   Graff and Wilcox, *A Freed Family History*, page 5.

1860-62 Lewes; 1862-3 Anemessex again; and in 1864, Seaford — where, owing to exposure to the severity of the weather, he was taken sick, and in a few days, just before the session of the present Conference, breathed his last in great peace. A devoted wife and six children, bereaved of the care and counsel of a pious husband and father, mourn his removal. His fellow laborers, and the people, wherever he was known, feel a sense of keen sorrow, as they think of him as no more among the living.

As a preacher, brother Freed was earnest, deep, and powerful. He studied assiduously to "show himself approved before God and man, and rightly divining the word of truth." He had a systematic mind, well stored with varied information. His congregations were interested, and savingly edified, by his expositions, and close application of the word to the heart and conscience. He was a faithful pastor; following the directions of the Book of Discipline, and fulfilling in every point the round of duties it enjoins.

In our National troubles [the Civil War] he never failed to show his loyalty to the Government, and his love for the Union. This cost him friends, and support; but life itself could not have induced him to compromise with wrong.

He was led to hope his illness would be but temporary, that his work would not terminate so soon; but God saw best, and took him home.

In weariness and pain he talked much of the sufficiency of Christ, and the preciousness of his sustaining grace. Blameless in life and conversation, pure in heart, he had no fear, no doubt. He "walked with God." Among the last expressions that fell from his lip, were the strains of the familiar stanzas:

My happy soul would stay
In such a frame as this;
And sit and sing herself away
To everlasting bliss.[7]

Rev. Freed served as President of the Philadelphia Conference of Methodist Ministers and was still in that office at the time of his death.

Finding herself widowed and with six children, Mary Singer Freed returned to Pennsylvania and took up residence in Williamsport at 132 Washington Boulevard, a log cabin on what is now part of the land belonging to Lycoming College. Her son William was in charge of the family, and providing for so many was not easy.

---

7   Minutes of the Philadelphia Conference of Methodist Ministers, 1865, pp. 35-36.

Mary Singer Freed, the daughter of a preacher, was herself a respected member of the Methodist Church, as evidenced by her own obituary:

> At the age of 13 at a camp meeting she gave her heart to God, and in her father's tent while praying alone one night she was happily converted. This experience was a reality to her, and she loved to speak of it to her children and friends. ... [With Abraham Freed] she shared the blessings and labors of the itinerancy for nearly twenty years. To them were born six children, five sons and one daughter. ...
>
> Sister Freed, at the time of her death, had been a Christian for 51 years and a widow for 28 years. She was a devoted Christian and faithful in attending God's house. Her love for Zion was deep and constant and genuine. Often she went to the sanctuary against the protests of her children, they thinking she was not well enough to attend. She was really interested in the spiritual and temporal welfare of Christ's cause and did all in her power to advance his kingdom. Her almost dying request was that her children give $5 for her to the Missionary Society.
>
> She was a devoted wife and mother. Her children loved her tenderly and now rise to call her blessed. She was the kindest of neighbors and the most faithful of friends. No sacrifice was too great for her to make for another's comfort, and she never seemed more delighted than when doing something to make others happy. She had been more or less afflicted for years, but bore her sufferings uncomplainingly. As she approached the end she seemed impressed she would soon depart. She made all arrangements concerning her effects and her funeral, bade her children and friends good-bye, gave unmistakable testimony of her implicit and satisfactory hope in Jesus, and then went to sleep.
>
> Her funeral services were held in the Mulberry Street M. E. Church, November 11, 1893.[8]

William had his father's body moved from Delaware to Williamsport. Mary and her husband are buried in Wildwood Cemetery, Williamsport, Pennsylvania, second lot north of the second intersecting road north of the Civil War soldiers' lot.

The Christian fervor of this dedicated couple was transmitted

---

8   Newspaper clipping from the *Williamsport Sun*, November 12, 193, found in William Walton Freed's scrap book.

to their children. Four of the five sons preached. Alpheus, the eldest, attended college, adopted the ministry as his profession, and went on to Kansas to preach for his entire career. William served as a "supply preacher," filling in in communities throughout the west until he reached San Francisco, then returned by ship to New York. The account of that voyage is included in this book. Two younger brothers, Benson and Summerfield, also preached at camp meetings and died of diseases contracted among these crowds.

The twins stayed with their mother throughout their lives and did not marry. Laura kept house for her mother, Milton worked as a plasterer.

It is the sons of Abraham and Mary Singer Freed whose sermons are preserved in this book. What is most important to remember from the lives of Mary and Abraham Freed is the intensity — nay, severity — of their religious fervor. Their lives were almost totally dedicated to evangelical Methodism. Only two of the six children married. They passed along to their children their parents' dicta of spiritual and temporal piety and propriety.

Rev. Abraham Freed (1817-1865), about 1860. Family collection.

Mary Singer Freed, 1865-70, about age 40. Family collection.

INTRODUCTION

You are about to read the work of four young men of the 1880's who sought to preach the gospel.

As we approach their work, we look back across one hundred years in America. Life as they knew it then no longer exists. Their culture, their ethics, are gone now, and it is hard for us to understand them.   This introduction is intended to help bridge that gap — to help you look back across that span of years with more knowledge and understanding of the context within which they lived and thought and wrote.

They were Methodists, Revivalists. They were Pennsylvanians. They were children of one father and one mother. That much we can talk about. More than that, they were children of an epoch when life was hard, when there was no assurance of tomorrow. From the stock market crash of Black Friday (September 24, 1869) through the Panic of 1873 and beyond, there was a depression which was not outdone until 1929. The Civil War, so recently past, had taken fathers and sons from every family. That war, so destructive of the land and the economy, was the last war fought on American soil. Fortunately, we who are alive in the 2020's's do not know first-hand the burning of our homes, the ruin of our cities, the roar of cannons and the bursts of light along the horizon which meant the battle neared. But for these men that was a harsh reality.

The West was young then, inviting Eastern youth to try a new territory and challenge Nature and lawlessness and Indians to carve out a new life. It offered endless challenges, not the least of which was the prospect of new territory to conquer for Christ.

Death was a living reality. It was not unusual for a perfectly healthy person — friend, brother, child — to fall sick and die within days. Measles, mumps, whooping cough, typhoid, diphtheria, smallpox, tuberculosis — all were very real, incurable, usually fatal. Christianity offered a way of coping with death — seeing it as the doorway through which one reached the Heavenly Life Beyond, better by far than anything one experienced on earth. But that portal led to another place as well, and Christians had to be wary of their conduct here in order to win a place in Heaven and avoid Hell Fire.

ABRAHAM AND MARY SINGER FREED

The parents of these young people were both devoted followers of Methodism. "From his earliest youth, [Abraham] was remarkable for more than ordinary seriousness and gravity of character, induced, no doubt, by convictions of the exceeding sinfulness of sin, and the necessity of spiritual regeneration; and by his habitually devout deportment, was marked as one that feared God."[1] Abraham died in 1865, leaving his young wife with six children, the oldest of whom was 16.

Mary, also the daughter of a preacher, was herself a respected member of the Methodist Church. "At the age of 13 at a camp meeting she gave her heart to God, and in her father's tent while praying alone one night she was happily converted."[2]

You can readily see that they would have communicated to their six children a strong love of God and a fervent hope in the Hereafter. They had their eyes firmly fixed on Eternity—so much so that they did not teach their children much about life in this world at all. Only two of their sons seem to have developed a high degree of skill—William and Alpheus—and one of those in preaching. Milton apprenticed as a plasterer and continued in that trade throughout his life. The other three seem not even to have had a well-developed trade. Only two of the children married—William and Alpheus. Four of the six children chose to preach.

METHODISM

Protestant Christianity takes many forms. John Wesley (1703-1791), an English cleric, founded the Methodist movement, disagreeing with the belief of the Calvinists that life was predestined, and preaching that men need to strive for Perfection. He appointed itinerant, unordained evangelists to spread the Word.

During the period 1840-1890 Methodism underwent a considerable change. All religion was challenged by the theory of evolution. Methodism responded by granting a place to modern science, while at the same time stressing the need for moral and religious institutions. There was also a strong stress on common sense.

Ministers of the church traditionally came to their calling through the Power of the Holy Spirit alone. Few were formally trained.

---

1   Minutes of the Philadelphia Conference of Methodist Ministers, 1865, pp. 35-36, as quoted in Graff and Wilcox, *A Freed Family History*, p. 2.
2   Obituary published in the *Williamsport Sun*, November 12, 1893.

If someone heard The Call, he could soon be a preacher. Beginning in 1844, however, the church began to set up a system for training its ministers. In 1844 the General Conference listed specific theological texts which would be used for examining aspiring preachers. The widespread suspicion of college education among Methodists began to decline. The Methodists soon began to establish advanced theological institutions, whose influence increased throughout the century.

> After the Civil War, Methodism gave more and more attention to the challenge of science, particularly as expressed by Darwin and the evolutionists. Methodism's response varied from outraged rejection to cautious acceptance.[3]

The doctrine of moral responsibility was a major theme. It required men to examine the doctrines and biblical revelation and grasp it through their own intuition and understanding. Methodism also sought to clarify and publish its doctrines so that it could more clearly instruct its members and its preachers.

REVIVALISM

Methodism in the 1880's was strongly evangelical. The great Revival of 1857-58 had seen the conversion of thousands of people through the camp meetings. During the Civil War revivalism continued, and Abraham and Mary Freed were both born-again Christians who were moved to follow Christ during camp meetings. During the 1870's a number of evangelists toured America, notably Dwight Moody, whose stirring sermons were complemented by the beautiful singing of Ira Sankey, a marvelous tenor who sang solos and led throngs of people in rousing old hymns. They led mass meetings in the largest auditoriums of the cities they visited. Their approach was interdenominational, entrepreneurial, and sincere. They drew large crowds, and never asked for compensation for themselves beyond payment of their expenses.[4]

The preaching needed in revivals was a particular kind of preaching aimed at converting the audience. In 1901 the Rev. Louis Albert Banks wrote an essay on this subject. In it he outlined ten requirements for effective revival preaching.

1. Revival preaching must be positive. There is no room for doubts or equivocations. Revival preachers have to be "cocksure of their ground" and "speak with authority."

---

3   Chiles, *Theological Transition in American Methodism*, pp. 49-51.
4   Sizer, *Gospel Hymns and Social Religion*, pp. 3-6. Also, Beardsley, *Religious Progress Through Religious Revivals*, pp. 61-66.

2.   Revival preaching must be direct. "He must get on to some basis by which he can make that man feel as well as understand the message."

3.   Revival preaching must be sympathetic. "It must get at men from their human side. The preacher must find a man's heart and warm it to himself, as well as to the Christ whom he preaches."

4.   Revival preaching must be directed toward the heart and not the head. "The heart must be aroused; they must feel the baseness of their ingratitude; they must see the heinousness of their sins; they must appreciate the certainty of punishment and feel that, hanging over their guilty heads, even now, is the weight of condemnation of guilt. Get hold of the heart, and the head yields easily.

5.   Revival preaching must be simple and clear. "There is no time to let a man study about it for a week and reason out what you have just told him."

6.   Revival preaching must be illustrative. "It must be in pictures. It must seize hold of the imagination. ... Sermons are strong that pull down the works of the devil and capture sinners for Jesus Christ."

7.   Revival preaching must be intense. "It must be more than earnest; it must be charged with suppressed moral electricity."

8.   To preach effectively in revivals the preacher must absorb a great deal of the Bible. "The sermon must be saturated with the Bible. ... Illustrations drawn from the Bible are peculiarly effective in times of revival."

9.   The preacher must be conscious that he is God's man. "If the preacher feels sure that God is with him, that he stands in the presence of the living God, there will be a glorious independence of speech, mingled with a deep and tender love for the people to whom he speaks, that will be marvelously effective.

10.   He must be sensitive to the Holy Spirit. "The presence of the Spirit of the living God in our hearts, giving holy unction to the message, is the crowning glory of the revival preacher."[5]

Rev. Torrey adds that the Holy Spirit must be present in the preaching and the testimony at a revival, and that the Holy Spirit must convict men of sin.

> Jesus said in promising the Holy Spirit to the disciples, "and He, when He is come, will convict the world in respect of sin." A revival without conviction of sin, deep, pungent, overwhelming, is not a true revival. It is true that a great many may be converted and born again without the deep and overwhelming conviction of sin on the part of many. It was so on the day of Pentecost; as Peter preached in the power of the Holy Ghost a loud cry went up from men who were pricked

5   Rev. Louis Albert Banks, "The Preaching Needed in Revivals," article from *How to Promote and Conduct a Successful Revival* by R. A. Torrey (New York, 1901), pp. 32-37.

in their heart, "Men and brethren, what must we do to be saved?" There has been similar conviction of sin at every genuine and lasting revival since.[6]

Once men are convinced that they are sinful and without hope, the Holy Spirit then revives and regenerates them. "Revival is new life, and new life to the unsaved comes through regeneration, and it is the Holy Spirit's work to regenerate. Men are saved not through works of righteousness which they themselves have done, but according to God's mercy, who saves us by the washing of regeneration and renewing of the Holy Spirit (Titus 3:5)."[7]

William James studied the phenomenon of conversion from a purely psychological point of view and came to much the same conclusion, totally apart from any particular denomination, or even from Christianity. Conversion is common to Hinduism, Buddhism, Islam, and to the religions of Greece, Rome, Egypt, and Japan.

> "Is there, he asks, "under all the discrepancies of the creeds, a common nucleus to which they bear their testimony unanimously?" He answers immediately in the affirmative. "The warring gods and formulas of the various religions do indeed cancel each other, but there is a certain uniform deliverance in which religions all appear to meet. It consists of two parts:
>
> 1. An uneasiness; and
>
> 2. Its solution.
>
> 1. The uneasiness, reduced to its simplest terms, is a sense that there is *something wrong about us* as we naturally stand.
>
> 2. The solution is a sense that *we are saved from the wrongness* by making proper connection with the higher powers."[8]

Methodist revivalism is typified by instantaneous conversions, marked by a combination of emotional and ethical elements. Wesley himself noted that conversion "is commonly, if not always, an *instantaneous* work."[9] These conversions, however, had to be followed by classes of instruction to insure that the newly converted would not revert to their old habits once the emotion of the moment was passed.

---

6   R. A. Torrey, "The Holy Spirit in a Revival," article from *How to Promote and Conduct a Successful Revival*, pp. 13-14.

7   Torrey, "The Holy Spirit in a Revival," p. 14.

8   William James, *The Varieties of Religious Experience*, pp. 505-506, as quoted in Sydney G. Dimond, *The Psychology of the Methodist Revival* (London, 1926), p. 160.

9   Charles Wesley, as quoted in Dimond, *Psychology of the Methodist Revival*, p. 163.

519 LUX BENIGNA. 10 4. 10 4. 10 10.   Rev. J. B. DYKES, 1867.

Rev. J. H. Newman, 1833.

LEAD, kindly Light, amid the encircling gloom,
    Lead thou me on;
The night is dark, and I am far from home,
    Lead thou me on.
Keep thou my feet; I do not ask to see
The distant scene; one step enough for me.

2 I was not ever thus, nor prayed that thou
        Shouldst lead me on;
I loved to choose and see my path; but now
        Lead thou me on.

I loved the garish day, and, spite of fears,
Pride ruled my will: remember not past
    years.

3 So long thy power hath blest me, sure it still
        Will lead me on,
O'er moor and fen, o'er crag and torrent,
    till
        The night is gone;
And with the morn those angel faces smile
Which I have loved long since, and lost
    awhile.

Lead Kindly Light. *The Book of Common Praise, being the Hymn Book of the Church of England in Canada. Oxford, 1938.* Hymn #519. This hymn was a particular favorite of William and Amelia Freed.

CALLED TO PREACH THE GOSPEL

After Abraham died in 1865, Alpheus and William, the two oldest children, went to work in Philadelphia. Alpheus worked in the printing trade, William as a steelworker. Mary received a widow's pension of some $300 per year from the Philadelphia Conference.[10]

The children all went to grammar school, and Alpheus "attended college in Philadelphia,"[11] possibly Dickinson College in Carlisle, Pennsylvania, the college supported by the Philadelphia conference of Methodist ministers. William and Alpheus made up their minds to embark on a preaching career in imitation of their father.

The first step in becoming a preacher is to get The Call. A man must be called by the Holy Ghost to preach. Secondly he must be examined by the conference of ministers to determine the validity of his Calling. Once the conference was convinced that his Calling was indeed genuine, he could be permitted to speak as a Local Preacher at local events and camp meetings, without pay.

Those who were serious about becoming a career preacher were then admitted as Traveling Preachers on trial. A Traveling Preacher on trial was a sort of apprentice who served as a substitute for regularly appointed preachers during times of illness or other absence from their duties. As they advanced, they might be appointed to serve in itinerant work on circuits, in stations, or in education. Depending on the place where they served, they were paid little or nothing; usually only room and board.

After two years on trial, a preacher could be examined or admitted into "full connection", or could be continued on trial. Once received into full connection, they might be appointed to a regular position. However, if there were more preachers than paying jobs, they might be listed as "supernumerary preachers" and employed only as substitutes.

---

10   The Widow Freed is listed by name in the Minutes of 1865 through 1871. After that time, the claimants were grouped together so we do not find her name. She received $179.79 in 1865, $400 in 1866, $325 in 1867, $325 in 1868, $300 in 1869, $310 in 1870, and $325 in 1871. *Minutes of the Conferences*, 1866-1873.

11   *Minutes of the Annual Meeting* of the Kansas Conference of Methodist Ministers, 1912.Philadelphia here means Greater Philadelphia. Alpheus attended Dickinson College in Calisle, Pennsylvania, outside Philadelphia, in preparation for going on to Lycoming College in Williamsport.

The Ministry

The Examination of those who think they are moved by the Holy Ghost to Preach.

¶ 99. In order to be moved by the Holy Ghost to preach, 1st the following questions be asked, namely: --

§ 1. Do they know God as a pardoning God? Have they the love of God abiding in them? Do they desire nothing but God? And are they holy in all manner of conversation?

§ 2. Have they gifts (as well as grace) for the work? Have they (in some tolerable degree) a clear, sound understanding; a right judgment in the things of God; a just conception of salvation by faith? And has God given them any degree of utterance? Do they speak justly, readily, clearly?

§ 3. Have they fruit? Are any truly convinced of sin, and converted to God, by their preaching?

¶ 100. As long as these three marks concur in any one, we believe he is called of God to preach. These we receive as sufficient proof that he is moved by the Holy Ghost.

Rules for a Preacher's Conduct

¶ 101. *Rule 1.* Be diligent. Never be unemployed; never be triflingly employed. Never trifle away time; neither spend any more time at any place than is strictly necessary.

¶ 102. *Rule 2.* Be serious. Let your motto be, *Holiness to the Lord.* Avoid all lightness, jesting, and foolish talking.

¶ 103. *Rule 3.* Converse sparingly with women. (1 Tim. v. 2.)

¶ 104. *Rule 4.* Take no step toward marriage without first advising with your brethren.

¶ 105. *Rule 5.* Believe evil of no one without good evidence; unless you see it done, take heed how you credit it. Put the best construction on every thing. You know the judge is always supposed to be on the prisoner's side.

¶ 106. *Rule 6.* Speak evil of no one; because your word, especially, would eat as doth a canker. Keep your thoughts within your own breast till you come to the person concerned.

¶ 107. *Rule 7.* Tell every one under your care what you think wrong in his conduct and temper, and that lovingly and plainly, as soon as may be; else it will fester in your heart. Make all haste to cast the fire out of your bosom.

¶ 108. *Rule 8.* Avoid all affectation. A preacher of the Gospel is the servant of all.

¶ 109. *Rule 9.* Be ashamed of nothing but sin.

¶ 110. *Rule 10.* Be punctual. Do every thing exactly at the time. And do not mend our rules, but keep them; not for wrath, but conscience's sake.

¶ 111. *Rule 11.* You have nothing to do but to save souls, therefore 'spend and be spent in this work' and go always not only to those that want you, but to those that want you most.

¶ 112. Observe! It is not your business only to preach so many times, and to take care of this or that Society, but to save as many as you can; to bring as many sinners as you can to repentance, and with all your power to build them up in that holiness without which they cannot see the Lord. And remember! a Methodist preacher is to mind every point, great and small, in the Methodist Disciple! Therefore you will need to exercise all the sense and grace you have.

¶ 113. *Rule 12.* Act in all things not according to your own will, but as a son in the Gospel. As such, it is your duty to employ your time in the manner in which

Doctrines and Discipline of the Methodist Episcopal
Church, 1876, pp. 75-86.

we direct: in preaching, and visiting from house to house; in reading, meditation and prayer. Above all, if you labor with us in the Lord's vineyard, it is needful you should do that part of the work which we advise, at those times and places which we judge most for His glory.

¶ **114.** Smaller advices which might be of use to us, are perhaps these: 1. Be sure never to disappoint a congregation. 2. Begin at the time appointed. 3. Let your whole deportment be serious, weighty, and solemn. 4. Always suit your subject to your audience. 5. Choose the plainest text you can. 6. Take care not to ramble, but keep to your text, and make out what you take in hand. 7. Take care of any thing awkward or affected, either in your gesture, phrase, or pronunciation. 8. Do not usually pray *ex tempore* above eight or ten minutes (at most) without intermission. 9. Frequently read and enlarge upon a portion of Scripture; and let your preachers often exhort without taking a text. 10. Always avail yourself of the great festivals by preaching on the occasion.

The Duty of Preachers to God, Themselves, and One Another.

¶ **115.** The duty of a Preacher is --

1. To preach. 2. To meet the societies and classes. 3. To visit the sick.

¶ **116.** A Preacher shall be qualified for his charge by walking closely with God, and having his work greatly at heart, and by understanding and loving discipline, ours in particular.

¶ **117.** We do not sufficiently watch over each other. Should we not frequently ask each other, Do you walk closely with God? Have you now fellowship with the Father and the Son? At what hour do you rise? Do you punctually observe the morning and evening hours of retirement? Do you spend the day in the manner in which the Conference advises? Do you converse seriously, usefully, and closely? To be more particular: Do you use all the means of grace yourself, and enforce the use of them on all other persons?

¶ **118.** The means of Grace are either instituted or prudential.

¶ **119.** The INSTITUTED are: --

§ **1.** *Prayer*: private, family, and public; consisting of deprecation, petition, intercession, and thanksgiving. Do you use each of these? Do you forecast daily, wherever you are, to secure time for private devotion? Do you practice it every-where? Do you ask every-where, Have you family prayer? Do you ask individuals, Do you use private prayer every morning and evening in particular?

§ **2.** *Searching the Scriptures*, by 1. Reading: constantly, some part of every day; regularly, all the Bible in order; carefully, with notes; seriously, with prayer before and after; fruitfully, immediately practicing what you learn there. 2. Meditating; At set times. By rule. 3. Hearing; Every opportunity. With prayer before, and, after. Have you a Bible always about you?

§ **3.** *The Lord's Supper*: Do you use this at every opportunity? With solemn prayer before? With earnest and deliberate self-devotion?

§ **4.** *Fasting:* Do you use as much abstinence and fasting every week as your health, strength, and labor will permit?

§ **5.** *Christian conference:* Are you convinced how important and how difficult it is to order your conversation aright? Is it always in grace? Seasoned with salt? Meet to minister grace to the hearers? Do you not converse too long at a time? Is not an hour commonly enough? Would it not be well always to have a determined end in view? And to pray before and after it?

¶ **120.** PRUDENTIAL means we may use either as Christians, as Methodists,

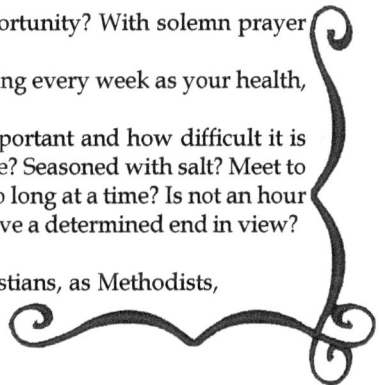

or as Preachers.

§ 1. *As Christians:* What particular rules have you in order to grow in grace? What arts of holy living?

§ 2. *As Methodists:* Do you never miss your class?

§ 3. As Preachers: Have you thoroughly considered your duty? And do you make a conscience of executing every part of it? Do you meet every Society and their Leaders?

¶ **121.** These means may be used without fruit. But there are some means which cannot: namely, watching, denying ourselves, taking up our cross, exercise of the presence of God.

§ 1. Do you steadily watch against the world? Yourself? Your besetting sin?

§ 2. Do you deny yourself every useless pleasure of sense? Imagination? Honor? Are you temperate in all things? For instance, in food. 1. Do you use only that kind and that degree which is best both for body and soul? Do you see the necessity of this? Do you eat no more at each meal than is necessary? Are you not heavy or drowsy after dinner? Do you use only that kind, and that degree of drink, which is best both for your body and soul? Do you choose and use water for your common drink? And only take wine medicinally or sacramentally?

§ 3. Wherein do you take up your cross daily? Do you cheerfully bear your cross, however grievous to nature, as a gift of God, and labor to profit thereby?

§ 4. Do you endeavor to set God always before you? To see his eye continually fixed upon you?

¶ **122.** Never can you use these means but a blessing will ensue. And the more you use them, the more you will grow in grace.

The Necessity of Union among Ourselves.

¶ **123.** Let us be deeply sensible (from what we have known) of the evil of a division in principle, spirit, or practice, and the dreadful consequences to ourselves and others. If we are united, what can stand before us? If we divide, we shall destroy ourselves, the work of God, and the souls of our people.

¶ **124.** In order to a closer union with each other — 1. Let us be deeply convinced of the absolute necessity of it. 2. Pray earnestly for, and speak freely to, each other. 3. When we meet, let us never part without prayer. 4. Take great care not to despise each other's gifts. 5. Never speak lightly of each other. 6. Let us defend each other's character in every thing as far as is consistent with truth. 7. Labor in honor each to prefer the other before himself. 8. We recommend a serious perusal of *The Causes, Evils, and Curses of Heart and Church Divisions.*

How we can Employ our Time Profitably when not Traveling, or engaged in Public Exercises.

¶ **125.** As a general method of employing our time, we advise you, — 1. As often as possible to rise at four. 2. From four to five in the morning, and from five to six in the evening, to meditate, pray, and read the Scriptures with notes, and the closely practical parts of what Mr. Wesley has published. 3. From six in the morning till twelve, wherever it is practicable, let the time be spent in appropriate reading, study, and private devotion.

¶ **126.** Other reasons may concur, but the chief reason that the people under our care are not better is, because we are not more knowing and more holy.

¶ **127.** And we are not more knowing, because we are idle. We forget our first rule: "Be diligent. Never be unemployed. Never be triflingly employed. Neither spend any more time at any place than is strictly necessary." We fear there is altogether a fault in this matter, and that few of us are clear. Which of us spend as many hours a day in God's work as we did formerly in man's work? We talk—talk—or read what comes next to hand. We must, absolutely must, cure this evil, or betray the cause of God! But how? 1. Read the most useful books, and that regularly and constantly. 2. Steadily spend all the morning in this employment, or at least five hours in the four and twenty. "But I have no taste for readiing." Contract a taste for it by use, or return to your former employment. "But I have no books." Be diligent to spread the books, and you will have the use of them.

Of our Deportment at the Conferences

¶ **128.** It is desired that all things be considered on these occasions as in the immediate presence of God; that every person speak freely whatever is in his heart.

¶ **129.** In order, therefore, that we may best improve our time at the Conferences, up in that holiness without what they cannot see the Lord. And remember! a Methodist preacher is to mind every point, great and small, in the Methodist Discipline; therefore you will need to exercise all the sense and grace you have. 1. While we are conversing let us have an especial care to set God always before us. 2. In the intermediate hours, let us redeem all the time we can for private exercises. 3. Therein let us give ourselves to prayer for one another, and for a blessing on our labor.

The Matter and Manner of Preaching

¶ **130.** The best general method of preaching is, 1. To convince; 2. To offer Christ; 3. To invite; 4. To build up; And to do this in some measure in every sermon.

¶ **131.** The most effectual way of preaching Christ is, to preach him in all his offices; and to declare his law, as well as his Gospel, both to believers and unbelievers. Let us strongly and closely insist upon inward and outward holiness in all its branches.

Camp meeting of Methodists, historical woodcut, circa 1870. Alamy stock photo.

Camp Meeting Rules.

1. Applications for license to erect a building or tent, from persons not members of the Association, must be accompanied by a written recommendation signed by three official members of the Methodist Episcopal Church nearest the place of residence of the applicant, or three members of the Association.

2. The ground within the circle of tents is sacredly set apart for religious worship; and during public service at the stand, all walking to and fro, or gathering together for conversation, is strictly prohibited.

3. At the ringing of the bell for public service, all loud conversation or other exercises in the tents and cottages must cease.

4. The hours for preaching shall be ten o'clock A.M., and two and seven P.M.

5. There shall be family devotions in each society tent morning and evening, with the reading of the Scriptures; and occupants of cottages and private tents are requested to attend regularly upon the same.

6. The bell will ring each morning at half past five o'clock for rising, and each evening at ten o'clock for retiring, when all vocal exercises must cease, and all persons not having lodgings within the encampment must immediately retire from the ground.

7. There shall be no smoking of tobacco in the society tents, or within the circle of said tents.

8. A light shall be kept burning at each cottage and tent all night, whenever said cottage or tent is occupied.

9. The occupants of each cottage and tent, before retiring at night, shall cause a bucket of water to be placed outside of the same, near the front entrance, during the entire occupancy of the said cottage or tent, for use in case of fire.

10. There shall be a superintendent appointed by each tent's company, whose duty it shall be to preserve order in his tent, in accordance with the regulations of the meeting.

Appendix to Camp Meeting Chorister.

Alpheus Singer Freed
1849-1912

Family Photo.

William Walton Freed
1850 - 1928

Family photo.

Laura E. Freed
1853 - 1932

Photo by Dean Studios, Williamsport, ca. 1880. Family photo.

Milton Freed
1853 - 1919

Photo by Dean Studios, Williamsport, ca. 1880. Family photo.

James Benson Freed
1856 - 1887

Photo by Dean Studios, Williamsport, ca. 1880. Family photo.

Wesley Summerfield Freed
1858 - 1882

Photo by Dean Studios, Williamsport, ca. 1880. Family photo.

FAMILY CHRONOLOGY

compiled by John C. Freed

We are fortunate that his travels are referenced in both a book[12] and the Minutes of the Philadelphia Conference.[13]

1817 Abraham is born in Pottstown, Pennsylvania.

1843 He is admitted to trial to the Philadelphia Annual Conference as a traveling preacher.

1844 Assigned to Oxford, Strasburg Circuit, Chester County, Pennsylvania.

1844 Assigned to Kent Circuit, Kent County, Maryland, Delmarva Peninsula

1844 Nottingham, Maryland

1845 He receives "full connection" into the ministry, age 28.

1845 Cecil, Maryland

1845 Marriage to Mary Singer, 9 Nov 1845.

1846 Denton, Maryland, Delmarva Peninsula

1847 Stoddartsville, Luzerne County, Pennsylvania, near Wilkes-Barre

1848 Tremont, Schuylkill County, Pennsylvania

1849 Abraham assigned to Lehman's Chapel circuit, now Lehman Methodist in Hatboro, Pennsylvania. Hatboro is in Montgomery County, which was part of Philadelphia County until 1784.

1849 birth of Alpheus Singer Freed, 30 July 1849

1850 Census showing Abraham Freed living in Middletown Township, Bucks County, Pennsylvania, with wife Mary and son Alpheus (Hatboro is 10 miles west of Middletown)

1850-51 The family is living in Attleborough (now Langhorne, Bucks County, Pennsylvania.)[14] William Walton Freed was born 5 Nov 1850 in Attleborough. Note that the Red Book incorrectly places his birth in Attleborough, Maryland.

1852-53 Abraham assigned to Springfield Circuit, Penna.; Strasburg and Chester Circuit, Penna.

1852 "Waynesburg" probably Wayne, which is next to Springfield in Delaware County, Penna. Also Strasburg and Chester.

---

12   *History of Chester County, Pennsylvania, with genealogical and biographical sketches*, by J. Smith Futhey and Gilbert Cope (Louis H. Everts, 1881, Philadelphia). Chapter on Methodist churches, p. 279ff.

13   Minutes of the Philadelphia Conference of the Methodist Church (1865).

14   See   https://www.livingplaces.com/PA/Bucks_County/Langhorne_Borough/Attleborough.html

1853-54 birth of Louisa Stephenson, later to marry Alpheus S. Freed, in Ohio. (Her parents are Alfred, age 52, farmer, and Elmira, age 40, according to 1860 Census, Brown County, Union Twp., Dwelling 86. The parents are buried in a family plot in Ripley, Ohio, Union Twp., just east of Cincinnati on the Ohio River.)

1854 birth of Laura E. Freed and Milton Freed on 27 April 1854.

1854-55 Bethel, Pottstown Circuit, Penna.

1854-55 Spring City, Chester County, Penna.

1856 Birth of Benson, 24 August 1856, in Pennsylvania according to the census.

1856 Abraham assigned to Delmarva Peninsula. The children are: Alpheus, age 7; William, 5; Laura and Milton, 2; Benson, infant.

1856-57 Anamessex Circuit, Maryland

1858-59 Church Creek Circuit, Maryland

1858 Birth of Summerfield, 10 Jan 1858, in Maryland.

1860 Census, Lewes and Rehoboth Hundred, Sussex Co., Delaware

1860-62 Lewes Circuit, Delaware

1862-63 Anamessex Circuit, Maryland

1864 Seaford Circuit, Delaware

1865 Abraham dies 28 Feb 1865 in Bridgeville, Delaware, leaving his wife and six children: Alpheus, 15; William, 14; Laura and Milton, 10; Benson, 8; and Summerfield, 7.

1865-1870 Mother, Mary Singer Freed, moves to Halifax, PA, with her family. Alpheus finds work as a printer "in Philadelphia". William finds work in a steel mill in Philadelphia, living at the YMCA.

1870 census, Milton is listed as a laborer, no doubt apprenticing and living with the family of David Hershberger, plasterer, in Plymouth Borough, Luzerne County, Pennslvania, near Wilkes-Barre.

1871 Alpheus goes off to college "in Philadelphia" (probably Dickinson College in Carlisle, Pennsylvania). For people in Kansas, this was nearly Philadelphia.

1874 William, about age 23, visits the South before returning to Halifax. See "Travels in the South."page 283.

1875 Alpheus becomes a travelling preacher.

1876 His brother, William, heads west as a supply preacher, spending eight months in Norfolk, Nebraska, eventually reaching San Francisco.

1877 Alpheus receives "full connection" into the ministry, age 28.

1878 Alpheus moves to Kansas, part of the "Wild West," leaving behind his mother, the twins and Benson. In Cincinnati, he meets Louisa Stephenson, age 25, who leaves for Kansas with the wagon train. The rest of the Stephenson family remains in Ripley, Ohio.

1878-89 William sails from San Francisco (19 Sept 1878) to Cobh (15 Jan 1879), thence to Dublin, London, Liverpool and New York.

1879 William finds work at an iron foundry in Danville, Penna.

1880 Alpheus marries Louisa K. Stephenson in Louisburg, Kansas, on 4 March 1880 in Ottawa, Franklin County, Kansas. Her name is Lida on the certificate. Her name is Eliza in the census dated 22 June 1880.

1881 Eldorado S. Freed, daughter of Alpheus and Louisa, born in Kansas. She is named after Louisa's younger sister.

1882 Summerfield dies at age 24, apparently of tuberculosis. Buried at Wildwood Cemetery in Williamsport.

1884 Mary Singer Freed moves to Washington Boulevard in Williamsport, Penna., with Laura, Milton and Benson. Her land is now part of Lycoming College.

1884 Esther Freed, daughter of Alpheus and Louisa, born in Kansas

1884 William, age 34, marries Amelia Doebler, 23 November 1884.

1885, Walter Curtin Freed, son of William and Amelia, is born in Danville, Pennsylvania, 2 October 1885.

1886-89 William and Amelia move to Lehighton, Pennsylvania, and run a general store,

1887 Benson dies at age 31 on 8 November 1887 and is buried at Wildwood Cemetery. Abraham Freed's body is brought from Bridgeville, Delaware, and reinterred at Wildwood Cemetery.

1889 Wilbur Freed, son of William and Amelia, born in Lehighton, Pennsylvania 15 February 1889; died 11 July 1889. Family moves to Williamsport. Buried at Wildwood cemetery.

1890 Mary Ella Freed, daughter of William and Amelia, born 3 June 1890, Williamsport, Penna.

1892 Coffeyville, in southeastern Kansas, is the site of a failed bank robbery by the Dalton Gang in which four citizens and four gang members died in a shootout. Alpheus and his family may have been present at the time; they are found in Coffeyville in the 1895 Kansas State Census and his obituary states he was a pastor in Coffeyville for five years in the "early nineties." Coffeyville had a population of about 3,200 in fewer than 600 households at the time.

1893 Mary Singer Freed dies 9 November 1893, age 65. Buried at Wildwood Cemetery. Laura and Milton continue to live in the house and Milton continues as a plasterer.

1895 Alpheus and Louisa living in Coffeyville, Kansas.

1900 Alpheus and Louisa living in Pittsburg, Kansas.

1900 US Census lists Milton and Laura, born April 1854, living on Washington Blvd in Williamsport. Milton's occupation is listed as Plasterer. They no doubt inherited the home upon Mary's death.

1906 Alpheus, age 56-57, visits Pennsylvania for the last time, according to notebooks of his nephew, Milton.

1910 Alpheus and family living in Coffeyville, Kansas.

1918 Alpheus dies at age 69 on 1 November 1918. Buried at Fairview Cemetery, Coffeyville, Kansas.

1919 Milton dies 16 March 1919, age 64. Buried at Wildwood.

1928 William dies at age 77 on 8 September 1928. Buried at Wildwood Cemetery.

1832 Laura dies at age 78 on 11 September 1932. Buried at Wildwood.

1935 Louisa Stephenson Freed, widow of Alpheus, dies at age 81 or 82 on 8 July 1935. Buried at Fairview Cemetery, Coffeyville, Kansas.

1939 Amelia Doebler Freed dies at age 89 on 20 August 1939. Buried at Wildwood Cemetery.

JAMES BENSON FREED AND WESLEY SUMMERFIELD FREED

Benson and Summerfield were local preachers of the Methodist church. Their tombstones dub them "Rev." yet they never reached full connection. We do not know of any other jobs they may have pursued. Local preachers were paid only when they substituted for a regular preacher. When they assisted with camp meetings they did not receive pay. However it must be remembered that this family cared little for things of earth. A meagre existence was all that was to be expected in this life. Their aim was fixed on the life hereafter. Benson died at the age of 31 of typhoid contracted at a camp meeting; Summerfield died at 24 apparently of tuberculosis.

We have only two little essays by Benson, neither of them very impressive. They seem rudimentary attempts to mimic his brothers or other preachers he admired.

Of Summerfield's work, we have no extant documents. Laura and Milton, the twins, are pictured here to complete the family.

ALPHEUS SINGER FREED

All seven of Alpheus' sermons included here are similar in paper, handwriting, and style, I believe them to have been written within a few years of each other. Judging by the stage of his development, I would place them between 1875 and 1878.

His spelling and grammar are very good. Except for an over-abundance of commas (which was customary in those days) there were very few grammatical corrections to be made. In addition, he has studied the Bible and a number of texts in great depth. He has his eyes firmly fixed upon the Hereafter.

In these sermons especially we see the need to *convict* his hearers of sin. This was as essential element of the revival meeting. He likens it to the experience of Saul of Tarsus who was convicted of his sin and lay blind for three days before his conversion. Thus, he reasoned, conviction was essential to the conversion process.

Throughout Alpheus' writings there are exhortations to concentrate on the Hereafter and give up everything of this earth. "The Penitent, as much as possible, should have his eyes closed to every thing of earth. … Avoid mirth, avoid being trifling. Close your eyes when praying. The mind then will be more fully fixed upon God and upon

Christ." And again, "All of this world's princely pageantry are but like the deciduous foliage of the forest tree, doomed to perish. Why then should we be so enamored with the ephemeral pleasures of earth which, like Jonah's gourd, come and depart almost simultaneously, while religion offers us joy under all circumstances?"

Of the seven sermons we have, all deal directly with his three strong primary themes: conviction of sin; repentance and conversion; sin, pain, and temptation here and joy in the Life Eternal. The sermons are not uplifting. They are full of the hellfire and damnation he must have learned at his father's side.

Here we can see clearly the kind of childhood and upbringing the six Freed children had. In essence, they had no childhood. They were expected to be upright Christians, striving for Perfection, responsible for their own place in Glory, accountable to God for every infraction. Their parents' love was based totally in Christian fervor and tightly bound by Christian virtue and purity.

Since children learn best by mimicking an idol, and since it seems clear that Mary and her children all idolized Abraham Freed, we can interpolate some of the characteristics of Abraham Freed's style by examining the rhetoric of his eldest son.

First, on the mechanical side, he takes a verse — usually only a single verse — from the Bible and weaves a fabric from it for his sermon. William refers to this as the "rock" or foundation for his sermon. Alpheus develops three or four major points to be made from this verse, and divides his sermon into as many major parts. He then builds a structure which aimed at convincing his hearers of the truth of his message, of their own sin and hopelessness, and of their need for Christ.

He then "draws the net" so as to bring his hearers to conversion, with a rousing plea for them to partake of the joys of heaven later by adopting Christ now.

Alpheus' sermons are carefully researched, carefully footnoted. They may well have been done in the course of his studies for some professor. In many ways they have the look of a research paper.

It would be interesting to contrast these early sermons of his with his later writing to see how he developed. He continued in the ministry until his death in 1912, and from such a beginning he must have developed into a powerful preacher. He was certainly highly esteemed in Kansas, where he preached for 40 years.

Will Freed (left) with Louisa and Alpheus Freed, seated with their Bibles, about 1880.

FROM THE MINUTES OF THE ANNUAL MEETING
OF THE KANSAS CONFERENCE, 1912.

ALPHEUS S. FREED.

Alpheus S. Freed was born in Philadelphia, Pa., July 30, 1849. In his younger days he worked at the printer's trade. He attended college In Philadelphia and entered the ministry forty-one years ago, preaching one year in Pennsylvania before coming to Kansas in 1878 and taking up the work at Labette City. From that charge he went to Louisburg, and until his retirement last spring served with fidelity important charges in the old South Kansas Conference and later the Kansas Conference. His appointments included Coffeyville, Pittsburg, Parsons, Iola, Chanute, Galena, Burlington and Howard. He was district superintendent of the Independence District for six years, giving up that work three years ago last spring, when he was sent to Howard. After one year at Howard, he served the Lane charge two years, then returned to Coffeyville, where be owned a home.

Dr. Freed was highly esteemed wherever known. Besides his invalid wife, he leaves two daughters, Mrs. John H. [Esther] Davies and Miss Eldorado Freed, both of Coffeyville, and a brother and sister [Will and Laura] in Williamsport, Pa. His death occurred at Coffeyvllle, Kansas, Nov. 1, 1918.

HISTORICAL SKETCH.

Methodism was introduced into Kansas when the Shawnee Indians were moved into the territory, and in 1880 Rev. Thomas Johnson appointed a missionary to them and established his headquarters first near where Turner, Kansas, is now located, and then south of the present site of Rosedale. When the Southern branch of the church seceded in 1884 Mr. Johnson went with the secession, taking all the mission property with him, but in the meantime the Wyandotte Indians had been located at the mouth of the Kaw River, bringing with them their church organization.

In 1854 the board of bishops commissioned Rev. Wm. H. Goode of the Indiana Conference to investigate the needs of Kansas and Nebraska territories. The following year he was appointed Superintendent of all the work in the two territories, and on October 23, 1856, Bishop Osman C. Baker organized the Kansas and Nebraska Conference in a tent at Lawrence, Kansas. The territory of the new Conference extended west from the Missouri River to the Rocky Mountains and from the Indian Territory north to the Dakotas. In 1860 Nebraska was set off as a separate Conference, and in 1863 what had been known as the "Rocky Mountain District" became the Colorado Conference. In 1873 the work in the state had grown so large that it was thought wise to divide the Conference, and the South Kansas Conference was formed, taking in all the state south of the south line of township sixteen, there being certain exceptions in regard to towns located on that line.

In 1882 the work in both Conferences had so developed that it was thought the part of wisdom to again divide the Conference, and the Northwest Kansas Conference was formed out of that part of the Kansas Conference west of the sixth principal meridian, and the Southwest Kansas Conference was set off from the South Kansas Conference, comprising that part of the old Conference west of Chase, Greenwood, Elk and Chautauqua counties.

It was not long until a movement for the uniting of the work in the east of the state into one Conference was started. At least two General Conferences in the 1880's passed enabling acts which were not ratified by the Conferences, but in 1912 both Conferences by a large vote requested another enabling act, and the General Conference having granted It. In 1913 each Conference voted to unite and appoint a joint commission to work out a plan of union. Bishop Shepard, who presided at both Conferences, gave his official concurrences, and on March 18, 1914, in Chanute, Kansas, the first session of the new conference was held.

The obituary published in the Coffeyville newspaper includes more warm memories:

Rev. A.S. Freed, a pioneer Kansas Methodist Episcopal minister, died at the family home, 709 West Eighth, last night at 10 o'clock as a result of heart trouble. Mr. Freed was up and about yesterday and ate a hearty supper but on retiring complained to his wife and daughter that he was not feeling well. In a short time a physician was called but nothing could be done. He sank rapidly and in a short time lapsed into the sleep that knows no waking. ...

The death of Rev. Freed removes one of the best known Methodist pastors in Southeast Kansas. Since his coming to the state, 41 years ago, he has been engaged in pastoral work except for two terms which he served on the district as superintendent (presiding elder). His work as a Kansas pastor started at Labette City and promotions came in due order until the highest pastorates in the conference were awarded him. Rev. Freed was district superintendent of this district for six years ending in 1915. In the early nineties, he served as a pastor of the local church for five years and this city has been like home to him since that time.

The past year and one-half he has held a superannuated [emeritus] connection with the church. He was generally beloved by all who knew him and his death will bring sorrow to a good many hearts.

Mr. Freed is survived by an invalid wife and two daughters, Miss Eldorado Freed and Mrs. John H. [Esther] Davies, both of this city. Two brothers and a sister, also survive. They [Milton, Laura, and William] are residents of Williamsport, Pa., and have been notified but probably will not be here for the burial.

WILLIAM WALTON FREED

We have the greatest number of sermons of William Freed, so by default they have taken the spotlight in the collection. In addition, I find his sermons the most readable of the lot. His themes are more varied than Alpheus', and he seems more human. I am able to relate to him more and understand his theme, even when I disagree with his theology.

Looking back to Banks' list of requirements for good revival preaching, I would rate William's sermons above the sermons of Alpheus we have here. Alpheus is certainly the more scholarly, and better schooled of the two. Yet William has a touch of warmth, and relates stories from everyday life which touch his hearers more closely. Alpheus concentrates on conviction of sin and leaves the forgiveness for a brief mention at the last. He leaves his hearers in the depths. William, however, uplifts and brings the listener with him higher.

Then too we have among the pieces some non-theological pieces which give us another side of William. He was a curious young man, thirsty for knowledge and experience. While he set out to preach the gospel, he kept eyes and ears open and drank in as much as he could. The talk about his trip through the South is a good example. His lecture about his voyage from San Francisco to Dublin[15] is another.

The trip through the South took place somewhere in the early 70's, approximately 1874. After that William returned to Pennsylvania for a short time.

Between 1876 and 1878 William spent most of the time in the West. We do not know his full itinerary, but family tradition says that he visited all 46 states and the territories which became the 47th and 48th. That was a lot of territory to cover in the 1870's. In September 1878 he boarded ship in San Francisco, and in 1879 he was back home in Pennsylvania.

He had left home to serve as a supply preacher in the West, serving his apprenticeship as a Traveling Preacher in hopes of being received into full connection. He served eight months in Norfolk, Nebraska. Written on the back of one of his sermons is the following undated letter of recommendation:

---

15   Graff and Wilcox, *A Freed Family History* (1981), pp. 94-109.

Norfolk Charge
        Madison County
        Nebraska

To all whom it may concern:

We the undersigned members of the M.E. Church on the Norfolk Charge, being fully aware of the Rev. W. Freed's gifts, grace, and usefulness as a minister of the Gospel (he having been our pastor for the past 8 months) do recommend him as a proper person to preach the Gospel wherever he may go.

S. W. Denel
Josie Denel
I. Karns
M. Karns

However by 1878 he had changed his mind about a career as a preacher and returned home to develop his skill as an iron worker. My mother, June Freed Wilcox, remembered him saying that when he returned to New York, he wanted to cross the Brooklyn Bridge, but could not afford the toll. He did not have the nickle required.[16] He vowed then to never be so poor again. From that time until his death he served only as a supply preacher in the Williamsport area, and assisted at camp meetings. He worked hard, was frugal, and purchased some modest houses to create rental income for his family.

In his sermons and talks, William shows the same speaking style we saw with Alpheus of taking a single verse and weaving an entire sermon around those few words. He is obviously well read, and brings in references particularly from history and biography where Alpheus brings the kinds of books he would have read in a seminary. Alpheus tells us about the details of farming in ancient Egypt, while William talks about Franklin, Napoleon, and experiences from his personal life.

Many of William's sermons are aimed at converting non-Christians. Many more, however, are aimed at fellow Christians. These are sermons which uplift, that tell of God's love and how He cherishes and blesses his people. In these there is a gentleness which we have not

---

16   "If you wanted to cross the bridge on foot, you had to pony up one cent. It cost five cents to cross on horseback and ten cents to cross with a horse and wagon. If you were transporting cattle it would costs five cents per cow and two cents per sheep. Pedestrian tolls went away in 1891 and all other tolls where rescinded by 1911." Source: untappedcities.com To put this in context, the average daily wage in 1870 was $2.20. United States. Bureau of Labor. "Wages in the United States and Europe, 1870-1898," in United States. Bureau of Labor. "September 1898 : Bulletin of the United States Bureau of Labor, No. 18, Volume III," Bulletin of the United States Bureau of Labor, Nos. 1 - 100 (September 1898) : 5-33.

seen with Alpheus.

If there is one major theme in William's sermons, it is Death. He is constantly grappling with how to cope with death. He is fully aware of the presence of death—his own and others'—and leans on Christianity as a means of dealing with it. When his little son Wilbur died at the age of five months, the printed funeral card read:

> There is no Death! what seems so is transition;
>   This life of Mortal breath
> Is but a suburb of the life elysian,
>   Whose portal we call Death."

We must also note the Victorian prejudices which appear periodically in his writing. In "Travels in the South" he speaks for a long time with a black man. There is obviously a great deal of respect for the man as a hard worker, patient and persistent. Yet toward the end of the lecture he begins to speak of blacks in politics, and begins to show more than a little disdain for their ability to function as equals in the society.

His relationship with Jews is similar. Christianity has always had a problem with its relationship to Jews. They share a common heritage, a common Bible. The Old Testament is the Jewish body of sacred books. Yet since the Jews are living proof that not everyone has readily embraced Christ, there is also a certain anger. William's anger seems not unlike the anger engendered in the Civil War. Those who fought were brothers—of the same race, language, culture—yet they fought and killed each other over a group of political ideas. While William rails at "Christ's most inveterate enemies—the Jews" he fails to look at the fact that Jesus and his original group of followers were all Jews. Christianity was but a new sect within Jewry, a sect which differed in its emphasis on and definition of the Messiah.

Over time, as Christianity was taken to the Gentiles, it moved away from its Jewish roots. The Gentiles saw what was pure Judaism as revolutionary new thought. They incorporated themes and concepts from their own cultures. However at its source, Christianity is Judaism. Jesus was a Jew; he taught Judaism. And the Jews, as fellows in the worship of God, as fellow preservers of the Word of God and the same basic principles which Jesus taught from the Torah, are brothers.

It is somewhat unfair to judge William's prejudices. He was a product of his time. Much of what he knew as Truth then has been modified by new discoveries. The Dead Sea Scrolls have changed our vision of the events of two thousand years ago. Medicine has changed life expectancies and reduced the number of diseases which wantonly claim our children and our friends. Hymnals of the 1870's were filled with hymns of death and resurrection and hope of eternal life. Modern hymnals have few hymns which face death squarely. Most Americans prefer not to think about death at all.

As you read the sermons, think of the life and times of these men. Try to place yourself among their hearers, and judge them not by the standards and ethics of the 21st century, but by the context of their own times.

SEQUENCE AND CHRONOLOGY

There were, of course, a number of ways I might have arranged the William's sermons. I might have arranged them in order by their Biblical references, or in some sort of proposed chronology. It seemed most pleasant to arrange them thematically, as I have done.

There is little chronological evidence to go on, but nonetheless I propose a possible chronology here. One of the clues is the paper he used. There are three distinct formats: a 14 inch paper which is very weathered and brown, an 8x8 format, and a smaller format. In each case the paper is double that size, and folded together to make booklets which are then sewn down the fold enough to keep them together. He wrote out the entire sermon, then made an outline for himself on the back of the booklet which he used while speaking.

Using the paper as a means of grouping the sermons, and adding historical clues, the get the following proposed chronology:

Sermons in Chronological Order
        Topic, Title, Location (if known)
Early – before 1876, possibly about 1870
extra large format
        Travels in the South
1876, in the east, small format
        Zechariah 1:5, Where are your Fathers?
1876-1878 , in the west, large format
        Luke 2:11 etc, On the Nature of Greatness
        Exodus 20:7, On Swearing, up near Buffalo Creek

Exodus 20:8, Keeping the Sabbath "while coming to the west",

Mark 9:33-37, God is Love

I John 4:8, The Comfort of His Love, letter of recommendation, Norfolk Nebraska

Matthew 13:11, The Kingdom of Heaven, talks about pioneer life, western prairie

I Cor. 15:55, Victory over Death

Daniel 6:20, God will Deliver us

Music, Church Music, back in Pennsylvania

Tobacco, Tobacco, talks about childhood in Maryland

James 1:5 - Wisdom

II Kings:11 - Help in Time of Trouble

After 1879, in Pennsylvania, small format

Before the Mast - talks about sailing around Cape Horn

James 1:25 - Law of Liberty; these times of wild speculation; in traveling o'er this broad land our ours you will see…

Romans 5:2, Access of Grace; protracted camp meeting

Job 38:11 - The Breakwater; talks about Cape May, Delaware Bay, Maryland

Luke 15:18 - Father, I have Sinned; his return to Pennsylvania; joy at seeing home

Genesis 13: - The Promised Land; talks about the beauty of the Susquehanna Valley

Dating the work of James Benson Freed was fairly easy. The one manuscript is dated with his flourishing hand—1880—when Benson was 24. He died at the age of 31. The other must have been an earlier effort since it is less well written.

The seven sermons of Alpheus Freed were much more difficult to deal with. Based on the level of learning they demonstrate, and knowing that Alpheus attended college in Philadelphia and preached one year before going west in 1878, I would place them in the first years of his ministry, or during the end of his college years, 1875-78. One sermon is clearly signed Alpheus S. Freed.

A date appears at the bottom of his "Fast Day Sermon"—July 1864. It is not likely that it was prepared by a 15 year old boy. There were many National Fast Days declared by the various Presidents, beginning with John Adams for 25 April 1799. Others followed: 14 May 1841, last

Thursday of September 1861, 30 April 1863, 4 August 1864.

So my best theory at this point is that the date written at the bottom of the "Fast Day Sermon" is not the date of writing, but the date being commemorated. There were two fierce battles of the Civil War that month — Petersburg, Virginia, and Atlanta, Georgia — in which thousands lost their lives. Even more plausible, however, is that the date was intended to be July 1863, which would have been the date of the Battle of Gettysburg, an even greater defeat for the North.

Therefore I will continue under the assumption that these sermons were written by Alpheus Freed in the period 1875-1885.

O For a Thousand Tongues to Sing

1

AZMON CM
CARL G. GLÄSER, 1784-1829
Arr. by LOWELL MASON, 1792-1872

CHARLES WESLEY, 1707-1788

1. O   for   a   thou - sand   tongues to   sing   My
2. My   gra - cious Mas - ter   and   my   God,   As -
3. Je - sus!   the   name   that   charms our fears,   That
4. He   breaks the power   of   can - celed sin,   He
5. He   speaks, and listen - ing   to   his   voice,   New
6. Hear   him,   ye   deaf;   his   praise, ye dumb,   Your

great Re - deem - er's   praise,   The   glo - ries of   my
sist   me   to   pro - claim,   To   spread thro' all   the
bids   our sor - rows   cease, 'Tis   mu - sic   in   the
sets   the pris - oner   free;   His   blood can make the
life   the dead re - ceive;   The   mourn - ful, bro - ken
loos-ened tongues em - ploy;   Ye   blind, be - hold your

God and King,   The   tri - umphs of   his   grace!
earth a - broad   The   hon - ors of   thy   name.
sin - ners' ears, 'Tis   life, and health, and   peace.
foul - est clean;   His   blood a - vailed for   me.
hearts re - joice; The   hum - ble poor, be - lieve.
Sav - ior come;   And   leap, ye lame, for   joy.   A - men.

Alternate tune: RICHMOND

"O for a Thousand Tongues to Sing." *The Methodist Hymnal.* Nashville, 1966.

COURSE OF STUDY FOR PREACHERS[1]

FOR ADMISSION ON TRIAL.

Candidates must be acquainted with –
The common branches of an English education.
Ancient History. *Rawlinson*
Scripture History, Old and New Testament. *Smith*
History of the United States. *Ridpath.*
History of Methodism (Abridged). *Stevens*
Rhetoric. *Haven*
Logic. *True.*
Discipline of the Methodist Episcopal Church.
{Read -- Wakefield's Theology; Watson's Life of Wesley; Whitney's Handbook of Bible Geography; Foster's Christian Purity; the Student's Gibbon.}

First Year.

Theological Institutes. *Watson* (Part I)
Plain Account of Christian Perfection. *Wesley*
Church History. *Waddington*
Homiletics. *Kidder*
Mental Philosophy. *Upham*
Written Sermon.
{Read -- Wesley's Sermons; Stevens's History of Methodism; New Testament Theology, Von Oosterzee; Early Years of Christianity. *Pressensé*}

Second Year.

Statement and Scripture proofs of Bible Doctrine.
Theological Institutes. *Watson* (Part II)
Baptism. *Hibband*
Moral Science, *Wayland*
Written Sermon
{Read -- Whedon on the Will; Emory's Defense of our Fathers; Porter's Compendium of Methodism; Gaussen's Origin and

Inspiration of the Bible; Rawlinson's Historical Evidences; Shadd's Homiletics and Pastoral Theology.}

Third Year.

Theological Institutes. *Watson* (Parts III and IV)
Introduction to the New Testament. *Nast*
Analogy of Natural and Revealed Religion. *Butler Cummings's Edition.*
Hand-Book of the Bible. *Angus*
Logic. *Whately*
Written Sermon
{Read -- Hagenbach's History of Doctrines; Hurel's History of Rationalism; D'Aubigné's History of the Reformation.}

Fourth Year.

PERSONAL RELIGIOUS LIFE AND HABITS.

1. State your views of the character and source of the Christian life.
2. How may we know that we are partakers of this life?
3. What are the evidences of a divine call to the ministry?
4. State what you consider to be the main duties of the ministerial office, and the necessary qualifications for the discharge of them.
5. By what means may these qualifications be cultivated?
6. Give your views of the nature and importance of Pastoral Visitation, and state the amount of attention you give to it.
7. Inform us of your general habits of study.
8. Name all the books you have read each year since your admission on trial in the traveling ministry.
9. How much time do you devote to the study of the Scriptures, and with what method do you study them?

EXAMINATION ON THE BIBLE

1. In what sense do you consider the Bible to be the word of God, and by what arguments do you sustain your views?
2. Explain what is meant by the

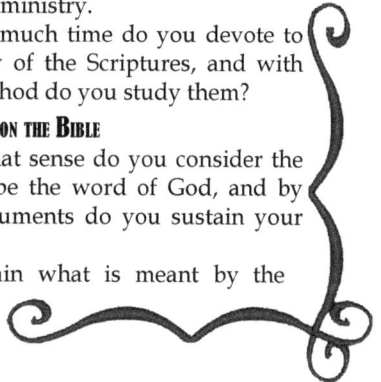

---

1 This *Course of Study for Preachers* is transcribed from the Appendix to *Doctrines and Discipline of the Methodist Episcopal Church*, 1876, pages 351-361. It is the framework for the preparation of Preachers, which would have been used by the Freed Brothers. {} here are [] in the original.

phrase "Canon of Scripture."

3. Distinguish between the genuineness and authenticity, and credibility of a book.

4. Give a synopsis of the argument by which the genuineness of the books constituting our received Canon of the Old Testament is established.

5. Give a synopsis of the argument establishing the genuineness of the books contained in the received Canon of the New Testament.

6. In what sense do Protestants affirm and Romanists deny that the scriptures form a complete and infallible rule of faith and practice?

7. State when the authorized version of the Bible appeared, and how it was produced.

8. Give an epitome of the history of the Israelites from the time of the Exodus to the death of Joshua.

9. Recount the leading facts connected with the revolt of the Ten Tribes.

10. Name the great Annual Festivals of the Jews; and also state what they were designed to commemorate, and how they were observed.

11. Name the principal prophets, the periods in which they prophesied, and the particular burdens of their prophecy.

12. Give from the life of our Lord some illustrations of his regard for the Old Testament Scriptures.

13. What predictions relate to Christ, especially to the time of his coming? His character? Office? Death?

14. Of what periods of the life of our Lord have we historical records? And over how long a period did his ministry extend?

15. Describe the principal events and localities of his ministry.

16. State the leading facts recorded in the Acts of the Apostles.

17. What is a miracle? In what way do miracles authenticate a divine revelation?

ON THE DOCTRINES OF THE BIBLE

1. In what manner does the Bible make known the existence of God?

2. What Scripture proof is there of a Trinity of Persons in one Godhead?

3. Enumerate the attributes of God, and give Scripture proofs of each.

4. Give the scriptural doctrine of the Incarnation and show how it is connected with the Gospel scheme.

5. Give a summary of the Scripture argument for the Divinity of Christ.

6. Give the Scripture proof of the Personality, Divinity, and Work of the Holy Spirit.

7. What was the effect of Adam's sin upon himself? Upon his posterity?

8. What is the relation of the vicarious death of Christ to the forgiveness of our sins?

9. State the proofs by which the resurrection of Christ is established.

10. Show the nature and value of Christ's intercession as taught in the Scriptures.

11. What are the doctrine and proof of the Witness of the Spirit?

12. State concisely the doctrine of Christian perfection as taught by Mr. Wesley, and support it by Scripture proofs.

13. Explain the difference between regeneration or the new birth, and entire sanctification.

14. State the Arminian doctrine respecting the perseverance of the saints, and show its harmony with the Scriptures.

15. State the nature, design, and obligation of Baptism; and the proofs of each.

16. State why baptism of infants should be retained in the Church.

17. What are the phrases used in Scripture to designate the Lord's Supper; what their import? What the ground of obligation on Christians to observe this sacrament?

18. State the Romish doctrine of Transubstantiation; also the Lutheran doctrine of Consubstantiation; and give an outline of the arguments by which each is disproved.

19. How do you prove that the wicked will not be annihilated?

20. State the Scripture doctrine of the resurrection of the body, and give the proofs.

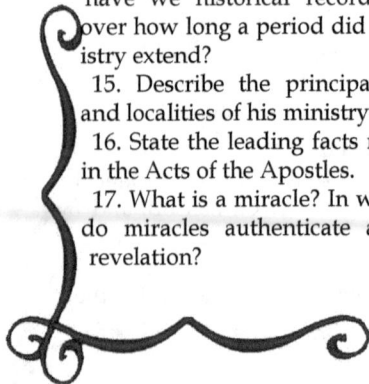

CHURCH ORGANIZATION AND GOVERNMENT

1. State the different forms of Church government.

2. State the character of the organization in Great Britain; in what respects it differs from, and in what it agrees with, that of the Methodist Episcopal Church in the United States.

3. What are the respective duties and powers of the General Conference and of the Annual and Quarterly Conferences in the Methodist Episcopal Church?

4. What are the peculiar duties and powers vested in the following officers of the Church respective namely: Bishops, Presiding Elders, Elders, Deacons, Preachers in Charge, Local Preachers, Stewards, Trustees of Churches, and Class Leaders? And how is the limitation of the power, and the amenability of each for its proper exercise, fixed?

ECCLESIASTICAL HISTORY

1. Enumerate and describe the principal Jewish sects existing at the time of Christ.

2. Give some account of the early persecutions of the Christians.

3. Mention some circumstances in the state of the world which assisted the early progress of Christianity.

4. State the doctrines of the Gnostics, and show their evil influence upon the early Church.

5. State the chief causes which led to the separation of the Greek from the Latin Church, and the period when it took place.

6. Give an account of the religious state of the world immediately prior to the time of Luther.

7. Give an account of the Great Reformation – the causes that led to it, and the principal characters engaged in it.

8. Give an account of the Reformation in England; also of the Puritans.

9. Give an account of the origin and rise of Methodism in Great Britain, and the leading characters in the Wesleyan movement.

10. How did Methodism take its origin in this country? Who were its principal founders? What were the principal characteristics of the movement?

11. What were the circumstances that led to the organization of the Methodist Episcopal Church? What were the time, place, and circumstances under which that organization was effected?

{Read -- Thomson's Evidences of Revelation; McClintock's Methodology; Kidder's Cristian Pastorate; Hervey's Christian Rhetoric; Conybeare and Howson's Life and Epistles of St. Paul.}

Books of References -- Fleming's Vocabulary of Philosophy; Smith's Classical Dictionary; McClintock and Strong's Cyclopaedia; Haydn's Dictionary of Dates.

For Local Preachers who are Candidates for Deacon's Orders.

THE BIBLE – DOCTRINES.

The Existence of God – The attributes of God, namely: Unity spirituality, eternity, omnipotence, ubiquity, omniscience, immutability, wisdom, truth, justice, mercy, love, goodness, holiness; the Trinity in Unity; the Deity of Christ; the humanity of Christ; the union of Deity and humanity; personality and Deity of the Holy Ghost; depravity; atonement; repentance, adoption, the witness of the Spirit; growth in grace; Christian perfection; possibility of final apostasy; immortality of the soul; resurrection of the body; general judgment; rewards and punishments.

THE BIBLE – SACRAMENTS

The sacrament of baptism; its nature, design, obligation, subjects and mode. The Sacrament of the Lord's Supper, its nature, design, and obligation.

{The examination on the above subjects is to be strictly biblical, requiring the candidates to give the statement of the doctrine and the Scripture proofs. To prepare for this, he should read the Bible by course, and make a memorandum of the text upon each of these topics as he proceeds.}

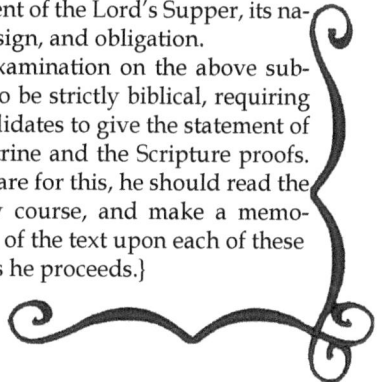

John C. Freed

OUR IMMIGRANT FREEDS

A Freed Family History, otherwise known as the Red Book, written by my aunt, June Freed Wilcox, and her daughter, my cousin, Joyce Graff, traced my family history back to the Civil War. Beyond that was impossible, given the research constraints of the 1970s. They went as far back as Abraham Freed, a noted Methodist minister in Eastern Pennsylvania and the Eastern Shore of Maryland, then hit a brick wall. Abraham was an extremely popular name at the time, and Freed was not a rare name. There were several families that could claim an Abraham Freed of about the right age. So where to go from there?

The answer came from Milton Haldeman, a Mennonite genealogist who wrote the book *Descendants of Christopher Haldeman.*[1] The Red Book noted that Milton Freed's notebooks contained a lot of interesting stories about the family, and referred to his aunt, Mary Shirk. "We were unable to find the connection, and leave this to further scholars."

Milton Haldeman recognized the name immediately, and was able to make the connection to the previous generation. In fact, Abraham is one of the children listed in a sampler by Lydia Freed, now on display at the Lancaster Mennonite History Museum. Knowing who Abraham's parents were enabled us to make the connection to the book of Charles Heiberger, *Descendents of Johannes Friedt/Freed,* which meticulously documents the chain from Abraham Freed's father back to John Freed, my immigrant Freed ancestor.[2] To seal the deal, we recently obtained DNA confirmation that Lydia's father and brother are indeed the men named Abraham Freed in my lineage.

We are lucky to have a lot of information on John Freed (1682-1744), the immigrant. In addition to his tombstone, in the Lower Skippack Mennonite Church graveyard,[3] there are extensive land

---

1   Milton S. Haldeman, *Descendants of Christopher Haldeman: son of immigrant Nicholas Haldeman.* Masthof Press, Morgantown, Pennsylvania, 2008.

2   The history is detailed in an article in *Pennsylvania Mennonite Heritage* (Vol. 34, No. 3, July 2011, p. 42ff.) by James H. Wilcox and Joyce W. Graff. This is the same Joyce W. Graff who is co-author of the Red Book. James H. Wilcox is her brother, and both are first cousins of mine.

3   A photograph of this headstone appears in Heiberger's book. A survey in 2020, however, found no trace of it; a group of John Freed's descendants are trying to locate it or replace it.

records showing his neighbors' property. From tax records, we know he owned 223 acres in Skippack. His will had been transcribed and published. What we did not know, however, was what happened to the deed to his land.

So I paid a visit to the Eastern Pennsylvania Mennonite Museum, where the curator, Joel Alderfer, spent some time with me, for example, pointing out an exhibition they had mounted about the barn of Peter Freed, a son of John Freed, which was built in 1761 and is still standing. He showed me a copy of the will of John Freed, and something I had never seen before—the inventory of his estate.

Until then, I had thought of John Freed as a man of average means. Yes, his farm of 123 acres was a little larger than most, which were typically either 50 or 100 acres at the time, and yes he did own another farm of 100 acres, but nothing extraordinary, especially when compared with the farm of Solomon Dubois, a whopping 500 acres.

So you can imagine my surprise when I learned that, in addition to John Freed's 223 acres in Skippack, he owned an additional 400 acres in Bucks County, several miles east of his main farmland. Far from being a man of modest means, John Freed was one of the most important land owners among the Mennonite settlers.

This led me to take another look at a reference in the 1714 books of the Penn family. They had granted a request by one John Fred to take an option on 500 acres of land in the Valley Forge area.[4] That option never went to an actual survey and sale, however, and there was a claim by the Fred family of Ireland that their ancestor, John Fred of Dublin Township, was the person who made the request. They explained that it never went to survey because John Fred had decided to return to Ireland and not pursue the matter.

However, when I looked more closely, I discovered that John Fred never returned to Ireland—his son did—so that cannot explain

---

4   Penn's Minute Book H, p577, 27 March 1714 John Fred obtains warrant for 500 acres in Chester County, price 10 pounds per Centum (per 100 acres), quit rent 1 p. C. This is apparently the same transaction listed in the Philadelphia County Old Rights Index, Book D65, page 196, where John Fred obtains a warrant for 500 acres on 27 Jan 1714. (In the calendar in use in 1714, the first month was March, so if the transaction was recorded as being in the first month, a later transcriber might easily reach the wrong conclusion that this was in January.) According to a county history, the warrant went to a John Fredd and the purchase was never completed because he returned to Ireland, leaving behind his sons Benjamin and Eli. In fact, however, John Fredd remained behind in Chester County; it was Benjamin who returned home. Valley Forge, where Hans Stauffer settled, is in Chester County, about 5 miles southwest of Skippack. Maria Fried, daughter of John Fried, married Peter Roth and settled in Vincent Twp., Chester Co.

why he would have let the option lie dormant.

Now armed with the fact that John Freed had enough money to buy 500 acres and that he arrived sometime between 1710 and 1727, I considered whether he might have been the mysterious purchaser of the option. What reason would he have to let it lapse?

To answer this question, I needed to understand more about the Mennonite immigrants, their community, their culture, and the legal systems they encountered. The Freed[5] families lived in the upper Rhine valley in what is now Germany three centuries ago. Many of the records from that era were later destroyed, so we know little about their European life or how they came to America.

From scraps of information, though, it seems they traveled in the company of two families, the Wismers and the Stauffers. We know, for example, that Paul Freed was married to Elizabeth Hiestandt Stauffer and set off for America with his wife, daughter, and father-in-law, Hans Stauffer, along with the rest of the Stauffer family. As they left Worms, their ultimate goal may have been America, but since America was a British colony, they needed permission of the monarch (Queen Anne at the time), who required all immigrants to pass through England *en route*. And so they arrived in London.

About the same time, Jacob Wismer also headed to London. He was married to Maria Freed, living outside Bruchsal, upriver from Worms. We know that Jacob and his wife (possibly a second wife—some accounts say Maria died in Germany) were in London in 1709[6] and in New Bern, Carolina, by 1711. If they traveled with the Stauffers, it seems likely that they were one of the "Poor Palatine" families aboard the *Maria Hope*, which stopped in Philadelphia on its way to New Bern. Jacob Wismer and his son were among the few survivors of

---

5   Variant spellings include Fried, Friedt (especially in Europe), Frid, Freit and Fritt. The families in Switzerland used the name Fridli or Friedli. I have normalized the surname of the most important family members using the spelling Freed.

6   Jacob Wismar is in the "First London List", an effort to make a census of the flood of Palatinates arriving in the city. Taken May 6, 1709, in St. Catherine's Parish, it shows him as a tailor, 50 years old, accompanied by his wife, a son age 22 and a daughter age 20. That puts the year of birth of Jacob Jr. as 1688 or 1689, so he was 98, not 103, when he died on 4 February 1787. It is my belief that the wife listed in the census was Maria Fried, mother of the two children, and that she died in the New Bern Massacre along with her daughter. See "Lists of Germans from the Palatinate Who Came to England in 1709: Board of Trade Miscellaneous. Vol. 2 D. 57", *The New York Genealogical and Biographical Record*, Jan. 1909, p. 49. See also *Even More Palatine Families: 18th Century Immigrants to the American Colonies and their German, Swiss and Austrian Origins*, by Henry Z. Jones, Jr. and Lewis Bunker Rohrback (Picton Press, Rockport, Maine, 2002). Heinrich Kolb and Gerhard Clemens, future neighbors of Paul Freed Sr. and John Freed, are on the list.

the New Bern Massacre in September 1711—he reportedly walked and ran ninety miles in one day. He eventually reached Philadelphia, and was an early member of the Deep Run Mennonite Church.[7]

Paul Freed first makes an appearance in the land records of Pennsylvania in 1714, when he bought land in Skippack, then known as Van Bebber's Township. It's possible that beforehand, he was a squatter. Several years later, when the Pennsylvania Legislature was having debates about how to deal with the flood of German immigrants, the legislators heard many a tale about the shiftless, lazy squatters who would never amount to much.

But to buy land posed a huge risk for these immigrants, as I learned through a magazine article in 2019, because by law, only British subjects were permitted to bequeath real estate to their heirs. In short, if you died while owning real estate, your family would inherit nothing. Needless to say, they had a strong motivation to become naturalized, and a strong aversion to owning land until then.[8]

The influx from Germany[9] led the governor of Pennsylvania to

---

7   Christoph von Graffenried of Switzerland sailed to the Carolinas in 1710 with 650 emigrants from Bern and the Palatinate; each family was promised 300 acres, free clothing and ocean fare, 1 cow and 2 pigs. He founded New Bern, which was destroyed in September 1711 while he was a prisoner of the Tuscarora tribe, and he recounted stories of women impaled on stakes, more than 80 infants slaughtered, and more than 130 settlers killed. Jacob Wismer (b. 1659, probably in or near Bruchsal) and his son were outside the settlement at the time of the attack, so they survived. (His daughter and wife did not.) According to *Deep Run Mennonite Church East: A 250-Year Pilgrimage, 1746-1996*, by Timothy Rice (Deep Run Mennonite Church East, Perkasie, Pennsylvania, 1996) father and son walked and ran ninety miles in one day. They eventually reached the Quaker community of Byeberry on the northeastern edge of Philadelphia. A Wismer family story recounts that the people who brought them from Byeberry to Bedminster by 1726 left Jacob Wismer, his son, and their possessions under a large tree in the woods and advised, "Now, Wismer, work or die." The Wismers were among the earliest members of the Deep Run church, and Jacob Jr. (1684-1787) is buried there. See *A Brief History of Jacob Wismer and a Complete Genealogical Family Register With Biographies of His Descendants from the Earliest Available Records to the Present Time,* by A J Fretz and Eli Wismer (self-published, 1893)

8   For a fuller discussion of this legal difficulty, see "Who for Conscience Sake Cannot Swear at All: The Quest of the Lancaster County Mennonites for Naturalization," by Allan A. Garber, *Pennsylvania Mennonite Heritage*, July 2019. Garber focuses on the struggle to pass the Naturalization Act of Feb. 14, 1730, giving rights to a number of Lancaster Mennonites. A nearly identical law, which he mentions only in passing, was approved the following year, and the bulk of those approved were Mennonites in or near Skippack, including John Freed and Paul Freed Sr. *Pennsylvania Archives*, series 2 vol. 7, p. 119.

9   Thousands of Palatine immigrants flooded London starting in 1709 and continued into 1710. Many of them apparently believed rumors that Great Britain would provide free passage to America and land when they arrived. The rumors, no doubt, were based on the real promise made by Christoph van Graffenried to the New Bern settlers.

order records of all ships arriving from Europe beginning in 1727, so we know the Freeds arrived before that. So now back to the question: Was the "John Fred" who got permission to try to buy 500 acres of land in 1714 the same John Freed who arrived sometime between 1710 and 1727?

I think it is, and here's why. The "Poor Palatines," as the British press dubbed them, were not necessarily poor at all.[10] The Whigs, who supported immigration, however, decided to play the sympathy card for political reasons, and painted the immigrants as freedom-loving Europeans fleeing oppression by the hated French.[11]

John Freed, however, was not a poor man. In my early research, I knew that he owned an average farm in Skippack—123 acres, slightly larger than most (which were 60 to 100 acres) but smaller than the biggest (which were 400 to 500 acres). He also owned an adjoining tract of 100 acres. What I didn't know until later was that he owned an additional 400 acres of land in Perkasie,[12] about 15 miles northeast of Skippack, making him one of the wealthiest individuals in the region, with 623 acres. So it makes sense that he would seek to buy 500 acres after his arrival in 1711, only to suspend his purchase when he learned about the inheritance laws.

Instead, what he did, I believe, was to lease land in Vincent

---

10 The writer Daniel Defoe (of "Robinson Crusoe" fame) was among those favoring immigration from the Continent. Pro-immigration forces coined the term "Poor Palatines" to describe the Germans, to contrast them with the hated French. Most of the Mennonites in the Palatinate were of German-Swiss origin, and as pacifists they had to contend with the constant warfare of the French and the Prussians over the land they farmed. See *Becoming German: The 1709 Palatine Migration to New York* by Philip Otterness (Cornell University Press, 2006).

11 The floodgates opened when the Whig-dominated Parliament passed a bill to encourage immigration by foreign Protestants, reducing the naturalization fee to just one shilling. That bill went into effect when it received royal assent from Queen Anne on 23 March 1709. See "The Poor Palatines and the Parties" by H. T. Dickinson, *The English Historical Review*, Vol. 82, No. 324 (July 1967), pp. 464-485.

12 Philadelphia County Deed Book F.8, page 318, Johannes Fried from Thomas Freame. This is 400 acres in Rockhill Twp., Bucks County, omitted from his will but included in the inventory of his estate. Purchased for 180 pounds on 3 Sept. 1735. Original indenture issued 6 Aug. 1735. See Heiberger, p. 31. Also in Bucks Co. deeds, vol. 23, pp. 279-283. Passed to John Freed, youngest son of the immigrant, after release from other heirs. Full deed in Heiberger book from sale of 200 acres of land to Jacob Kinzig on 11 May 1748 for 100 pounds. Land is adjacent to Henry Freed and Anthony Haynes(?) Funk(?). Recorded March 26(?) 1787 in Norristown. Resold by John Kinzig and Mary Kinzig Kraut in March 1787 upon death of their father, Jacob Kinzig, husband of Catherina Freed, who was a daughter of Johannes Fried. The agreement by the heirs provides crucial evidence of what happened to the children of Johannes Freed.

Township,[13] just north of Germantown, until moving to the new tract of Matthias Van Bebber, later known as Skippack Township. The first to take the plunge was John's brother, Paul Freed Sr., who bought 50 acres in 1714 and 50 more in 1721. A year later, John bought 100. The brothers no doubt knew about the proposed legislation to allow Mennonites to become citizens, and thus gain the right to bequeath land. Such a law was finally passed, after years of debate, in 1730, and was the subject of the Garber article in 2019.[14] The article laid out in great detail the debate in the Pennsylvania General Assembly, along with the Lancaster County Mennonites who benefitted. What the article omitted almost entirely, however, was that a nearly identical law was enacted the following year for the Mennonites of Skippack Township—including John Freed and Paul Freed Sr., who became British subjects.

Armed with the assurance that they could will their land to their children, Paul and John continued to make additional purchases in Skippack, so that John eventually owned 223 acres and Paul 242. Unknown to me, however, was that John was also buying land in Bucks County, bringing his total to 623 acres.

There is further indirect evidence to support the idea that John Freed arrived around 1711. His oldest son, Heinrich Friedt, born in 1712, bequeathed land to his children. This would not be possible unless Heinrich was a British subject, yet there is no record of his naturalization. This supports the idea, then, that Heinrich was born in America and thus had no need to be naturalized once his father became a British subject.

When John Freed died in 1744, he left a will naming his youngest son, John, as executor, and his "dear beloved friends" Jacob Crader and Paul Freed as administrators. It was highly unusual to name both an executor and an administrator, but it makes sense when you consider that John had not yet turned 21 when his father wrote the will. One Freed family history speculates that John was not in his right mind

---

13 I have two main reasons to believe they might have settled first in Vincent Township. First, it is close to the area where the Stauffers reportedly settled, the Valley Forge area, and also close to Skippack. The evidence for Vincent Township specifically is that John Freed's daughter Mary married Peter Roth of Vincent Township about 1740. How did they meet? I believe they grew up together. Peter Roth anglicized his name to Peter Rhoad, and the old Vincent Mennonite Cemetery, also known as Rhoad's Burial Ground, is named for his family. Joel D. Alderfer of the Mennonite Heritage Center in Harleysville has written about this family.

14 "Who for Conscience Sake Cannot Swear at All: The Quest of the Lancaster County Mennonites for Naturalization," by Allan A. Garber, *Pennsylvania Mennonite Heritage*, July 2019.

when he wrote the will, because Paul, his brother, had died in 1743. But in fact it was not Paul Sr. who was named as co-administrator; it was Paul Freed Jr., who had not yet moved to Allentown. The other adminstrator, Jacob Grater, was the son-in-law of Paul Sr. This explains why he referred to them as his dear beloved friends, which was simpler than saying "my brother's son-in-law and my first cousin once removed." Everyone knew what he meant.

Johannes Friedt signature, from
Last Will and Testament of Johannes Friedt (1682-1744)

Another interesting aspect of John Freed's inventory included a box for holding land deeds. What happened to the deeds? There was a clue in an article by Governor Samuel W. Pennypacker of Pennsylvania written in 1907. He stated that he had the original of John Freed's deed in his possession,[15] because it had been countersigned by his ancestor, who was a land agent for Matthias Van Bebber.

So I contacted the Pennypacker Museum in Eastern Pennsylvania, and I am happy to say that this Freed artifact, too, is a museum piece. The curator of the museum was kind enough to send me a photograph of the original, which includes the signature of John Freed.

---

15 "Bebber's Township and the Dutch Patroons of Pennsylvannia", by Samuel Whitaker Pennypacker, *Pennsylvania Magazine of History and Biography*, 1907, Vol. 31, No. 1, p. 6.

THE FREEDS IN EUROPE

Thanks to the extensive research of Richard W. Davis,[16] we have some notion of the Mennonite Freeds in the Palatinate. The records are sparse indeed; as he explains, many of them were destroyed during the Second World War.

We do know a few things, however. There was a Heinrich Friedt who was one of the first Mennonites to arrive in the Palatinate. I had learned he had written to the church elders in Amsterdam, so I visited the Mennonite Archives at the University of Amsterdam, where the director, Professor A. J. Plak, broke into a broad smile when I told him what I was looking for. "Perhaps," he said, "you would like to see this." After a minute or two scouring the top shelves of the library, he pulled down two books of transcriptions of letters.

He showed me correspondence from 1690[17] between the Mennonite elders of the Palatinate and senior church officials in Holland, who pledged to give financial aid to the refugees who had begun flooding out of Switzerland about 1670. The signatories in the Palatinate included Heinrich Friedt and Valentine Hütwohl, a minister born about 1642. He is important for genealogists because he had compiled lists of the refugees around 1672 at the request of the church leaders in Holland. In a prefatory letter in late 1671 he described the conditions.

---

16 Richard W. Davis is considered perhaps the leading expert on Mennonites in the Palatinate. His works include *The Stauffer families of Switzerland, Germany, and America (including Stouffer and Stover)*, self-published, 1992. Paul Freed Sr.'s father-in-law was Hans Stauffer.

17 From *Documents of Brotherly Love: Dutch Mennonite Aid to Swiss Anabaptists, Vol. 1, 1635-1709*, by James W. Lowry, edited by David J. Rempel Smucker and John L. Ruth, Ohio Amish Library, Millersburg, Ohio, 2007. Document 54. December 11, 1690. Committee members in Amsterdam transmit money through Peter d'Orville at Frankfurt for the Palatinate and make an offer of ongoing help to Mennonite ministers there. Document 77. March 3, 1709. Copy of a letter from the Palatine Mennonite churches about the dispatch of their delegates, Peter Kolb and Hans Bechtel, to Holland to discuss the Pliem affair. According to Lowry, "This letter provides a valuable list of twenty-six ordained Mennonites from the Palatinate with German names, unfortunately, not always accurately spelled in this copy by a Dutch secretary. The ministers gathered to sign this letter at two places, Immelhäuserhof on March 3 and at Ibersheimerhof on March 13." Heinrich Friedt was among those who signed on 13 March 1709.

"These are scattered among the fellow believers throughout
the region over a twelve-mile territory. Among these you
will find those who need canes, being 70, 80 and 90 years
old. On the whole they need clothing sorely; they didn't take
more along than what they had on their backs. With little
bedding, we don't know how to keep them warm. Some
amongst us have seven, eight or nine living with them.
When you speak of their property, they sigh, wishing that
they had their houses and farm land here as before. There
are men who left their wives and children, and women,
older as well as younger, who have left husbands and
children; others who brought along some, leaving the rest
with the husbands, also expectant mothers; also children
who left father, mother, brothers and sisters behind".[18]

The 1690 letter appears twice in the Mennonite archives in
Amsterdam, with slightly different wording, apparently because of a
different transcriber. Here is the translation:

Since because of the destructive war here in the country,
great ruin and damage has taken place, so that many people
will have to leave the country because of lack of bread; and
considering that a heartfelt comfort has been promised to us
from you our dear brethren, on the advice of ministers and
elders, we have commissioned these men as fellow ministers
and elders to make a journey to you people, namely Jonas
Lohren, Johan Schumacher, and Christiaan Plein, to consult
with you about where each of us who cannot remain here
in the country might be able to go to earn his bread, and
then further to speak with you about what they have been
commissioned to; trust the aforementioned men, they will
describe and tell you orally about all the situation of this
country, and then expect all brotherly advice from you,
about which we comfort ourselves sincerely: remaining then
always your well-inclined brothers

in Christ Jesus our lord, willing to serve
 written in the Palatinate, 18 June 1690
  was or is signed [sic]

Michiel Christoffel	Hans Meijer
Severin Haan	Nicholaas Ellenberger
Hans Lutteweiler	Ulrich Eicher

18 Richard W. Davis, *The Stauffer families of Switzerland...*, Part 1, pp. 26-28

Valentyn Hutwaal	Nicolaas Gram
Hans Hoogennauw	Hans Haage
Hans Jacob Hiestand	Ulrich Burchholter
Ulrich Stauffer	Hendrik Friedt
Hans Muller	

It appears that "Christiaan Plein" was in fact Christian Pliem, another senior Mennonite in the Palatinate. The elders' reply was dated December 11, 1690:

> We have received your welcome letter of the 22nd of last month in good time. To which this serves as a friendly answer, that the last bill of exchange has not only been accepted by Mr. Peter d'Orville of Frankfurt, but shall be paid at the proper time. Meanwhile we give the friends the further useful report that approval has been granted to Mr. d'Orville by the general and united group of delegates to withdraw 1000 rixdollars more, if you have need. In any case you must not think that is the end of it. No, we have still more for the service of the brothers. And when they have need, they should simply report it without embarrassment. Then we will supply the requirements so that you do not suffer from your troubles. We are reporting this quietly so that the friends can handle matters accordingly — etc.

Your affectionate friends and brothers in Christ,
    Willem Heisterman —
    Johannes Kops —
    commissioners of the Mennonite congregation
holding meetings in the church called the Sun.

A third letter, dated 3 March 1709,[19] concerned a scandal uncovered after the death of Christian Pliem, who apparently was entrusted with the funds from Holland. His accounting of the funds was — how do I put this diplomatically? — irregular. Apparently fearing that the news would reach Holland from disgruntled churchgoers, the

---

19 From *Letters on Toleration: Dutch Aid to Persecuted Swiss and Palatine Mennonites, 1615-1699*, by Jeremy Dupertuis Bangs, Picton Press, Rockport, Maine, 2004. Document 158: Mennonite Church Archives in the Amsterdam Municipal Archives, inventory number 1426 (18 June 1690). Letter to the clergy throughout Holland and elsewhere from the clergy in the Palatinate. Document 159, a copy of the same, with slight spelling variations: Mennonite Church Archives in the Amsterdam Municipal Archives, inventory number 1131(b) (18 June 1690), but inserted in a letter of 10 August 1690, inventory number 1131(a).

Palatinate elders gathered in two places to sign the following letter:

After God, the Lord, by His mighty hand summoned our brother Christian Pliem from this world and his temporal life ended, his charity funds were examined and there was some inaccuracy present. This news spread somewhat broadly among the people, and there was much restless talk. Also some were agitated and declared that they would accuse us to you and could indeed cause you sorrow. However, to avoid this and to have you properly informed in everything, we as reported above in general consider it good and advisable to send some ministers and elders to you. Peter Kolb from Kriegsheim has been named for this purpose and Hans Bechtel from here, a confirmed deacon, ministers ready for the journey, whom we send to you out of love. They will visit you in many locations and wish to indicate our thanks for the manifest love and great benevolence, which you have demonstrated from brotherly love toward us and all in need. We hope that the Lord will accompany them with His holy angels there and back again. To confirm this the more, we the abovementioned have signed this with our own hands.

Jacob Landes
Sammel Meyer
Christian Beth
Jacob Gut
Hans Henrich Baer
Peter Bledtli
Michel Meir
Samuel Meyer
Ulrich Neukommet
Hans Cheurts

[page two]
We, the ministers and elders from the Palatinate in our meeting acknowledge the above as appropriate, good, and advisable. In witness whereof we have signed with our own hands. Ibersheimerhoff, March 13, 1709.

Hans Muller   Henrich Friedt
Hans Mayer   Valentine Hütwohl

Casper Gut	Christian Nvustur [sic]
Tielmann Kolb	Hans Jacob Schutblÿ
Peter Lemen	Hans Brubacher
Heinrich Hiestant	Christian Kruns
Hans Busshaler	Hans Schinner
Jacob Müller	
Christian Seikommet	

Those were the first records I could find of any Friedt. Considering his companions, I strongly suspected he was originally Swiss. The name Friedt does not appear in the Swiss records,[20] but there are several Friedli families in the 1600s in Canton Bern. It was common for Swiss families to drop the "li" suffix when they moved to Germany—Schnebli becoming Schnebel, for example, or Baerli becoming Baer. So I thought to look there, without immediate success.

By the late 1600s, Richard W. Davis found, several Friedt families were established in the Palatinate, including Heinrich Friedt (b.1656), and his father Rudiger, who lived in Aspisheim. Rudiger, like Hans, is a nickname ("The Red" or "Redhead"). I believe this Heinrich is the father of the brothers John and Paul who lived in Skippack, because of German traditional naming conventions. Ordinarily, the firstborn son was named after the father's father. We know that Heinrich had two sons who emigrated. One is our immigrant ancestor, John (or Johannes) Freed. The other is Paul, who emigrated with his wife and daughter. Paul had no sons, but John did, and his firstborn was named Heinrich (b.1712). So if he followed tradition (and this family seemed to do so), John's father's name was Heinrich.

The two other Mennonite Freeds who were on the 1734 tax roll north of Philadelphia were Paul Junior of Skippack (who later moved to Allentown) and Johann Jacob "Hans" Friedt of Salfordville. Both had firstborn sons named Johannes. So we would expect their father to also be named Johannes.

Thanks to data compiled by Bruce Fosnocht and released in 2019 by the Lancaster Mennonite Historical Society,[21] I believe I have

---

20 Private correspondence, Hanspeter Jecker. He was of the opinion that a connection between the Fridli and Friedt families was unlikely.

21 "Swiss Surname Finding Aid", compiled by Bruce Fosnocht, 2019, published via the "Members only" section of LMHS.org.

found the Swiss family from which we Freeds descend.[22] The initial couple were Peter Fridli and his wife Catharina Wundt, and it appears that they baptized their children as infants, in violation of Mennonite practice. They might have converted, but if so, it was after the births of their four children. Their eldest, Peter, was born in 1603. He married Barbara Schaller in 1634 and was a Mennonite.

His son, also named Peter Fridli, was born about 1634 and was expelled from Biglen, Switzerland, to Holland in 1660. It appears he returned to the area from Holland, and he is next found in 1672 in the Palatinate, then a part of the Holy Roman Empire and today part of southwestern Germany.[23] He appears on a refugee list as Peter Frieder. On the same list are Christen Frieder, who I believe was Peter's brother, next to Barbara Frieder, who I think was Christen's wife. By this time, Rudiger Friedt, who I believe was a third brother, had already settled in Aspisheim, having appears on the 1664 census. Among the three families, they had four small children: Peter (son of Peter, born 1655), Heinrich (born 1656, son of Rudiger), Paul (born 1657, son of Rudiger), and Maria (daughter of Christen, born 1664 in Bruchsal, near Karlsruhe).

By 1690, the Fridli children are spelling their surname Friedt, and most have moved down the Rhine:

- Peter moved with his father to Obersulzen. His son, Peter (b. 1677), is the father of Heinrich and Johann Paul who emigrated on the bilander *Vernon* in 1747.
- Heinrich settled in Aspisheim with his father, nicknamed "Rudiger." Heinrich became an important figure in the Mennonite community and was a contemporary of Valentine Hütwohl. His children included my immigrant ancestor, Johannes "John" Freed (b. 1682) and Paul Freed (b. 1684), who emigrated about 1710 and eventually settled in Skippack. He had another son, Heinrich (b. 1693), who remained in the Palatinate.
- Paul settled in Weinheim bei Wallertheim. His son, Johannes

---

22 This connection is necessarily speculative, as there are no common ancestors traced via DNA. However, it could prove productive for future researchers to look at Freedley families, especially any with Mennonite roots, to see if this theory can be confirmed or refuted.

23 Amsterdam Municipal Archives, inventory number 1199, translated by Richard W. Davis. This list is dated 1672 but does not provide a location for the refugees. A companion document, Amsterdam Municipal Archives, inventory number 1196, was described by Charles Whitmer in "Swiss Anabaptist Refugees from Canton Bern in the German Palatinate in 1671", *Pennsylvania Mennonite Heritage*, April 2001. Whitmer notes the existence of Document 1199 and says he hopes to have it translated and published in the future.

(b. 1680), was the father of Paul Freed "Junior" of Skippack (later known as Paul of Allentown) and Johann Jacob "Hans" Freed of Salford Township. Johannes remained in the Palatinate, and is found in Hamm in 1732 with his three youngest children. His two eldest, Paul and Jacob, emigrated about 1723.

- Maria married Jacob Wismer and stayed in Karlsruhe. They emigrated about 1710 and settled in New Bern, North Carolina, where Maria and their daughter were killed in a massacre.

All these conclusions are fully consistent with the census data compiled by Richard W. Davis and the results of the Freed DNA Project,[24] which showed that Paul Freed "Junior" and John Freed shared a common ancestor who is not their father. That common ancestor was Peter Fridli of Biglen, Switzerland.

PERSECUTION OF THE MENNONITES

Switzerland exerted increasing pressure on its Mennonite citizens over the course of several decades. There was a mass expulsion in 1671, but even before that Peter Friedli was expelled in 1660 to Holland. The usual practice was to send them to Holland under armed guard and dump them there. In at least one case the Dutch sent them back to Switzerland, saying in effect, how dare you try to solve your religious problems on our backs.

Switzerland had two principles that meant the Mennonites were troublemakers. The first required all able-bodied adult men to own a gun and know how to use it, to help defend the country from potential invasion. The second was their main way of raising money for the government, a "head tax," based on the number of adults and children, which in turn was based on the baptismal records from the churches. The Mennonites refused to own weapons, and they did not baptize their infants.

The Swiss tried persuasion, then force. Many of the lovely Swiss castles have towers where Mennonites and others were held prisoner. Their land was confiscated. Eventually the Swiss began

---

24 I am indebted to James M. Freed of Delaware, Ohio, who died in April 2019, for creating this project, http://familytreedna.com/groups/freed/. Jim was a selfless man who helped Freed genealogists of all stripes, regardless of whether they were related to him. I, for instance, am not related to him.

executing Mennonites, who were considered traitors, not just heretics. They were often executed through drowning—the idea being that if you won't baptize your children, we will baptize you by dunking you in the lake until you are dead.

After the great expulsion of 1671, William Penn came to the area of Germany where they were living, along the Palatinate (now part of the German state of Rhineland-Palatinate), to promote his idyllic land where all religions could live in harmony. Today we call it Pennsylvania. The first Mennonites to heed his call founded Germantown, Philadelphia, in 1683. The first Freeds arrived around 1710.

Grave marker: "In Memory of Johannes Freit who Departed this Life Dec 31 1744 Aged 62 years." Photo taken in 1984 by Charles A. Heiberger. This marker is now missing.

IN SUMMARY: THREE CENTURIES OF FREEDS

John and Paul Senior arrived about 1710 and became landowners in the new township of Skippack. Their influence was substantial, and the evidence remains to this day in the layout of the roads in the area. Both John and Paul Senior became British subjects in 1731, allowing them to bequeath land to their descendants. There are no roads or monuments in Skippack in their memory, however, because the male line of the Skippack-based Freeds died out quickly. Only Heinrich and Peter, who lived elsewhere, had sons to carry on the name. Paul Senior had one child, a daughter, and John Freed willed his Skippack land to his youngest son, John, who had five children, all daughters. Paul's land went to Jacob Grater, after whom Graterford is named, while John's land went to a granddaughter's husband, Henry Wismer. Its outline remains clear, as the new Phoenix State Prison is built on the site. John also owned 400 acres of land near Perkasie, where several roads are named after his family and where the Peter Freed barn, built by his son in 1761, is still standing at the Heckler Plains Farmstead. His great-grandson, Abraham (b.1785), converted to the Methodist Church in 1830 and became president of the Philadelphia conference of ministers. Abraham's grandson, William Walton Freed, is the starting point in the *Freed Family History* written by Joyce Graff and June Wilcox.

Here, then, are the connections between Peter Fridli of Switzerland (b.1570), through the immigrant John Freed, to Abraham Freed (1817-1865), president of the Philadephia Conference of Methodist Ministers:

1. **Peter Fridli (1580-).** Lived in Canton Bern, Switzerland. Not Mennonite. He married Catharina Wundt.

1.1 **Peter Fridli (1603-).** Born in Biglen, Switzerland. He married Barbara Schaller in 1634. Mennonite.

1.1.2. **Heinrich Fridli (1635-).** Born in 1635, Biglen, Switzerland.

1.1.2.1. **Heinrich Friedt (1655-c. 1710).** Born in Biglen, Switzerland. Died after 1710, Aspisheim, Palatinate. Prominent Mennonite Minster who signed correspondence with church elders in Holland.

1.1.2.1.1. **John (Johannes) Friedt (1682-1744).** Born in Aspisheim, died 31 Dec 1744 in Skippack Township, Pennsylvania. Buried at Lower Skippack Mennonite Church. Subject of a book by Charles A. Heiberger. Married Christianna, (1688-1746) Skippack Township. Presumed buried next to her husband; tombstone illegible.

1.1.2.1.1.1. **Heinrich Fried (1712-1786)** Born 30 Oct 1712, probably in Skippack, d. 30 Jan 1786, West Rockfill Township. Buried at Jerusalem Union Cemetery. Married Anna (1718-1803), buried at Methocton Mennonite Cemetery. Two of their children followed the Funkite Mennonite tradition.

1.1.2.1.1.1.3. **Heinrich Fried (1754-1820).** He fought in the Revolutionary War, and his children were Funkites, but he is buried in the Germantown Mennonite Cemetery, Philadelphia, so apparently all was forgiven. Married Veronica Schlieffer (1755-1839). Buried at Methacton Mennonite Cemetery.

1.1.2.1.1.1.3.5. **Abraham Schlieffer Freed (1785-1840).** Born a Mennonite, he converted to Methodism. Married Catherine Ecker (1775-1854) after the death of her first husband, Jacob Wanger. Their daughter Lydia's sampler in the Lancaster Mennonite History Museum was an important link in the family history. Abraham and Catherine are buried at the Mayer Graveyard, Lancaster County, which is adjacent to the Shoppes at Belmont Mall.

1.1.2.1.1.1.3.5.6. **Abraham Freed (1817-1865).** Methodist. President of the Philadelphia Conference of Methodist Ministers. He is the first entry in the *Freed Family History* by Graff and Wilcox. Married Mary Singer.

To add to these nine generations, append a number dependent on the birth order in the family (first, second, third child etc). Thus:

1.1.2.1.1.1.3.5.6.1 Alpheus Singer Freed or
1.1.2.1.1.1.3.5.6.2 William Walton Freed

which makes us
1.1.2.1.1.1.3.5.6.2.1.2.3. John C. Freed
1.1.2.1.1.1.3.5.6.2.1.1.1. Joyce Wilcox Graff

THE FREEDS AND DIVIDED LOYALTIES

It's not written about often these days, but Americans were far from unanimous in supporting the split from England in 1776. Perhaps the greatest effect on churches was the forced separation of the American Episcopal Church from the Church of England. But it had a profound effect on the Mennonite Church as well.

The Mennonites, like the Quakers, were strict pacifists and opposed anything that would support war. They refused to bear arms, for example. But the Pennsylvania General Assembly had imposed a tax to support the fledgling Revolutionary Army, led by General George Washington, and the Mennonites had a problem.

Bishop Christian Funk of Franconia opposed taking up arms, but he felt morally obligated to support the revolution by any other means necessary. About four dozen of his fellow worshipers agreed with him, and he was excommunicated. Henry Freed (b.1712), the eldest son of John Freed, my immigrant ancestor, apparently sympathized with the Funkites. Radically breaking with Mennonite tradition, he enlisted in the army in early 1776, even before the Declaration of Independence. He was wounded in an early skirmish with the British and sent home to recuperate, where he married and started a family. Henry later rejoined the fight and was captured in battle but survived the war, which is lucky for me, because his son, my ancestor, Abraham S. Freed (b.1785), was born after the war. Henry's children, apparently, were all Funkites. Two of them married relatives of Bishop Funk, and others married into another Funkite family, the Rosenbergers.

After the war, and even during it, a number of people who supported England (often referred to as Tories) left for another American English colony, Canada. And in fact, in one Freed family, we see every single sister leave with her husband for Canada around 1802.

Not so with my Freed line. While they remained in the United States, they gravitated away from the Mennonite Church. Abraham S. Freed, born in 1785, converted to Methodism, joining the United Brethren in Christ. He followed in the footsteps of Bishop Martin Boehm, a Mennonite who had co-founded the United Brethren in Christ in 1789. Abraham Freed became a well known Methodist preacher, holding revival meetings around eastern and central Pennsylvania. It was at one of these meetings where his son, also named Abraham (b.1817), met Mary Singer, who hailed from Halifax, Pennsylvania, not far from Harrisburg.

Abraham and Mary traveled various circuits for the Methodist Church, mostly around Montgomery County, Pennsylvania, and on the Eastern Shore of Maryland. It was while serving in one of those circuits that Abraham suddenly took ill and died. His widow returned to Halifax with her seven children, including Alpheus, William, and Benson, whose sermons and talks we are about to explore.

Refugees from Switzerland fled up the Rhine River to the Palatinate, now part of the German state of Rhineland-Palatinate. Map from Walter Allen Knittle, *Early Eighteenth Century Palatine Emigration*. Philadelphia, 1937.

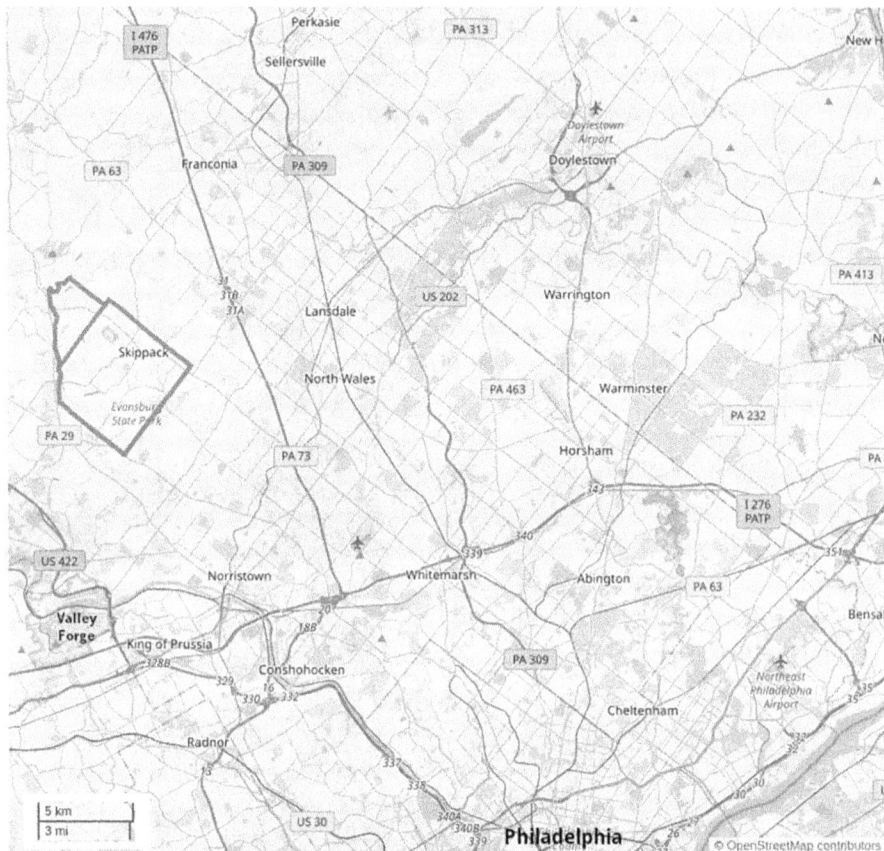

Skippack Township, 2020

This is a modern map of the area northwest of Philadelphia where John Freed settled. The square to the west marks the original Van Bebber's Township. The irregular area to the west was later added to create modern Skippack Township.

From Skippack it is 30 miles southeast to Philadelphia, 15 miles northeast to Perkasie, or 20 miles south to Valley Forge.

On the next page you will find Van Bebber's Township as it appeared about 1727.

Today it takes only an hour to drive to Phildelphia, or two hours by train. In 1727, by foot or horseback, on dirt or nonexistent roads, fording the streams you see on the map, the journey was measurable in days.

Map copyright OpenStreetMap Contributors.

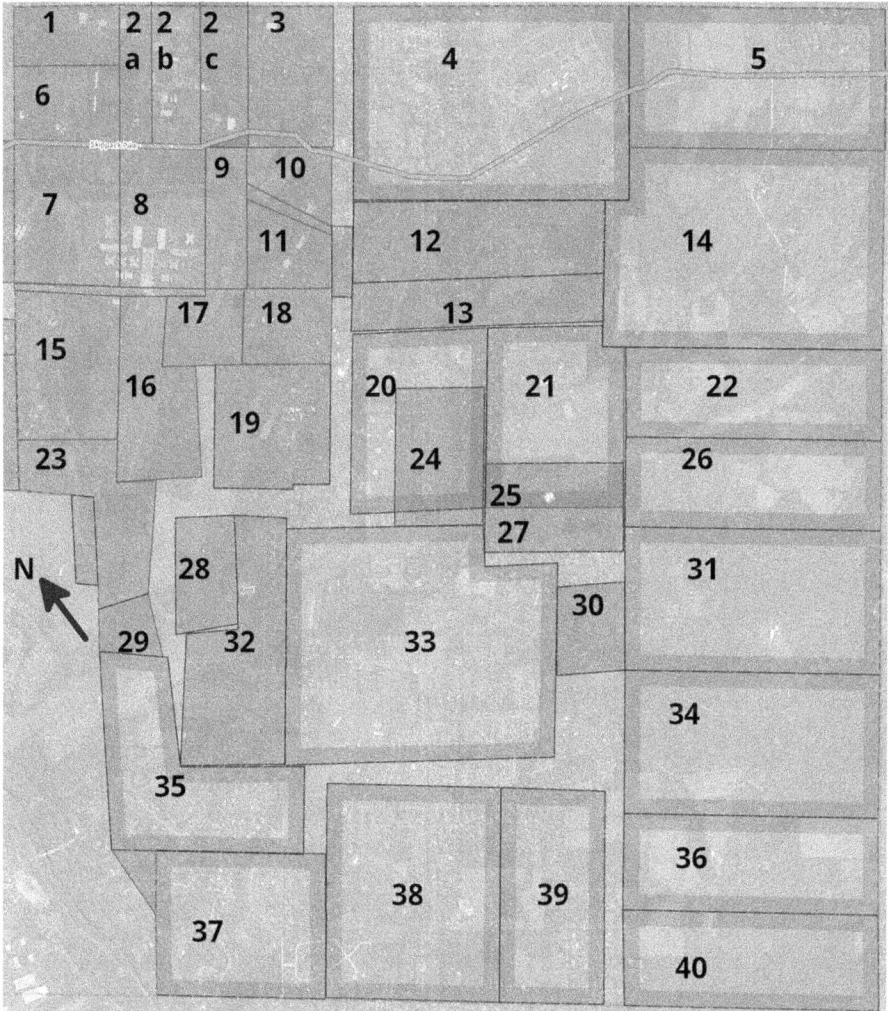

Van Bebber's Township, about 1727

Any historical map of Skippack Township is necessarily a snapshot in time, because the residents were continually buying and selling their land. My map is more or less how the township, recently renamed from Van Bebber's Township, looked in 1727, when Matthias Van Bebber sold his remaining interests to Ludwig Sproegel, "except for 120 acres reserved" to Paul Freed Jr. The roadway near the top is Skippack Pike.

Key to Map:

1. Jacob Kolb. He purchased this land from Sproegel about 1728, so I included it in the map with him as the owner. Interestingly, this lot, along with all the land in a straight line to the point where Skippack Pike enters the township at the right of the map, was outside the original purchase by Van Bebber. In short, he sold land he did not own. This was later rectified

by the Pennsylvania General Assembly, and to this day there is a "notch" visible in maps of the township that takes this error into account.

2. Jacob Kolb's original purchase, 15 Dec 1709. Lots 2(b) and (c) were inherited by his sons Henry and Dielman in 1748. This Henry Kolb was known as "Henry Kolb, bludier". A bludier, or blue-dyer, was an expert in dyeing cloth. Henry bludier also purchased Lot 2(a) from his father in 1739.

3. Michael Ziegler, 14 Feb 1718.

4. Gerret Inden Hoofen, 1706.

5. Dirk and William Renberg, 9 Dec 1706. These men eventually divided this property along the Skippack Pike. I believe that John Renbury, who obtained a warrant on the Allentown property that Paul Freed Jr. eventually bought, is a close relative of these men.

6. Martin Kolb, 1724.

7. Johannes Friedt, 1 April 1723. This became the Freed homestead, and two generations later the Wismer homestead. John Freed later purchased the small strip of land under Lots 7 and 8, which is now Mokychic Road.

8 and 9. This land was originally purchased by Jacob Kolb. On 1 Feb 1722, he subdivided the land, selling 100 acres (Lot 8) to Johannes Friedt and 50 acres (Lot 9) to Henry Kolb (not his son). This other Henry became known as Henry schreiner, to contrast with Henry bludier. A schreiner is a joiner or cabinetmaker.

10 and 11. Michael Ziegler bought Lots 10 and 11 from Gerhard Clemens on 18 Dec 1722. He and Paul Freed Sr. split the land along a diagonal, each winding up with 50 acres (Lot 11 for Paul). Later, Paul bought another 10 acres of this land from Michael, the small strip running between the two lots. The segment to the right of Lot 11 was eventually purchased by Paul Freed, and it was right in the middle of the planned road to what was later known as Grater's Ford. For centuries, the road made a zig-zag around this lot.

12. Daniel Desmont, 12 June 1708.

13. Christopher Zimmerman, 12 June 1708.

14. John Newbry, 26 October 1706. Here was another case where Van Bebber sold land improperly (I doubt it was intentional—metes and bounds are tricky). Newbry bought 450 acres, supposedly a rectangle 225 perches by 300 perches (a perch, or rod, is five and a half yards). However, when he paced it out one day, he noticed that it was in fact smaller than what he had bought. He sued Van Bebber, who worked out a deal where some land was taken from Lots 12 and 13, which were then pushed slightly west, into the supposed right of way for a future road. It was this land, which Paul Freed Sr. later purchased, that led to the zig-zag.

15. Paul Freed Jr., 1727. It took me a few years to track this one down.

16. Hans Detweiler, 8 Apr 1724. Hans is the father of Susan Detweiler, who later married John Freed, ancestor of Isaac G. Freed.

17. Henry Kolb, schreiner, 1 Feb 1722. He purchased this land the same day he bought Lot 9. The Upper Skippack Mennonite Church and graveyard sit on part of this lot.

18. Paul Friedt Sr., 3 May 1721. This was the first Freed to settle in Skippack.

19. Jacob Updegrave, 8 Apr 1724.

20 and 24. It is difficult to sort out this property using metes and bounds. Apparently, Lot 24 was purchased by Richard Gabell in October 1706. Lot 20, which overlaps it, was purchased by Johannes Scholl on 10 June 1708. How exactly that was resolved is not clear in any deeds recorded at the time.

21. Herman Kuster, 10 June 1708. His initial purchase was 200 acres, but he sold 50 acres back to Van Bebber, who then deeded it as a gift to the "Mennonist Society" on 8 June 1717. Those 50 acres are marked as Lot 25 on the map.

22. Edward Beer, 9 Dec 1706. This land was sold to William Dewees in 1708.

23. Peter Reiff, 4 Sept. 1728. This was part of the unsold land that went to Ludwig

Sproegel in 1727. The small adjoining lot of 16 acres was purchased by Isaac Dubois about 1716; it fell right along the township line and might have been outside Van Bebber's Township.

24. See Lot 20, above.

25. Mennonist Society land, originally part of Lot 21. Christopher Dock's schoolhouse was approximately in the middle of this land.

26. Thomas Wiseman, 12 Dec 1706. This land was subdivided, with the part adjoining Lot 22 going to William Dewees in 1708 and the rest retained by Wiseman.

27. Mennonist Society land, deeded as a gift by Van Bebber on 8 June 1717. This lot of 50 acres has the Lower Skippack Mennonite Church and graveyard, where the immigrant John Freed is buried.

28. William Weirman, about 1724.

29. John Jacobs Jr., 1724.

30. Claus Johnson, 12 June 1708.

31. Claus Johnson, 11 Dec 1706.

32. Nicholas Hicks, 12 June 1723. Hicks defaulted on this land, which was sold at auction to John Heizer (or Keizer) and eventually bought by Yellis Kolb.

33. Isaac Dubois, 1716. At 500 acres, this was the largest single property in Skippack.

34. John Krey, 25 Feb 1703. Krey was the first person to buy land and remain in Van Bebber's Township. A couple of others bought lots around the same time but soon sold them back to Van Bebber.

35. John Jacobs Jr., 8 March 1724.

36. Henry Pannebecker, 12 June 1708. Pannebecker eventually succeeded Sproegel as the owner of the unsold Van Bebber land. A small creek runs through this lot, and Peter Bon bought the part of the lot to the west of the creek.

37. John Jacobs Sr., 31 October 1704. He bought the small triangle to the west of this lot the same year. I believe this reflected the limit of arable land before reaching the banks of Perkiomen Creek, which this property adjoins.

38. Derrick Jensen, 2 May 1721.

39. John Umstat, 1717.

40. John Umstat, 9 June 1708. This land went to his sons, Herman and Henry, upon his death.

SERMONS BY
ALPHEUS SINGER FREED

ALPHEUS FREED

FEW ARE CHOSEN

Matt. 20:16, For many be called, but few chosen.
Lesson: Isaiah 53:1-10. Acts 10:34-44.

Hymns 89, 562, 572.

In the preceding verses, the Saviour says, the kingdom of heaven, that is, Christ's kingdom on earth, is like unto a man that is a householder, which went out early in the morning to hire laborers into his vineyard. He agreed with them for a penny a day, and sent them into his vineyard. He sent also others, agreeing to give them what was right—some at the third hour, some at the sixth, some at the ninth, and some at the eleventh hour (v. 1-7). In the evening the lord of the vineyard commanded his steward to call the laborers, and give them their hire, beginning with the last, and regularly paying them, to the first, with a penny given to each laborer. Those who went first into the vineyard supposed they would receive more, though they had agreed to work for a penny.

When their expectations were disappointed they murmured against the good man of the house, Saying, these last have wrought but one hour, and thou hast made them equal unto us, which have borne the burden and heat of the day. But he answered one of them, and said, Friend, I do thee no wrong: didst not thou agree with me for a penny? Take that thine is, and go thy way: I will give unto this last, even as unto thee. Is it not lawful for me to do what I will with mine own? Is thine eye evil, because I am good? So the last shall be first, and the first last: for many be called, but few chosen." (Matthew 20:12-16) This parable was doubtless designed to teach the Jews that though they were first called into the covenant, and had to bear the burden and heat of the day in sustaining a very costly system of religion, yet, under the Christian dispensation, the Gentile nations should be made equal with the Jews, and would be first brought into the favor of God, while the dissatisfied Jews, as a nation, would be rejected. And further, that while God called many, in calling nations, yet few would be chosen into his favor.

I. Let us inquire, Who are called? Answer: All. All nations, and all individuals. Every individual that hears the Gospel is called. There is no mortal in reference to whom the blood of Jesus is inefficacious to his salvation. When Satan fell, his sin was an inexpiable sin. It hurled him into inextricable ruin. But happy for man, his sin has been atoned for. But though atoned for, it will inevitably drag the soul to hell if not repented of and pardoned. The inexorable justice of God demands that the soul that sinneth, it shall die. And Christ is the only Palladium,[1] the only effectual defense, protection, and safety to save us from being destroyed by the two-edged sword of justice. He desires you to come to him that he may save you. As the husbandman went out and hired all he found in the market place, where those wishing employment presented themselves. So Jesus goes out in the person of his ministers into the world to call all into his vineyard. He has called you at the third, the sixth, and the ninth hour, and now he is calling some of you at the eleventh hour. But the eleventh hour is not the dying hour. Those who were called at the eleventh hour were yet able to labor.

The Gospel of Christ, the child of heavenly birth, the brightest star that ever shone on our earth, offers light, life, and peace to all. As the stars offer light to every traveler in the darkness of the night, so the Gospel offers light and life to every traveler passing through the dark night of his pilgrimage here. Yea, even the infidel, who would so gladly proscribe Christianity and blot out the Sun of Righteousness for ever.

But he who will turn a deaf ear to the call of Christ will be eternally banished from his presence. A man's imperious demeanor here will not command respect for him hereafter, but will only serve to sink him ingloriously into the jaws of eternal death. Your heart may now be impervious to the truth of God. You may refuse to allow the Gospel light to penetrate your soul. But, by your present conduct, you are only treasuring up wrath against the day of accounts. Oh, turn from sin ere it ruins you! Look at the evils sin has already brought upon us. Sorrow, tears, and suffering are the inalienable heritage of all the children of Eve, all of which in our primeval state we were free from. The sufferings which sin now inflicts upon man are but the presage of the poignant sufferings which it will inflict in the world to come. You may cavil[2] now, and by various pretexts endeavor to justify yourself in your refusal to obey the call given you. But in the day of account your prevarications will not screen you from the now impending stroke of inexorable justice. Then the fiat [command] of the Almighty will strike consternation through every fibre of the body, and every sensibility of the soul, with the doleful sound, "Depart," etc. (Luke 5:8-11)

---

1   Palladium. Anything believed to provide protection or safety. Comes from the statue of Pallas Athena in the City of Troy, on which the safety of the city was supposed to depend. Random House Dictionary.

2   Cavil. Make petty or unnecessary objections, grumble.

II. Who are chosen? Ans: Those few who are willing to forsake all sin. It is supposed there is here an allusion to the manner in which the army, among the Jews, supplied with new recruits. Among them it was customary to speak, not of levying troops, but of choosing them. All the men from 20 years old and upwards that were able to go to war, were liable to serve as soldiers (Num. 1:3,20,45.) Hence they had always a great number, more than they needed. When the ranks were to be filled, the people were called together by the sound of the trumpet and, on passing in review before the officer, those were chosen who were deemed most fit for service. Out of the many that were called, but few were chosen. (Bush on Matthew 20:16). And thus the Gospel calls many, but few are chosen, only those fit for service in Christ's army. Only those who are willing to forsake all for Christ, join his army and fight under his banner. As a general, going to meet a foe, could not choose those to fill his ranks who were willing to do no more than to strew his path with flowers, but he would choose those who were willing to forsake all and follow him to distant fields, so Christ chooses not those who are willing to do no more than pronounce their eulogies upon Christianity and acknowledge that it is good and true, but he chooses those who will follow him, and follow him till death.

Every true Penitent will be chosen, every such one attracts the eye of Jesus as the world passes in review before him. No pains will be spared on the part of Christ to bring such into the vineyard. Look at the case of Cornelius, the Centurion at Caesarea. He was a true Penitent. But at Caesarea the Saviour had no one to call this true Penitent into his vineyard. Hence he sent an angel to him to command him in a vision, evidently about the ninth hour of day, to send to Joppa,[3] 30 or 40 miles down the coast of the Mediterranean, to call Peter to him. The same day Cornelius sent three men, two of his household servants and a devout soldier, to call Peter. As they drew near Joppa, Peter went to pray on the housetop. While there he fell into a trance, saw heaven opened, saw a vessel, as it were a great sheet [sail] knit at the four corners, and let down to the earth: "Wherein were all manner," etc. (Acts 10:12-16). While he doubted what this should mean, the men, sent by Cornelius, made inquiry for Simon's house, where Peter lodged, and stood before the gate. And "the Spirit said unto him, Behold, three men seek thee. Arise therefore, and get thee down, and go with them, doubting nothing: for I have sent them." (Acts 10:19,20a). Peter went down to them, heard their report, next day went with them to Caesarea, and became the instrument of leading Cornelius into the vineyard of Christ.

---

3   Modern Jaffa, Israel.

Here we may learn the interest Christ feels in every true Penitent. As the rays of the sun in the heavens penetrate every fissure of the rock in the mountain precipice, so the healing, genial rays of the Sun of Righteousness will penetrate the heart through every chasm which the hammer of his word, and the sword of his Spirit shall open there, and give life and peace. O that you may be chosen!

III.　　Those who are chosen must labor till the end of the day, not be at ease in Zion. It was not till even[ing] was come that these laborers received their hire (v. 8). And it is not till the evening of life shall close in upon us, and the nightfall of death settle down upon the body, not till the sun of life shall go down in death, that we shall receive our full reward. While we are here, in the wilderness, we have a foretaste of the fruits of the goodly land. As the spies, whom Moses sent to search out the goodly land, brought one cluster of grapes to Israel, in the wilderness, and some pomegranates, and figs (Num. 13:23-26) and thus gave them a foretaste of the fruits of the land, so we have, by the way, grapes of Paradise, pomegranates and figs of heaven. But at the end of the world we shall have our full reward. It will be, not a penny, but a crown of Everlasting Life.

Oh, will you not labor for so rich a reward? Oh remember, death will soon be upon us all. Every pain we feel is indicative of our approaching dissolution. And will you continue to be idle? To procrastinate? Oh what a destroying monster is Procrastination! It is the Amazon upon which the souls of innumerable millions have floated to the unfathomable ocean of Eternal Damnation! Oh, come, seek your happiness in God! The world cannot give you real happiness. Life, what is it, but a tissue of sorrow, disappointment, pains, and tears, from the cradle to the grave? And how brief is life! Soon the tragic scene will close.

Come into Christ's vineyard and you shall be happy here and hereafter. You shall not be deprived of any pleasure of earth excepting that which would be for hurt. Christ does not restrict his people beyond what is for their real benefit. Come to Christ, and the currility[4]—the low, vulgar, abusive language of malignant foes—shall never harm. Oh Christians, let us be inflexible in our purpose to labor in the vineyard till death! Let us avoid every infraction, of the holy, the infrangible [unbreakable] law of God! Then shall our last enemy be an informidable foe.[5]

Soon we must die. Neither wealth nor power can elongate our days, nor enable us to elude the stroke of death. Let us be faithful,

---

4　　currility or scurrility, the state of being scurrilous, like a curr

5　　In other words, if we follow God's laws carefully, we will be able to defeat our foes.

and soon our souls will make their egress from these bodies into the effulgence of the kingdom of God, and the entire domain of Jehovah will be our possession! Then let us labor for Christ, let not sin dominate over our souls. Let us so live and labor, that in death we may hear the plaudit of "Well done, [thou] good and faithful servant." etc. (Matt. 25:21).

Nearer, my God, to thee, Nearer to thee;
E'en though it be a cross That raiseth me;
Still all my song shall be, Nearer, my God, to thee, Nearer to thee.

2   Though like the wanderer, The sun gone down,
Darkness be over me, My rest a stone;
Yet in my dreams I'd be Nearer, my God, to thee, Nearer to thee.

3   There let the way appear Steps unto heaven;
All that thou sendest me In mercy given;
Angels to beckon me
Nearer, my God, to thee, Nearer to thee.

4   Then with my waking thoughts, Bright with thy praise,
Out of my stony griefs Bethel I'll raise;
So by my woes to be
Nearer, my God, to thee, Nearer to thee.

5   Or if on joyful wing Cleaving the sky,
Sun, moon, and stars forgot, Upwards I fly,
Still all my song shall be Nearer, my God, to thee, Nearer to thee.

"Nearer, my God, to thee," by Sarah Adams, 1841. *The Book of Common Praise.*

ALPHEUS FREED

FUNERAL SERMON

Psa. 90:12 "So teach us to number our days, that we may apply our hearts unto wisdom.

Lesson: Psa. 103. Matt 25:1-13.

Our days on earth are very few compared with the lifetime of man in days of old. Adam lived 930 years, Seth lived 912 years, and Methuselah lived 969 years. Now few are our days compared with theirs. The Psalmist, in his day, could say "As for man, his days are as grass: as a flower of the field, so he flourisheth. For the wind passeth over it, and it is gone; and the place thereof shall know it no more." (Psa. 103:15,16.) How oft death calls us together to weep over the departed ones whom we loved. And how soon will our friends thus weep over us. It is said of Scipio, the Roman General who took the city of Carthage, that when its walls were broken down, and its palaces were on fire, he shed tears over the scene of general devastation, and exclaimed, "It will one day be thus with Rome." (Rollin, vol. II, p. 26. D. Aubignes, vol I, p.26.) And while we shed our tears over our loved ones who have fallen by the stroke of death, we should remember that it will one day be thus with us. We may well say, "So teach us," etc. text.

I. We are prone to put death far in the distance. We are too much like the rich man whose goods increase. "And he thought within himself, saying," etc. (Luke 12:16-20.) He intended to make great arrangements for long life, and then say to his soul, "Soul, thou hast much goods laid up for many years; take thine ease, eat, drink, and be merry." Let us not fall into his error.

The Psalmist doubtless felt that he and his brethren were in danger of this error, hence he prayed in the language of the text. We are like the warrior who goes to the field of battle. When first the cannon begins to roar and his ears are saluted with the groans of the dying, he feels that he is exposed to danger, but soon he is accustomed to the cries of his fellows, loses sight of danger, and is fired with a burning desire for victory. So we enter upon the battlefield of life. While young we feel our danger, we soon lose sight of danger, and thirst for victory on the battlefield of life. Well may we then say, "So teach us ..."

II. What is wisdom? "The right use or exercise of knowledge." (Webster.) We know that in this world we must prepare for the world to come, and he is a wise man who makes a right use of this knowledge. When Solomon would teach us a lesson of wisdom, where does he find the instructor? In the king upon his throne? In the warrior? Nay, he sends us to the ant who knows that in summer she must provide for winter, and who makes a right use of her knowledge. He says, "Go to the ant, thou sluggard; consider her ways, and be wise: Which having no guide, overseer, or ruler, Provideth her meat in the summer, and gathereth her food in the harvest." (Prov. 6:6-8.) Thus let us be wise.

"The fear of the Lord is the beginning of wisdom." Psa. 111:10.

Let us be wise, as the wise virgins. Matt. 25:4.

Let us be like the wise man who built his house upon the rock, Matt. 7:24.

III. The heart must be applied to Wisdom, or Religion.

1. By Repentance. "A broken and a contrite heart, 0 God, thou wilt not despise." (Psa. 51:17.) As the husbandman breaks up the earth before he sows the seed, so must the fallow ground of the heart be broken up before the Spirit of God can there produce any fruit. (Gen. 4:3.)

2. By Faith, "With the heart man believeth unto righteousness; and with the mouth confession is made unto salvation." (Romans 10:10.) Oh seek him, then, with a sorrowing heart, as Joseph and Mary did. And as they found him in the temple, sitting in the midst of the doctors, "Both hearing them, and asking them questions," (Luke 2:46), so shall you find him in the temple of his mercy both to hear your prayers, and to grant you the desire of your heart.

Notice the Deceased. Address Friends.

Alpheus S. Freed

ALPHEUS FREED

ON PRAYER

> I Timothy 2:8. I will therefore that men pray every where, lifting up holy hands, without wrath and doubting.

> Lessons: Psalms 116; Luke 18:1-14.

> Hymns 1:331, 1:335, 2:331

The privilege of praying is an inestimable privilege, bequeathed to man by the vicarious death of Jesus Christ. It is a privilege from which devils are for ever cut off. But to man there is a throne of grace ever accessible. Hence, "I will therefore that MEN pray everywhere." Prayer is to be made for all men. "I exhort therefore that first of all supplication, prayer, intercessions, and giving of thanks be made for all men: for kings, and for all that are in authority; that we may lead a quiet and peaceable life in all godliness and honesty." (verses 1,2) We should pray for all men, because God will have all to be saved. "For this is good and acceptable in the sight of God our Saviour; who will have all men to be saved and to come unto the knowledge of the truth," (v. 3,4). Happy for us that we have the privilege of praying! Man, by his fall, has destroyed the beauty of the temple of creation and driven the dove of people from his soul. And now, by Faith and importunate [persistent] prayer, he is to recall to his fallen spirit the dove of celestial peace and be made the happy participant of the benediction of heaven.

I.   Where may we pray acceptably? Answer: Anywhere. "I will therefore that men pray everywhere." In ancient times God was frequently in a grove. "Abraham planted a grove in Beer-Sheba, and called there on the name of the Lord, the everlasting God," (Genesis 21:33.) Probably he intended this grove to be a representation of Eden, where under the boughs of the trees Adam worshiped. (Reito, vol. I, p. 244.) Heathens also worshiped their idol gods in groves. Hence the Israelites were strictly commanded to destroy the altars, break the images, and cut down the groves of the nations whom God should drive out before them. (Exodus 34:13).

In the days of Christ, Jews entertained the notion that at Jerusalem men ought to worship God. And the Samaritans contended that Mt. Gerizim, upon which they had a temple, was the proper place to worship

God. (Clarke on Genesis 4: 20), as we learn from the conversation of Christ with the woman of Samaria at Jacob's well. But Christ teaches that we may worship any place: in the solitary plain, or in the opulent city; on the mountain top, or in the lonely glen. "I will, therefore, that men pray everywhere." (Text) But though we may pray acceptably on any part of God's footstool, yet we are commanded not to forsake the assembling of ourselves together "as the manner of some is." (Hebrews 10:25). By prayer we gain the victory.

The Lord has been pleased to put great honor upon prayer. When the Amalekites came out and fought against Israel, at Rephidim, some 20 miles from Mt. Sinai (Exodus 17:8) before they reached Mt. Sinai, (Exodus 2), Moses sent out an army under Joshua to fight them while he took Aaron and Hur, and went up to the top of a hill, where with outstretched hands he implored help from God. But his strength failed, his hands dropped. Then Amalek prevailed. Now Aaron and Hur seated Moses upon a stone, and one on each side stayed up his hands until the going down of the syn, and Joshua discomfited Moses and his people with the edge of the sword (Exodus 17:8-13).

Here in their first battle God honored public prayer on the hilltop in the sight of the two contending armies. But not only has God stamped public prayer with his peculiar approbation, but also secret prayer has been sanctioned with his peculiar favor. When the Israelites were encamped at Mount Horeb (Exodus 33:6,7), Moses pitched the tabernacle without the camp, afar off. And when it came to pass that every one [who] sought the Lord went out unto the tabernacle of the congregation (Exodus 33:7). When Moses went out, all the people stood in their tent doors and looked after him until he was gone into the tabernacle. As he entered, the cloudy pillar descended and stood at the door of the tabernacle,

"And the Lord talked with Moses ... face to face, as a man speaketh unto his friend." (Exodus 33:10,11) While in these tabernacles we abide, let us call upon God—"Everywhere."

II.   How should we pray? Answer: We should pray, "Lifting up holy hands, without wrath and doubting," (Text) as Moses did. He was not filled with wrath, neither did he give place to doubting. We must pray in spirit. "God is a spirit: and they that worship him must worship him in spirit and in truth." (Genesis 4:24) We cannot worship God in Spirit if the heart is full of wrath.

Hecatombs[6] of victims and rivers of libations avail nothing; with

6   In ancient Greece and Rome, a hecatomb was a public sacrifice of 100 oxen to the gods. It can refer to any great slaughter.

these we cannot worship God. Neither does prayer depend for its value upon the vociferousness of the individual. To worship God properly, the spirit must be engaged in worship. It should be a time of feasting to the spirit. The Jews regarded feasting upon the animal sacrificed as part of the sacrificial service (Smith, vol. I, pp. 223, 226) And when we offer up sacrifice of prayer and praise, it should be a time of feasting to the soul. This should ever be regarded as part of the sacrificial service.

To go through the form of worship without having the spirit engaged in worship is but mockery. The Jews fell into this sin. "This people draw near me with their mouth, and with their lips do honor me, but have removed their heart far from me." (Isaiah 29:13) Let us divest ourselves of indifference in the worship of God, as this is exceedingly blamable.

Among the Athenians it was considered very blamable for a member of the court of Areopagus to laugh during the sitting of the court. (Robbins, p. 179. Ancient.) The Areopagus was a court held at Athens, famous for its justice and impartiality. Their sessions were in the night that they might not be diverted by objects of sight, or influenced by the presence and actions of the speakers. (Webster)

And how much more blamable is indifference in the presence of God? O for that fervence of soul the Psalmist had when he said, "My soul waiteth for the Lord more than they that watch for the morning; I say, more than they that watch for the morning." (Psalm 130:6) As the watchman, after a long watch in a cold winter's night, would anxiously look toward the east for the dawning of the morning,with such fervency should the soul wait for the Lord, yea "More than they that watch for the morning."

We must lift up holy hands without doubting. We must believe that we receive. "What things soever ye desire when ye pray, believe that ye receive them, and ye shall have them." (Mark 11:24) Believe that ye receive the grant of them in the mind of the Deity, and ye shall have them in the proper time. But we must patiently wait God's own good time to give us the evidence of his having heard us by giving the thing we desire. The Lord may delay a little, as when Abraham requested that God would give him some evidence that his seed should inherit the land of Canaan. He was commanded to take a heifer, a goat, and a ram, each to be three years old, and a turtle dove, and a young pigeon, to be offered in sacrifice to God. Abraham prepared them. The animals he divided, and laid the halves over against each other.

This was the most solemn of all forms of ratifying a treaty,   or covenant, among ancient nations—to divide the carcass of a victim lengthwise and place the halves opposite each other. Then the covenanting parties entered at the opposite extremes of the passage thus formed, met in the middle, and there took the oath. (Reitto, vol. I, p. 199, 200).

When Abraham had thus prepared the victims and was ready to receive the evidence that his seed should inherit the Promised Land, God did not immediately come to give the evidence. Abraham patiently waited. The fowls came to feed on his offerings, but he drove them away. (Genesis 15:11) And it was not till the sun was going down that the evidence was furnished. Had this token been given at noon day, it would not have shown so brightly—God delays till the blessing will be most beneficial to us—"And when the sun went down and it was dark, behold a smoking furnace and a burning lamp that passed between those pieces," (Genesis 15:12-17) Thus we must patiently wait, and keep the fowls of unbelief from devouring our sacrifice. "I waited patiently for the Lord; and he inclined unto me, and heard my cry," (Psalm 40:1). Thus let us cry unto him, and patiently wait his own good time.

III.   Why should we Pray? Answer: Because Christ "gave himself a ransom for all," (v. 6) By the use of Prayer we are to secure to ourselves the forgiveness of our sins and the blessing of God. As Solomon prayed at the dedication of the temple, that in case the heaven should in future days be shut up and there should be no rain, that if they should pray toward the temple and confess the name of God and turn from their sins that then God might hear them in heaven and forgive their sin and send rain. (I Kings 8:35,36) So when the heaven is shut up and spiritual blessings are withheld on account of our sins, if we pray toward heaven, his temple, confessing the name of God and turning from our sins, then we shall be forgiven and receive the grace of life. Hence we should pray, that we may be the happy participants of the riches of heaven, purchased for us by the ransom paid for our Redemption --
> "Prayer is appointed to convey
> The blessings God designs to give ..."
> -- riches that are imperishable.

Riches of this world Christ has not promised in abundance to his people. Though our bread shall be given, and our water shall be sure (Isaiah 33:16), yet in respect to riches it is the lot of many of Christ's disciples in this respect not to be above their Master—who, though he created the heavens and spangled them with suns and moons. and stars; though he created the earth and placed the cattle upon a thousand hills; though he created the fowls of the heavens and the fishes of the sea and creeping things; yet, when he was upon earth, he could say, "The foxes have holes, and the birds of the air have nests; but the Son of Man hath not where to lay his head," (Matthew 8:20).

But Jesus has a kingdom just beyond this vale of tears that shall remain when the light of the sun shall be lost in the conflagration of this world, a kingdom whose durability shall be eternal. To this kingdom the child of Jesus is heir. "Blessed be the God and Father of our Lord Jesus Christ, which according to His abundant mercy hath begotten us again unto a lively hope by the resurrection of Jesus Christ from the dead, to an inheritance incorruptible and undefiled, and that fadeth not away, reserved in heaven for you who are kept by the power of God through faith unto salvation, ready to be revealed in the last time." (I Peter 1:3-5).

> "There we shall see his face,
> And never, never sin;
> There from the rivers of his grace
> Drink endless pleasures in."

There "They shall hunger no more, neither thirst any more; neither shall the sun light on them, nor any heat. For the Lamb which is in the midst of the throne shall feed them, and lead them unto living fountains of waters: and God shall wipe away all tears from their eyes." (Revelation 7:16,17.) "There shall be no more death, neither sorrow, nor crying, neither shall there be any more pain; for the former things are passed away." (Revelation 21:4) 0 let us pray everywhere; wherever the providence of God may cast our lot, till we quit this vale of tears and meet in glory.

542 God Be with You Till We Meet Again

1 God be with you till we meet again; lov - ing
2 God be with you till we meet again; un - seen
3 God be with you till we meet again; when life's
4 God be with you till we meet again; keep love's

coun - sels guide, up - hold you, with a shep - herd's care en -
wings pro - tect - ing hide you, dai - ly man - na still pro -
per - ils thick con - found you, put un - fail - ing arms a -
ban - ner float - ing o'er you; smite death's threat - ening wave be -

fold you:
vide you: God be with you till we meet a - gain.
round you:
fore you:

After writing the first stanza of his "Christian Good-bye," the author sent it to two composers, one celebrated and one unknown, to see how each would set it. This is the second person's tune, which the author found more effective and used for the hymn's first publication.

TEXT: Jeremiah Eames Rankin, 1880, alt.
MUSIC: William G. Tomer, 1880

GOD BE WITH YOU
9.8.8.9
(German tune: RANDOLPH, 541)

ALPHEUS FREED

SIN NOT FORGOTTEN

> Numbers 32:23. But if ye will not do so, behold ye have sinned against the Lord: and be sure your sin will find you out.

Lesson: Psalm 4   Luke 10:1-16.

Hymns 1:193, 2:190, 2:250.

Among the children of Israel there were two tribes, Reuben and Gad, that were very rich in cattle. They "had a great multitude." (Numbers 32:1) When the Israelites were encamped in the plains of Moab (their last encampment. Numbers 25:1. Benson) these tribes came to Moses and to Eleazar and unto the princes of the congregation (Numbers 32:2) desiring that, as the land east of the Jordan was a land for cattle and as they had cattle, their possession might be given to them there. Moses was much displeased with their proposal, as this would discourage the people from going over the Jordan. (Numbers 32:1-15) But they proposed to leave their cattle and families and go armed before the children of Israel till they had brought them unto their place. (Numbers 32:16-19) Moses now agreed that if they would do this, they and half the tribe of Manasseh (v. 33) should have their possession on the east of the Jordan, as they desired. Then he said, in the language of the text, "But if ye will not do so, behold ye have sinned against the Lord: and be sure your sin will find you out."

I. In what would their sin consist? Answer: in failing to fulfill the solemn promise they had made. Thus many sin against the Lord. They solemnly promised to serve the Lord all the days of their life, but alas, they have long since forsaken him. This is a great sin. He who enters as a partner into a solemn business transaction with another party breaks the engagement and forsakes the other party to his injury without any fault on his part. Such a man would be considered guilty of a great wrong. How much more is he guilty who engaged to serve Christ and has forsaken him? Was there any fault on his part? You are injuring his cause. You have promised your dying friends to meet them in heaven. You have often promised the Lord and yourself that you would become religious, but still you fail to come up to your promise. Will you continue to neglect and injure Him who broke down the powerful fortification

Satan had thrown around the hopes of man to hold his soul in eternal despair? What a work this was! When the walls of Jericho were to be brought down and the city given to the Jews, they marched round it each day once, for six days. Seven priests marching before the ark, bearing seven trumpets of rams' horns. The seventh day they were to compass the city seven times. The priests were to blow with the trumpets, the people were to shout, and the walls were to fall. And thus it was. (Joshua 6:3-6,20). But when the wall Satan erected was to be brought down, not six days only of preparation were necessary, but four thousand years before the gospel trumpet could be blown to all to excite shouts of joy in every part of the world. Now angels and men can say, "Glory to God in the highest, and on earth peace, good will toward men." (Luke 2:14).

II. Be sure your sin will find you out. You may now imagine that all these broken promises are forgotten, but they will find you out at the day of judgment. How will you escape them? When the Saviour sent out the seventy disciples to preach, he commanded them that in whatsoever city they should enter and the people refuse to receive them, they should go into the streets of the same and say, "Even the very dust of city which cleaveth on us we do wipe off against you." And Jesus says, "It shall be more tolerable in that day for Sodom than for that city." (Luke 10:1, 10-12) They had only refused to receive Christ, but broke no promise. You have promised to receive him, but break the promise, and still refuse. Will you hide under the plea of ignorance of your duty? Here your sin will find you out, and will proclaim to you that you had Moses and the prophets. (Luke 16:29)

Will you hide under the plea of inability to comply with the requirement of Christ? Here your sin will find you out, and proclaim to you that he said to you, "My yoke is easy, and my burden is light." (Matthew 11:30) You cannot hide from your sin. The swift winged angel of God's corning judgments will find you out. Are you like Pilate who forsook Christ for fear of offending the Jews? He was persuaded Jesus was a just person. (Matthew 27:24) And when he was on the judgment seat his wife sent unto him, warning him not to have anything to do with that just man, as she had suffered many things that day in a dream because of him. (Matthew 27:19) Yet to please the Jews he scourged Jesus and delivered him to be crucified. (Matthew 27:26) Will you thus scourge him and crucify him to please your fellows?

III. Unless you find out your sin and repent of it, it will be sure to find you out and ruin you for ever. As Pharaoh's sins brought such hosts of locusts upon Egypt that the land was darkened and every green thing was eaten through all the land of Egypt (Exodus 10:15), so your sins will darken your future state and devour every prospect of happiness and leave you to say, "The harvest is past, the summer is ended, and we are not saved." (Jeremiah 8:20) You may now be eating and drinking and making merry, while ruin is just at hand. Thus it was with Israel in the days of Solomon. They were numerous as the sand of the shore, "Eating and drinking and making merry." (I Kings 4:20) But their prosperity and mirth were soon followed by a fall, for no sooner were Solomon's days ended than the nation drifted upon the rock of ruin, split asunder and bade adieu for ever to their former prosperity. So will the tide of time soon take you upon the rock.

You know your duty, and if you do it not your destruction will be certain. You remember that in ancient days a prophet was sent out of Judah to Bethel to prophesy against the altar upon which Jeroboam sacrificed unto the golden calf he had there set up. (I Kings 13:1), as also he set another up at Dan, (I Kings 12:29). Jeroboam stretched out his hand against the prophet. It withered. The prophet prayed, and it was restored. The king desired the man to go home with him, be refreshed, and rewarded. He refused, saying that he was commanded not to eat nor drink nor turn by the same way that he came. So he returned by another way. An old prophet went after, found him sitting under an oak, belied him, saying that an angel commanded him by the word of the Lord to bring him back that he might eat bread and drink water. The prophet obeyed the lying prophet, went back, ate and drank, but on his way was met by a lion and slain on the highway. (I Kings 13:1-25)

You know your duty. If you do it not, be sure your sin will find you out, and will slay you. The lion of sin will meet you on the highway to eternity and slay all your hopes of future happiness and leave you to lie in despair to all eternity.

674   There is a green hill

HORSLEY   CM

Words: Cecil Frances Alexander (1818-95)
Music: William Horsley (1774-1858)

There is a green hill far a-way with-
-out a ci-ty wall, where the dear Lord was
cru-ci-fied, who died to save us all.

1 There is a green hill far away
   without a city wall,
   where the dear Lord was crucified,
   who died to save us all.

2 We may not know, we cannot tell
   what pains He had to bear,
   but we believe it was for us
   He hung and suffered there.

3 He died that we might be forgiven,
   He died to make us good,
   that we might go at last to heaven,
   saved by His precious blood.

4 There was no other good enough
   to pay the price of sin,
   He only could unlock the gate
   of heaven, and let us in.

5 O dearly, dearly has He loved,
   and we must love Him too,
   and trust in His redeeming blood,
   and try His works to do.

Complete Mission Praise, 1999.

ALPHEUS FREED

FAST DAY SERMON

July 1864[7]

Jonah 3:5. So the people of Nineveh believed God, and proclaimed a fast, and put on sackcloth, from the greatest of them even to the least of them.

Lesson: Psalm 46.

Hymns 2:609, 2:600, 2:611

This great humiliation on the part of the people of Nineveh was brought about by a short sermon preached to them by the Prophet Jonah. This was his sermon: "Yet forty days, and Nineveh shall be overthrown." (Jonah 3:4) The people were terrified and quickly took these words to the king. (v. 4) Jonah had not yet reached the royal palace, and as a stranger most likely could not have approached the king, but God sent him the message. When he heard it, he arose from his throne, laid his robes from him, covered himself with sackcloth, and sat in ashes and caused it to be proclaimed throughout Nineveh by the decree of the king and his nobles that neither man nor beast, herd nor flock should taste any thing—food nor drink—but that man and beast should be covered with sackcloth and that the people should cry mightily to God. (v. 6-8) The king and his people believed that ruin was at hand. "So the people of Nineveh believed God, and proclaimed a fast, and put on sackcloth, from the greatest of them even to the least of them." (Text)

I. Nineveh was a great city. It was one of the first founded cities of the world. It was built by Asshur, the son of Shem (Genesis 10:11,22) and grandson of Noah. At the time of Jonah it "Was an exceeding great city of three days' journey" (Jonah 3:3) in its circumference, not closely built. (Ful. Proph. p. 231) It contained more than 120 thousand persons that could not discern between their right hand and their left hand." (ch. 4:11) Children of this age are generally reckoned to form one-fifth of the inhabitants of any place (Ful. Proph. p. 231) The population of Nineveh, then, may have been above 600,000. But though Nineveh was a great city

---

7   Editor's note: This sermon was for a fast day, declared state-wide or perhaps nationally, probably remembrance of the anniversary of the Civil War battles of Petersburg, Virginia, and Atlanta, Georgia, resulting in thousands of casualties, which occurred at the end of July 1864. This sermon was written much later.

and an ancient city, yet God purposed to destroy it. We may learn here that the most exalted position to which a nation can rise will not exempt it from the judgments of God, nor from entire destruction. Where is Tyre? Babylon? We are a great nation, raised up, doubtless, for special purposes among the Nations of the earth. But if we betray our trust, our greatness will not shield us from the sword of a sin-avenging God.

Battle of Atlanta, July 1864. Niday Picture Library / Alamy Stock Photo

II. They fasted and turned from their sins. (Jonah 3:8) Fasting has been practiced by different nations, from very ancient days, in times of affliction and mourning. (Wat. Die. on Fasting) Joshua and the elders of Israel, soon after they crossed the Jordan, prostrated themselves before the ark, putting dust upon their heads, and remained there without eating till the eventide. (Joshua, 7:6,7) It was a time of mourning to them. One of their number had sinned when they took Jericho. God had warned them against taking anything that was cursed except the gold and silver, and vessels of brass and iron. They were consecrated unto the Lord, and were to come into the treasure of the Lord. (Joshua 6:17-19) So they destroyed the city and burnt it (6:24) But Achan saved to himself a goodly Babylonish garment, 200 sheckels of silver, and a wedge of gold of 50 sheckels. (Joshua 7:20,21) Soon after Jericho was destroyed Joshua sent about 3000 men to destroy Ai. But the men of Ai chased them and slew 36 of them. (Joshua 7:25) Then Joshua and the elders mourned and fasted. And God assured them that they could not stand before their enemies till the accursed thing was taken away from them. (ch. 7:13) And Achan and his sons and daughters (which doubtless were in the secret) and all that he had were stoned and burned with fire. (Joshua 7:24,25) As Achan's sin brought Israel into trouble, so doubtless we have had Achans whose sins have brought on our troubles. And as the 36 innocent men suffered death, so have many suffered who were innocent of the sin that brought the trouble. And as Joshua and the Elders of Israel humbled themselves, so it behooves us to humble ourselves. As the people of Nineveh fasted and prayed, so it becomes us to fast and pray. As they turned from their sins and from the violence that was in their hands, (Joshua 3:8) so must we. In this is our hope, that the great sin, and the violence, is being put away.

III. Nineveh was not destroyed because the people humbled themselves. When Jonah was commanded to preach that the city should be destroyed in 40 days (ch. 3:1-4) it was a conditional threatening. Otherwise it would have been useless to send them a warning. Had they refused to heed the warning they would have been destroyed. At a later day they were destroyed, and Nineveh long since has been in ruins. But at this time they were saved from the threatening ruin. We see then that in such cases prayer and fasting can change the purposes of God. Hence, let us be encouraged. The course of events for years have indicated that God had a quarrel with this nation, and that our ruin was a thing not impossible. But as the nation this day is called to humiliation and prayer, we hope that God will be gracious unto us and spare us.

Not Devoured {Conditions}

Refused {Destroy}

Later Day

Prayer first {Change}

Encouraged {gracious}

Practiced {Office}

Josh. Elders {Ark}

Achan {3 000} {36}

As Achan's {trouble} (36)

As Josh. {King} {sins vic.}

Hope

Great City {1st Ath}

3 Days {120,000} {600,000}

Exalted {Type} {Baby}

We Great {special}

Betray {Shield}

Jonah 3:5. "So the people of Nineveh believed in God, and proclaimed a fast, and put on sackcloth, from the greatest of them even to the least of them."

Humilia. {Sermons} "Ezek 46."

To King {strangers}

Robes. Sack. {Ashes}

Fast. Decree {Man. Beast} {Cry}

Believed

"So the." Text

Alpheus' speaker notes for his Fast Day Sermon.

Jesus, lover of my soul, Let me to thy bosom fly,
While the nearer waters roll, While the tempest still is high;
Hide me, O my Saviour, hide, Till the storm of life is past;
Safe into the haven guide. O receive my soul at last.

2   Other refuge have I none; Hangs my helpless soul on thee:
Leave, O leave me not alone; Still support and comfort me:
All my trust on thee is stay'd; All my help from thee I bring;
Cover my defenseless head With the shadow of thy wing.

3   Thou, O Christ, art all I want: More than all in thee I find:
Raise the fallen, cheer the faint, Heal the sick, and lead the blind.
Just and holy is thy name; I am all unrighteousness;
False, and full of sin I am; Thou art full of truth and grace.

4   Plenteous grace with thee is found,——Grace to cover all my sin:
Let the healing streams abound; Make and keep me pure within.
Thou of life the fountain art; Freely let me take of thee:
Spring thou up within my heart; Rise to all eternity.

Jesus, lover of my Soul," Hymns for the Use of the Methodist Episcopal Church, revised edition, 1870.

ALPHEUS FREED

THE KINGDOM OF HEAVEN

> Matthew 13:44. Again, the kingdom of heaven is like unto treasure hid in a field; the which when a man hath found, he hideth, and for joy thereof goeth and selleth all that he hath, and buyeth that field.

> Lesson: Proverbs 3:1-18, I Peter 1:1-16.

> Hymns 1:250, 2:261, 2:552.

The kingdom of heaven mentioned in the text is the inward kingdom which Christ sets up in the soul. It is the kingdom of which St. Paul speaks, saying "The kingdom of God is not meat and drink; but righteousness and peace and joy in the Holy Ghost." (Romans 14:17) Why is the inward kingdom of Christ like "Treasure hid in a field?"

I. Because it is of very great value, as the treasures were which were hid in the field. Men would not hide that which was of no value. No practice, it is said, was more common than that of hiding valuable articles in a field or garden because the people had not any place of safety in which to deposit their riches; and because their rapacious rulers were sure to find a pretext for accusation against them in order to draw their riches from them. Hence men of great wealth often affected great poverty and walked about in mean apparel in order to deceive their neighbors.

And hence arose the practice of hiding treasure in the earth. It is supposed that without a doubt there are immense treasures buried in the earth at this day. It is related of a certain individual who ascended a Palmyrah tree[8] to lop off the upper branches that one of them struck into the ground. On taking it out, he saw something yellow. He looked, he looked and found an earthen vessel full of gold coins and other articles of value. (Bush on Matthew 13:44)

As these treasures are of great value, so is religion. It ameliorates the condition of men in this life. It assuages the grief of earth by bringing men into an amicable relation with their Creator. And after death it will introduce them into the ambrosial joys of heaven. It is antidote to the atrophy of sin, the wasting disease of sin which wastes away the sensibilities of the soul. And when the soul is riven [split apart] with sorrows of earth it points the aspiring spirit on high. It comforts when

Satan assails us.

What would we be without the religion of Jesus? Look to heathen lands and you have the answer. Our souls would be in the power of the devil, and doomed to look only downward for ever and ever, like the poor woman in the gospel whom Satan had afflicted eighteen years and who could in no wise lift up herself. (Luke 13:11-16) But Jesus breaks the power of the devil. The soul rises as the cork rises to the surface of the water when the thread is broken which held it under the water. The soul then looks to things eternal where the joy of one day shall more than countervail the sufferings of life. There we shall wear the diadem of unfading glory.

II. Religion is like hid treasure, because it must be sought for in public or private. It cannot be purchased. These are the things which are hid from the wise and prudent, and are revealed unto babes. (Luke 10:21) Religion is not like hid treasure in this respect: that its possessor is to retire into solitude, seclude himself, and live the life of a hermit. "Let your light so shine before men that they may see your good works, and glorify your Father which is in heaven." (Matthew 5:16) We are to show ourselves, and not fear Satan, our clandestine foe, nor the whole clan of his emissaries.

Religion is hid from the impenitent and must be sought for earnestly. There should be compatibility between our desire for and our effort to obtain religion. We should concentrate every power of the soul in our effort to obtain religion, and saving our souls from sinking into the abaddon,[9] the bottomless pit, the abode of woe. While devils meet in their pandemonium to concert secret schemes for our ruin, let us be intent in our effort to obtain the favor of God.

We must seek earnestly, as Solomon says, speaking the knowledge of God, "If thou criest after knowledge and liftest up thy voice for understanding; if thou seekest her as silver and searchest for her as for hid treasure; then shalt thou understand the fear of the Lord and find the knowledge of God." (Proverbs 2:3-5) There must be an earnestness.

See the Thirsty Hart upon the mountain ready to perish with thirst. With what eagerness does he seek for water. So the soul is to seek after God. "As the hart panteth after the water brook, so panteth my soul after thee, O God." (Psalm 42:1) It requires effort to break loose from the power of the wicked one. He will not easily allow his prey to escape. You recollect that when Jesus commanded the unclean spirit to

---

9   Abaddon: A place of destruction; the depths of hell. Job 28:22, Revelation 9:11.

come out of the man, it was not till he had torn him and cried with a loud voice that he came out. (Mark 1:25,26) The Penitent, as much as possible, should have his eyes closed to every thing of earth. As Saul was without sight for three days from his conviction to his conversion, (Acts 9:9) so should the Penitent close his eyes to all things but Christ, the great light. Avoid mirth. Avoid being trifling. Close your eyes when praying. The mind then will be more fully fixed upon God and upon Christ.

But we are not to suppose that because earnestness required that it is because of any intricate questions or things hard to be understood or because the scriptures darken the subject with a circumlocution of words. Nay, the disconsolate soul in quest of the bread of life has no perplexing difficulties to solve, but may quickly realize the verification of the gracious promise of Christ which says, "Seek and ye shall find." (Matthew 7:7)

III. We must seek by Faith, as the Saviour said to the man whose son had a dumb spirit When he besought Christ to cast him out, Jesus said unto him, "If thou canst believe, all things are possible to him that believeth. And straightway the father of the child cried out, and said with tears, "Lord, I believe; help thou mine unbelief." Christ commanded the spirit, and he came out. (Mark 9:17-26) Faith has power to remove the mountain of sin from the soul, and fill the troubled spirit with the peace of Eden. As Paul and Silas said to the trembling Philippian jailor, "Believe on the Lord Jesus Christ and thou shalt be saved." (Acts 16:31) Faith in its triumphant march beats down every rampart of the wicked one, and conducts the light of the Sun of Righteousness into the soul, as a triumphant conqueror leads his army into the city which has trembled and fallen before his conquering arm. Victory will perch upon the banner of faith in spite of all the powers of hell. "He that believeth and is baptized shall be saved." (Mark 16:16)

IV.   He who obtains the favor of God has joy, as he who findeth the hid treasure, "And for joy thereof goeth and selleth all that he hath and buyeth that field." (Text) Part with all sinful pleasures, for at death they will part with you. They will leave you, and when the storms of life are in eternity you will find yourself like [the] wreck of a vessel on the sea shore after a dreadful storm * a hopeless and depraved being. O that the blessed Spirit of God may find you out before it is too late! God invites. The Angel of Heaven says "Come to the Spirit;" the bride says "Come to this beautiful and cleansing fountain open in the blessed side of Jesus; to the house of [the Lord] I will [go] for sin and uncleanness.[10]

10   From the * to this point, this insertion is written in another hand, with grammar and syntax which are definitely not Alpheus'. It appears that it may have been Summerfield, or possibly his mother, adding a fiery flourish.

Christ fills the soul with life and joy. He does not raise a soul from spiritual death, as the witch of Endor raised Samuel who, though he was raised, still was of the dead. (I Samuel 28:12) He raises the soul, as he raised Lazarus, to life. And as Lazarus, after his resurrection sat at the table with Christ as Bethany where they made him a supper, (John 11:43,44; 12:1,2) so is the soul to sit at the table with him and feast upon the pure perennial peace and bliss of heaven. We shall have joy. This joy shall be eternal. Well may we sacrifice every thing of earth "For joy thereof." (Text) All of this world's princely pageantry are but like the deciduous foliage of the forest tree, doomed to perish. Why then should we be so enamored with the ephemeral pleasures of earth which, like Jonah's gourd, come and depart almost simultaneously (Jonah 4:10), while religion offers us joy under all circumstances? You may imprison the Christian in the darkest and most solitary grotto [cave] of the most barren mountain, and still he has joy unspeakable and full of glory. For the genial rays of the Sun of Righteousness shall transform solitude into a Paradise. His presence can inspire the soul with bliss in darkest days. O that the soul may even gravitate toward the city on high, the center of creation!

There we shall wear a sparkling diadem of unfading glory. A crown which shall emit rays of glory, the faintest of which shall eclipse the richest costumes of earthly glory and grandeur. A crown of rejoicing which will infinitely more than counterbalance all the loss we sustain in the sacrifices we make to secure the hid treasure. Then, like the man who found the hid treasure, let us part with every thing which hinders us from obtaining and retaining the treasure after we have found it. And soon we shall range the delectable fields of glory. Religion causes the fields that spread out before us in the future to bloom with bliss and fills the soul with glory. O that you may seek and find the treasure and never with it part!

366 Love Divine, All Loves Excelling

1 Love divine, all loves excelling, Joy of heaven, to
2 Breathe, O breathe thy loving Spirit into every
3 Come, Almighty, to deliver; let us all thy
4 Finish then thy new creation; pure and spotless

earth come down, fix in us thy humble dwelling; all thy
troubled breast; let us all in thee inherit; let us
life receive; suddenly return, and never, never-
let us be; let us see thy great salvation perfect-

faithful mercies crown. Jesus, thou art all compassion;
find the promised rest. Take away the love of sinning;
more thy temples leave. Thee we would be always blessing,
ly restored in thee: changed from glory into glory;

This text and this tune occur in almost all English-language hymnals (though not always together). The transforming power of love motivates the unending praise of the life to come, and this fine Welsh tune (whose name means "delightful") gives us a foretaste of endless song.

TEXT: Charles Wesley, 1747, alt.
MUSIC: Rowland Hugh Prichard, 1831, alt.

HYFRYDOL
8.7.8.7 D

Glory to God: The Presbyterian Hymnal, 2013.

ALPHEUS FREED

JOURNEYING TO CANAAN

> Numbers 10:29. We are journeying unto the place of which the Lord said, I will give it you: come thou with us, and we will do thee good: for the Lord hath spoken good concerning Israel.

> Lesson: Psalm 91. Genesis 12:1-18.

> Hymns 2:8, 1:284, 2:553.

These words were spoken by Moses to Hobab at the foot of Mt. Sinai. The Israelites left Egypt on the 15th day of the first month of their ecclesiastical year, beginning some time in our March. Their civil year commenced in our September. (Clarke on Exodus 12:1-12) They were 45 [days] from the time they left Egypt until they reached Mt. Sinai. (Clarke on Exodus 19:1) At Mt. Sinai they remained encamped 11 months and 20 days (Clarke on Numbers 10:11) Here Hobab (father-in-law to Moses, (Judges 4:11) visited them, and when they were about to depart,

> "Moses said unto Hobab, the son of Raguel the Midianite, Moses' father in law, We are journeying unto the place of which the Lord said, I will give it you: come thou with us, and we will do thee good: for the Lord hath spoken good concerning Israel. And he said unto him, I will not go; but I will depart to mine own land, and to my kindred. And he said, Leave us not, I pray thee; for as much as thou knowest how we are to encamp in the wilderness, and thou mayest be to us instead of eyes. And it shall be, if thou go with us, yea, it shall be, that what goodness the Lord shall do unto us, the same will we do unto thee. (v. 29-32)"

It appears that he now yielded to the request of Moses and accompanied them, for we find in the book of Judges (chapter 4:11) that his descendants dwelt among the Israelites in the days of the Judges.

As Moses said to Hobab, so do we now say to you. "We are journeying unto the place of which the Lord said, I will give it you: come thou with us, and we will do thee good: for the Lord hath spoken good concerning Israel."

I. We find here that the great burden that rested most heavily upon the heart of Moses was the welfare of the church of God. For the good of the church it was that he desired the services of Hobab. Hence, "Thou mayest be to us instead of eyes." (v. 31) He felt deeply interested for the prosperity of the church. This was the burden of his soul, even down to death. For when God commanded him to go up into the Mount Abarim and view the promised land, and informed him that then he should die and not enter the land, (Numbers 27:12-15) he at first entreated the Lord that he might enter the holy land. (Deuteronomy 3:23-26) For this privilege he suffered in Egypt—in the wilderness. For near 40 years this hope gave buoyancy to his soul under the most herculean difficulties. But when he received a positive denial, what was his next concern? Not any interest of his family next occupied his mind. The welfare of the church immediately occupied his attention, and we hear him saying, "Let the Lord, the God of the spirits of all flesh, set a man over the congregation which may go in before them and which may lead them out and which may bring them in; that the congregation of the Lord be not as sheep which have no shepherd." (Numbers 27:16,17)

How different is the conduct of very many! How many who, for a little self-interest or sinful gratification, will stab the church. How many by their inconsistencies dishonor the God whom they profess to love, for St. Paul says, "Thou that makest thy boast of the law, through breaking the law dishonorest thou God. For the name of God is blasphemed among the Gentiles through you." (Romans 2:23,24) Some conduct themselves as though a Christian's main business was to accumulate money, to imburse [fill] his coffers. They have no care for the church. O for zeal! Is the zeal of Moses no longer imitable? Has it become altogether inimitable in these days? Let us not sacrifice Christ upon the altar of the world. Let us not immolate principle upon the altars of mammon. Let us glorify God, and seek the good of the church, and we shall soon be admitted to all the immunities which the immutable promise of God sacredly guarantees to every child of Jesus.

Let us exhibit the zeal for the glory of Christ's kingdom which men exhibit for the glory of their cities or their states. Look at the spirit of emulation abroad. The great emporiums of the land are expending vast sums in constructing public works to facilitate trade and draw the wealth of nations into their bosom. And shall we be inactive and feel no interest in the honor and glory of Christ's kingdom? In disseminating the truths of the Bible far and wide? O let us labor for Christ, that at his coming the high encomium[11] of "well done" may salute our ears and we may enter into the enchanting home of the faithful which is already so endeared to our heart:—where Jesus is—whither friends have gone.

II. Let us notice the good that would accrue to Hobab by going

---

11   Encomium: A formal expression of high praise.

with the Israelites. The good contemplated was that he should share in the land of promise, which was goodly land. Moses said to Israel, "The land whither thou goest in to possess it is not as the land of Egypt from whence ye came out, where thou didst sow thy seed and didst water it with thy foot as a garden of herbs." (Deuteronomy 11:10) Where they should be free from toils to which they were exposed in Egypt.

In Egypt very little rain ever falls, never sufficient quantities to fructify the land. (Wat. Dic. on Nile) But this want of rain is supplied by the annual inundations [floods] of the Nile. Such vegetables however as require more moisture than is supplied by these inundations are refreshed with water drawn out of the Nile and deposited in cisterns with plugs fixed in the bottom. The fields are generally ploughed in rills[12] and when the gardener wishes to water the field he removes this plug and conducts the stream from rill to rill, and thus sends it over the whole field. When he wishes to turn the stream from one trench to another, he opens a new trench with his mattock,[13] at the same time turning the earth into the old trench with his foot. (Horne vol. II, p. 176) The whole land of Egypt was anciently sluiced in this manner with innumerable canals and water courses to carry the water of the Nile through every part of the valley through which it runs. (Bush on Psalm 1:3)

But in the land of Canaan they rested from this toil. It was a land of hills and valleys, a land that drank water of the rain of heaven. (Deuteronomy 11:11,12) And in this land Hobab was to share if he would but go with the people of God. And if you, dear unconverted friend, will go with us, good shall accrue to you. You shall share in the land of Canaan on high, which is a land of hills of pleasure, a land with fertile valleys of undying joys, a land that drinks the fertilizing waters of Jehovah's presence for ever. There we shall rest from labor for ever. We are going to a county upon which the curse of God has never yet fallen. Our present place of abode is one upon which the curse of God has pressed for near 6000 years! Here we are doomed to eat our bread in the sweat of our face till we return to the ground. (Genesis 3:19) But upon that country the smile of Jehovah has ever played. No cloud of gloom has ever rolled over the territory of the eternal kingdom whither we are journeying.

> When shall I reach that happy place
> And be forever blest?
> When shall I see my Father's face,
> And in his bosom rest?"

---

12   2   Rills: Long narrow trenches. Here, irrigation ditches.
13   3   Mattock: An instrument for loosening the soil in digging, shaped like a pickaxe, but having one end broad instead of pointed. *Random House Dictionary*.

O will you not pursue that course which will cause Jehovah to look with complacency upon you in this world, and which will conduct you to happiness eternal in the world to come? Here we all are heirs [of] pain and disappointment from the day we enter upon the arena of life to the day of death! But soon a brighter world will loom up to the vision of the soul! Then, with lowliness of heart let us press onward. Come, go with us! We will do thee good.

III. The want of a disposition on the part of Hobab to go with the people of God is characteristic of man. Will you go with us, or will you refuse? Remember, sirs, soon the comedy of your merry life in this world will close for ever. O strive to retrieve the loss you sustained in Adam, and conciliate the favor of God. Do not excuse yourself by saying that you do not feel like going. Your want of feeling will not excuse you. Suppose I were to see a man drowning and refused to rescue him, would I be excused should I declare that I felt no inclination to assist him? Your soul is sinking — you know it — and you should at once take that course which will save it. Do your duty, and God will do the rest. Every man has the power of fixing the destiny of his own soul.

Man, what is he compared with the holy angels who at the bidding of Jehovah wing their way to this earth to perform the will of the Supreme One? He is but dust and ashes (Psalm 103:14) to be laid in the balance. He is altogether lighter than vanity. (Psalm 62:9) And yet he possesses a power which might well make an angel tremble — the power of saving or ruining a soul. O then come to Christ. Come with us. Lay up your treasure in heaven. The gospel says to each, "Come thou with us." It casts an eye of mercy to every part of the world. As the twelve oxen which bore up the molten sea which Solomon made in the temple looked toward the north, south, east, and west (I Kings 7: 23-26) so does the Bible, which bears the sea of God's mercy to a fallen world. It casts an eye laden with richest mercy to every mountain top and every valley deep, and bids all drink and live forever.

O Repent and forsake your evil ways or you never can enter the Land of Promise. God has so taught, and is not this then a cogent reason why you should be deeply concerned to have your soul, now so callous, freed from the pestiferous disease of sin? Has your heart become so petrified by your flagrant crimes as to remove you beyond the possibility of being made to feel? Is every avenue that leads to the soul so guarded as to make your heart impervious to gospel light? Will you continue to drink the opiate of sin and pleasantly sleep till the soul sinks into the opaque regions of endless woe?

Come with me. We are journeying through this rough and thorny vale of tears to fairer worlds on high. There we shall possess mansions, for Jesus has said, "In my Father's house there are many mansions; if it were not so, I would have told you. I go to prepare a place for you. I will come again and receive you unto myself; that where I am, there ye may be also." (John 14:2,3) There the journey shall end. There we shall find a place of rest.

645   Faith of Our Fathers

1. Faith of our fa - thers! liv - ing still in spite of dun - geon,
2. Faith of our fa - thers! we will strive to win all na - tions
3. Faith of our fa - thers! we will love both friend and foe in

fire, and sword: oh, how our hearts beat high with joy
un - to thee, and through the truth that comes from God,
all our strife, and preach thee, too, as love knows how,

when-e'er we hear that glo - rious word! Faith of our fa - thers,
the world shall then be tru - ly free: faith of our fa - thers,
by kind - ly words and vir - tuous life: faith of our fa - thers,

ho - ly faith! We will be true to thee till death!
ho - ly faith! We will be true to thee till death!
ho - ly faith! We will be true to thee till death!

WORDS: Frederick W. Faber, 1849
MUSIC: Henri F. Hemy, 1864; James G. Walton, 1874

ST. CATHERINE
8.8.8.8.8.8

Celebrating Grace Hymnal, 2010.

Rev. Alpheus Freed with his wife, Louisa Stephenson Freed, and daughters
Eldorado (above) and Esther. About 1889, Coffeyville, Kansas

SERMONS BY
JAMES BENSON FREED

BENSON FREED

THE POWER OF INFLUENCE

I.   Its effect upon the mind, upon the eye, ear.[1]

Mind and matter are the chief spokes in the great wheel of the universe. Detract from the latter the rich wealth of beauty that possesses it and the former sinks into a deplorable leanness. Here would be the gem without deep development. Mind could scarcely ever exist where matter did not. The mind must have an object after which to aspire. If that sought for something is as the savory bubble upon the sea, it becomes lean and mean. Close the eye to the rich wealth of nature and mind will reach out and beyond, not that vision has any present object but it had a fore knowledge. Where sight is void, appreciation of natur[al] beauty fails. Can I be fascinated with that I have never seen? There may stir a quick inward emotion at the recital [account] of a land bathed in perpetual sun light.

[That sought-for something] would be as the kernel in the acorn left to blanch and weather on the burning sands of Africa. The barbarian is not ignorant of the fact that as the crystallizing wave of civilization rolls on, that he is to possess this golden gem of universal admiration. He soon launches his frail barque upon the boundless sea of futurity, flings her silken sails to the quivering breeze, scans the crystal waters of America's proudest oceans and seas to swell the lofty anthems of the sweeping millions. Thus by the influence of impression he has learned to appreciate, in part at least, the wealth and grandeur of life.

Any object presented to the mind influences it to a greater or lesser degree. Varied and many reasons may be advanced to claim that those upon whom its shadows have fallen are far from such impressions. The assassin's knife has scarce sundered the cord of 1ife ere the mind that plotted mischief is paralyzed in hopeless horror. The whole land is bathed in terror. All sit upon the throne of judgment to condemnation.

We claim that evil makes no impression upon the mind of him who is far from it. [But] impression is made without effect. If no influence is made, why meditate upon it? However insignificant and frightful an object may be in itself, it carries an influence. We see the serpent. It is removed from our sight. Yet the form, color, and all connected with it lingers in the memory so distinctly and irresistibly fixed we could not, if we would, forget it. Through the long line of prophecy the golden corridors of time have echoed with the good, the worthy and the true. That I possess a power called the human will is no proof that I can rid myself from thought. However little the spark may be it will grow, if fanned, into a bright brilliant flame until its curling form wraps the azure brow of heaven [in] horror. So also will the powers of the mind, counteracted by evil, become as great insurpassive [unsurpassable] mountains to stay future glory.

--*Benson Freed*

Conversation.

Thought remains as dead upon its throne where speech is void.

It may wander out in imagination, through floating seas, and beyond rolling planets, fixed stars, fiery suns, and pale moons. Hail the Invisible. Take its stand upon the golden throne of meditation, when it is heard to pour fourth the sublime strain.

Benson Freed, an excerpt from the manuscript of "Conversation."

BENSON FREED

CONVERSATION

Thought remains as dead upon its throne where speech is void. It may wander out in imagination, through floating seas, and beyond rolling planets, fixed stars, fiery suns, and pale moons, hail the

Invisible, take its stand upon the golden throne of meditation. When it is heard to pour forth the sublime strain:

"Let the words of my mouth, and the meditations of my heart be acceptable in thy sight, O Lord, my strength and my Redeemer."[2]

Man may commune with God but God alone, as we cannot understand the flow of human thought.

We may trace it to thought, and thought to mind, and mind to its giver, who is God, and God to his Godhead, when we are lost in the boundless sea of mystery. Communing with one another we learn to know and are known. Then "let our conversation be as becometh the gospel."[3]

Systems begin, and end, eternity rolls on [its] endless years, bearing its millions of victims down the broad current of time. Men become entangled in worldly pursuits. The love of fortune and of fame leads them to do that which is unjust. Floods of heart rendering oaths burn upon their polluted tongue as they converse with their friends.

Who can estimate the unlimited power of the evils growing out of conversation! It is beyond man's highest conception. The bright and blazing sun with its orient locks the moon and twinkling stars with man. And all created matter are approaching that period when they shall mantle themselves in the drapery of destruction and fall beneath the marching ages of unknown eternity, never to be unchained from their slavery. But pure or impure conversation will leave lasting impressions upon the heart and mind of friends or foe which shall never be erased by the flight of years. Hence we should cultivate good morals, thus becoming holy in all manner of conversation.

Man is the only being endowed with powers to act in accordance to his own will. With these superior powers the Deity was pleased to create him. The powers man possesses are imitative of the higher and more sublime powers. He holds in check or sways at will the unlimited pen of thought until from the blazing watch-tower of his mind there roll forth words of honor or disgrace.

We see the amazing grandeur and beauty of heaven's greatest blessings resting upon all creation, from the parching sands of this lower world to the loftiest throne of the star-set heavens. But how often we see all the glories of God's natural world polluted by the foul tongue of man. The eternity that rolls in endless years cannot bury the great deeds of good men. So also, evil thoughts expressed in words cannot be erased.

No force of natural law is so great. The golden blaze of the sun reflected through the window upon the wall lasts but a moment and then vanishes away. The flinty rock which has stood immovable amid the charging centuries must give over at last the struggle. But our words will live on to testify against us throughout the endless ages of eternity. Our words are the index of our thought. That which we speak is supposed to be that which we mean. Men do not always speak of that which they mean. Neither do they always think of that which they speak. We find the once fair pages of the past polluted with our crime, arising from the indulgence of self-gratification in unapproved conversation.

Many of the richest and deepest thoughts are brought to light by conversing with each other. Who is the person that has not been inspired and electrified as he had stood upon some lofty eminence [hilltop] conversing with his friends, as his eager eyes penetrated beyond rolling hills and green valleys until he caught a glimpse of the silvery waters of old ocean, as they have intermingled with the golden beams of the setting sun. Much of the training and culture of youth depends upon home conversation. The child who has never learned to distinguish the letters of the alphabet may in a few years talk fluently by being in company with persons who are well versed in the languages.

Our words should be accompanied by the purest thoughts, for they shall ascend like sweet perfume or be mixed with the blackness of polluted crime.

J. B. Freed Nov. 6th, 1880

Much of the training, and culture of youth depends upon home conversation.

The child who has never learned to distinguish the letters of the alphabet, may in a few years talk fluently, by being in company with person who are well versed in the languages.

Our words should be accompanied by the purest thoughts, for they shall ascend like sweet perfume, or be mixed with the blackness of polluted crime.

J. B. Freed
Nov. 6th 1880.

Benson Freed, an excerpt from the manuscript of Conversation, with his flourished signature.

SERMONS AND TALKS BY
WILLIAM WALTON FREED

TEN COMMANDMENTS

ON THE NATURE OF GREATNESS

Luke 2:11. For unto you in born this day the city of David a Saviour, which is Christ the Lord.

Matthew 1:21. And she shall bring forth a son, and thou shalt call his name JESUS: for he shall save his people from their sins.

Great men are often born in a very obscure manner, seemingly buried away only to shine out with more brilliance when they take their proper place among the illustrious ones of earth. One of the greatest men this country ever produced was born in a log cabin (I refer to Abraham Lincoln) and sometimes, my dear hearers, in riding over this circuit I see in imagination that old log cabin far away in the state of Kentucka [sic]. These cabins of our pioneer fathers with mud roofs and a hole in the roof for the smoke to go out are fit representatives of the birth place of one of the most illustrious men this country has ever produced. Napoleon was born on an insignificant island in the Mediterranean, and yet he rose to be a dispenser of sceptres and thrones. And so, my hearers, some of the most illustrious men that earth has produced have been born in poverty and obscurity.

Christ who in this passage is called the Saviour of the World, whose name shall live through the ages of eternity, was born where this word declares – in a manger among the beasts of the field, where browsing cattle stood at their stalls and fed on their frugal meal. Have you ever, my hearers, calmly contemplated that scene? Have you ever thought of the old barn where the pale moonlight glistened through? Where ever and anon the rude wind swept by? Have you thought, my hearers, of browsing cattle and neighing horses stamping their feet -when all was stillness? Again, have you pictured to yourself the stalls filled with hay and the old barn door with its wooden pin? If you have done all this you have some conception of the birthplace of one of the greatest men that ever lived, our Lord and Saviour Jesus Christ, whose birth will in a few days be commemorated by the Christian nations all over the habitable Globe. Yea, my Christian friends, and wherever a Christian man is found—whether on Africa's torrid plains or in frigid zones, whether among the heathen in all his blindness or the infidel in his wretchedness — wherever, my brethren, the devoted Christian man is found he will be found observing this day and reverencing it.

I have thought, my hearers, sometimes when I see this nation honoring Washington's birthday, of other nations that have honoured the birthday of their illustrious men. I have thought of Rome paying homage to her Caesars, of Macedonia honouring her Alexander, of Persia rendering homage to Cyrus, of Carthage, of Athens, of Sparta, of all the ancient nations honouring their great men, and then the question has come with all its power: Where are the people that paid homage to these illustrious men? They have passed away. And well might we exclaim in the language of Black Hawk, Who is there to pay homage to me now? None their lives, like the bones of his Indian braves, lie scattered on the plains of many hard fought battle's field.

But while, my hearers, the nations that honoured these men have passed away, the Christian nations have not disappeared.   The   wise men that honoured the birth of Christ in Bethlehem have not disappeared. Their number, my hearers, has gone on increasing for eighteen hundred years. This grand old army of Christian men and women have been swelling their ranks from Bethlehem in Judea. The tide has been rolling on. It has swept over Europe with its teeming population. It has crossed the blue waters of the Atlantic. And the spires and domes of every city and town in this land of ours tell that his kingdom is established here. And in India and China, in the dark places of the earth, this kingdom is being established. Surely our Lord hath gotten to himself a great name from an insignificant handful of followers. Well may the poet exclaim, His kingdom spread from pole to pole till moon shall wax and wane no more.[1]

Let us consider Christ first as a great man. Great men have established their reputation on different standards. Some of the great men of the earth have been only great as warriors. Some have been not only victorious in war but they have been doubly so in peace. Washington will be honoured by his countrymen with more devotion than ever when they remember that he might have been a king instead of a President. And when, my hearers, I contemplate that illustrious hero at Annapolis, surrendering his sword, surrendering the command of invincible legions and retiring to private life again, his greatness as a man swells out to far more wonderful proportions in my mind. Surely this was a great man. There beat beneath his sunburnt countenance a heart that was superlatively great beyond the reach of finite men.

---

1   A line from the Hymn, "Jesus Shall Reign Where'er the sun."

Think you, my hearers, if you had stood at the head of a victorious army, where a sceptre might be had for the asking, think you in that tremendous hour you could have buried self and retired to the old farm again as a private citizen for your country's good? Few men, I venture to say, could have withstood that ordeal. And here is a type of greatness the world has seldom seen. Napoleon was a great man. But, unlike our loved Washington, his greatness consisted in blood and carnage instead of peace and happiness. It is estimated that Napoleon in his desperate efforts to achieve renown sacrificed the lives of two millions of men. Surely, my brethren, there is a ghastly spectacle for one man to establish his fame over the bloody bodies of .two millions of his fellow men. And yet, my hearers, as the lover of history reads the life of this wonderful man, a romantic interest compels him to acknowledge his greatness. When he contemplates him [Napoleon] at the bridge of Lodie,[2] catching up the flag of his fallen standard-bearer and leading his victorious army over amid a storm of shot and shell. He must acknowledge his greatness as a leader when he contemplates him crossing the Alps and defying difficulties, when he views him on his return from his first imprisonment, when he views him amid death and destruction leading on the Imperial guard at Waterloo. He cannot but say he was a great man.

But his greatness, my hearers, was wrapped up all in himself. It was "I" with him all the time. For this he tore himself away from one of the best wives; for this he sacrificed an army of almost 500,000 thousand men on his Russian campaign; for this he crowned himself Emperor of the French and King of Italy. For "ME" he did all this. His greatness, my hearers, stopped all in the man. And when you have told that, you have told the whole story of the man.

And so, my hearers, I might go on enumerating the different men who have left a name behind them. I might tell you of Caesar, who was a great warrior, a great statesman, a great orator, and a great writer. I might tell you of Alexander, of Cyrus, of Hannibal, of Pyrhuss. But I will drop all these and strive to convince some hearts here today that Christ our Saviour was not only a great man but a great God above all other gods. That he was a great man his most inveterate enemies will not deny—the Jews—and the only objection they had against him was that he did not place himself at the head of their armies and lead them on to victory.

---

2   Battle of Lodi, (May 10, 1796), small but dramatic engagement in Napoleon Bonaparte's first Italian campaign, in which he earned the confidence and loyalty of his men, who nicknamed him "The Little Corporal" in recognition of his personal courage. *Encyclopedia Brittanica.*

His kingdom, my hearers, was not of this world. He declared his kingdom was a spiritual kingdom. He wrought not with sword and staves. He did not require strong armies and invincible men to establish his kingdom. The heart was his battlefield, and he contained within himself the power to batter down all opposition and win the hearts of his hearers to himself. And as you contemplate Christ as a man of sorrows and acquainted with griefs, as you, my hearers, depict yourself a poor man that had not where to lay his head, with twelve followers, you ask yourself, Where does this man's power lie? Is this the man that proposes to establish a universal kingdom? This, my unconverted brother, is the man. His power, like that of Samson, lies within him. He has the power of heaven at his command.

This man does not rest his fame on his own followers. His most bigoted enemies record the fact that such a man did live and performed many wonderful miracles to attest his power. And when I read this, my hearers, I turn to this word with more love than ever and trace the deeds that have established his fame. I contemplate him as the sick and suffering are piled around on every side. Here, my brethren, I view him establishing his fame in the hearts of his hearers. I see him in thought standing on the deck of the old ship on a dark and stormy night at sea when old ocean is roaring with majestic grandeur and commanding the waves to be still. I see him by the side of Lazarus' grave, with weeping friends and streaming eyes, commanding the dead man to come forth, and I acknowledge his greatness. And you, my hearers, must acknowledge the same. He is not establishing his fame on the bleeding bodies of his victims. He is not deluging the land in blood to found his empire. He is not filling happy homes with misery and despair. He is not, my brethren, tearing loved ones from home but, on the contrary, he is filling saddened homes with joy and gladness. The palsied one is coming home again with buoyant step, the lame man is greeting wife and children without his wooden leg. The arm that lay powerless by my side is strong once more. Happiness and peace is following in the wake of this man instead of misery and woe.

And this, my hearers, is enough of itself to establish his fame. But these wonderful deeds are but the prelude to greater achievements. This is but the commencement of this man's word. He proposes to abolish sin—a Herculean task—and these wonderful works are wrought that ye may know that the Son of Man hath power. For what, my unconverted brother, hath power on earth to forgive sins? I believe, my brother, he has that power. The man that can unstop the dumb man's mouth, that can calm old ocean, that can raise up the dead, can, I believe, forgive my sins.

But before preceding farther, let us consider this man as a great God that has power on earth to forgive sins. Mahomet tells in his Koran where and how, on a certain dark night, he left his wife and, traveling on his white horse, ascended to heaven, talked with God, and came back to earth again before the break of day. But he has none to corroborate his statements. He forces it down the throat of his hearers on his bare assertion. And by the power of sword and saber compels unwilling men to believe it.

Not so with our Lord. Other men, both sacred and profane, record his deeds. We have very meagre accounts of Christ outside this blessed book, but what we have are enough to establish its veracity. Josephus, the Jewish Historian, in his history of the Jews writes these significant words in regard to our Saviour: "Now there was about that time Jesus, a wise man if it be lawful to call him a man, for he was a doer of wonderful works, a teacher of such men as receive the truth with pleasure. He drew over to him both many of the Jews and many of the Gentiles. He was the Christ, and when Pilate at the suggestion of the principal man among us had condemned him to the cross, those that loved him at first did not forsake him for he appeared to them the third day alive again as the divine prophets had said. These and a vast number of other wonderful things concerning him, and the tribe of Christians so named from him, are not extinct to this day."

This, my hearers, is the testimony of a Jewish historian whose veracity cannot be questioned. I might recount others, but this is sufficient. He hesitates to call Christ a man. He admits he rose from the dead, and many other wonderful things that he did. His Godhood is established outside this blessed Book, and we can, my Christian friends, read over the story of our Great God and Great Man with more love than ever before.

His divine power to forgive sins was established when he rose from the dead. Not all the marshalled legions of Rome, not all the seals and signets around his tomb, could keep our imprisoned Lord in his grave. His father God sent down the myriad hosts of heaven to roll away the stone, to strike down the mailed warriors as dead men and to liberate the Saviour of mankind. His claim as the son of God was established on the cross when earth and heaven conspired to render him divine honours. His claim to be equal with the Father was established when he ascended through ether's [highest] space to the throne of God. And we may well, my hearers, honour this great man and Great God with all the love it is possible for us to display. Men honour that man most who does the most for them. And who, might I ask, has done more than Christ for us? He proposes to save us from our sins. He proposes to save us from eternal misery. He proposes to prepare a mansion in heaven for us when earth and its cares are over.

Let us consider the first proposition: a saviour from sin. And just here, my hearers, I might remark that Christ does not propose to drive down our throats the idea that he can forgive sins without a tangible proof of the same. It would be an easy matter for me to travel up and down this world like some modern Texel[3] forgiving sins by the wholesale. I might by a few strokes of my hand declare that your sins were forgiven. But the heart of man wants more tangible proofs than all this, and our Saviour as he stands by the bed of the sick man, asks of the unbelieving Jews which is the easiest to say: "Thy sins be forgiven," or to say "Rise up and walk"? Which, my hearers, would you think was the easiest task for me, if I stood by the side of the palsied man that had lain for long years on his bed? And say "take up your bed and walk" or "thy sins be forgiven"? I would have an easy task in the one case. I could go through a great hospital filled with sick and suffering humanity and say to each one "thy sins be forgiven". That would be an easy task, my brethren. But that ye may know, says our Saviour, that ye may know that I have power to do the little act in your estimation, I will give you a tangible proof by doing the hard one. Take up thy bed and walk!

My unconverted brother, if I had lived in that day and saw such an act I couldn't have helped but believe that he had power to forgive sins. He has that power, and he proposes first to transform the man in this life. He proposes to enter such dens of vice as Five Points in New York City and convert drunken men and women that lie around on the streets like demons of the lower regions into good men and women. He proposes by the aid of his followers to establish a universal kingdom of love instead of blood and carnage. He proposes to tear down the heathen temples of China and teach her teeming millions to worship

---

3   Under Pope Leo X a system of "indulgences" was established in the Roman Catholic Church whereby people could buy forgiveness for major sins by making a large donation to enrich the Pope's finances. "One Texel, a Dominican friar, particularly distinguished himself in pushing the sale of these indulgences. Among other things, in the sermons and speeches he made on this occasion, he used to say, that, even if a man had lain with the mother of God, he was able, with the Pope's power, to pardon the crime; and he boasted that he had saved more souls from Hell through these indulgences than St. Peter had converted to Christianity through all his preaching." *An History of the Corruptions of Christianity*, by Joseph Priestly, 1793, (reprinted 1871), vol. 2, p. 166.

God instead of wood and stone. He proposes, my hearers, to save the struggling infant of some heathen mother in India from the jaws of an alligator and teach her darkened mind that there is a more tender and loving God than that. That there is a religion that does not require the fond parent to sacrifice her very life blood to such hideous monsters. He proposes finally, my hearers, to teach men to love God instead of Satan, to plant the cross over the heathen temple, to transform the Rum shop where men damn their souls, into a house of prayer, to break up the dens of vice where innocent women are sunk into the lowest depths of hell, to teach men to love each other instead of hating them, and to establish his kingdom in the hearts of the people where all true power must exist.

This religion, my hearers, that Christ has established, has accomplished wonderful things in the darkened places of earth. This religion drives out the earnest man of God into the darkened places of earth to publish the glad tidings of a Saviour and his love and the transformations, scenes that have ensued under its divine power, are wonderful to contemplate. It is related of the Sandwich Islands that before their conversion the most horrible forms of heathenism were practiced. Captain Cook on his last voyage around the world was murdered here, and his fellow voyagers received his bones mutilated in a horrible manner. Before their conversion they [the natives] thought nothing of roasting and eating their victims. The brightest and fairest were sacrificed to their gods like so many cattle. But, my brethren, there has been a transformation scene since that time. The illuminating torch of Christianity has lighted up those darkened parts of the earth. Their wooden gods have been burnt. Churches have been established. Schools have been founded. The people now dress like men instead of like wild beasts. And the Sandwich Islands of today is like light is to darkness.

To be a Christian is to teach men how to live like men, to bring out the noblest attributes of their nature, to transform the murderer at heart into a follower of the meek and lowly Jesus, to transform the thief who would rob and if need be murder you, into a good [man], to set up a standard for men to live by. The mechanic must have some rule to work by; the carpenter cannot build a house without a plan; the farmer must have some method in planting his crops; and religion sets up a standard for men to live by. The rules are laid down in the Ten Commandments, and if people would live by them, what a blessed thing it would be for this world of ours! Let us, my hearers, examine these rules and ask ourselves, are we living up to them?

Let us commence at the first commandment: "Thou shalt have

no other gods before me." That teaches men to know that there is but one God, the Father, and commands them to love Him with all their hearts and soul and strength.

"Thou shalt not make unto thee any graven image." That strikes a blow at every heathen temple in this world of ours.

"Thou shalt not take the name of the Lord thy God in vain." That teaches the man whose mouth is filled with oaths and curses all the time that every oath is a sin against God.

"Remember the Sabbath day to keep it holy." That strikes a blow at every violation of the Sabbath day.

"Honour thy father and thy mother." That teaches children to love and respect their parents.

"Thou shalt not kill." That teaches men that murder is wrong and wherever or in whatsoever form it is practiced it is a sin deep and damning against them.

"Thou shalt not commit adultery." That strikes a blow at every house of ill fame in this land of ours and teaches men to love and honour the virtuous man.

"Thou shalt not steal." That teaches the thief that it is wrong for him to rob his fellow man.

"Thou shalt not bear false witness." That teaches men to detest the liar and slanderer wherever he is met.

"Thou shalt not covet." That teaches these men and women that are always wishing for every thing but their own that they should be satisfied with what God has given them.

Are not these enough, my hearers, to teach men how to live? It seems not. Our Saviour has added one more: "Thou shalt love the Lord thy God with all thy heart and with all thy soul and with all thy mind . This is the first and great commandment. And the second is like unto it: Thou shalt love thy neighbor as thyself." This, my hearers, is the standard that Christ has set. It takes in every case, it meets every want, it teaches men how to live like the children of a God. Under its divine influence, civilization has been advancing with gigantic strides. For eighteen hundred years, under its enlightening power, men have proved themselves worthy of such a God as our God. Under the Christian dispensation printing has been invented, steam has been discovered, electricity has been unearthed—all the wants of men both spiritually and temporally have been supplied. Men have learned how to live under this. And if for no other reason, my hearers, men should honour Christ for leaving them such an excellent example in this life. The Spartans honoured Lycurgis for leaving them laws that were rigid to the last degree. Let us on the corning Christmas honour Christ for leaving us laws that deprive us of nothing but sin.

But Christ has taught us not only how to live but how to die. Confucius taught his followers how to live. But Christ goes farther than that. After having preached for three long years, after having filled the land with joy and gladness, after having raised up suffering humanity in this life, he proposes to raise them up to eternal life in the world to come. The great heart of this Great man and Great God seemed to be studying out some greater heights for your enjoyment, my brother. After the most unselfish love and greatness of soul has been displayed, after enduring the ridicule and persecution of selfish and ungrateful men, he sacrifices himself on the cross for you and me. My brother, he goes down into the tomb beneath a lost and ruined world and raises them up to everlasting life.

It was not enough for him, my brother, to teach us how to live. But his great heart took in all our wants. He goes down, deeper down than ever fallen humanity went, and raised them up to life again. Like the balloon that carries her occupants far up from mortal sight, so this eternal Saviour of our race went down to the depths of hell and raised us up to everlasting life. And, my hearers, we may not only live a happy life now, but die a triumphant death. We may bid goodbye to fathers and mothers now in hope of meeting in a better land. We may [view] the imprisoned soul struggling in this mortal tenement now in the joyful realization of the fact that this mortal will put on [immortality]. I can, my hearers—now though hard it may seem—I can take the hand of my dying father cold in the embrace of death and bid him goodbye with joy and happiness. I can bend over the loved form of my mother and whisper in her ear, "Farewell! Meet beyond the swelling floods of Jordan!" I can bid goodbye to sister or brother if I know they are Christ's, in hope of meeting where parting shall be no more forever.

I can do all this, my hearers! Christ has made it possible for me. After living a happy and joyful life in this world of sin and sorrow, to shout victory over death at last! Christ has made it possible for me to bid goodbye to father and mother, to sister and brother, with joy and in the joyful realization of the fact that we shall meet again. Christ has done all for you and me, my brother, that an infinite God could do. And let me urge you in conclusion, you that are fathers and mothers, to consecrate your lives to Him. Let me urge you to love this great Saviour Jesus Christ because he has wrought such wonderful works in your behalf because of your little ones who are singing around his throne today, because of your old father and mother whose parting words were "Meet me in heaven,"—because of all these reasons, let us love this Great man and Great God of our race.

And then, my hearers, we shall see our Saviour as he is. We shall not see him then nailed to the cross, we shall not behold him with bowed form and weary step. No, no, my hearers, he has been transformed long ere this. He commands the armies of heaven now. And when we behold him in all his glory we shall see the infinite man and infinite God who performed all his wonderful acts for you and me in this earth.

Faith sees the final triumph

Am I a soldier of the cross,—
    A foll'wer of the Lamb,—
And shall I fear to own his cause,
    Or blush to speak his name?
2 Must I be carried to the skies
    On flowery beds of ease;
While others fought to win the prize,
    And sail'd through bloody seas?
3 Are there no foes for me to face?
    Must I not stem the flood?
Is this vile world a friend to grace,
    To help me on to God?
4 Since I must fight if I would reign,
    Increase my courage, Lord;
I'll bear the toil, endure the pain,
    Supported by thy word.
5 Thy saints in all this glorious war
    Shall conquer, though they die:
They see the triumph from afar,--
    By faith they bring it nigh.
6 When that illustrious day shall rise,
    And all thy armies shine
In robes of vict'ry through the skies,
    The glory shall be thine.

Hymns for the Use of the Methodist Episcopal Church, revised edition. New York, Carlton & Lanahan, 1870. # 734.

Ten Commandments

On Swearing

> *Exodus 20:7.* Thou shalt not take the name of the Lord thy God in vain; for the Lord will not hold him guiltless that taketh his name in vain.

In the first verse of this chapter we read these words that God spake all these words saying: Thus and so shalt thou do, thus and so shalt thou not do. This short sermon of ten commandments seems to have been the guiding star of the Christian world both under the Old and New Testament dispensation for ages. Never was there a sermon that fell from mortal lips that has commanded the reverence and respect of men and as to his relation to God? Here is the explanation. Is he in doubt whether to do this or that? Here is the solution of the problem, uttered with authority as coming from One that is All Powerful. It falls on the human ear in the form of a stern and imperative command.

God, in speaking these words to Moses, assigns a reason for almost every command in relation to our duty to him, except the first which is so apparent that because love to one that has done so much for us would prompt us to pay homage to Him. In the second command He assigns a reason for not bowing down to wood and stone; and in the third he exclaims, Thou shalt not take the name of the Lord thy God in vain because He will not hold him guiltless that taketh His name in vain. No other reason is assigned. The condemnation of God is supposed to be enough to stay the countless oaths that come, like the sweeping tornado from the mouth of men. But it is not enough. The condemnation of God, the fearful punishment that is threatened and the dire effects produced on men by this baleful sin is not sufficient to stay the oaths of wicked man.

Let me ask why do men swear? Some men imagine that a terrible oath at the end of every sentence will make a more lasting impression, that it serves as a kind of wedge to drive home their words, that it serves to convince their hearers that they have to do with a man here that has soared above finite men, up into the blue of ether,[4] higher — yet here is a man that is above God. And to hear him talk, the question would arise in your mind whether the command "Thou shalt not take the name of thy

---

4   Ether: the higher atmosphere, beyond air.

God in vain" would not sound better transposed in his favor and read: thou shalt not take this man's name in vain.

I once knew a man that was a terrible swearer and he seemed to delight in the thought that he could outdo his fellows in oaths. He would swear and swear and swear till you could almost feel that there were devils in the room – till the air fairly seemed to flash out oaths – till the place was made terrible by the fearful language used. He thought he was a smart man for that. His wicked companions looked up to him as chief in all their wickedness and like Spartacus the Roman gladiator that exclaimed "Ye call me chief and ye do well, him who for twelve long years has stood in the arena and met all kinds of men and beasts!" So with this man. He had cursed God so long that the Devil had given him a premium and he was chosen to preach the tidings of a slandered God to among his evil associates. Men may pay a wicked respect to such a man, but they cannot, my hearers – they cannot love him.

Boys swear because their older companions indulge in the same, and here is the power of influence. Children are learning every day. The world is a school for them, and with some a very bad school. There seems to be a higher course, where boys learn from their older companions true nobility, and insensibly commence to rise. And there is a lower course whose steps take hold of hell. Here the boy learns to smoke. It is repulsive to him. It makes him sick and pale. But like the native of the Fuji Islands that suffers himself to be tattooed till his body is a mass of sores so that he may be a man among his fellows, so the boy persists until he is a full grown man as far as smoking goes, and tells his older companions that he cannot possibly do without it .

In this lower school, boys learn to swear, and I and you have seen some little fellows that could hardly walk, yet commence to use the name of God in vain. And by the time they arrive at an age when they know right from wrong they are steeped in sin – coated over as it were in a garment of oaths – and noble man one that is ready to steep his hands in all kinds of wickedness – a cold, selfish and cruel man that has no heart, no sympathy for others' woes.

Swearing, my hearers, is useless. Like Booth[5] when he held up his hands in death and exclaimed in death "Useless, Useless!" so I will hold up before your minds in imagination these hands of oaths – blackened and begrimed with all the vile catalogue of oaths that men have ever

---

5   A reference to the last words of John Wilkes Booth, who assassinated Abraham Lincoln. His death, April 26, 1865, was widely reported in newspapers at the time. As quoted in Smith, Gene, *American Gothic: the story of America›s legendary theatrical family, Junius, Edwin, and John Wilkes Booth.* New York: Simon & Schuster, 1992, pp. 23, 210-213.

uttered and ask you in the name of humanity, in the name of the rising generation who are following in your steps, What earthly use have they? They do not make men better. They do not make boys better. But they do make all that use them worse.

This is an era of retrenchment. Men are talking on every hand about the hard times, about the extravagance of the nation and the woe and want caused thereby. And they are reducing down their expenses to the lowest possible terms. Let us turn this same [kind] of argument on the side of language. The English especially. This language is made up of almost every other language. The languages of earth have, as it were, been flowing right into the lap of the English language for centuries. And like Germany that was flooded with French gold,[6] so our language is flooded to overflowing, running over. And would God that we could have a panic once that would break up every vile seller of oaths so that we might take these terrible and useless oaths and bury them so deep that they would never have a resurrection.

Not only is swearing useless, but men are in the inmost depths of their hearts ashamed of it. They will swear among their associates, but they will not do it around their fireside, and if it will not do at home it will not do abroad. There are, it would seem, two different men that we are conversing with — often a man within a man, a man for home and a man for the world. And hanging up in their office closet there is in imagination a suit that has been specially made for home. Oaths have besplattered it sometimes in walking home, but the mud is carefully washed off, and by various patches of good resolutions it has kept its color. But peering out beneath that suit of outward purity, there are a legion of peering devils in the shape of oaths that only wait till they lose the sacred radius of home to issue forth in all darkness. Well has the Saviour exclaimed, "Your outward part is fair to behold but the inward part is full of dead men's bones."[7] The heart is gone, in other words. The fire of these terrible oaths have burnt it into a shapeless mass.

Not long since, up here near Buffalo Creek,[8] a prairie fire burnt up some cattle till they looked like pieces of charcoal. And so I have thought that some men have been caught in this terrible prairie fire the

6   Referencing news reports of the time. Global markets in silver and gold were manipulated in 1871-73 through a process of shifting reserves of gold and silver called "monetary dislocation," causing the U.S. to pass laws in 1873 and 1878 to stabilize the currency. See *Coinage Laws of the United States 1792-1894*, by US Congress Committee on Finance, 53rd Congress, report number 235, 1894, pp 668-670.

7   Matthew 23:27.

8   While there is a Buffalo Creek in Pennsylvania, it is safe to assume that in every pioneer state throughout the plains there was also a Buffalo Creek.

veriest trash. It does not add one jot or tittle to your words, and it does not diminish its force. I do not know, my hearers, one sentence that will convey an intelligent idea that is made up of oaths. I have studied it over and endeavored to think of one, but I cannot. And I cannot think of one sentence that you cannot utter without using an oath. I cannot find any rules laid down in grammar that should govern us in taking the name of God in vain. After looking all over this terrible mountain of oaths and striving to think of one that we could not get along without, I am constrained to utter the language of our Saviour, "Be thou removed and cast into the sea as utterly worthless." We are not satisfied with the necessaries of life, but the cry is for the luxuries. The poor man is striving to surround his home with new beauties, and the rich one is increasing the attractions of home. But swearing does not even make our language beautiful, but horrible. It does not increase our stock of virtue, but it sears it over with a hot iron and leaves the man heartless. Like the drone bee that is eating up the labor of the industrious, so these worthless oaths are soaring around like the drone bees, recognized by our God in heaven, by the grammarian, and by all Christian men, as utterly worthless and only fit to be cast out and trodden under the feet of men.

When God conferred on man the power of speech, he gave him a language free from oaths. But when this text was uttered from the heights of Sinai I suppose the Jews had commenced to curse God. They were the most ungrateful people that ever trod the face of the earth, and as we read over their history we cannot fail but see the all-pervading spirit of love that punished when they sinned and forgave when they repented. Swearing was one of those sins. A heartless and ungrateful people, they cursed that God that watched over them in Egypt. They cursed that God that delivered them from Pharaoh's hand. They cursed that God that smote the waters of the Red Sea. They cursed on and on until amid the flames and rumbling, amid thundering and lightning of smoking Sinai, they received the imperative command of God in the form of my text: "Thou shalt not take the name of the Lord thy God in vain." That command applies to you and me. And as the curse of God was pronounced on the Jews for taking his name in vain, so the curse of God is pronounced today on the man or woman that takes his name in vain.

All men believe there is a God that is watching over the destinies of the earth, that is watching over them. And to basely slander that God is a crime of the blackest character. Men will sue a man for telling an untruth about themselves, and to slander a God whose every act toward you is that of love is the basest of crimes. The laws of the state will not sanction them in it; the laws of common sense will not sanction you in it; and the laws of God will not sanction you in it.

Swearing entails a curse on him that uses oaths. It may not be apparent. His boys may hear him swear for long years. He is doing that that he would not want them to do, but though he may not see its evil effects, though he may die and pass away, still the mother will see it at last and it will sadden her declining years. The boy will take it up as a manly art that is necessary to his development, and it will sear his nobler manhood. It will teach him to despise a loving God that has tenderly loved him. It will teach him to break the Sabbath. It will teach him to despise the Church and associate with evil companions. And it will follow him like a fearful nightmare to darken and blight all his nobler resolutions.

"Thou shalt not take the name of the Lord thy God in vain." That command is to you, my brother, that have sons and daughters growing up. That command is to you that are thrown out on your own resources to battle with the world. And if you heed it, the blessing of God will be upon you. I shall not mention the ladies. No true lady will swear. And men could not respect the women that would curse God. Women seem to be in a charmed circle where oaths do not come. And while men never imagine that a true lady would be guilty of such an offense as swearing, while they shrink from taking God's name in vain before them, they yet hide the serpent beneath an outward garment to bring it forth at a more convenient season. The thief would not steal in public. He does his deed amid the darkness of the midnight hour. And the man that swears steals from God. And women, while they as he supposes are unconscious of the fact - they may deceive women but they cannot deceive God. And this fact should ever be before us.

The more we study God's goodness to men and women, the more thoroughly should we shrink from taking his name in [vain]. The Psalmist exclaims, "When I survey the heavens, the moon and stars, what is man that thou art mindful of him?" And when, my hearers, the Christian man and woman—when the lover of religion, no matter whether he is in the church or not—when he considers the wonderful blessings that he has bestowed upon him, how he should revere and love him! When we consider that man is ruler over created life, that he is the husbandman of this exhaustless field of the world, filled with the fish of the sea and the fowl of the air and the beasts of the field; that he is destined to an immortality of life beyond the grave—How we should love such a Father!

And to crown all other blessings we have the power of speech, one of the grandest gifts conferred on man. We can walk and talk with our fellow men. We can sing of the love of God because of this power of speech. We can talk of the love of God because of this power. We can sit beneath the eloquent appeals of men because of this power. And we can rejoice to know that the Great Giver of all Good has given us the power of expressing our thoughts intelligently. The Infidel has said that this power has come to man through centuries of time, that in the earliest stages of the world men expressed themselves by the shortest monosyllables, and that there has been a gradual improvement to the present day. But leaving all these vain theories, we as Christian men have the consolation of knowing that God talked with Adam, and that he has been continuing that conversation through the ages of the world, and that we are enjoying the same grand power of speech. Then, my hearers, if this is so, if God has given us this grand power of speech, should we basely use it? The man that has a valuable machine and deliberately misuses it until he finds it is worthless, is a foolish man—and the man that has the power of speech should be careful to use it properly.

The old Puritan fathers taught their sons and daughters to reverence the name of God. They punished the swearer as severely as the thief, and from that old Puritan law, almost every state has framed laws against swearing. But like the rotten ship that lies in port dismasted and useless, so these laws seem to be useless. Swearing has entered into the Judge and juries, and God's name is slandered with impunity. A power that ought to be a grand civilizer is in a great many instances a terrible debaser. God has given men the power of speech to use, not to abuse. He has expressly forbidden us to take his name in vain. But upon bended knee we are to call upon God, as did the poor publican with the exclamation, "God be merciful to me, a sinner!"

Would that I could, my hearers, depict to your mind this grand power of speech that is used in too many instances to slander God! We cannot realize it. Behold the dumb man, and if possible put yourself in his place, and ask yourself the question, if there is anything so dear to you that you would not sacrifice it to avert such a disaster? Not far from my native home there is a little boy, strong and healthy, happy, apparently, but dumb. He cannot speak. His tongue lies like the tongue of the ox, useless in his mouth. Think you, my hearers, if it were possible for him to have this power of speech! Would he not sacrifice every oath and every idle word so that he might but touch the hem of the garment of language? Oh, my brethren, I venture to say that he would be satisfied with the child's prattle. He would be willing to pick up the crumbs that fall from this grand banquet of language that you and I enjoy.

Language enables us to converse with friends far away. It enables you to sit down and pen your thoughts to an old father or mother in some far distant land. It enables you to flash it over hill and dale and under Ocean's gale to the shore of your native hills. Once more it enables men like Morse to tell of the wonders of the electric flash.[9] It enables men like Fulton to tell of the wonders of steam. It travels through the earth like the air, unseen yet powerful, stronger than the mountain heights. It crosses over and under her mighty bed and laughs at her hoary heights. It bids defiance to Ocean's gale and lightning's gleam and sends her on harmless in her course.

This, my brethren, is language. We cannot describe it, but like poor blind Bartimaeus[10] who exclaimed one thing: "I know that whereas I was once blind, now I see," so we know that we can talk to our fellow man and send on a thought like Morse Telegraph forever. I cannot tell you how you do it. I do not understand how you can utter words and the dumb man is powerless to utter. But one thing I do know — that you and I have this power conferred on us by the immortal God himself, whose name is blasphemed by that same power. Thou shalt not take the name of the Lord thy God in vain. Can you, my hearers, grasp the idea of that Almighty God who, amid the flames and smoke of Sinai uttered that command? Can you conceive that God sitting amid sun and moon and stars and guiding on their revolutions? Can you conceive that God on the foaming crest of ocean's wave, commanding her to go thus far but no farther? Can you conceive of that God going before the Jewish multitude as a pillar of smoke by day and a flaming fire by night? If you can conceive of that almighty God, let me whisper in your ear the awful and yet grand thought that God is your God – a God of love, and yet a God of Justice, who has commanded you not to take his name in vain.

If we had a king over this nation that could at his command cut off a right arm or pluck out a right eye, how we would fear him! If we lived under the Russian Emperor who could at a word consign us to the mines of Siberia at hard labor for life, how we would fear such a ruler! And let me ring in your ears in conclusion, my hearers, the thought that that God whose command has gone forth not to take his name in vain is mightier than them all! His kingdom is above every kingdom. That at the name of God every nation shall bow low. He holds our life as he

9   The telegraph.
10   Mark 10:46 ff.

holds the ocean wave. A word and tis done! Man yields up the ghost and returns to dust. A word and, like the engineer shutting off his steam, so the brittle thread of life stops. Man pants and catches at an element that God has withdrawn and is no more.

This, my hearers, is the God that is our God and Father, that has [so] loved us as to give his only son to die for us, that has given us all that heart can wish and that has exclaimed, Thou shalt not take His name in vain. Let us resolve this day to heed that command. Let us resolve never to breathe that Name but on bended knee, to come before His presence with thanksgiving and praise for his blessings. God has not said that we shall not call on his name. We may take that name in our polluted lips and ask whatsoever we will and He is faithful and just to forgive us.

Let us come then with our wants and wishes, with our sorrows and burdens.

[The following two newspaper clippings were enclosed in this sermon booklet.]

SIBERIAN EXILES[11]

The exiles who live in the mines are convicts of the worst type, and political offenders of the best. The murderer for his villainy, the intelligent and honest Polish rebel for his patriotism, are deemed equally worthy of the punishment of slow death. They never see the light of day, but work and sleep all the year round in the depths of the earth, extracting silver, or quicksilver, under the eyes of taskmasters, who have orders not to spare them. Iron gates, guarded by sentries, close the lodes or streets at the bottom of the shafts, and the miners are railed off from one another in gangs of twenty. They sleep within recesses hewn out of the rocks — very kennels — into which they must creep on all fours. ... They have only two holidays a year — Christmas and Easter — and all other days, including Sundays, they must toil until exhausted nature robs them of the use of their limbs, when they are hauled up to die in the infirmary. Five years in the quicksilver pits are enough to turn a man of thirty into an apparent sexagenarian, but some have been known to struggle on for ten years. No man who has served in the mines is ever allowed to return home. The most he can obtain in the way of grace is leave to come up and work in the road gangs, and it is the promise of this favor, as a reward for industry, which operates even more than the lash to maintain discipline.

---

11   From *Christian Treasury*, a weekly periodical for evangelical preachers.

[second article, untitled]

Quick and terrible retribution followed the wicked oath of a poker player at Grand Island one day last week, the particulars of which have just found their way into print, and the following we take from the Omaha *BEE*: "A dispute arose as to the game, when one of the parties made use of an expression about as follows: "I hope Christ will kill me if it isn't so." He had dealt the cards, and the betting on the hands was over, when he passed the pack to the next man on his left to deal. The dealer shuffled the cards and handed them back to the man to cut, at the same time giving him a light slap to attract his attention. The man did not move. He was found to be stone dead. He had died in his chair immediately after uttering the oath above quoted. The deceased was a well known citizen of Grand Island. There was no more poker playing that day among that party. Some people may account for the singular death by saying that it was a visitation of Providence; others will declare it a case of "just retribution."

TEN COMMANDMENTS

KEEPING THE SABBATH

Exodus 20:8. Remember the Sabbath day, to keep it holy.

There is, my hearers, a peculiar style about this commandment [which] there is about no other and which at first sight impresses the mind of the reader. The first three commandments are uttered with authority: Thou shalt have no other gods before me. Thou shalt not make any graven images. Thou shalt not take the name of the Lord thy God in vain.

And as if forgetting something in regard to man's duty to his God, he exclaims in the language of my text, Remember this also about the sacred Sabbath day. As if Moses were almost gone, he calls him back and gives him further instruction in regard to himself. Remember how often, my brethren, have you as fathers and mothers called back your children and given them further advice. I can recall today vividly the incidents of my childhood in this direction. I can see my father or mother standing on the old door step just as I was about to pass the corner of the street and calling me back to tell me something they had forgotten, to give me new instruction. I can see them in thought as I draw nearer, calling to me in the language of my text, Remember! Don't forget this or that. And is there a man or woman, is there a father or mother, is there a boy or girl who cannot remember the same incident in their life?

We can all remember, I venture to say, such an experience. And so, my brethren, I have thought that God has dictated the law in regard to the Sabbath in this forcible style. Remember! For as all parents fully realize the fact that children are not apt to remember long, so God— recognizing the fact of the proneness of man to forget and also that his heart is fully set in him to do evil—cautions him with all the entreaties and warnings of this word to remember the Sabbath day.

Let us for a short time consider how men follow the injunction of this text. Some men, as you are well aware, have forgotten it altogether. They are something like an old woman I heard of during the war that heard for the first time of Washington's death. They never seemingly by their actions have heard of this day. They are something like the disciples of John that told Paul that they had not so much as heard whether there be a holy ghost or not. So these men seem to be living in Egyptian darkness on this question when you meet them on the Sabbath. They are all at work as busy as a bee in summer. The farmer will be seen way back in his field plowing. The carpenter has his shop door closed, but if you look through the window you will see him planing[12] away the sacred Sabbath day. The merchant takes account of stock on that day or looks over his books, while some throw the door wide open to invite the world to look at their wares. It is as they suppose a general holiday. And when do goods sell so well as on such a day to sell goods?

Then, my hearers, there is another class that plans out all the amusement of the week for this day. When Sabbath comes, John with his hook and line is seen making his way to the nearest stream, soon to be joined by a goodly company. And there they sit all day long, laughing and joking and ever and anon congratulating themselves on their good or bad luck until night draws her mantle over them. Some go out for a long drive on this day, some to take a sail, and some — alas that I should announce it as a living fact! — look upon this day as the best in the week to go, as they call it, "on a good drunk". There are, my hearers, thousands of hard-working men in this land of ours who toil and sweat for the scanty pittance they get, that spend it on the Sabbath day for rum and then take Monday to "straighten up" as they term it.

Then there are a class that look on the Sabbath day as emphatically a day of rest. They generally rise about ten o'clock with slippers on. They take an early dinner, and then retire to rest again, getting up about 3 o'clock, when perhaps they will take a walk with their family and go to church in the evening. These may be termed half-Sabbath Christians. And as I think over this word, I have thought it would be well not only to keep it holy in the sense of the text, but also wholly in the sense of an entire consecration of this day to the service of God, from the dawn till the close of day.

And finally, my hearers, there is one more class who have preserved this blessed day to us in all its purity, who have stood on the ramparts and beat back the hosts who have desolated its purity. And they, my brethren, are the devoted Christian men and women who rise with a song of joy on their lips, who spend a short time in prayer on its opening, who sit beneath its sacred portals all day long and drink at the fountain of living waters. These men and women, my brethren, have bequeathed this day as a sacred legacy from sire to son to the present day. And though the powers of darkness have prevailed against its

12   Using a carpentry tool with a sharp metal plate to "plane" or smooth the surface of a wooden plank. This was manual labor, frowned upon on the Sabbath.

purity in many portions of our world and of our own land, yet still like the immortal three hundred at the pass of Thermopylae,[13] the Christians of today propose to die, sword in hand, on this question.

The sanctity of the Sabbath day. I remember to have seen this struggle of the Christian army beautifully illustrated in the city of Philadelphia some years ago. There was a terrible struggle to have the street cars run on Sunday. The poor women and children wanted fresh air, said the advocates of Sabbath breaking, and they proposed to ride roughshod over the lovers of the Christian Sabbath. But these men, my hearers, were not to be bought or sold. They could not argue or convince the Christians of that city that it was not wrong to drive the noble and faithful horse seven days a week and three hundred sixty-five days a year. And finally it was appealed to the courts, and a decision was granted allowing the running of the cars on Sunday, but it was carried from court to court until the Supreme Court decided in favor of the cars. The Christian men and women of that city were defeated, but they died at their post, contending for the right to the last. And now, my hearers, let me ask what was the effect of that decision, and of every decision of like character? As the child is molded by his parents, so communities are molded in their relation to this day. The father molds his son as surely as the sun molds the seasons. If the father works on Sunday, his son will not regard it with less respect. If he indulges in baseball and all other amusements of the Sabbath, the son will do the same, and proudly point to his father and say: he does it, why should not I? This truth will hold good the world [over]. The good man will leave his example as a pattern for his son and if the father has contended for the Sabbath day, the son will grasp the falling weapon from his sire and be found in the same course.

And so with these men in Philadelphia. They were molded by the cities around them. And as greed of gold makes man to man unjust, they sought an excuse for their actions. Twas not long till they found one. And, my brethren, this day has been profaned so much by the nations of the world that they can find an excuse now for almost any action they contemplate in regard to the Sabbath day. Why, said they, New York allows cars to run on Sunday, why not Philadelphia? They pointed with exultation to almost every city in this land of ours as an example for them. St. Louis was a pattern; Chicago set them an example; Baltimore

---

13   Reference to the battle of Thermopylae, where King Leonidas of Sparta defeated the much larger Persian army of King Xerxes in 480 BCE. In military history, this is a famous example of a patriotic army defending its own soil, and as a symbol of courage over overwhelming odds.

and Washington joined the glad song; and Philadelphia must succumb.

It did succumb, my hearers, and the next petition was one from the Lager beer men. They said, beer was like soda water and they wanted the privilege of keeping open on Sunday too, and proudly pointed to Germany for their standard of this day. And at this rate, my hearers, we can get a standard for every violation of the Sabbath under the sun. Spain regards the Sabbath as a holiday, and while the son and daughter of Rome will go to mass in the morning, they with far more pleasure see a bull fight in the afternoon. And in France, the afternoon is one grand gala day. Theaters and dance hall throw open wide their doors to welcome the devoted Catholics to their portals. How the children of thugs are brought up to look at murder! France was not always as it is.

Thanks be to God, my brethren, the Protestant Christians of this land of the free and the home of the brave propose to fight it out on a different principle! They believe that the salvation of their sons and daughters is at stake. They believe the very bulwarks of this republic are being undermined by such pernicious doctrines. The world does not care whether the cars run on Sunday or not, but it is only a stepping stone to tear away all the hallowed principles that the Christians hold near and dear to their hearts. Let us then, my brethren, remember this sacred day with more love than ever before. Let us elevate the standard of God our father "Remember the Sabbath day to keep it holy" and with one voice and heart let us crowd around its shrine and battle for its principles. Let us remember in this land that as ignorance increases, vice increases; and as knowledge grows, men recognize the fact that God governs the nations of the world and not men; that sin is a reproach deep and lasting; and that righteousness exalteth a people.

The question naturally occurs, why did God specially designate this day as a day of rest? The answer is because God rested on that day from his labor. But, my brethren, there is a deeper reason than all this. Our Saviour asks his disciples in one place: Can ye not discern the signs of the times? And we might well ask, Cannot the man or woman who studies this word perceive a lesson from this text? God has a far reaching object in view when he commands his children to keep the Sabbath day holy. Think you the infinite God who performs his wonders on the deep had need of rest on the seventh day? I cannot believe it. But as the Lord's supper was instituted for a perpetual remembrance of Christ's death, so I believe, my hearers, that this day was instituted for a perpetual remembrance of our dependence on God's all-wise providence. Each week as it passes away brings us to another Sabbath day. And if the traveler is in a country village or in the crowded city, he cannot fail but be impressed with the solemn fact that God rules and man must obey. All laws pale before God's laws. And as the traveler walks the street he must exclaim as the centurion at the cross of Christ, Surely this is God's day! The busy hum of business is hushed. No more do you behold the rumbling cart and care-worn driver. No more the hammer of ceaseless workmen. All has changed, and solemn stillness pervades the community. Man acknowledges God as over all, and we are the creatures [of His] hands.

God has not only commanded us to remember the Sabbath day, but He has placed it in such a position that no matter how steeped in sin the man or woman is, he must remember it. Every seven days this day confronts him anew with its solemn message. And while he may discard it, he cannot forget it. Like the top the boy pushes under water, it comes to the surface again, and no amount of pushing will keep it there. So this day he may deride and defy, but he cannot, my hearers, he cannot forget it.

Is there a man who would discard this day, let me tell him that in a temporal view this day is necessary. It is as necessary, my hearers, for this day as for the air we breathe. If men worked always and forever they would soon lose their reason. This is a proven fact. All work and no play would unfit a man for all business. He must have recreation. And here comes the Sabbath and presents her claims to your consideration. You cannot only have rest from your labors, but you can thank and worship God in the beauty of holiness. You can draw your minds away from the world and thank God for all His goodness and mercy, you can contemplate Him in His Love, in His tenderness, in His compassion. And leaving all the troubles of life behind, you can for one day walk and talk with God.

And then, my hearers, did you ever think of the amount of good this day performs in this world of ours? This day is indeed the leaven that leavens the whole week. The stillness it exerts induces consideration and thought. If you can get a man to think, you have accomplished a great work. And what the world wants is calm consideration of their relation to God. And the stillness of the Sabbath day does this. It induces thought. Have you ever, my hearers, been alone in a dark room or far out on the prairie by yourself? If so, how soon do you commence to think deeply and earnestly? If you have done wrong, conscience is reproving you. Its still, small voice will there assert itself. You may try to banish it, but it will not be driven away. And whatever affects a man most, that will he think of soonest.

If you are at a political meeting, your thoughts for days will turn in that direction. You will imagine you can hear this candidate praised or this one reproved. If you have been lately investing in goods, this will be the theme of your thoughts. If you have heard a grand and eloquent speech, this will be uppermost in your mind. And because of this fact, the Sabbath day was established to draw men's minds towards God. God wants some of your thoughts, my unconverted brother and sister, and if you will only study your loving Father's goodness you will acknowledge Him as your God and Father.

The stillness of the Sabbath, like the morning cloud, lingers on the breath of Monday, and the Sabbath day and that alone has by its hallowed influence saved thousands of men and women that never would have been saved in any other. There are men, my hearers, that have been saved by this day that never went to church. They perhaps have desired to fly away, but they could not. This day, like God, was everywhere. In the dance hall among lewd women, and in the theater, in the work shop and store, the sacred Sabbath knocked for admittance and presented by its very stillness and quietness its plea for God. Cursing would not drive it away. Work could not send it off. Like the dove of peace, it has been hovering over you all your life. And it asks [you] to love God because God loved you.

I was peculiarly impressed with this fact while corning to the West. We arrived in St. Louis on Saturday night and the next day was the Sabbath day. I knew it before I rose from my bed. I listened in vain for the tramp of busy feet. The cart horse and his driver had vanished away, as it were, and universal stillness reigned around. And then the old church bell commenced to ring, telling the Sabbath breaker this was God's day. It rang out the glorious news, my hearers, all over that great city. The sound of that bell went down to the wretched hovel where poverty reigned supreme. In the prisoner's cell it came through iron bars to cheer his heart. The sick man knew the sound thereof. It floated out like the night air all around, telling the sleeper to arise and go up to the house of God and he will teach them of his way.

And then, my brethren, the next thought that impressed the beholder was the little children wending their way to the Sabbath school. Those, my hearers, that God declared are the representative of heaven on earth, they were going before the Christian army. They were to me presenting their plea first, leading off the procession to the house of God, with happy hearts and cheerful voices, with all the care that loving mothers could bestow upon their darling boys and girls. They were coming from near and from far — from the palace where broad and spacious avenues greeted the eye, and from the dark and dismal alley. They were coming in all the pride and love of a mother's heart. Some of them were dressed in purple and fine linen, some of them came with clean faces and coats of many colors so poor perhaps they had no shoes to cover their little feet.

But though they came in poverty their songs were just as sweet. Beneath the tattered garment there flowed the love of God. And as their voices joined in the hymn

I'll away, I'll away

To the Sabbath school with the morning light,

Their hearts were just as happy as those who never knew what it was to suffer want.

But there [was] another scene yet to that Sabbath day, my brother, as the old church bell rang out her call again the father and mother in Israel join the procession to the house of God. They came like the children from the palace and from the hovel. They came from spacious avenues and from the crowded alley. They came in purple and fine linen and in poverty, with careworn faces and sorrow stamped on their brow. Some of them have worn the old coat and hat for a long time. The wife ought to have a new shawl, the boy a new pair of shoes. But leaving all these things behind, they, my hearers, come to worship God, to drink in the glorious news of salvation, to find out about that better land where sorrow and sadness shall flee away forever and forever.

And so, my brethren, I have thought that just like that from the Atlantic to the Pacific, from New York to San Francisco, from Chicago to New Orleans, all over this land of ours in every village and hamlet, the Christian army is marching to the house of God. From 40,000 pulpits the news of salvation is proclaimed of this the sacred Sabbath day.

And think you, my hearers, men are not impressed by these weekly scenes? I believe they are. The Sabbath day is a day in which Christian men and women can let their light shine above all other days. Said a man at one of Mr. Moody's meetings, "I was converted and led to see my danger by a little child going to Sabbath school." That man, I venture to say, would never have been converted in any other way. You could not get him inside the house of God. But the little one with her bright and happy face touched his hardened heart. And as the Christians of this land of ours cherish this day, as they keep it holy, as they keep it in all its original purity, in just that proportion will the Sabbath day impress men and draw them by its power to the cross of Christ.

I believe, my hearers, we should keep it not only holy in the sense of worship but wholly in the sense of the entire consecration of this day to God. You will not keep a man in your employ who works only half the time. You want a man that will work all day long. And God wants such Christians. Men and women above all others to keep this day to hand it down as a precious legacy from son to son so that the world may be led to the foot of the cross. Such men will preach Christ to the perishing ones around as they walk the street. And though they may like Moses be slow of speech, still the falling shadow of the devoted Christian will be a far more effectual sermon to that man or woman who desecrates this day than all the eloquence of Demosthenes.[14]

Finally, my hearers, we should keep this day holy first because God rested on the seventh day from all his labors. What stupendous work he performed for you and me, my brother, in the six days preceding this day! This book declares that God created the heaven and the earth. He made the light and the darkness. He separated the sea and land. He divided our seasons and caused the earth to bring forth her fruit in its season. He made the sun and moon and stars. He filled the air with birds and the sea with fish and the earth with every living thing for man's convenience and comfort. And finally, to consummate all, He made man in His own image. He gives him dominion over the fish of the sea, over the fowls of the air, and the beast of the field. And as each day rolls around, let us remember that God rested. On that day He surveyed the works of his hand. Let us turn to it with sorrow and sadness as did the Jews towards Jerusalem, and remember that there was a time in our history when we appeared before our maker in all the purity of our creation, ere sin had marked us as her victim. Yet disease had no power over us then. Let us remember it, my hearers — you that are fathers and mothers — because of your children. Consecrate this day to God for their sake. Show them by your example that you love this day. And as you wish them to be good men and women, leave behind you a living legacy of your devotion to the Sabbath day.

Remember it finally, my hearers, because God has commanded you to keep it holy. Tis but a small sacrifice He asks of you. You love to see your services appreciated. God wants you to show your regard and thankfulness to Him for all His mercies conferred on us by keeping this

---

14   A famous orator of ancient Athens, 384-322 BCE.

day holy. Let us then, my hearers, resolve to consecrate this day anew to His service for our children's sake, for the sake of perishing humanity, and to show our love for God.

Our gratitude. Let us not be ungrateful. We detest it in men. We scorn to see the benefactor insulted by that one who has received a favor at his hand. Men have reared many temples and statues to commemorate the name and fame of the great men of earth. Let us then rear anew the sacredness of the Sabbath day. Let us commemorate this day as a living witness of God's goodness. Let us rally with one voice and heart around its standard and God will own and crown your labors with success.

Then, my hearers, this seventh day of our week shall shine out as some bright comets in the heavens, untarnished by one blur to mar their beauty. Monday shall be robbed of her returning cares and sorrows. Tuesday shall be bathed in the light of heaven instead of the darkness of earth. Wednesday shall be the central star around which all the rest shall circle. Thursday shall be lighted by the sun of righteousness instead of the darkness of death. Friday shall no more be darkened by the hangman's halter and Saturday shall be but the beginning of another Sabbath. They, my brethren, we shall not only be changed, but these week days shall be changed also. The angel of God shall inscribe Sunday over Monday and Tuesday and Wednesday and Thursday and Friday and Saturday and one eternal Sabbath shall roll on forever and forever.

Man frail—God eternal.

O God, our help in ages past,
  Our hope for years to come,
Our shelter from the stormy blast,
  And our eternal home:——
2 Under the shadow of thy throne
  Still may we dwell secure;
Efficient is thine arm alone,
  And our defense is sure.
3 Before the hills in order stood,
  Or earth received her frame,
From everlasting thou art God,
  To endless years the same.

"O God our help in ages past," *Hymns for the Use of the Methodist Episcopal Church*, revised edition. New York, Carlton & Lanahan, 1870. # 1059.

BEATITUDES

LAW OF LIBERTY

> James 1: 25. But whoso looketh into the perfect law of liberty, and continueth therein, he being not a forgetful hearer, but a doer of the work, this man shall be blessed in his deed.

In this beautiful passage of scripture filled with so many subjects for thought and reflection, one of the first thoughts is that of perfection. The apostle declares this law to be a perfect law and have we not every reason that can convince the human understanding that he declares truthfully? Perfection is stamped upon all the handywork of God. The sun that shines so beautiful is no more perfect than the blade of grass that ripens beneath its luster. Look where you will upon nature's works or upon nature's God and the answer comes back that His work is a perfect work and that His law shall last while the rolling ages roll.

The apostle urges upon us the injunction to look. And Oh, my Christian friends, how essential it has proven in these times of wild speculation when the whole world seems to be turned into a kind of vanity fair and the guiding star of man's ambition seems to be fortune and fame! When this sacred word filled with the knowledge of life and of the Life to Come lies as an ornament — perhaps on some richly furnished table, or perchance upon some neglected shelf covered with dust and rubbish. It lays neglected and forgotten, its pages are never unfolded, its truths are never read before the family altar or in the secret chamber, and the souls of all within that sacred circle are perishing for heavenly food.

Every man, especially that man whose confiding wife and loving children hang upon his grin, drinking in all his words and taking lessons from his every action, occupies the position of the candle so beautifully portrayed in this volume, and shed a light either for good or evil to all within that happy home. There are those here present who fill that position. And I would urge them in the name of that loved home, with all its sacred scenes, to add one more scene and gather in the boys and girls. And while John sits on one knee and Lizzie on the other, and wife perhaps is keeping the baby, unfold this sacred word and read those things which will make for their eternal happiness. Draw their young lives toward the Saviour of mankind and sow that heavenly seed that shall make not only your life happy but the lives of all around. Then indeed will you send forth ministering angels to scatter joy and gladness to all the desolate ones within their reach. By studying this word, we have the glorious assurance that we shall be blessed. Oh my Christian friends this is an assurance that will doubly repay all the labor and time devoted to this study.

Let me this evening, in the name and by the authority of this holy word, urge upon that man who tonight feels that he has no talents to give to the Lord, who serves him like trembling Peter afar off, ready at any time to fall a prey to the adversary of souls, to take courage and be strong in the Lord. Let me urge you to this fountain of life! Bring forth your long neglected Bible! And as you read it you can feel, like that one who took up his bed and walked, the vital power of God flash through thy palsied soul. As you read its sacred pages you can hear, heralded back from the far off mount of Galilee by thy Saviour, the blessed assurance: Blessed are the poor in spirit for theirs is the kingdom of heaven. Then indeed will the cloud that hovers o'er thy soul making all around dark and gloomy, melt and pass away, chased by the glorious power of God's eternal day.

No more will thy soul be burdened with care
And tremble and shrink on the verge of despair.
But the perishing ones that circle around
Will draw from thy heart the life-giving sound
That Jesus has saved thee and shed o'er thy soul
A power and light that forever shall roll
And the kingdom of heaven thy portion shall be
There to rest with the Saviour forever more free.

Time would fail to tell of all the rich promises of God that shine out all over His inspired word like the glittering star far away in the blue of heaven. So these promises can be viewed. And as your desire is to view one star in heaven, you naturally turn that way.

Let me this evening speak to you, a company viewing the sacred heaven, let me draw you away from life and its turmoils and like a company far away, viewing the rich gift of some friend, let me present to you this blessed gift. And as you spread it out in imagination, looking at its beauties and admiring this star and that, let me point you to one near and dear to every soul, that takes in the saved and unsaved of this life. And as you look at it, its light shines down into thy troubled soul, and comfort cheers thy bleeding heart. And as you look still nearer you may read: Blessed are they that mourn, for they shall be comforted. Oh take courage, you that are sorrowing for loved ones! And in this sacred word find comfort to thy soul. Remember that tears fell from the eyes of heaven's dear son as he viewed the sorrows of Lazarus' friends.

But let us look at that one, seemingly forgotten and lost in all this brilliant collection. And glimmering out are the words: "Blessed are the meek for they shall inherit the earth." That is a star of hope in these dark hours of pride and arrogance—a promise that may yet save our loved land from ruin and desolation, a promise that cheers that man dressed in humble garb. Be encouraged. God's word declares that the world's wealth is thine and eternal wealth hereafter.

But as you look, shining out more brilliant than all the rest is that star of hope to the thirsty soul, the burden of whose cry is: I drink and yet am ever dry! He reads: Blessed are they that hunger and thirst after righteousness, for they shall be filled. This promise, like some welcome rain upon the poor traveler journeying over some desert Sahara fills the soul with joy and gladness, and he is enabled to go on his way rejoicing. So, my Christian friends, we are traveling in a great desert where dangers stand thick through all the ground to drag us down to eternal death, where sin and iniquity abound on every hand. And sometimes in our journey we come across some poor traveler, almost ready to lay down and despair of ever reaching the eternal city. The longings of his heart are, oh! that I had wings like a dove! Then would I fly away and be at rest. Be encouraged, ye that hunger and thirst. There is an abundant feast prepared for you. God's word declares you shall be filled.

I love to think of that man, my Christian friends, whose whole life seems to be a study how to perform the will of God. As he walks the street, the mantle of God seems to be resting upon him. His hand is ever ready to save the perishing ones of earth. He speaks while he is walking and sitting. A heavenly halo goes forth from him that is constantly doing good and drawing men toward Calvary's cross. These men have been declared by our blessed Lord as the salt of the earth; and none, I venture the assertion, will contradict it. Imagine what a vast amount of good will be accomplished by such soldiers! These are the kind of warriors that shall shake the walls of sin to their foundation. Imagine an army of such men, clothed in all the panoply of God, marching every day around this sin-cursed earth ; marching on not only seven times as did the army of Joshua, but seventy times seven! And think you their prayers and tears will fall powerless to the ground? No, No! I have the authority of this sacred word to say that they will rise up, though after many days, and bring forth an abundant harvest to the honor and glory of God.

And now, my Christian friends, in conclusion remember that

heaven's blessings are standing out in bold relief all over this glorious heaven. You may look and read of the blessings awaiting all the sons of earth. Hear the inspired words of Christ:

> Blessed are the merciful for they shall obtain mercy. Blessed are the pure in heart for they shall see God. Blessed are the Peacemakers for they shall be called the children of God. Blessed are they which are persecuted for righteousness sake for theirs is the kingdom of heaven. Blessed are ye when men shall revile you and persecute you and shall say all manner of evil against you falsely for my name's sake. Rejoice and be exceeding glad, for yours is the kingdom of heaven.[15]

And there is one other promise that shall cheer all those that are heavy-laden down to life's latest breath. And when the trembling soul is hovering o'er the dark abyss, and sin's dark wave shuts out the home of bliss, tis then he can turn his eyes and view the Savior of mankind and hear him saying: whosoever will may come and partake of the waters of life freely, without money and without price.

And now, my Christian friends, my text declares that "whoso looketh into the perfect law of liberty and continueth therein, he being not a forgetful hearer ..." And just hear at the word "forgetful". Let us stop and think how truthful it is and how prone to forget is man. This is the great thorn in the flesh of all mankind. Forgetfulness. People will sit down and read this word from a conviction of duty — good men and women — and after they have closed the book they hardly know what they have been reading, or if they have been reading. Or if they remember it, they do not live out its counsels. To remember is to obey. And it matters little if the world were blazoned all over with the warning "Thou shalt not kill" if every man followed his own judgment and killed notwithstanding.

How eagerly do men remember the passing events of each day, especially that which concerns their own business. No man sells his goods but what the ledger is brought forth and it is written down, while the heavenly ledger — that book which has recorded within its pages the accounts of eternity — is forgotten and life's race is run. And as he comes down to the brink of death he remembers that there is such a heavenly journal within his house. All hands engage in the search for the lost treasure. Tis at last found, the dust is wiped off, and on a dying bed he commences that work which should have occupied his whole life. The

---

15   Matthew 5:7-12.

account is found wanting, and his soul passes on to live forever in bliss or woe.

In traveling o'er this broad land of ours you will see at the crossing of every public road with the railroad, the warning "Look out for the locomotive" nailed up high so that every one may see it. And this Bible has a warning for every traveler through life's pathway — at every crossing from the straight and narrow way there is a warning. I see in imagination some soldier of the cross in this narrow path come to the broad road that leads to eternal death, and sin holds out the tempting prize. Earth and hell conspire to draw him in this broad way but as he turns and looks up he sees written in characters that shall live forever "Escape for thy life" and he forgets not its truths but crying "Get thee behind me, Satan!" presses on.

And so all through life's journey are the finger boards of heaven pointing upward and calling this way. The pleading voice of God is knocking at every heart and its cry is "Turn from your evil way and do good." Oh my dear hearers let me urge you once again in the language of my text to look into this blessed word.

Tis heaven's own weapon, tis the Savior's bright sword
That he wielded on earth when he fasted and prayed
And that crowned him victorious o'er death and the grave
Tis offered to you as the Father's rich blessing
'Twill save you from death and crown you in heaven.

There is one other thought and I have done and that is the thought of liberty. The text declares that the Bible is a law of liberty. Now as you know the Bible declares that the wages of sin are death and in thinking o'er this passage how beautiful and yet how truthful is the thought of liberty. We are enabled by the power of this law to shake off the shackles of sin, which by nature is our lot. We are born slaves, held in a tighter grip than was ever slave before. No pains have been spared to keep us from the light. Earth with all its allurements draws us by nature from this liberty, and we are prone to wander from the right way. The longings of man's soul are ever naturally from God, and it requires some effort on our part at first to submit to the pure law of light. But having at last looked into this law of Liberty and seen how rich are its promises and how great are its rewards, who can fail to accept this law as his rule of life? This law declares that we shall have eternal life at God's right hand, while the law of sin is that we shall live forever with the lost. This law of liberty declares that we are the children of God.

As we view the good man that takes the Bible for his chart, we may almost see the blessing of God resting upon him. His step is firm and his countenance bears upon it the impression of youth. Even in age his silvery hairs tell of a youth well spent and he rejoices in hope of soon bidding adieu to earth and its cares and living with the angels in light. How different that man whose life has been spent in all the allurements and its pleasures! He too can be told as he walks the street, and as you view him you cannot fail to see a slave to his own appetites. His life has been wasted, and no ray of hope cheers him on as he nears the tomb.

Oh, my dear hearer, there is life within this law! There is death outside its walls! Step into that law and be saved — saved from the sins of the world — and made new creatures in Christ Jesus. Life will be happy then, and death will lose its terrors. You will be enabled to look forward in death's dark hour and say, "Though I walk through the shadow of death I will fear no evil, for thy rod and staff do comfort me." Heaven is waiting, angels are calling, and God's word is pleading, "Come!" And I would urge you once again in the language of my text,

> Whoso looketh into the perfect law of liberty, and continueth therein, he being not a forgetful hearer, but a doer of the work, this man shall be blessed in his deed.[16]

Pass me not, O gentle Saviour,[17]
Hear my humble cry;
While on others thou art calling,
Do not pass me by.

2 Let me at thy throne of mercy
Find a sweet relief;
Kneeling there in deep contrition,
Help my unbelief.

3 Trusting only in thy merit,
Would I seek thy face;
Heal my wounded, broken spirit,
Save me by thy grace.

4 Thou the spring of all my comfort,
More than life to me;
Whom have I on earth beside thee?
Whom in heaven but thee?

---

16   James 1:25.
17   "Pass me not, O Gentle Saviour," by Frances Jane Van Alstyne, 1870. *The Book of Common Praise*, Oxford, 1938.

LOVE

GOD IS LOVE

> **Mark 9:33-37.** And he came to Capernaum: and being in the house he asked them, What was it that ye disputed among yourselves by the way? But they held their peace: for by the way they had disputed among yourselves by the way? But they held their peace: for by the way they had disputed among themselves who should be the greatest.
>
> And he sat down, and called the twelve, and saith unto them, If any man desire to be first, the same shall be last of all, and servant of all.
>
> And he took a child, and set him in the midst of them: and when he had taken him in his arms, he said unto them. Whosoever shall receive one of such children in my name, receiveth not me, but him that sent me.

This, my hearers, was the first act that proved God's love to man beyond all doubt: the promise of a Saviour—an immediate promise. Love is not ready to wait for a favorable opportunity and then help, but "Now!" is her cry. Today is the accepted time. Does a helpless and unfortunate being present himself at your door and ask for help, and if you have the power to help, are you going to stop and ask: Are you of my creed? Do you belong to my church? And if he does help him, and if he does not refuse? That is not love. That is not God. For He sends his rain on the just and the unjust alike.

Love, according to my text, is the certificate of the Christian man, the only token of his sonship. He that loveth not, knoweth not God. And though it is impossible to describe the new birth of the soul in the image of Christ, though I cannot tell you how the still small voice always speaks to burdened souls, this I can say, my brethren, that the fruit of that new birth is love. As you can tell a tree by its fruit, so you can tell if a man has been taken up by the power of God and planted in his church. Does his every action breathe out the same old spirit that you saw in him before, does he delight now in sin as he did before, does no ray of this heavenly attribute breathe out from his nature to fallen humanity does he, in a word love now where he hated before? If he does not, my hearers, he is not born again. He knoweth not God by an experimental religion.

He that loveth not is not of God, and on the same principle, he that loveth is of God. "And though the man be poor, so poor that he can but give a cup of water in my name, he is my disciple," says Christ. "Though so poor that she can give but one penny in my name, she is my disciple." God, my hearers, is gathering in these loving ones from every clime. Do you love, you are mine. The heathen in all his darkness may still be a disciple of Christ if he love his fellow man. From the Creation to the present day, Love has been circling round and round this globe, gathering in the loving ones into heaven. God is love. Heaven is love. He that loveth not is not of God and is not bound for heaven. Heaven is peopled with the loving ones of earth. Hate cannot enter there; malice cannot enter there; pride cannot enter there; ambition cannot enter there; but only love – only one attribute – no discord – a universal blending together.

I have thought sometimes, my hearers, of the woman who came to Christ with her two sons. She was ambitious, but ambition could not enter heaven. "Grant, Lord," said she, "that this son may sit on the right and this one on the left." But Christ could not grant it. And then the question among the disciples: "Who shall be the greatest," said they to Christ, "in thy kingdom?" And he took a little child and sat it in the midst of them. And said, "He that is least among you, the same shall be the greatest." And then again we read he took the little ones up and blest them and said, "For of such is the kingdom of heaven." What more loving than a little child? That seems to be its whole store of knowledge: Love. No more does it possess.

And we are to become as little children in the sense of love. Dictionaries may define love to mean thus and so, men may define it to mean this and that, but if you want to find out the meaning of this word love in all its grand and heavenly attributes, go to the child in all its innocence, and there see your definition. Christ might have preached for three long years on love to God, he might have told how the inhabitants of heaven loved one another, he might have enlarged on the beauties of love till he carried his hearers to the other world, but when he took the little child in its innocence and purity and sat it in the midst of them and exclaimed: Here is heaven, heaven is like this little child, God is like this child, the angels are like this child, the ransomed of the Lord are like this child – when he explained it in that way, every heart could comprehend. It was not too high for the poor, they could go up. It was not too low for the rich, they could come down. All could comprehend the meaning there.

He that loveth not in this life, my hearers, how unhappy he is!

That man or woman who cultivates this quality of love is a happy man or woman wherever he is. There are some old log cabins, my brethren, that look rough on the outside, that look like the picture of woe, but they are heaven for all that. And there are some palaces robed in all the beauty that art and wealth can put upon them, that are prison houses of despair for all that. Love can fare sumptuously on the crust of bread; hate will famish with all the market will afford. God is love, and man ought to be love.

The heart of man naturally is like God. Hate must be cultivated. Just like the boy cultivating a taste of tobacco. He does not like it at first, but if he keeps on, he will acquire the habit. Hate is not natural with the child or with the man, but it can be cultivated till it becomes a second nature with him and he goes forth to spread a dark miasma all around. He is not happy himself. He sees nothing he loves. He pines and frets and worries at everything. He is ready to find fault with every man and woman. He never speaks a good word for any person, and he is not only unhappy himself, but he makes every person he comes in contact with unhappy.

Not so with love that is ready to look on the bright side of everything, always ready to forgive, always happy. One of the grandest proofs of man's divine origins is his longing for something to love. God is love, and his love is displaced on every hand to man. And we are the children of God because we as naturally desire to love as God. Love seems to be the spontaneous outgush of the Father – the river of life that flows from the throne of God down to earth and fills and thrills every part of our fallen nature is the spirit of the Father. I care not, my hearers, how far the man may have sunk in sin; I care not though like one of old Satan has taken full possession of his heart, though he has bound him with a thousand cords; though the artillery of hell may play from a thousand batteries the shot and shell of the evil one; still he cannot drive out love from the man's heart. There is always, my hearers, a small breastwork amid the ruins that like old Fort Sumter still holds a valiant guard. The prisoner at the bar may laugh at Justice, may stalk forth to meet his doom with sullen despair, but his old mother will bring the tear to his eye. He may have cultivated hate till he seems to hate the whole world, but you can never drive out his love for his father or mother if you lock him up in his prison cell for ten, fifteen, eighteen years, or for life, and give him nothing to love. How wretched beyond all description is he! His cry is for something to twine his affections around. Nothing too low, nothing too mean. Now a mouse will be a welcome guest and many a long and weary hour has been beguiled away, my brethren, by such an insignificant companion, while perhaps some of you were among scenes of the brightest joys.

This love, my brethren, that is a part of God's nature and ours, reaches out like the arms of the cuttlefish in every direction. It must have something to twine around. Men will love something, and if that is so, my hearers, how important it is to the little one, that one that Christ has declared is the representative of heaven! And twine its affections around lovely things. Never was there a nobler work that engaged man or woman than that. This innate love in the Child is reaching out on every hand, and the father and mother must watch the course it takes with greater caution than ever the husbandman took.

Imagine, my hearers, a vine that is planted in a grove with only one tree to twine around, and think you it will follow the course marked out? If it is not watched, I venture to say no. Ever and anon it will take hold of other trees, and he must be constantly watching its course. And so, my hearers, I have thought of the child. He is planted in a grove where thistles and thorns and briers abound on every hand, and with all the care of the father and the love of the mother, she finds to her sorrow that these arms of love have twined around wrong, have found something that is not right, and she must be constantly watching to keep her boy in the right path. And God, my brethren, has planted you and me in a grove where sin abounds on every hand, where our affections are liable to be drawn away from God, and if we want to stay in the straight path, how constantly we must be watching ourselves! We are to twine around Christ. We are to cultivate his spirit. Christ is the vine, and we are the branches, and if we follow the chart that is given, we need not be at loss, for the royal way to heaven is the royal way of the cross.

God is love; Heaven is love, a vast ocean of heavenly bliss. And Christ is love; Christ is the way to this port. And never did nobler study engage man or woman than the study of Christ. We only know God through Christ. And as Christ is the exemplification of God's love to man on earth, let us for a short time consider the grand lessons that he has left us in regard to this study. Love seems to be his theme to man all the time. Did he heal the sick? Did he weep over the dead? Did he sorrow over the woes of Jerusalem? Did he die on the cross?

It was for you and me. Did he leave a new commandment? It was to love one another. Did he sum up the ten commandments? It was love God and your neighbor. Tis only a God who could have centered in four words every commandment.[18] Those words "Love God" sweep away

---

18   Matthew 22:37-40, quoting Deuteronomy 6:5 and Leviticus 19:18.

every image, sweep away every oath, teach us to revere the Sabbath and to worship God in the beauty of holiness. "Love your neighbor" sweeps away every sin of whatever form and teaches us to love Him as we would love our own bodies. And is it not a noble ambition to cultivate and aspire to all the love that was in Christ.

Men may study this love in this life. They may commence when they are boys in years. Like one of the great preachers of our church, Alfred Cookman,[19] they may go deeper and deeper, higher and higher, till they fairly beam forth with this heavenly attribute, and still exclaim in death sweeping through the gates to the ocean of love beyond.

Every man is the architect of his own fortune in a certain sense of the word. They carry within themselves the power to achieve renown or shame. The murderer started from the same cradle that the good man did. God gave him the same passions that he gave the good man, but he misused them. Does he hate, so God hates evil and cannot look on sin with the least degree of allowance. Hate is a good thing in its place. 'Twould be a poor man that could not say no in time of danger. I hate to do wrong. Daniel Webster would not fight a duel because he dreaded the thought of imbruing his hands in innocent blood. Such hate as that is Godlike hate. If this passion of hate that God has given you will twine around Christ, around the great vine, it will shine out in beauty instead of shame; while, on the contrary, if hate is left to run wild, as it were, it will indeed of all men make you the most miserable.

Do you have ambition, so God has ambition. The ambition of God in regard to man is that he shall love and serve him as a poor man that has no ambition. Ambition in this world has elevated the race to her present standard. Ambition has saved this republic of ours from being torn asunder. Ambition has clothed an army of men into invincible legions. Ambition has sent forth the praying women of our land into the dark and dismal den of woe to seek to save them for God and heaven. Ambition is the nerve that strengthens the arm. And if a man [who] enters into business has no ambition, he never will succeed. That clothes his store in beauty, that sends forth his salesman into every corner of our land. That element in his nature floods the land with bills and advertisements. That element, that attribute, is a twin brother to love.

19   Rev. Alfred Cookman (1828-1871) was a successful businessman and an ardent Methodist who often spoke at various Methodist Camp Meetings in Maryland and surrounding states. While in Ocean Grove, New Jersey, in 1871, he raised $200.00 from the Ocean Grove Camp Meeting audiences, to help found a new Methodist sponsored school for freed black males in Jacksonville, Florida. The money was used to put up the school's first building, and the school was called the Cookman Institute. This school is now the Bethune-Cookman Institute in Daytona. *The Life of Alfred Cookman* by Henry Ridgaway; 1873, Google Books

And if instead of letting it run wild, as it were, it is trained for God and heaven. What a world of good it will do! Ambition, my hearers, is one of the weapons that God designs to conquer the world. That attribute has sent forth the missionary to foreign lands, has clothed the land with houses of worship, and filled the darkened places of the earth with joy and gladness.

Do you have pride, so God has pride. Behold the temple that Solomon built for the residence of our God. It could not be too grand, too noble for the residence of God. Pride is a good thing, and if it is blended with love tis a heavenly attribute. Does not this word say that cleanliness is next to Godliness, and the slovenly man will not do good himself nor do others good? Pride embellished God's house in beauty. Pride spurs men on to keep this grand old gospel in the front ranks all the time. Pride knows no superior. And if this attribute of pride is taken from the world, if it is turned around God and Christ, tis a mighty engine for good. But if the world takes possession of that element, then, my hearers, farewell to religion, farewell to suffering humanity, farewell to all that is good and pure. If Satan takes possession of the heart, then pride instead of bringing forth good fruit will bring forth nothing but thorns and thistles. How important then, my hearers, that this element of our nature is trained around Christ.

Do you love? So God loves. And love seems to be the grandest attribute that God has implanted within us. Woe[ful] indeed is that man that has no love. Better had it been for him had a millstone been hanged about his neck and he been cast into the sea! Love, like some sweet messenger of peace, is soaring up and down this world, seeking to save. Does suffering humanity appeal for help? She [Love] cannot say no. Give, Give, Give willingly. "Give" is the burden of her song and she is ready to share the last crust of bread to alleviate others' woes if this love of God takes full possession of the man. He seems to be helpless before its power. Loves unlocks his pocket and brings forth dollars where cents were before. Love, my hearers, is the angel of peace that knows no surrender. Love will batter down the hardest citadel that ever Satan erected. You cannot drive some men, you cannot force them, but you can draw them by this element. Like the bird that circles round the great fire till it falls helpless beneath its power, so my brethren, this fire of love will draw where all else will fail. God is love; Christ is love; and every professing Christian should beam out with love to God and man. That weapon is the weapon that he designs to conquer the world with. No other will do. Hate is a good thing in its place. But you cannot conquer the world with that. You cannot conquer it with pride or ambition. But when you bring love, that is the invincible legion that does the work.

Mr. Murphy[20] could never have accomplished the grand temperance work that he did, had he not convinced his hearers that he loved them. He could, tis true, tell them how he was found in the fetters of intemperance. He could tell them how he almost broke his old mother's heart. He could tell them how he filled his home with sadness and woe. But when the poor inebriate came to him and told him that he was in need of bread, the first act he did to convince that man that he had his welfare at heart was to clothe and feed him. And when he had convinced him that he loved his outward man, then the poor man was ready to surrender his soul. He knew that he loved him then, he knew that he had his interest at heart. And by that means and that alone this grand old temperance wave has gone on swelling and widening all over this land of ours. Tis not by the magic of eloquence that great popular movements are inaugurated, but by the magic of love. The women of our land that inaugurated this great temperance movement before Mr. Murphy did not do it by their eloquent prayers but by their tears, by their earnest appeals for their welfare.

And so, my hearers, with this salvation by faith in Christ. It was not inaugurated by long sermons, but by deeds of kindness. His cure of the leper was a far more effectual sermon than words that went down in the hearts of his hearers. And as miracle after miracle was performed, his hearers were more ready to believe that he was indeed and in truth God. God is love, and no more worthy representative could have been

---

20   An Irish immigrant, Francis Murphy was a reformed alcoholic whose drinking had destroyed his family and successful hotel and saloon business. Murphy found religion and temperance in 1870 while jailed in Maine for violating the state's prohibition law. After his release, he spent the next five years telling his story and promoting temperance in New England and the Midwest. Everywhere he traveled, he encouraged people to sign pledges not to drink, which he emblazoned with his motto, "With malice toward none and charity for all." Murphy advocated "moral suasion" rather than prohibition as the solution to America's drinking problem, believing the decision not to drink had to be a personal one, not imposed by a legal ban. Pittsburgh in 1876 was still recovering from the Panic of 1873 and its saloon business was booming. A group of concerned Pittsburghers formed the Young Men's Temperance Union (YMTU) and hired Murphy to deliver eight temperance lectures, hoping he could alleviate the city's drunkenness and idleness. In addition to his words, Murphy also provided community and social welfare, believing temperance workers "must offer the drinking man something better than he finds in the saloon before we can make any progress." In Pittsburgh, he organized free holiday dinners for the homeless at the Old Home and raised money to open a shelter for recovering alcoholics. Murphy did so despite church trustees' objections to the large expenditures and prejudiced complaints that Murphy's lower class converts broke windows, ruined the carpet, and disordered the pews. His Blue Ribbon movement was highly successful. *The Heinz History Center* blog, February 28, 2018.

sent into the world to prove his love to man than Christ.

The next thought is how are we going to obtain this spirit of love by kindness? That is the only way that God has left on record for us. Well has it been said tis more blessed to give than receive. Kindness is the tree from which love emanates. And as you cultivate the tree, as you tear away every root and dig around it, in just that proportion will it bear this glorious fruit. Let us then, my hearers, cultivate this glorious fruit with renewed ardor. Not that kindness that never goes farther than the door — for you must know that in all this grand orchard there are more trees that bear a stunted fruit than that bear the luscious fruit. Some men are all that can be desired at home. Home is indeed their heaven. But they never go farther. They will embellish home, they will make every sacrifice to make home happy, but they never get beyond the door. That, my brethren, is not Godlike love. The publicans and sinners will vie with you. Then Christ goes farther than that. His love took in not his own family but the whole world. And if we love only our own and have no tear of sympathy for others' woes, we are not God's.

What a grand world this would be, my hearers, if love was the controlling power! How often have we heard the expression that some poor woman has been cast on the cold, cold charity of the world. No sympathy may she expect. How many there are in this land of ours that have been raised in affluence that must toil at hard labor, while their more fortunate neighbor looks on with cold pity. Perhaps by the midnight light she sews for some unfeeling merchant to keep soul and body alive. Perhaps she toils over the wash tub while her only boy is on the street selling papers. Sad, sad is that man's or woman's condition! I read only the other day of a man that died in Norfolk, Virginia, that was born to titles of honour and power in France — died so poor that he literally starved to death. The world pities him, of course. Pity, vain pity, unfeeling pity did not minister to his wants. Pity, in the language of Shakespeare, is trash. Pity is worse than mockery. Pity, unless accompanied by something more substantial, is worse than an insult.

"How much do you pity this man," said Stephen Girard, as some pitying friends were standing around a poor man that had lost his horse. "I pity him ten dollars." That kind of pity will convert more souls for God, will save more starving men and women, than all the empty pities of the world. That pity emanates from a heart filled with love. And if that divine attribute filled the hearts of men and women instead of this sordid, selfish, cold, unsympathizing pity, there would be happy homes now where there are miserable hovels of woe. If love burned in the hearts of men and women instead of hate and selfish sordid passions, then there would be no need for another heaven after this world was past. Then this would be heaven indeed below. Then we could erect, like Peter of old, permanent tabernacles and abide forever. But where there is one lovely spot now in this great Sahara of the world, there are a thousand sand hills. There are a thousand hearts wrung with anguish and pierced with woe. Instead of being the attribute that fills the mind of men, and instead of treating every man as a brother, they will grind him to powder, follow him remorselessly until he stands like the deer at bay, helpless before his foes. And then, in exultation and unpitying fury, they will fall upon him and strip him of every cent, leave his family penniless to endure the cold, cold pity of the world. From such pity as that, I pray God to deliver you and me.

We shall never, my hearers, know what God and heaven is here below. We do not seem to be able to soar as high as that. Love is an impenetrable problem, but hate in all its worst forms seems to be the monarch of this earth. I care not where you go, she rules. Go with me to China, and you will find that the Chinaman hates the white man with a deeper hatred than ever a white man hated him. Travel with me to India and a high caste Indiaman would as soon touch a rattlesnake as shake hands with you. Let us go to Europe among our own race and the titled nobles cannot be convinced that you [are] as good a man as he. So with religion, with business, with nationalities. Hate and pride rule on every hand and have drawn lines that admit of [permit] no reconciliation. Love, Godlike love, can only be seen among the little ones. The white man's son and the black man's boy will play together without a thought that one is better than the other. You can rear them up together in innocence, but the time soon comes when the one commences to realize that he is a little above his black companion, and hate and pride commence to draw their lines.[21] But, thank God, my brethren, there are no lines in heaven. God is love, and he that loveth not is not, cannot see God, cannot enter there. No hate nor envy can enter there.

Heaven, my Brethren, is like the little one in all its innocence. And though I should preach with the tongue of angels, I cannot give you a better meaning. Though I should draw a thousand paintings and pave the streets with gold, I could not define heaven to your mind as the innocent child can. If you want to see heaven below, look at the little one in all its purity. Take it in your arms and press it to your bosom. And then look at this Book and see "for such is the kingdom of heaven."

---

21   The two children are innately equal, but in the social structure of the times they were not equal.

If I were going to draw heaven before your minds in all its beauty and glory, I should send to China for an infant. I should take one from India. I should take the Indian's babe and the black man's. I should travel to the north pole and find one there, and then to the south pole and find one there. I should gather in the little ones from every corner of the earth and put them all together and exclaim, "Here is heaven!" No jarring-nor discord can be found in that company. None are above the other. They are all on a par. And everyman may understand the interpretation.

Finally, my hearers, let me ask you in conclusion, is not such a grand inheritance worth seeking after? We seek for wealth and honor here, but they must pass away. We see the sorrow and woe there is in this world on every hand. We see the contending passions of men on every hand in business, in religions, in the different races of men, and it seems to be impossible to rid ourselves of it. Is it not then worth a struggle to attain a land where all this will be done away? Where there will be no pride or hate or envy? Nothing but love? I venture to say had I the suffering sons of men before me now I would hear a responsive "Amen" to that. I care not what his religion or caste, such an inheritance would be a joyful change. That inheritance, my hearers, is for us. And it remains for you to accept the grand offers of salvation. Strip yourselves of the pleasure of the world. Throw away the carnal man and put on the new man which is Christ the lord, and become like him in every sense of the word. And though, my hearer, we shall not in this life know what this Godlike love is in all its significance, yet still we shall be enabled to get a foretaste. We shall know more of this love as we sink deeper into the fountain, and finally we shall go home to an inheritance where all is love.

Alas! and Did My Savior Bleed   341

1. A - las! and did my Sav - ior bleed, and did my Sov -'reign die!
2. Was it for crimes that I had done he groaned up - on the tree?
3. Well might the sun in dark - ness hide, and shut his glo - ries in,
4. Thus might I hide my blush - ing face while his dear cross ap - pears;
5. But drops of grief can ne'er re - pay the debt of love I owe;

Would he de - vote that sa - cred head for such a worm as I?
A - maz - ing pit - y! Grace un - known! And love be - yond de - gree!
when Christ, the might - y Mak - er, died for man the crea - ture's sin.
dis - solve my heart in thank - ful - ness, and melt mine eyes in tears.
here, Lord, I give my - self a - way, 'tis all that I can do.

Isaac Watts, 1707
Alt. 1961

MARTYRDOM C.M.
Hugh Wilson, 1800
Arr. Robert A. Smith, 1825

LOVE

ACCESS TO GRACE

> Romans 5:2 - Therefore being justified by faith, we have peace with God through our Lord Jesus Christ: By whom also we have access by faith into this grace wherein we stand, and rejoice in hope of the glory of God.

The apostle Paul in the preceding chapters of this epistle, after recounting to the brethren of the church at Rome the glorious works of his ministry, urges upon them constancy and devotion in their high calling. He tells them in the language of my text how they were brought into this grace, and how they may have admittance to a throne of mercy. His language is by whom also we have access by faith into this grace. In the first verse of this chapter we read that we have peace with God through our lord Jesus Christ. Therefore we have access to a throne of mercy.

Also "by Jesus Christ" is the soul-absorbing theme. The inspired apostle hangs upon the story of the cross as the drowning man hangs upon the passing lifeboat. And what, I ask, is there for sinking humanity, tending toward the grave with lightning speed, to take hold of, but the all atoning blood of Christ. Take away Christ from this word and you take away the word itself. Take away Christ from perishing souls and you knock out the only prop that cheers them on in life's dark hours. What would that poor woman who is surrounded by her innocent children do without the comfort of Christ, as she lives on day after day, struggling to keep the wolf of want from her door? For her children's sake she feels that nothing but them bind her here to earth. And when that chain is severed, life has lost its charm to her and she looks forward by faith in Christ to her heavenly home. Christ then is her all in all.

Who has not read the story of the babe of Bethlehem? How lowly was his birth! But though he was born in a manger, heaven was illuminated with his glory. His star was seen in the east, and the heavenly host sounded his praises all over its wide extent. His life was filled with privations and suffering. While his daily work was the comforting of the lost children of the house of Israel, their sole intent was his destruction,[22]

---

22   This is a great exaggeration. All the early followers of Jesus were themselves Jews.

until at last we view him expiring upon the cruel cross amid scoffs and ridiculing.

This then was the Saviour Jesus Christ, by whom we have access to a throne of grace. Though his life and death were filled with cruel persecution and torture, his resurrection has opened our way to a throne of grace. His mission was to the Jews first, but it has descended to the Gentiles also, and we rejoice today that we can look up and say "Abba, Father!" through Christ our living head.

This, my dear hearers, is a legacy that can never be taken away. The rich man may lose his riches. They may take the wings of the morning and fly away. But if he has Christ in his heart he has that wealth that shall stand when all things earthly shall have passed away. The thirsty one may drink the cooling waters but, Ah! he comes back again to that same old well for more. But this word assures us [that] if we have Christ within us we shall never thirst. Infidels may ridicule the saving power of the blood of Christ. Argument after argument may pile herself in massive columns before his mind to pull down the stronghold of Christianity. But the silent tear and warm embrace of a heart filled with the love of Christ will break through all his reasons and go down to the depth of his soul with convincing force in the efficacy of the blood of Christ.

Have you ever stood before a body of men who had met for the sole purpose of vilifying and slandering the name of Christ? Have you ever heard the arguments they have given for denying the power of his atoning blood? If not, let me tell you this evening my experience in one of these meetings. After arguments had been presented pro and con for Christ, after the stirring appeals of Christians had been laughed down — for if an unbeliever cannot convince you by reason he will ridicule you and try and drive off the champions of the cross by jeers and scoffs — there arose way back in that audience a woman whose trembling voice almost failed to be heard at first. But warming up as the power of God fell upon her, she made an appeal to those hard hearts that was unanswerable for Christ and his kingdom. She did not attempt to go into a learned version of why Christ should possess our hearts' affection, but simply told what great things God had done for her. And I venture the assertion that more than one of that audience were constrained to become Christians from her address.

Ah! my dear hearers, who can be found so small or weak who cannot rise and tell of the love of Jesus? Who cannot stand up and testify

---

Jesus was preaching to his own people, the Jews. The Romans and certain factions wanted to be rid of this upstart teacher for political reasons.

of the power and efficacy of the blood of Christ? It has been said that the Methodists of today are unlike their shouting forefathers. That no more are the classrooms packed and crowded with the veterans of the cross. That no more can the loud hallelujah of the days of yore be heard, and the thrilling appeals of hearts filled with the love of Christ be listened to.

This ought not to be. Those that claim the high privilege of followers of Christ ought at all times to be ready to testify of the love of Christ of how they have access into this grace. Oh how zealous are those who have just tasted of the love of Christ to testify of how they were made whole! Tis no trouble then for them to wade through snow and mud to meet their Christian brethren and sisters in a classroom and make the walls of that consecrated place resound with the praises of God. Then they will be found at every opportunity testifying for Christ. But soon, ah soon a change comes over them. Like the Children of Israel, they look back and long for the fleshpots of old Egypt. Once more their ardor dies out almost as soon as it was kindled, and not many days elapse before they are found once more far away from Christ, far away from this grace, and plunging into the deepest depths of sin. And as you view them, my unconverted friend, you ask yourself the question, why is it that so soon they return once more to their companions in sin? You ask yourself the question why they have lost so soon their love for the classroom, for the secret chamber, and for the people of God. And let sound back the answer, they have lost sight of this holy word. They have lost sight of the means of grace. They have lost sight, in a word, of Christ by whom they have access into this grace, wherein we stand.

Oh my dear hearers, let me urge you to greater devotion and love for Christ. Christianity does not consist in idle forms, but the master call is for workers in his vineyard. As mighty oak becomes rooted and grounded by every hurricane that sweeps its breast, so the Christian becomes established by every good word and work. Tis the laborers that shall gather the harvest. If you want to grow up into this grace wherein the Christian stands, unfold your arms that have hung for so long listless and inactive, and put your shoulder to the wheel of the gospel car.

Shake off the lethargy that has so long bound you to the groveling things of earth. Cast your eyes toward the heavenly harvest that is waiting all around you to be gathered into the garner of the lord. Rest not with halting experience that never changes itself but may be heard Sunday after Sunday, year after year, in these words: I am still striving to serve the Lord in my weak way and manner. There are greater heights than this to be attained. Let your motto, like that of Napoleon's legions when crossing the Alps, be: Excelsior! And like his youthful standard-bearer who, as he sank beneath the everlasting snows of those rugged mountains, sank with his motto [banner] grasped in his hand, so, my dear hearers, you that stand in this grace, as you sink beneath the stroke of death, sink with your face turned toward the new Jerusalem! Sink with the banner of Emmanuel grasped in your hand and your steps on heavenly mounts! And as your comrades meet around your lifeless form, they will feel and know that you have had an abundant access into this grace.

My text declares that by faith in Jesus Christ we are admitted into this glorious fellowship. What more simple and plain explanation than this! But it seems to be a greater mystery today to understand this simple truth than ever before. As time advances, the followers of Christ seem to be at a greater loss to understand its simple meaning. No more as in the days of Christ are his followers found gathered in one place with one mind and one heart. No more are they found grasping hands and hearts together for the salvation of souls that shall live forever. No, no, these simple truths — so plain that they may be understood by a child — have been twisted and turned into a thousand shapes and shades to suit all classes and tastes, until the poor seeker after the love of Christ who is seeking an admittance into this grace stands lost in the labyrinth of doctrinal points that are presented to him on all sides, and cries in utter amazement, "Where shall I go to find rest to my burdened soul?" Let me tell that one that this word declares by faith, Are ye admitted into this grace? There is nothing more simple. God does not require you to make a long journey to some far distant land to find this grace. He does not require you to go through a thousand forms and ceremonies to find this pearl of great price. You can believe that the winds sway and move the ever-bending trees, and yet you cannot see the power that drives it on, nor tell whither it is bending. You can hear the muttering thunders and view the lightning bolts of heaven descending and tearing the mighty oak from top to bottom as though it were a feather, and yet you cannot see the force that does the work.

Mystery stands all around. You are a mystery to yourself. As soon as frail humanity commences to fathom the mystery all around him they commence to grow more mysterious than ever before. The heart of man can feel the movings of God's holy spirit, calling him to accept Christ and step into the grace. And oh! As you value your soul, do not stop and commence to reason with God's holy spirit. The destinies of Eternity are involved in that frail reasoning. Accept its call and be saved.

Believe on the Lord Jesus Christ, whose witnesses stand all around you, whose power and love has been felt and tasted by so many thronging millions for eighteen hundred years. And then, and not till then, will you find an admittance. into this grace and be enabled to tell what a dear Saviour you have found.

But not only does the Christian have the consolations of religion in this life, but he rejoices in hope of the glory of God. What man or woman in this house this evening has not implanted within his breast the life-giving power of hope? It seems to be as natural for a man to hope for a higher end, a better business and greater wealth than he has, as it is for the sparks to fly upward. Have you ever seen a man that was satisfied that did not hope for something better? Are you satisfied tonight with your position in life? What man in this house tonight can rise up and say I am satisfied? I venture the assertion that the world may be searched in vain for such a man. If you find a man in the depths of poverty you will find a man that hopes to become rich or in good circumstances. If you find a man that is rich, you will find a man that hopes for greater riches. The wealthiest men in our land today are as eagerly pressing their claims for more as though they were depending on the charity of their friends and strove to avert that humiliating end.

Man, like the idle schoolboy pursuing the butterfly from bush to bush, is ever pursuing the phantom of fortune. If you find a man in the Assembly of your state you will find that his ambition is to represent the good people of his district in the Congress of the United States. Does he reach that body,[23] his hopes are that he will become President. And too many times he dies lamenting ruined hopes and prospects.

Have you ever stood in company with a lot of your companions and in their conversation the subject finally turns on some man's wealth? Oh, how his ease and luxury are extolled and envied! The burden of their song is, if I only had the one-half of what that man has I would be satisfied. Years roll around and the wheel of fortune has not only given them as much but more than that envied neighbor. Could you hear him talk now you would think he was the poorest of poor men. Now he has great projects on hand. Money is required to carry them on and he cannot get it fast enough to meet his wants, and deep lamentations are the result.

Ah, my dear hearers, Solomon has truthfully said, "Vanity of vanities!" This also is vanity. Let a man hope for earthly glory and fame, and he will die in despair. His pinnacle [goal] that he has marked out will

---

23   When he reaches that body ...

never be reached. But let him fix his hopes on heavenly understanding and knowledge, and when death overtakes him he will but just have commenced to realize the riches and power of this grace. He will just have taken his first lesson in this glory.

Man must have something to satisfy his longings and hopes. He will either be doing good or evil. He must do something. I care not how great a drone a man is, he will be found with his mind occupied. The greatest punishment that can be inflicted on a person is to give him nothing to do, nothing to occupy his mind. Take away all his tobacco, all his books, put him where he can see nothing but blank walls, and soon you will find his reason fled.

If then man must have something to do, and if he is never satisfied with the pleasure and fortunes of earth but wearies himself endlessly and forever more, Oh let me present to you this balm in Gilead that will ease thy burdened soul! Let me urge you to center your hopes on Christ. Labor in the vineyard of the Lord. There is an end here to your aspirations. You may go from strength to strength. You may know more of the power of religion every year down to life's last breath. And when at last you come down to death's cold stream you may look beyond its turbid waters and see the final reward. You may see your brightest hopes and prospects realized. You may behold the crown of eternal life that you have looked for so long, hoped for through so many weary years of your life waiting for you, and go into the marriage supper of the Lamb.

Man's hopes and prospects all perish in the grave. The mightiest warrior that ever waved his sword before his victorious army has closed his hopes and glories in death. But if we have a hope beyond the grave we have attained greater glories than ever the conquering hero wears.

Who in this house today can say they have no hope beyond this vale of tears? If such there be, let me tell you today to think where you stand. Oh stop and ask yourself the sober question what are my hopes beyond the grave? You have an immortal soul that must live forever. Do you intend to waste the precious hours and days of life in the fleeting bauble of this world's fame and when life's race is run take up the doleful lamentation, "I have no hope?" Remember, tis a fearful thing to fall into the hands of an angry God. Oh, as you view your dying companions who rejoice in hope of the glory of God, make up your mind to seek a crown of life. Make up your mind to gain the wealth and honor of eternal life. Ease your hopes toward the New Jerusalem and you will gain a name and fame that shall live forever. My text declares that they also rejoice.

Well may that man who has a hope of living forever with the ransomed of the Lord rejoice. As you view his glowing countenance and hear the loud hallelujah of the ransomed of the Lord, know that they have obtained the wealth of eternal life. Know that within their bosom beats the power of the Holy Ghost. Men may rejoice when the telegraph brings the news that their political party, after a long and heated canvass [vote], has triumphed over every foe. They may rejoice when they have been lifted out of poverty and wretchedness to wealth and affluence. But above all that they may rejoice when they can feel and know that they have a hope that when this mortal frame shall crumble into dust they have a home beyond its dark and chilling depths at God's right hand.

I love to view the streaming eyes and warm embrace of the heirs of eternal life. Oh how eager do they seem to gather in the wanderers around this consecrated spot and tell them of a hope beyond the grave! If there is a heaven on earth, it is around this altar, as one after another comes and kneels before her footstool. The songs of rejoicing ring out on their way to heaven, louder and clearer, and it would seem that the saints of God were rejoicing over a soul saved from eternal death.

Oh my dear hearers, religion is worth rejoicing over. We may rejoice when temporal blessings are ours, but above all that we may rejoice for the thought that we have a home beyond the skies. Were it possible, the song of rejoicing should sound from earth to heaven. It should be heard from shore to shore of this broad land. Every harp and trumpet should be called into the army of Christ to ring out its praises again and again that we have passed from death unto life and from the power of sin and Satan unto God.

Finally, my hearers, my text declares that we rejoice in hope of the glory of God. This is the final consummation of all the Christians' hopes—the glory of God. They that are zealous for the salvation of souls are equally zealous for the glory of God. Jesus Christ is our great commander. He has not stood afar off and left his followers to ...

[page missing]

... may embrace that Christ who is waiting to receive you. You may rejoice in hope of the glory of God. Oh step into this hope and be saved. Then will you be enabled to shout in death's dark waters.

"Unfading hope, when life's last embers burn."[24]

---

24   From "The Pleasures of Hope," a poem by Thomas Campbell (1777–1844)
UNFADING Hope! when life's last embers burn,

This is what the Christian is ever looking forward to. My Christian Brethren, the soldier of the cross can rejoice and praise God that he has the blessed promise; that he may view his great commander coming from the clouds of heaven, surrounded by the saints and martyrs of all ages; that he may see the heavenly host and hear the loud echo sounding all over the wide extent of heaven. "Hallelujah! for the Lord God Omnipotent reigneth!"

Perhaps you have seen the President of this great country traveling o'er this great land of ours.[25] Oh, how eager are the people to see him. They will travel for miles to catch a glimpse of him. And when they finally see him, they will stand spellbound to the spot until he has passed, and then the assembled multitude will make the air resound with the loud hurrah! And so he travels on. At each city he is welcomed by the mayor and common council, the hospitalities of the place are extended to him, and every person vies in honoring his illustrious person. And why all this honor? He holds the office of President of the United States. He holds the destinies of his country in his hands. And it is to him that the people look for the enforcement of her laws.

And shall I tell you that God holds the destinies of the world in his hands? He holds your destiny in his grasp, and it is for you to say whether you will form one of that insurmountable multitude that shall view his glory. It remains for you to say whether you will join that great choir composed of the countless millions of earth, inhabitants in that final day of his power and glory, when the earth shall melt away and sun and moon shall cover themselves in darkness. When the ransomed of the Lord shall come with songs of rejoicing to hail their great deliverer and sit down at God's right hand to sing of his power and glory forever, you want to be a sharer of that glory.

I know there is not one in this house that is not anxious to rejoice in this glorious hope. I know you expect to become a Christian. You don't

---

When soul to soul, and dust to dust return!
Heaven to thy charge resigns the awful hour!
O, then thy kingdom comes! Immortal Power!
What though each spark of earth-born rapture fly
The quivering lip, pale cheek, and closing eye!
Bright to the soul thy seraph hands convey
The morning dream of life's eternal day,—
Then, then, the triumph and the trance begin,
And all the phoenix spirit burns within! ...

25   Presidents and other dignitaries traveled by train, stopping at various towns and "whistle stops" to make speeches and visit with the leaders. People would come from their farms to the town to see and hear them.

intend to be lost. You intend to see our mighty commander Jesus Christ in all his power and glory. You are saying to yourself, as soon as the next protracted meeting is held I will become a Christian. Oh beware! Life is a terrible reality. You may tonight take up the wail "I am lost!" or you may rejoice in hope of everlasting life. Oh accept Christ whose witnesses stand all around you and when life's race is run you sing ...

SECOND TUNE

CAPETOWN   77 75

Arranged from a chorale in the
Choralbuch by Friedrich Filitz 1804–1876

When the day of toil is done,
When the race of life is run,
Father, grant thy weary one
    Rest for evermore.

2   When the strife of sin is stilled,
When the foe within is killed,
Be thy gracious word fulfilled --
    Peace for evermore.

3   When the darkness melts away,
At the breaking of thy day
Bid us hail the cheering ray --
    Light for evermore.

4   When the heart by sorrow tried,
Feels at length its throbs subside,
Bring us, where all tears are dried,
    Joy for evermore.

5   When for vanished days we yearn,
Days that never can return,
Teach us in thy love to learn,
    Love for evermore.

6   When the breath of life is flown,
When the grave much claim its own,
Lord of life, be ours thy crown,
    Life for evermore.

When the Day of Toil is Done, by John Ellerton (1870). Printed in 70 hymnals.

LOVE

The Comfort of His Love

> I John 4:8. He that loveth not knoweth not God; for God is love.

God has a great many attributes. He has mercy, for we read he will have mercy on whom he will; Justice, for he cannot look on sin with the least degree of allowance but above all things else Love is the predominating virtue, a leaven that leavens the whole lump. God's love to man is displayed from the time he placed him in the Garden of Eden till his fall. He stood then as the son of God in all his royalty and majesty. At this time, my hearers, he had dominion over animal and over every force of nature. No woe was his outwardly, and inwardly he was pure. Disease had not tainted his frame. Death had not bound him in his fetters. He was lord of all he surveyed, and stood in the garden of Eden as an equal with God, as God's steward and husbandman. And when he fell from high estate, when he rebelled against God, when he violated His law, he did not forfeit His esteem. No sooner had he fallen than Love, the animating motive of God, spurred Him on to devise a means for his rescue. And by the sacrifice of His own son he promises to fill in the chasm that separates him from his God.

What, may I ask, can describe the love of the father here? Who, may I ask, would be willing to sacrifice his son for one that had insulted all his fondest hopes? A love like this passes the bounds of man's knowledge, soars into a realm beyond his comprehension. Man is lost here. I cannot sacrifice my son, said a certain father during a terrible siege, for bread. He is John. I love him. He is my first born son. And here is Harry, the joy and pride of my heart. I cannot give him up. And Willy. We cannot let him go. And thus he went around. They were all dear to his heart. He could not give one of them up.

Yet what, might I ask, would be the feelings of that man who had but one son in such an hour when he felt that the time had come that he must give him up? How his heart would be wrung with anguish as he saw the only boy being carried away to suffer pain and woe! How the fond mother will cling to the last straw of hope! When her boy is in danger, how she will watch til tired danger succumbs around his bed. And terrible to her is the news that he is gone forever.

Yet God's love, my hearers, passes all these terrible thoughts in relation to his only begotten son. He saw not his son. He only saw perishing humanity.

Here is a rebellious subject, tis true. He has trampled all my love under foot. He has forfeited every plea to my mercy and ought to die. But I have destined him for higher enjoyments. I have made him in my image and he shall not die eternally. Here is my son, my only begotten son. He shall by his blood be his rescue. And willingly he sacrifices his son for his rebellious subject. From the hour of his fall to the present day he has been promised a saviour…

[page missing]

… many instances was he not mistaken. And as the philosopher watches the starry heavens and finds out here unknown stores of knowledge, so the wise man, no matter what may be his creed, watches these ideas of man in relation to God and proves to his satisfaction that there is a God.

The greatest infidel that ever lived believes that there is a God. He must believe it, my hearers. He [cannot] but believe it. And what, might I ask, have men wrought out of their imagination in relation to this supreme being? The Indian,[26] whose religion comes nearest to the Christian religion, believes that he is a great spirit; and he worships him in a spiritual form. The teeming millions of India have enshrouded their god Jugernut[27] with bleeding victims' blood and gore, and it is enough to curdle the blood with horror to think of such a god. Pizarro[28] found the simple natives of South America worshipping the sun. And it would be natural, for that man that had never heard of a god of love, to worship such a flaming ball of fire that lightens all the world, and ascribe to it divine honors. The sons and daughters of Africa have a host of gods such as snakes and animals of all kinds, and some imaginary gods that they pay the most horrid worship to, such as the sacrifices of human victims in countless numbers. And to crown all these other gods we

---

26   American Indians believe in one god, The Great Spirit.

27   Juggernaut is a rather minor avatar of Krishna in Hindu mythology, with very few references or myths. It is interesting to note that the fourteenth-century book *The Travels of Sir John Mandeville* popularized the notion in Europe that Juggernaut caused such a frenzy among devotees in Puri that they threw themselves under the wheels of his festival cart as human sacrifices. The book is filled with many such dubious claims, and is now viewed largely as a work of fiction. However, this description of Juggernaut was commonly used by European Christians as a way of illustrating the supposed backwardness of Hindus who had not accepted Christianity. Oxford University Press, encyclopedia.com

28   Francisco Pizarro González (1478-1541) was a Spanish conquistador who led the Spanish conquest of Peru.

have the God of the Christian, that is the God of love.

The higher man rises in the scale of intelligence, the more lovable his maker and preserver becomes. He believes He is a God of love from nature, from the world, which satisfies his every want. From the arrangement of the seasons that bring summer and winter, cold and heat, he views the earth receding from the sun, and argues that none but a God of love could devise such a plan to give rest to the toil-worn sons of men. And again he sees her coming nearer, and his heart is rejoiced to know that his God is about to provide for his returning wants by another kind dispensation of his Providence. The waving fields of grain tell him that God is a God of love. The ripening corn breathes out the same old song of love. The cattle on a thousand hills speak of a God of love, and nature teaches him on every hand that his maker and preserver is a being of love.

The Christian also believes that his maker is a being of love from revealed revelation that has come down to us through the long ages of the world. He sees here his love displayed by the promise of a savior, by the sacrifice of his only begotten son. For a rebellious subject he finds in this book the most excellent advice that it is possible to give: how to live; how he may shun the evil of this life; live a pure and virtuous life; and enjoy a blessed old age. He does not tell him in this book that you may engage in this sin and that one, and no harm will ensue, but the language of Holy Writ is to shun the least appearance of evil. This, my brethren, is another proof of that our God is a God of love.

And Christ comes into the world as the promised Saviour of the world, comes among men as a son of this God whose every attribute breathes out the spirit of love. How tremendous are his assertions! "I am God on earth." How we would shrink from the man that made that assertion today! We would expect that a lightning bolt from heaven would strike him dead at once. Some men shrink from the swearer who takes the name of God in vain with terror. States like old Massachusetts have made it a penal offense to take the name of God in vain, and even among refined people, especially the ladies, how repulsive it is to their ears to hear a man who uses his maker's name in vain! Yet here is a man who comes out boldly before his mother and father, his brethren and companions, his friends and relatives—the whole world in the crowded city—and by the well of Samaria, before unbelieving Jews and infidel gentiles and asserts it as a living fact that "I am God, I am the one that for centuries and centuries you have been loving." For I am the one that God declared to fallen Adam should bruise the serpent's head. I am the one that is to bless the whole world. I am the one that for three thousand years you have been looking for. I have come at last, and if ye believe not me, ye shall die in your sins.

No wonder, my brethren, that Pharisees and Saducees—the whole Jewish nation—were stirred   to their inmost depths by such a tremendous declaration. Here is the long looked-for messiah! But he must prove his pretentions. There is an old saying, some men are born great, some men have greatness thrust upon them, and some achieve greatness. The man that achieves greatness in any avocation in this life must battle for it. He will be criticized and watched in every possible way. He must prove his fitness for that high position before he can hope for success.

Christ came among men with the declaration: "I am he; I am God." How, might I ask, does he in the face of such overwhelming odds prove his assertion? He proves it first by prophecy. He declares that his Father bears record of him, and let us ask, where are the testimonies for his assertion in this particular? I shall only refer to old testimonies, predictions, to prove his mission here. In Isaiah we read he is despised and rejected of men—a man of sorrows and acquainted with griefs. Does not this prophecy coincide with the life of Christ? When we remember that he had not where to lay his head, that he was mocked and spit upon, that he was crowned with thorns and crucified? Cannot we say that his life was one that agrees with this prophecy? And in Micah we read these words in reference to Christ: "But thou, Bethlehem Ephratah, though thou be little among the thousands of Judah, yet out of thee shall he come forth" hath been of old from everlasting. This prophecy, my hearers, agrees with the birth of Christ in every particular. And again in Isaiah we read "For unto us (unto the Jews here in particular) a child is born, unto us a son is given, and the government shall be upon his shoulders and his name shall be called wonderful counselor, the mighty God, the everlasting father, the prince of peace." The government here referred to is a spiritual government and Christ still holds dominion all over this world, over the sons and daughters of men. He has, my hearers, been a wonderful counselor. The sorrowing ones of earth will acknowledge that he has proved himself to be a mighty God, the Everlasting father, the prince of peace to the sons and daughters of men. These are only a few of the Old Testament predictions and prophecies concerning Christ which he refers to in his arguments with the Jews to prove his divine character.

I remark secondly that Christ sought to prove his divine

character by his miracles. For, said he, if ye believe not me, believe me for the very works' sake. The God that Christ represented was a God of love, and the miracles which he performed were all to the poor and lowly. He did not seek out the high and noble families, and there work his miracles, but those that were poor, that could not afford the ministering care of physicians, to these [he] exercised his kindly offers and was continually healing them. His miracles, my hearers, will prove his divine character above all things else. His casting out of the devils, his raising of the widow's son from the dead, his midnight walk on the Sea of Galilee, his cure of the ten lepers, and his feeding of five thousand hungry, famished men and women on five loaves and two fishes and a host of other wonderful works are engraved in living letters to confirm the wonderful assertion of Paul that this is very Christ.

I remark in the third place that the life of Christ proved his divine character. When a man professes to be born into this grace, when he professes to have passed from death unto life, when he professes, in other words, to come out from the world and be separate from them, men are on the watch to see if he makes a misstep. And he may, my hearers. Men are only fallible, and they may fall from grace. Paul was afraid after having done all that he might become a castaway.

And some of us may know some of these castaways who have fallen from grace. But Christ, after having traveled this earth for three long years, after supping with publicans and sinners, after contending with them in discussions in every conceivable place, is brought at last to judgment spotless and pure. They could [not] tell one bad action he had been guilty of — he had not inbrued [stained] his hands in blood; he had not been guilty of theft; [he had not] broken a law of his king or country; and he stood before Pilate guiltless. "I find no fault in this man," is his [Pilate's] assertion. They could not prove an iota against him. And driven at last to the wall, they declare that he has made himself equal with God, a charge that Christ did not deny, a charge that he ever asserted, a charge that he had sought to convince the world of in his life, and now was ready to substantiate by his death. The purity of Christ's life has been the theme of the world. Well has it been said, Never was man like this. Poets and scholars have sung and written of the purity of Christ's life now for 1800 years, and still as the ages roll on the lustre of his fame increases. We love, my hearers, to read of character of our great men at the time they lived and as the years roll on it seems more precious to us. Let me then read to you the character of our great high priest, Jesus Christ the Righteous, written by Publicus Lentulus, President of Judea, to the Senate of Rome at the time of Christ.

"There lived," said this ancient historian at this time, "in Judea a man of singular character whose name was Jesus Christ. The barbarians esteem him a prophet, but his followers adore him as the intermediate offspring of the immortal God. He is endowed with such unparalleled virtue as to call back the dead from their grave and to heal every kind of disease with a word or a touch. his form is tall and elegantly shaped. His aspect amiable and reverent; his hair flows in beautiful shades which no whited colors can match, falling into graceful curls below his ears, agreeably couching on his shoulders and parting on the brown of his head like the head dress of the sect of Nazarites. His forehead is smooth and his cheeks without a spot, save that of a lovely red. His. nose and mouth are formed with exquisite symmetry; his beard is thick and suitable to the hair of his head, which reaches a little below his chin, and parts in the middle. His eyes are bright, clear, and serene. He rebukes with majesty, counsels with mildness, and invites with tender and persuasive language his whole address whether in word or deed, being elegant, brave, and strictly characteristic of so exalted a being. No man has seen him laugh, but the whole world has frequently beheld him weep. And so persuasive are his tears that the multitude cannot withhold theirs from joining in sympathy with him. He is very modest, temperate, and wise — in short, whatever this phenomenon may be in the end, he seems at present a man of excellent beauty and divine perfection, ever surpassing the children of men."

This, my hearers, is the testimony of this ancient historian. The divine attributes of God seem to shine out from Christ brighter than ever before. And as he stood before the world as the son of God, his divine character seems to shine out especially if he is noble and brave. He delights to introduce him to the world as his boy. He loves to think that when he is gone he leaves behind a worthy son, and Jesus Christ, as he stood before the world unheralded and despised, maintains the high reputation of a son of God. Caesar might have envied such a son. Rome might have proudly claimed him as her son. No king or nation need have been ashamed of such a representative. But when he stands before the world as the representative of heaven, when he declares that before the world was, I am; when he declares that he has seen God, that he has walked the streets of the new Jerusalem, that he has commanded the armies of heaven, that he has ranged the plains of paradise, the world commenced to look upon him as a celestial being, and his every motion is watched with eager interest. But he maintains the high character of a son of God, and history is emblazoned all over with his name and fame.

The high character of Christ was established in the fourth place by his noble birth. When Alexander the Great was born the celebrated Temple of Diana was burnt to the ground and this, it was claimed, was an omen of his future greatness. Kings are ushered into the world in our day amid the roar of the canons and the loud huzzahs of the multitude. But when the son of god came to earth, the powers of heaven were summoned to honor his birth. Angels chanted the song of peace and good will to men. The wise men of the East followed the star of the East till it stood over his lowly manger. And not only that but we find scattered all through this sacred word the glad tidings that he is coming. Prophets tell us he is coming. God the Father tells fallen man he is coming. Angels announce the glad tidings that a son of the immortal God is to be born, and all heaven rings with the acclamation that the promised messiah has come at last. Is not, my hearers, his birth a proof positive that he has come? No belching cannons announce his birth, but he is welcomed among the suffering sons of fallen, wretched, and lost humanity, amid the songs of celestial beings.

His assertion that he was the son of God was proved in the fifth place by his death. Tis true that such an ignominious death as the death of a malefactor was not becoming to the lofty assertion of a son of God. We would not, my hearers, be willing to pay divine honors to that man that suffered on the gibbet for supposed crimes, and we find the same spirit prevailing in that day. Peter and the rest of the apostles were ready to stand by him till they saw him being led away to execution, when they, to a man, left him. And with oaths and curses Peter declares that he never knew the man. Left alone amid the Roman guards and Jewish rabble of men thirsty for his blood, he is nailed to the cross. And amid the rumbling of Earth and the darkening of the sun, amid the weird spirits of the dead that burst the bars of death and walked the streets again, amid the terror stricken multitude who cries, "there is indeed the son of God," he dies and verifies his high assertion on the cross to be the son of the immortal God.

And finally, my hearers, Christ verifies his high pretentions to be the son of God by his resurrection and ascension. A poor man in life, so poor that he had not where to lay his head, he is thrown on the charity of his friends in death for a decent burial. No royal sarcophagus with emblazoned arms awaited him. In death he is buried as a good man who had given his life for the amelioration of his fellow man and the world is left in darkness once more in relation to the coming messiah.

Rancorous hate that had followed our lord in life pursued him to the tomb, and amid the stone walls of his prison tomb the Roman guards are stationed to watch not the living but the dead. But the powers of darkness had triumphed long enough and the assertion of Christ that "I am He" is again verified by his resurrection and ascension on high. He has gone up amid the shouts of celestial beings and is at God's right hand, pleading for you and me.

This, my hearers, is the Christ that we preach to you. He has proved his assertion that "I am he" on more than one occasion. And if ye believe not that he is the Christ ye shall die in your sins. God does not require you to do some great thing to merit eternal life, but his invitation is "Believe!" The Mohammedan thinks that it is necessary for his salvation to journey to Mecca and there view the tomb of the Prophet. But Christ does not ask you to journey to Jerusalem. He does not ask you to ascend the mount of suffering, but simply believe and you have the witness of the spirit that ye are born again.

The devotion, my hearers, that was displayed by the apostles after Christ's death is another proof that he rose from the dead and is a light to cheer the believing children of men. St. Matthew, the first apostle that write of Christ, was a Roman tax-gatherer when Christ chose him to follow him, a position that brought odium on him that held it. But we read that he left all the emolument of state and became a willing and obedient servant of this immortal being till death closed his labors. St. Mark was the same earnest and devoted servant that Matthew was, and continued so till death. St. Luke is found to be an earnest fellow laborer to spread this gospel after Christ's death. St. John, after leaving his fisherman's net, followed our lord in all his ministry, suffered the most awful punishment such as being thrust in a boiling cauldron of oil, escaping that only to be banished to the Island of Patmos. He died at last in the triumphs of this faith. St. Paul, after standing by the mangled form of Stephen and testifying to his death, after following his disciples with death and destruction, is converted at last and becomes a chosen vessel to bear this gospel to foreign lands. Death could not shake his resolution to go up to Jerusalem. He declares that he is not only willing to be bound, but willing to die for the name of the lord Jesus. And so, my hearers, with the rest of the disciples. They were willing to be burnt, to be sawn asunder, to be cast into the dens of wild beasts, to be crucified, because of the name of the lord Jesus.

Think you, my hearers, that these noble men had not a reason for their action? Think you that they would have been willing to die for nothing? Ah, my hearers, one of the grandest proofs that Christ was the son of God was the heroism that he breathed into his followers. We talk sometimes of the magnetic influence of some men. I remember one in particular that I had the pleasure to see in the city of Washington, the Hon. James G. Blaine.[29] He sat in the Speaker's chair and seemed to rule the House by magnetic influence almost. And when they adjourned, one great rush was made to grasp his hand. His bitterest foes politically seemed to be his best friends. Every man, is seemed to me, wanted to grasp his hand. A magnetic influence seemed to sway around his person. And so, my hearers, with some of our great generals. Men are willing to sacrifice their lives for them.

But Christ has left such an influence behind that 1800 years the tide has been swelling and widening until today the prophecy as being fulfilled that I will draw all men unto me. Christ has inspired his followers with such devotion that they are to leave home and friends and sacrifice life itself for his cause.

What, my hearers, is that power that holds the Christian church aloft amid the wave of infidelity? What magnetic influence has Christ left that cements his church together? The Holy Spirit is the animating motive. The Holy Spirit is traveling this earth now in the stead of Christ and kindling the devotion of men and women to do and dare and die for the name of the lord Jesus. 'Tis true, my hearer. We have not Christ with us today as the apostles had him. We cannot see his majestic form and heavenly look. We cannot grasp his hand and view the kindling fire of his eye. We cannot see him raise up the palsied one and command the dead man to burst the bonds of death and come forth. But there is an invisible Christ still. He is traveling up and down the world. He has perhaps knocked at the door of your heart, my unconverted brother. And let me ask you as an ambassador of God, will you let him come in? The same words that he spake to the unbelieving Pharisees he is ringing in your ears: "I am he." Will ye believe? or will ye reject and die in your sins?

Men are looking for a balm for their bodily ailments in this life. Go with me to Saratoga[30] and you will see the sickly invalid sipping its waters for health and strength. The ocean's wave is bearing on her bosom thousands of suffering ones that hope the salt sea breeze will drive away disease. The sunny clime of Florida is filled with suffering

---

29   James Gillespie Blaine was an American statesman and Republican politician who represented Maine in the U.S. House of Representatives from 1863 to 1876, serving as Speaker of the U.S. House of Representatives from 1869 to 1875, and then in the United States Senate from 1876 to 1881.

30   Saratoga Springs, New York, known as "the Queen of the Spas," has a rich heritage as a health resort in the 19th and 20th centuries. The area known as Serachtague, "place of swift water," was sacred to the Mohawks and other Native Americans.

humanity looking like DeSoto[31] of old for the waters of eternal life. California tells the same old tale and drug stores are filled with every imaginable medicine to heal suffering humanity but still they are dropping, dropping, dropping like autumn leaves, and the wretched sufferer looks out on a vast ocean of suffering that cannot be cured. He drags his weary limbs from America to Europe. He crosses the Alps and dies on the plains of sunny Italy at last. From suffering thousands the cry is going up.

Escape this terrible monster of despair! Money cannot save you. Kings must fall as well as the peasant. And it behooves me to prepare in life to meet death at last with joy and not with grief. Christ, my unconverted brother, is the Remedy. "If ye believe that I am he, ye shall live." That, my unconverted brother, is a balm for your every disease, a consolation for every wound. Is disease gnawing at your vital frame? And are you trying this remedy and that? Let me present to you the remedy of heaven, Jesus Christ the Righteous. He will carry you, my brother, on eagles' wings to a land where there is no suffering. He will raise you up to the delectable mountains where you shall be enabled to look away from earth and its woes and see a better land where there is no death and suffering. Let me then in conclusion, my unconverted brother, urge you to accept Christ as your saviour. Accept him because the prophets of God foretold his coming. Accept him because of the purity and heavenly character of his life. Accept him because of his angelic birth that angels and archangels heralded 1800 years ago. Accept him because of his mighty works to the children of men. Accept him because he has burst the bars of death and gone up to sit at God's right hand forever and ever. Accept him finally, my hearer, because of the devotion of his followers that count all things but dross so that they may win Christ. And my God's blessing rest upon you. Amen.

---

31   Hernando de Soto (1500-1542) was a Spanish explorer and conquistador who was involved in Pizarro's conquest of the Incas, but is best known for leading the first Spanish expedition deep into the territory of the modern-day United States. He famously sought the "Fountain of Youth" reputed to be in Florida.

What a friend we have in Jesus,
  All our sins and griefs to bear!
What a privilege to carry
  Everything to God in prayer!
O what peace we often forfeit,
  O what needless pain we bear,
All because we do not carry
  Everything to God in prayer.
2 Have we trials and temptations?
  Is there trouble anywhere?
We should never be discouraged;
  Take it to the Lord in prayer.
Can we find a friend so faithful,
  Who will all our sorrows share?
Jesus knows our every weakness;
  Take it to the Lord in prayer.
3 Are we weak and heavy-laden,
  Cumbered with our load of care?
Precious Saviour, still our refuge --
  Take it to the Lord in prayer.
Do thy friends despise, forsake thee?
  Take it to the Lord in prayer.
In his arms he'll take and shield thee;
  Thou wilt find a solace there.

"What a friend we have in Jesus," *Book of Common Praise*

65   Let the Lower Lights Be Burning

1. Bright-ly beams our Fa-ther's mer - cy   From His light-house ev - er - more,
2. Dark the night of sin has set - tled,   Loud the an - gry bil-lows roar;
3. Trim your fee - ble lamp, my broth- er: Some poor sail - or tem-pest tossed,

But   to   us   He gives the   keep-ing   Of   the lights a - long   the shore.
Ea - ger eyes   are watching, long-ing,   For   the lights a - long   the shore.
Try - ing now   to make the   har- bor,   In   the dark-ness   may   be   lost.

D.S.–Some poor faint-ing, struggling sea-man You may res - cue, you may save.

CHORUS

Let the low - er lights be burn-ing! Send a gleam a - cross the wave!

"Let the Lower Lights be Burning," written by Philip Paul Bliss (1838-1876) after hearing Dwight Moody preach a sermon about the sinking of the *Sultan* in 1864.

DEATH

THE BREAKWATER

Job 38:11. Hitherto shalt thou come, but no further:
and here shall thy proud waves be stayed.

What a grand a majestic passage is this, beautiful in its conception and signifying omnipotent power. It holds the minds of men in reverent awe as they read its words like the rumbling thunder in the heavens. Man is spell-bound with reverence as his eyes for the first time trace these lines. And I imagine no more grandly lofty passage can be found in this sacred word than the words of my text: "Hitherto shalt thou come but no farther: and here shall thy proud waves be stayed."

This passage forms a part of the conversation of God with afflicted Job. And as I read it o'er and ponder its meaning, I see behind its majestic form the healing wand of God's eternal love. Job, as you all well remember, has suffered as no other man can. His children have been slain, his possessions have taken the wings of the morning and fled. He has been stripped of all that the human heart can love. And worse than all that, his very person has been rendered loathsome and disgusting—a horrible mass of corruption. And he is driven out, as it were, from society. His friends forsooth come and add to his already terrible sufferings by standing afar off and giving him advice.

And Job, at last driven to despair, laments and bewails the day of his birth and calls upon God to deliver him from his misery and close his eyes forever in the sleep of death. And then our great Father in heaven, who sees and knows our every weakness and who was watching over his servant Job, reproved him for his want of faith and tells him of his almighty power in the language of my text. And I imagine, my brethren, as Job heard these words, his soul was stirred with joy. The waves of affliction had well nigh o'erwhelmed him. But thanks be to God, they can come no farther.

"Thus far shalt thou come but no further." I cannot for a moment doubt the almighty power of God. There is life in that word, my hearers. There is life for the Church. There is life for that one who is almost persuaded to give up forever the religion of Jesus for the vanities of the world. There is life for the down-trodden and oppressed who, like Job, are almost ready to curse God and die. Hold on to the old ship a little longer!

"Thus far shall thy proud waves come, but no further!" There is matchless power in that word. And as we read it., we think of the great God, holding the waves of the sea in the hollow of His hand. As I read it today, my brethren, I can see in thought the waves of old ocean lashed with foam and piling themselves upon each other in awful grandeur. I can hear the loud wind as it shrieks through the sails of the good ship and dashes its force upon the blue waters of the deep. I can see in imagination some huge wave far away coming grandly forward, marshalling all its force in one awful charge and lifting as an infant the great ship high in air and then plunging it again in the depth of the sea, mocking in derision its creaking timbers, and dying away in the distance only to be succeeded by another. This, my hearers, is but a faint picture of the power of old ocean at sea. But there is another scene yet. Thanks be to God, there is a harbor! My brethren, let us get the old ship in the harbor once more and then view the storm in all its grandeur.

Perhaps some of you may have seen a breakwater which consists of a stone wall built at the entrance of the ocean in some bay or river where vessels at sea may come to in case of storm. There is a very celebrated one opposite Cape May at the entrance of the Delaware Bay to the ocean, almost a mile long, built at great expense by the government of the United States. And in that small compass I have viewed a perfect forest of masts during a storm at sea. It has been my privilege to stand upon the deck of a noble vessel and see old ocean as it seemed to vie with all the powers of heaven and earth in tearing down that noble structure. I have seen the mad waves, lashed to a perfect foaming mass, dash up against that stone wall and disappear.

And as I think over it today I can exclaim in the language of my text, "Thus far shall thy proud waves come, but no farther!" All was calm on the other side, and it was a grand thought to know, my brethren, that all was peace behind its strong shelter. The mariner, as he viewed old ocean contending with that strong bulwark of safety, thanked his great Father in heaven for such a defense in his hour of peril. The praying wife far away in some distant land sent up her sincere thanks to her God for that strong tower of refuge. The loving mother joined in song of joy. The devoted sister and kind brother united in the chorus, and all rejoiced to know that God had provided such a shelter in time of danger.

And Oh, my brethren, as you hear these lines from sacred writ again, "Hitherto shalt thou come but no further, and here shalt thy proud waves be stayed," turn your thoughts for a moment from the great sea of water to that of the ocean of sin. Standing upon the good ship of Zion, I can see in thought the great wave of intemperance far away in the distance. Gradually it comes nearer, seething and boiling with all the vile mixture of men's ingenuity. It strikes the old ship at last and lifting it on high we come nearer to God. And then as the waves recede we sink again to the old level and view its ravages all around us, mocking in derision the tears of loving hearts at home. It dies away in the distance. Some of the planks may be strained to their utmost tension, but I believe the old ship is sound.

Yet the waves of pride and malice, of envy and contention, of every imaginable evil may swell up around us and, like Peter, we may cry out "Help, Lord, or I perish!" But there is the strong breakwater of God's eternal love all around, built upon the foundations of the prophets and apostles, and all is calm behind its firm shelter. The mariner across life's dangerous and stormy pathway rejoices to know that God has so loved us as [to] provide such a shelter. The praying mother seeks to guide the thoughts of her wandering boy in that direction. She wants her son on board the old ship. And we are all, my hearers, expecting to get on board this good boat at last. We see others going down to death in this terrible ocean of sin and yet we sail on, regardless of the danger to ourselves. We stand upon the shores of time and look out upon this vast sea of sin and see here and there and everywhere the spreading sails of the different denominations, all steering for the same harbor. And when the waves of contention rend them sore, you may [see] them safely anchored behind this strong refuge of God's eternal love. Here they find a sure support in time of danger. All the powers of darkness may beat against it, but it will stand through all the ages of time.

Let us resolve, my hearers, to embark our fortunes on board some of these good vessels, and we shall land at last safe, safe, on the evergreen shore. We may not all love one church, but I trust we all love Jesus. We may not all see things in one light, but we shall, I trust, all see our Saviour as he is. We all want to get to heaven. We come to church to hear and talk of that beautiful place, and our souls are stirred with a pentecostal shower. Sometimes we endure persecution for the prize at the end of the race. We read of that beautiful land in this sacred volume. We come to the place in St. Matthew where our great captain took refuge behind the shelter of God's sacred word. I can see the good ship of Zion today in that storm. I can see the great waves of temptations dashing against that devoted vessel. But they fall powerless behind the love of Jesus. And as the storm breaks away we may see gleaming out these glorious truths: Man shall not live by bread alone, but by every word that proceedeth out of the mouth of God. Thou shalt not tempt the Lord thy God. And that glorious passage, Thou shalt worship the Lord thy God, and Him only shalt thou [serve].

And so, my hearers, the Christians today take refuge behind this same old book. The waves of infidelity have dashed against its strong towers more than once. Satan's hosts have combined to destroy it. But it has come forth through all the storms of the ages that have passed brighter and purer, dearer to the Christian heart than ever before. And we may rejoice today to know, my brethren, that we have a strong tower who have flew for refuge, to lay hold on eternal life.

I remember to have seen a painting some years ago that left an indelible impression on my mind, and which, it seems to me, brings out the story of the cross contained in this sacred word with more beauty than anything I have ever read. A helpless woman is out on the stormy ocean alone with no eye to pity and no arm to save. But she drifts near the cross of Jesus, represented in the form of a rock. The Rock of Ages. She lays hold, and upon its strong shelter the foaming billows dash up against it, but they fall powerless at its feet. And as I looked at it I thought of that familiar hymn we sometimes sing:
I am clinging to the cross[32]

There was eloquence there more beautiful than mortal tongue can utter. The waves of sin fell back as did the Roman guard when they came to take Jesus. And the words of my text came back with all their force. "Thus far shalt thou come but no farther: and here shall thy proud waves be stayed." I love, my hearers, to think of that old painting. Yet in my hour of loneliness and sadness when the heavens seem to be as brass and my soul in burdened with temptations, I can see that painting again. I can view in thought the weakest child of Jesus clinging to the cross. I can see the pale face and eager eyes turned to high heaven in an earnest supplication for mercy. I can hear going up the simple prayer:
"Without one plea
But that thy blood was shed for me."[33]

But not only, my hearers, does this text suggest to us God's almighty power, but there are in the first words of this text "Hitherto shalt thou come" — an intimation that God permits us to be afflicted for our own good. Sometimes this is clearly seen in the case of Job. Job had, it would seem, always had uninterrupted prosperity. His faith had never been

---

32   "On a Hill Far Away," Methodist Hymnal, # 228
33   "Just as I am, Without One Plea," Methodist Hymnal # 119

put to the test, yet twas an easy matter for him to be good. But back of his seeming piety the devil saw a weakness, and God permitted him to be afflicted for his own good and to show him his dependence upon his Creator.

Prosperity, my hearers, is a good thing. But I believe adversity is sometimes better. That man who is carried as it were on the flood tide of prosperity from his cradle to his grave loses sight of God. He comes to think too highly of himself. He imagines he is a God himself in too many instances. This was the case with Nebuchadrezzar.[34] But at [last] God humbles his pride in a signal manner and he acknowledges the God of heaven above all other gods. In profane history we find that Alexander, by his uninterrupted successes, imagines at last that he is a god, and in order to prove his almighty power drinks such a prodigious quantity of wine that he dies in a drunken fit. And coming down still farther in the ages of the world to the late Napoleon, I read that he dictates one of his messages to the Emperor of Russia in these words when about to invade his Empire: "I come," says he, "guided by the god of fortune and the god of war." But Oh, my hearers, these fickle gods soon left him to his fate and he died a close prisoner upon the rocks of St. Helena.[35]

No man ever lived a happy life and died a triumphant death who ignored his father in heaven. And as adversity comes upon us, we get nearer the cross of Christ for refuge. We never know our weakness till affliction comes upon us. We never put forth our noblest efforts till trouble assails us. Tis then, my hearers, that we see the undaunted bravery and devotion of our race. Tis not the man who has been born to wealth that reaches the highest positions in our land, tis the poor and unknown youth that mounts the ladder of fame at last. Adversity seems to be the school that rouses up all the latent energies within them, and they come out more beautiful from its refining fire. Men set a higher value on that man who has fought his way up from obscurity and poverty to honour and power than upon that one who has been born to titles of fame and positions in society.

There is a great difference, my hearers, between Abraham Lincoln with his raft of logs going down the Mississippi and the heir to the throne of England who never did anything to merit that high position.

34   King of Babylon circa 605 BC - 562 BC. He was the monarch in the Book of Daniel. In those times the King of Babylon was considered to be a god, so discussion of One True God (other than the king) was a political offense.
35   Following his defeat by the British at Waterloo (1812) and subsequent pursuit by an alliance of European states (Great Britain, Russia, Austria, and Prussia), Napoleon surrendered to the British in 1815 and was exiled to the island of St. Helena in the south Atlantic ocean, 1162 miles from the west coast of Africa, where he died May 5, 1821.

In the one case we see a penniless boy in homespun dress toiling at hard manual labor during the day and at night while father and mother are sleeping the hours away he with a dim tallow candle is deeply engaged in study. Tis thus he fights his way up, inch by inch, little by little. He mounts at last the highest position in the gift of this great people.[36]

In the other we see an infant born to titles and honour, an heir to England's greatest gift. His tastes are pampered in every imaginable way, his slightest wish is gratified, liveried servants stand ready to wait on his every want. And thus he grows up. Tis not worth that makes the man in his case, but birth. And which, I ask, do you respect most? Tis not hard to answer. Every man and woman will pronounce in favor of our great Lincoln. Tis not enough, my hearers, for a man to be great after he reaches a high position, but in order to merit it he must show to his fellow citizens his greatness before entering the office.

And so, my hearers, in a spiritual sense we are serving an apprenticeship here below. The prize at the end of the race is a great one, and I believe God will [cause] all the latent energies in a man's nature to be brought out in order to gain that great life. Tis true we have been born to inheritance that is incorruptible at God's right hand. And it is equally true that every man may aspire to be President, but few reach that lofty position. And, my hearers, this sacred word declares that the way to eternal life is narrow, and few there be that go in thereat. I sometimes think, my hearers, as I see the lives of some professed Christians: How can they ever expect to get to heaven? No storms ever cross their pathway. They never reach out a helping hand to the oppressed and needy. They are seemingly unconcerned whether their children are saved or not. Life is one uninterrupted paradise to them.

And then as I turn my thoughts to the glorious lives of the apostles and prophets, I ask myself what have they done to inherit eternal life? When we think of the sacrifices that Christ made in our behalf, when we remember the devoted lives of his apostles, when we read the lives of good men and women who have lived in our day, we cannot fail but see through all this earnestness the great and fundamental truth of struggle to obtain that inheritance. I believe, my hearers, if there are some things which are great trials to us, I believe there is active, noble, earnest effort to be put [in] in order to obtain that reward. We cannot sit and sing ourselves away to everlasting bliss. I do not believe that God will crown us heirs at last unless we prove ourselves worthy here below, not only in prosperity but in the hour of adversity.

---

36   The highest office which can be given to any American by its people.

There is a scene in the life of Pilgrim[37] that beautifully illustrates this thought. Pilgrim is being shown the different scenes in the life of the Christian, and among others he sees a noble warrior come to the gate of the Celestial City. But there are innumerable foes in his way to its entrance. Nothing daunted, though, he presses forward and engages single-handed the whole host. The battle is a hard one. He is struck down more than once. But he pushes the battle to the gate itself and is admitted into the company not of society unworthy of such a man, but of noble warriors like himself. And, my hearers, we have seen scenes just like that. God will not permit the wave of affliction to come upon us more than we are able to bear, and it remains for us to fight the battle nobly. And we shall enter in at last if we faint not.

Finally, my hearers, my text not only suggests to the mind the strong power of God in our behalf in the words "Hitherto shalt thou come," but we ask ourselves how far shall we go in order [that] sin cannot enter into the Church of God's true believers. It will fall powerless at its doors. But we may go into the whole world. There are no bounds set for God's children. "Go ye into all the world preaching and teaching" is the language of Christ to his apostles. And let us, my hearers, as we look out upon this vast ocean of sin, resolve to do something for God, something for the Church, and something for the perishing ones around us.

Are there any fathers and mothers here unconverted? Let me, I beseech you, urge the claims of religion upon you. If your children die in their sins, doubly great will be your sorrow. You will regret that you did not show them the beauty of the Christian life by your chaste walk and conversation. You will regret to know that when the doctor pronounced their case hopeless you could not point them as Christian fathers and mothers to Christ, the Saviour of the world. And you will regret to think through all your life that you perhaps will be required to answer to their souls at the bar of God.

The Christian father and mother have the sweet consolation of knowing, like Martha of old, that they have done what they could. They have the consolation of knowing that they have carried their children as lambs to Abraham's bosom. They have the consolation of knowing that they have rescued them from the contaminating influences of sin. And

---

37   The story of Pilgrim (symbolizing everyman) is a Christian allegory, regarded as one of the most significant works of religious English literature, was required reading for school children of that time. John Bunyan, *The Pilgrim's Progress from This World, to That Which Is to Come*, W.R. Owens, ed., Oxford World's Classics (Oxford: Oxford University Press, 2003), xiii: "... the book has never been out of print. It has been published in innumerable editions, and has been translated into over two hundred languages."

above all that, my hearers, they have the consolation of knowing that they have some bright jewels around our father's throne.

O my hearers, let us resolve this day to come into the church of the living God. Let us get behind the bulwark of the cross, and we shall be safe from all danger while under its wing! The waves of persecution may assail us, adversity may come upon us, but it will only make us cling nearer to the cross. And in the hour of death we may look down into its cold and chilling depth and exclaim, "Hitherto shalt thou come but no further, and here shall thy proud waves be stayed!" We shall, my hearers, be enabled to shake off the shackles of sin in death and rise victorious in Christ our living head.

Tis a glorious thought to know, my hearers, that there is an end to all our trials here below. The poor woman struggling in poverty and want looks forward to a brighter future beyond these scenes of care and trouble. The suffering invalid wasting away day by day rejoices to know that there is an end to all his sufferings in the grave and immortal bliss beyond its dark waters. The waves of affliction may come upon him, but they cannot follow him in the grave. Thus far shalt thou come, affliction and trouble; thus far shalt thou come, poverty and want; thus far shalt thou come, disease and death, but no further! Here shalt thy proud waves be stayed!

We shall be free over there. We shall not all sleep, my brethren, but we shall all be changed. The scenes of anguish here will be scenes of joy and gladness over there. These hovels of want and wretchedness here will be mansions of eternal happiness over there. Disease and death will be changed to life and beauty over there, and we shall live at God's right [hand] forever and forever.

> Jesus keep me near the cross;
> There a precious fountain
> Free to all—a healing stream—
> Flows from Calvary's mountain.
>
> 2 Near the Cross a trembling soul,
> Love and mercy found me;
> There the bright and morning star
> Shed its beams around me.
>
> 3 Near the Cross! O Lamb of God,
> Bring its scenes before me;
> Help me walk from day to day
> With its shadow o'er me.

"Jesus keep me near the cross," *The Book of Common Praise.*

DEATH

THE KINGDOM OF HEAVEN

> **Matthew 13:11.** - He answered and said unto them, Because it is given unto you to know the mysteries of the kingdom of heaven, but to them it is not given.

This is the answer of Christ to his disciples when they came to him with the question, Why speakest thou to the multitude in parables? The answer seems to signify that Christ thought they were not able to comprehend his words by any other process. Parables seem to occupy a prominent place among public men in all ages of the world. And as the child cannot comprehend the language of grown people, so an illiterate man cannot understand a deep problem by an explanation that would be perfectly plain to the intelligent man. Parables also bring home with all its force the meaning of a declaration as no other can. And Christ, in preaching to the ignorant masses of those days in parables, follows the track of the wise men of those days.

We read in history of Socrates the philosopher of Athens reproving a young man for his inordinate pride in this manner: This young man was boasting of his wealth to Socrates when the old philosopher took a map in his hand and desired him to point out Attica, the province in which his great estates lay. The young [man] at last found it, but a mere dot as it were, and on being desired to point out his particular estate in that small province he was ashamed to confess that he could not find it. And then Socrates displayed to him his poverty and insignificance in the great world around. And Christ could explain to his illiterate hearers the kingdom of heaven by parables when he could explain it in no other way.

I desire, my hearers, this morning if possible, to unfold from this labyrinth of similitude the kingdom of heaven in all its beauty and grandeur. Christ is constantly holding out to his disciples and the pressing multitude of suffering humanity that crowd his path in every direction, the kingdom of heaven robbed of all sorrow, of all care, where there are no halting steps, no blind eyes and haggard looks. And as he goes through the world, he converts the desolate waste of broken hearts into joy and gladness, spreads happiness all around, and then whispers in each heart and ear the grand and consoling words that: I am of this kingdom, I am a representative of this grand kingdom whose power shall be without end. [He] seeks by every possibility to create a rivalry, a struggle, for this kingdom. Christ seeks to implant within them a personal knowledge of this kingdom by giving them tangible proof of the wonderful felicity and joy that awaits the residents of that delightful world.

And as the farmer would show you by actual and tangible proof the ease with which his machine will cut down the waving grain, and by that act create within you a desire to have such a wonderful machine, so Christ as a representative of the kingdom of heaven, as a son of the King of this kingdom, touches the eyes of poor blind Bartimaeus[38] before the whole multitude, tears off the scales of his sightless eyelids, to show the crowd that blindness was not one of the afflictions of that country. He commands the dead man to come forth to show that death was not one of the troubles of that country. He heals every disease to show that the inhabitants of that country are not afflicted as men in this world. And by every possible means he seeks to bring right before the multitude of a criticizing world a living exemplification of the kingdom of heaven, and to implant within men a desire to transfer their allegiance to this King of Kings; struggles to awaken in their minds a desire to better their condition; struggles if possible to awaken their cupidity for gain. For some men will make a venture if they think success is in view, that would have ventured on no other conditions.

This is proved by our western prairies that are settling up with hearty pioneers — because of what? Why do these men drag their families from Europe to Nebraska? Why do they leave comfortable homes in the East and live in log cabins in the West? Why do they endure their crust of bread when they might have the flesh pots of old Egypt? Why do they accept the conditions of the U.S. Government[39] to live on a trackless prairie without a tree as far as the eye can see — with howling wolves and treacherous savages on every hand to murder and scalp their defenseless ones — if there is not before them a hope of reward? Men in this life will do anything that you can think of if there is a chance of gain

---

38   Mark 10:46-52.

39   Signed into law by President Abraham Lincoln on May 20, 1862, the Homestead Act encouraged Western migration by providing settlers 160 acres of public land. In exchange, homesteaders paid a small filing fee and were required to complete five years of continuous residence before receiving ownership of the land. After six months of residency, homesteaders also had the option of purchasing the land from the government for $1.25 per acre. The Homestead Act led to the distribution of 80 million acres of public land by 1900. Library of Congress.

in it. And Christ is aware of that element in men's nature and presents this kingdom as the government presents her western prairie, in all the beauty of word and deed. Not only does he paint it as a country that has an eternal fountain of water, which if a man drink he shall never thirst, but he paints [it] as a land flowing with milk and honey. This is enough of itself to excite a desire in the minds of his hearers to settle in that country. He paints [it] as a land where there is no disease. Her cities are inhabited with men and women that are not like you. You don't see any blind eyes in that country. You look in vain for crutches. No haggard faces and sunken eyes. But he tells them that the inhabitants of that country are like the angels of heaven, are like the young man that told the weeping mother of Jesus: He is not here, he is risen.[40] See the place where he lay. And as you look at his garment of death that he has thrown off, take one look at the inhabitants of this glorious kingdom of heaven that have lived always and shall live forever.

Christ presented this kingdom, in every guise and urge, by his miracles and by his eloquent words, the importance of immediately deciding to become an emigrant to this glorious country, to leave all father, mother, sister, and brother, yea and even this body that must die and — like Lot[41] of old — never look back but press forward till you gain this delightful country.

In reading over this gospel of St. Matthew we see all through its pages kingdom of heaven. Christ is never tired of telling about it. "Kingdom, kingdom, my father's kingdom" is the burden of his soul all the time. The forerunner of Christ, John the Baptist, cries to the gaping and listless multitude in these words: Repent! for the kingdom of heaven is at hand! The world was on the lookout. Satan had his sentinels out on every hand to catch the first glimpse of this exalted resident of the kingdom of heaven. He did not meet the son of this king. Earthly monarchs welcome distinguished men of other countries. But the whole land is devastated with fire and sword to unearth this son of the kingdom of heaven. The infants are slaughtered and butchered on every hand. The land is filled with weeping and wailing mothers and the whole world is turned upside down by these earthly kings to find the first inhabitant of this better kingdom that dare tell men there is a better country than this suffering world. But John's prediction was verified. The kingdom of heaven was at hand. This grain of mustard seed in a crooked and wicked world lived through it all. The son of the King of the kingdom of heaven was preserved and comes forth at last.

40   Matthew 28:6
41   Genesis 18-19

And what was his first utterance that we find in sacred writ? We read that he commenced to preach repentance, for the kingdom of heaven is at hand. And going on a little farther we read that he blessed the poor in spirit, and told them that they should inherit this kingdom and they that are persecuted for righteousness sake come under the same head and are residents of the same kingdom. And as [he] closes his grand sermon that shall live while time shall last, he tells them who shall inherit this kingdom: They that do the will of my father which is in heaven, they that accept my declarations and immediately start for this kingdom.

Coming down still farther in the writings of St. Matthew we find him next commencing to teach the masses by parables in regard to this kingdom. It would be impossible in one sermon to present to you in every guise the kingdom of heaven as Christ presented it. The hunter of truth today must cull out from these various parables the true kingdom we are living in, a land of Bibles, untrammeled by any despotic rulers and with the declaration of Christ before us to search the scriptures. Let me then urge upon you the importance of sitting down and comparing the various parables to satisfy your own mind in reference to this kingdom. Leaving you thus as a jury to interpret this kingdom from an open Bible, let me bring before your minds a few thoughts which I believe will bear the light of the 19th Century.

And where, might I ask, is the commencement of this kingdom? And I would answer on the authority of this word, right in the hearts of men. Christ says the kingdom of heaven is within you. By that expression I understand the there is a colony of this country in the United States. That the kingdom has her citizens in England and France, in Italy and Asia, in Australia and the Isles of the Pacific. That the sun never sets on the possessions of the kingdom of heaven. The kingdom of heaven is within you. You are, in other words, a citizen of this glorious kingdom in a foreign realm, that you are like the child just commencing to walk on this pilgrimage to the better world. And like the Mohammedan that leaves the plains of Turkey and tramps and tramps over mountains and across valleys till he reaches Mecca, so you are a citizen of heaven, of the kingdom that shall never end. And from the time you first enter your name as an emigrant to this country, till you cross over the swelling floods of death, there is a constant progress through affliction and persecution, trouble and woe, till you enter the better land. And having established the proposition that this kingdom that is within you, [he] has reference to the earnest Christian man—that he [has] for his one desire the promulgation of the beauties of this heavenly kingdom, the other becomes plain enough. Having transferred this kingdom from earth to heaven, every parable is explained and brings forth this glorious kingdom with new beauties.

Christ had talked so long about this kingdom and on two occasions had displayed such royal bounty in feeding five thousand at one time and seven thousand at another that the multitude thought he was their long-looked-for king—Caesar and Pompeii fed the Roman citizens—and they were going to take him by force and make him an earthly sovereign,[42] but he withdrew from their sight. So firmly was this impression on the people that both his enemies and his disciples believed it. The Pharisees came to him with the question whether it was lawful to

---

42   Under the Roman conquest of Israel, crushing the independence of Judea, people longed for the Messiah to come and deliver them. The Talmud extensively discusses the coming of the Messiah (Sanhedrin 98a–99a, et al.) and describes a period of freedom and peace, which will be the time of ultimate goodness for the Jews. Several people claimed to be the messiah, led revolts against the Romans, and were conquered. Their influence was mostly local and temporary; some, however, succeeded in attracting large numbers of followers, and created movements that lasted for considerable periods. The effects of these Messianic movements were pernicious. Many of these Messiahs and their followers lost their lives in the course of their activities; and they deluded the people with false hopes, created dissensions, gave rise to sects, and even lost many to Judaism. Kaufmann Kohler, H. G. Friedmann, *Jewish Encyclopedia*. From Josephus it appears that in the first century before the destruction of the Temple a number of Messiahs arose promising relief from the Roman yoke, and finding ready followers. Josephus speaks of them thus: "Another body of wicked men also sprung up, cleaner in their hands, but more wicked in their intentions, who destroyed the peace of the city no less than did these murderers the Sicarii. For they were deceivers and deluders of the people, and, under pretense of divine illumination, were for innovations and changes, and prevailed on the multitude to act like madmen, and went before them in the wilderness, pretending that God would there show them signs of liberty" (Josephus, "B. J." ii. 13, §; 4; idem, "Ant." xx. 8, §; 6). Matt. xxiv. 24, warning against "false Christs and false prophets," gives testimony to the same effect. Thus about 44 CE, Josephus reports, a certain impostor, Theudas, who claimed to be a prophet, appeared and urged the people to follow him with their belongings to the Jordan, which he would divide for them. According to Acts v. 36 (which seems to refer to a different date), he secured about 400 followers. Cuspius Fadus sent a troop of horsemen after him and his band, slew many of them, and took captive others, together with their leader, beheading the latter ("Ant." xx. 5, § 1).

        Thus the persecution of Jesus which William discusses falls into three parts: (1) Herod, who was the King of the Jews appointed by Rome, was half Jewish and entirely paranoid. He built four cities at the four corners of his kingdom to be places for him to take refuge in case the people rose up against him. He was terrified of anyone who might displace him as King of the Jews. It was Herod who order the killing of Jewish babies who might fit the prophesies of a new King of the Jews. (2) The Pharisees and Sadducee were two sects of priests who had power under the Romans. They jealously guarded their political power, and worked against anyone with possible claims to displace them. They are the ones who bribed Judas to denounce Jesus. (3) The Romans themselves did not want anyone coming as the Messiah to lead an army and reclaim political power from the Romans in Judea.

pay tribute to Caesar — if, in other words, you are the rightful king, why do you not assert your power? Why cringe and fawn to Caesar? Why go about telling about "my kingdom"? If you are a king, assert your right to the high dignity. Publish to the world the grand truths that it is not right for the Jewish nation to pay tribute to a foreign despot. But Christ leaves them in ignorance as to his true character and tells them to render to Caesar the things that are Caesar's and unto God the things that are God's.

So also his disciples are in ignorance. The mother of Zebedee's children[43] came to him with her two boys asking him to grant that they may have a seat near the throne. She firmly believed that Christ would soon be crowned king of the Jews and then her boys would be rewarded because of her faith in believing that though it looked dark for him now, still he was sure to be their king. And the Apostles we find were wrangling together about who should be the greatest. And Christ takes a little child and places it in the midst of them and declares that except ye become as a little child ye cannot be my disciple. No doubt this was strange language to them. "The kingdom of heaven … like children." They had that saying in their heart, I imagine, and thought long and deep over it. What will a nation of children do when strong and valiant men attack their forts? Why the thing is preposterous! And as they could not understand how they were to eat Christ's flesh and drink his blood, so I venture to say that they could not understand how Christ would defend his kingdom with children.

But still they believed he was a king, and they waited to see the end. The whole world had imbibed the idea that this Jesus was a king, and all was in suspense. The world expected to hear that at any moment Christ had inaugurated his kingdom and overthrown the Roman power. But he goes on in the same course till the Jews could wait no longer. Suspense was intolerable. They made up their mind that Christ was an imposter and ought to die. They conspired for his destruction and captured him at last. The multitude that hung of his every word vanished in thin air. His disciples forsook him. There was sent a man that had the courage to come forward and speak the truth for Christ, and he is condemned on the naked declaration of his enemies that he said he was a king. This seems to have been their main charge against Christ. And Pilate asks the Saviour, "Art thou the king of the Jews? You have been going up and down the world some time now talking about the kingdom of heaven and tell us now, is there any truth in these men's assertions? Art thou really the king of the Jews?" And Jesus asked

43   The mother of James and John, Jesus' disciples.

him if the Jews told him to ask him that question. This seemed to be a damper to Pilate, and he exclaims, "Am I a Jew? Thine own people have delivered thee to me. You knew the charges before, and are you guilty? Is there any truth in their statements to me?"

Then Christ unravels the whole. All this long line of parables cuts the Gordian knot[44] and transplants his kingdom to heaven, tears the scales from the eyes of an ignorant and prejudiced people, and tells the, that "my kingdom is not of this world."

"I have, tis true, been conquering province after province for my father. I have been enlisting men in this army of mine, but I have armed the heart instead of the arm. I have placed this gospel in their hands to publish to the lands of the world, but I war not with outward but with inward weapons. I struggle to capture the heart instead of the bodies of men. I am a king, Most Noble Pilate. I shall not deny my royal ancestor. I stand before this jeering mob of men that are thirsting for my blood as a representation of the kingdom of heaven. I have been preaching that kingdom, and am willing now to die for that cause, but woe unto the man that sheddeth my blood! Better had it been for him had he never been born!"[45]

I imagine, my hearers, as Christ stood before that royal assemblage of priests and potentates that he was glorious in his fall. It is related of a certain great captain of ancient times that he was captured and condemned to die. A soldier was sent to dispatch him in his prison cell, but though he was bound hand and foot he rose before his assassin with his clanking chains around his form and cast such an awful look upon the soldier that he shrank from him. And then lifting his voice he cried, "Dost thou dare to slay Senna?" So I imagine that Christ's royal mien as he stood before Pilate with the declaration that he was indeed

---

44   The term "Gordian knot," commonly used to describe a complex or unsolvable problem, can be traced back to a legendary chapter in the life of Alexander the Great. As the story goes, in 333 B.C. the Macedonian conqueror marched his army into the Phrygian capital of Gordium in modern day Turkey. Upon arriving in the city, he encountered an ancient wagon, its yoke tied with what one Roman historian later described as "several knots all so tightly entangled that it was impossible to see how they were fastened."Phrygian tradition held that the wagon had once belonged to Gordius, the father of the celebrated King Midas. An oracle had declared that any man who could unravel its elaborate knots was destined to become ruler of all of Asia. According to the ancient chronicler Arrian, the impetuous Alexander was instantly "seized with an ardent desire" to untie the Gordian knot. After wrestling with it for a time and finding no success, he stepped back from the mass of gnarled ropes and proclaimed, "It makes no difference how they are loosed." He then drew his sword and sliced the knot in half with a single stroke. *The History Channel website.*

45   William here has taken liberties with the text. This is not Jesus' speech to Pilate, but rather to his disciples at the Last Supper. Matthew 26:24

a king struck terror in every heart. Pilate shrank from sacrificing such a royal personage and begs for his life, washes his hands before the multitude, exclaiming, I am innocent of this man's blood. And even in death the idea seemed to linger in the mind of Pilate that Christ was a king.[46] The inscription above his head was "This is the king of the Jews." They robed him in a purple robe and a crown of thorns to mock his kingdom. But all to no effect. For heaven at last asserted that a great prince had fallen when he gave up the ghost.

And, my hearers, after a lapse of 18 hundred years, we may look back and see if the prediction of Christ about this kingdom has been verified. This kingdom. Certainly all that we can glean is a kingdom of love, is a power among men that is only seen by its fruits, is a foretaste of heaven on earth. Every man believes that the inhabitants of heaven have but one song, and that is the song of love. We all comprehend that. And I would, if possible, initiate you in that kingdom here below. I know that men band themselves together in this world for an object. I know that Masonry[47] has an end in view. I know that Odd Fellowship[48] has an object. And I know that to find out that object you must become a member and pass every degree before you can say that you understand either. And I know that Christ has established a branch of heaven here on earth that he has said that we may be conscious of all the length and depth and height and breadth of love, but in order to understand that expression we must be initiated by actual experience. The oath of every member of secret societies swears secrecy and they cannot divulge the proceedings of any of their meetings.

---

46   This passage of course ascribes too much charity to Pilate the Roman governor of Judea. He was not in any way eager to see a new king of the Jews, but to preserve Roman rule.

47   Freemasonry or Masonry consists of fraternal organizations that trace their origins to the local fraternities of stonemasons that from the end of the fourteenth century regulated the qualifications of stonemasons and their interaction with authorities and clients. The degrees of Freemasonry retain the three grades of medieval craft guilds, those of Apprentice, Journeyman or fellow (now called Fellowcraft), and Master Mason. The candidate of these three degrees is progressively taught the meanings of the symbols of Freemasonry, and entrusted with grips, signs and words to signify to other members that he has been so initiated. The degrees are part allegorical morality play and part lecture. members of any of these degrees are known as Freemasons or Masons. There are additional degrees, which vary with locality and jurisdiction, and are usually administered by their own bodies (separate from those who administer the Craft degrees). *Wikipedia*

48   Odd Fellows, or Oddfellows, is an international fraternity consisting of lodges first documented in 1730 in London. Convivial meetings were held "in much revelry and, often as not, the calling of the Watch to restore order." Names of several British pubs today suggest past Odd Fellows affiliations. To this day, beyond recreational activities, Odd Fellows promote philanthropy, the ethic of reciprocity and charity, albeit with some grand lodges implying Judeo-Christian affiliation. *Wikipedia*

And the Christian man that is permeated with this grand doctrine of love is a sealed man to the world. He cannot tell you how it is. You may see the fruits of this kingdom of heaven that Christ has established on every hand, but you cannot understand the animating motive till you enter in through the grate, until the robe of sin is torn off and the new man Christ Jesus is transplanted within you. You may doubt whether there is such a thing as a man being initiated into the mysteries of this kingdom on earth, but I can tell you on the authority that there is, I can tell you on the authority of the noble Christian army that have sealed their faith with their blood that there is. There are some of these old veterans of this kingdom left yet that have been going from degree to degree till their whitened head and trembling step tell me they will soon take their last degree and disappear from mortal sight, join the invisible company of that higher kingdom whose reign shall last forever.

I have heard some men talking on this wise. Said they, "I believe this kingdom is on the earth, there will be a new heaven and a new earth. Grant it, my brother. We can shake hands over that chasm. It makes little difference to me whether I shall sing the praises of a saviour's love in a new heaven or a new earth. I do not care whether I shall soar above Saturn and Mars, whether I shall leave the Sun behind till he is powerless to throw his mighty ray any farther. It makes no difference me whether I shall see my Saviour here or there. But there is one thing that I trust we all shall all gain, and that is this grand kingdom of heaven. I trust we shall all be so happy as to see our immortal king that so loved us as to come to this vile world and implant within our hearts a hope that lifts us up above earth's sorrows and woes, a hope that lifts us up above a dying bed and transplants the trembling soul into a kingdom where all is love. Let me in conclusion, my unconverted brother, present to you this kingdom of heaven. Let me urge you to resolve to start at once to throw away the burden of sins.

Rock of Ages, cleft for me.
    Let me hide myself in thee;
Let the water and the Blood
From thy riven side which flowed,
Be of sin the double cure,
Cleanse me from its guilt and power.

2   Not the labours of my hands
Can fulfill thy laws' demands;
Could my zeal no respite know,
Could my tears forever flow,
All for sin could not atone,
Thou must save, and thou alone.

3   Nothing in my hand I bring;
Simply to thy Cross I cling;
Naked, come to three for dress;
Helpless, look to thee for grace;
Foul, I to the fountain fly;
Wash me, Saviour, or I die.

4   While I draw this fleeting breath,
When mine eyelids close in death,
When I soar through tracts unknown,
See thee on thy judgment throne
Rock of ages, cleft for me,
Let me hide myself in thee.

"Rock of Ages," tune by Richard Redhead (1820-1901), *Psalter Hymnal* #579.

DEATH

VICTORY OVER DEATH

> I Corinthians 15:55 - O Death, where is thy sting?
> O grave, where is thy victory?

… stalwart men and helped on the anger of a death. The gleaming saber has sown some of that hail, shot and shell until you would imagine that the Power had overcrowded this spot. He has sown too many grain here. They will never come up. Some of the seed will be choked and die. But that, we read, is impossible. Like the full grown head of wheat that drops in the ground and rises again, so these shall come up, though they be sown so thick that the whole valley is choked up with gory humanity. Though they are piled on top till they rise mountain high, still they shall bloom.

And oh, my hearers, how many has the angel of death sown on some ghastly battlefield! We have seen the wheat field sown in densely. We have heard of tremendous yields from one acre of land, but some of these battlefields of the world will yield a harvest on the last great day that shall startle the world! Every step will yield a sheaf. The harvest shall indeed be a great one. Who, my hearers, can point out the place where none of this seed has been sown? You can tell me that there will be a grand yield from the fields of Gettysburg. Some of you perhaps may have remembered some terrible battle where you saw men dropping like hail. You know there will be a grand harvest there. But that is all you can tell me, my brother. You cannot say that perhaps a bloody battle was not fought where we now stand. Time will level off the battlefields of our late war. Time has leveled off the battlefields of our American Indian. And perhaps there may be beneath this spot a harvest in the last great day that shall astonish you and me. Perhaps where we now stand ten thousand Indians with painted faces and demonic yells contended in deadly struggle. Perhaps the air has been filled with flying arrows and deadly scalping knives. Perhaps the sufferers lay in ghastly piles where you and I now stand. It may be, my brother. You cannot say it is not so. I can say that it may be so.

And thus I might go on. I might tell you of the thousands that have been sown on some pleasant hillside. I might tell you that some of this seed has been sown in the dark and dismal dungeon. I might tell you that the planting process is still going on, and that this angel of death is walking up and down this tremendous field of the world with gigantic strides and scattering the seed like copious rain in every direction.

But I shall stop. One thing cheers our heart, my brethren. This seed shall not always lie dormant, this corruptible seed, this sunken shriveled seed shall produce a crop, shall not wither, shall not die. The second crop shall always be the same. It shall come up fair. Like the waving grain and the green field, so it shall be green. But as the years roll on it shall continue the same. That seed shall live and live and live year after year, always the same. It shall, my brethren, live forever. This was the consoling thought of the apostle Paul. He examined death. He went through her wide halls. He saw her means of torture. He saw all her terrible armor. But back of all, he saw the teeming millions, brighter and fairer than ever before. And as he closes his rambles through this labyrinth of death he exclaims in the language of my text, "O Death, where is thy sting, o grave where is thy victory?"

That there is a sting in death, all will admit. That death is terrible to contemplate, all will admit. Some things have a bright side. Almost every avocation in life has connected with it a dark side and a bright one. But death has no bright side. You may hold it up in every light, but like the dark black ball it is dark, dark, dark on every side. I do not know one death I would like to die. You can present the pill of death to me sugar coated in every form. But like Socrates when he took the deadly cup of hemlock in his hand, so I know and you know that beneath its apparent innocence and purity there is death—a total separation of the soul from the body; a turning point, as it were, when this living, moving body will be like the piece of marble, unconscious, helpless, and inanimate. And that, my hearers, has no bright side and cannot be concerted into life by any possibility whatever. Well has the sacred writer exclaimed: the terrors of death got hold of me![49] Like Pilgrim[50] as he stood beneath the tottering mountain and felt the rumblings of earth, so we, as we contemplate death, see no means of escape. Death is flashing out her ominous shrike from the lightning bolts of heaven and from the depth of earth. She is clad in terrors on every hand without one glimmering ray of light.

What are the terrors of death, my hearers? The first terror that confronts the traveler to the tomb is the manner of his death. And oh, my brethren, how terrible is the array presented here! Imagine a thousand men in one regiment and every man with a different weapon, and say if <u>that would not</u> be a grand sight to behold! And then in imagination see

49   Psalm 55:4
50   *Pilgrim's Progress*

an unseen, invisible thousand of unknown inhabitants of that deathly world commanded by the angel of death, and every man with a different weapon, with death, death, death flashing out all along that deathly line! And say if that would not be a terrible sight to behold! Say if as they advanced toward your citadel of life with stately and ominous tread, the terrors of death would not take hold of you. Say as you saw them conquering the strongest fort and carrying everything before them, you would not flee in despair and cry for the rocks and mountains to hide you from such an army of men!

And that, my hearers, is the way this terrible monster is coming, clad in a thousand different ways. The soldier on the field of battle sees his comrade leap in air and drop dead at his feet, and expiring groan and the life blood ebbing from his heart. Tell him how he met this monster of despair! The traveler sees his fellow passenger drop beneath the stroke of death, and is told that it was heart disease and that is all he knows. An invisible, unseen monster is in this car, and he has deliberately killed this man before me! I may shudder at the deed, I may swear vengeance, but where is the foe? I cannot beat the air.

This invisible demon of despair may even now be standing before me with uplifted sword, ready to strike his fatal blow. And unconsciously, my brethren, we shrink in terror from such a foe. Brave men are ready to fight a living enemy, but they shrink before an unseen adversary. Braddock's troops[51] were brave men. They had met death more than once. But when from ten thousand unseen foes the rattling hail of death came pouring through their ranks with no enemy before them, the stoutest heart quailed, and they fled in despair.

And when, my hearers, this monster death attacks the strong man's brain, he quails before its advance. In life he can take the name of his God in vain. In life he can defy his fellow man. In life he can be a terror to all. But when this unseen foe comes stealthily up and knocks at the door of his vital frame for admittance, he will not be turned aside but knocks and knocks until he forces his way in, then like Belshazzar[52] his face assumes a deadly hue, his knees tremble and shake, and he cries in despair for help. He may fight a living foe with sword and stave, but here is a foe that comes not with visible but with invisible armour.

---

51   In April 1755 British Major General Edward Braddock (1695-1755) set out with 2500 men to advance against the Indians near Fort Duquesne, near Pittsburgh, Pennsylvania. Young George Washington was Braddock's aide-de-camp. He tried to warn Braddock of the danger of the Indians, but he would not listen. Suddenly bullets and arrows rained upon the troops from hidden positions in the trees. The troops scattered, and Braddock was defeated. Sarah Pendleton Lee, *A Brief History of the United States*, 1896, page 86.

52   Daniel, chapter 5.

Death, my hearers, will make a man think when all else fails. The terrors of death command attention, and will not take no for an answer. Men will make all kinds of promises if they believe they are on the point of death. With what terrible armour it sometimes presents itself! Horrible in its best form, it comes sometimes like the weary beggar, shoeless and hatless in rags and tatters. A form of horror as we first look upon it, it sometimes changes its shape till ten thousand horrors dance around the central form.

I dread death, my brethren. The thought of death is horrible enough, but I pray God to deliver you and me from the death of some men. I remember one that occurred not long since. A little boy. Death seemed to be playing around his form only to prolong his misery. It took possession of his feet, and they lay as dead as the piece of marble. It captured one of his limbs. It took possession of another. It struck his arm lifeless by his side. It seemed to crawl up from every part, little by little, till it reached his beating heart. Oh what a death was that! Dead yet living, living yet dead.

Who can tell the manner of his death? Who can tell with what deadly form this deadly monster will present the cup of death? It may be some of you will die suddenly. Some perhaps will linger between life and death for long years before your final death. And it is that thought, my hearers, that enshrouds this terrible monster in such terrible shades.

I have often thought I should love to understand in all its various workings this machinery of life as the physician understands it so that when the hour should come that I must enter the valley of death I might be conscious of the fact. That, it seemed to me, my hearers, would be one consolation. If there were no other, I should love to meet death as one lying down to pleasant sleep. I should love to meet it as did a certain celebrated physician. His medical friends stood around his bedside. He knew he was dying, and as they stood there, he held his pulse in his hand and described his feelings. But the pulsations of his heart grew weaker and weaker and suddenly he exclaimed with his dying breath "Stopped! stopped! stopped!" and all was over. Such a death as that comes the nearest to Shakespeare's description[53] that I have yet encountered.

It is a terrible thought to think of the manner of our death. But that is not the only terror that confronts men in the thought of death. Another terror is that their loved ones will be left alone in this cruel

---

53   There are many, but perhaps this from *Hamlet*, Act III, scene 1, line 60:
To die:—to sleep: / No more; and, by a sleep to say we end
That flesh is heir to, 'tis a consummation / Devoutly to be wished.
The heart-ache and the thousand natural shocks

world. There are thousands in this land that are living only for their children. We have heard the expression "I would willingly die if it were not for my children." And when death does come, they shrink in terror from it, not for themselves, but for another. The days of noble heroism are not past yet, and these struggling ones are living exemplifications of the same.

Some men shrink from death because of business. They actually seem to be so overcrowded with business that they never think they can take time to die. Like the man running a race and meeting obstacles on every hand, so these men seem to be running a race with death. Does it stop them today by sickness, impatience seems to mock delay and the thought never enters their mind that it is death. Vanderbilt was an instance [example] of this. An old man just ready to die, he stood piling gold on gold with the shovel of this world. He stood working steadily away, and he never once thought of death. His physician declared in open court that the man didn't believe that he was going to die, and death, my brethren, is a terrible thought to such a man. There are terrors there that you and I know nothing of. Treasures have been heaped on treasures all along this road of life till decrepit asserts its power, till death looms up. And instead of being a warning to the man to prepare to meet it with joy and not with sorrow, it only increases his trouble. Death seems to be a vexatious delay. He would pass by if he could. He would buy an exemption if he could. But as he cannot, he goes on adding on to his already increasing store till he enters the valley of death, and here he clings in despair to his gold. Death is not so terrible as the thought that he cannot take his property with him.

Why, my hearers, there are men living in this world that would sooner die a thousand deaths than lose their property. I remember of reading of one not long ago, a grasping miser that carried his gold around his neck. And when death seized his frame he clutched to it with the energy of despair. But at last he apparently died. His eyes closed, his face assumed the hue of death, and all thought he was dead. They prepared him for burial by first removing his golden collar. But its rattle seemed to put life into that cold frame once more, and with a deathly zeal he clutched his gold again. I cannot tell his terrors, but I imagine his departing spirit came back from the spirits of the dead at the first rattle of that golden belt he could not brook [bear] to lose, and he would have carried it with him. But sad to relate the laws of gravitation compelled him to let go his belt.

There are more than one of such deaths as that. Business engrosses men so long that it seems to carry them to the realms of Immortality and they convert their heaven to this lower sphere. These, my brethren, are the thoughts that fill the unbiased beholder. View the marble palace that some man has erected, and you would not suppose that a mortal and corruptible man that must molder to dust resides there. See him as he hurries to and fro along the street, and you would imagine he was more than mortal. Hear his conversation, and tell me if you can hear aught else but dollars and cents and how he may make money coming forth. Talk to him of Religion, tell him that he is a mortal man, urge upon him the importance of preparing in life to meet his God, and like of old he will turn from you in disgust with the exclamation,"Go thy way for this time, and at a more convenient season I will send for thee."[54] And when at last death seizes his frame, impatience clouds his brow and not till the last moment can you convince that man that he must die. Death is terrible but to such a man it is double terrible.

To the unconverted man, death has here terrors when he contemplates his hereafter, and men have twisted this into all manner of shades and shakes. He believes he has a future state. He finds a consciousness of that fact in his own heart. He argues it from the past history of men who have believed it, and from the savage tribes around him and from an inward consciousness of the fact that seems to be part of his nature. From all this proof he believes he has a future state, and it is a terrible thought to him to think what will be his future state. There is a sting here that asserts its power over him. If he is a wicked man, he shrinks from the thought of endless punishment. And some have devised an intermediate state between heaven and hell[55] to suit such a troubled man. As for my part, my hearers, I believe I should choose the safe side.

If I knew that in a certain business there was a safe way and a probable safe way, that perhaps I could take this course and succeed and perhaps I should love all, I would not be long in making my decision. And there are thousands of men and women venturing [betting] their eternal happiness on a mere quibble. The thought, like some fearful nightmare, haunts them that this way may be wrong. It adds to their misery in life, and it is doubly terrible in death, but still they persist.

If there is a doubt, my unconverted brother, in your mind that there is such a place as an intermediate state, why not ascend higher?

---

54   Acts 24:25b.

55   The Catechism of the Roman Catholic Church says this about Purgatory: "All who die in God's grace, but still imperfectly purified, are indeed assured of their eternal salvation; but after death they undergo purification, so as to achieve the holiness necessary to enter the joy of heaven" (1030).

Heaven looms above that, and if there is the least spark of ambition in your heart, you will not be willing to enter an intermediate state when you can enter heaven at once. The bad man in this life, or a great man of them, think that possibly—by the merest accident perhaps—they may enter heaven, that some way or other they will be dragged in. They are living here in a region of hope and despair—hope that they will be saved, but fear they will be lost. And death is terrible to them, as they will finally be thrown out on an ocean of chance where they will drift, no one knows where.

If there is such a thought, my unconverted brother, in your mind, if you are in doubt whether there is a hell where there is all misery, whether there is an intermediate state where the wicked man has another chance for life, or whether there is a heaven where all is happiness—if, I repeat, there is such a doubt, decide for heaven! Carve your name in the Lamb's Book of Life! And if religion is all a myth in your mind, you will lose nothing; while, on the contrary, if religion is a vital reality you will gain everything.

And finally, my hearers, to come to my text, Paul seems to be unconscious of the sting of death. He believed there was such a thing, but where is it? There was no sting in death to him as we view him in his ministry. We find him fearless before death all the way. Let us follow the course of this good [man] for a short time, my hearers, and find, if possible, why he uttered in such fearlessness the words of my text. Behold him first at a city called Iconium[56] among a raging mob, fearlessly declaring the truth. See him again at Lystra being stoned almost to death, yet dauntless still. Follow him, my hearers, in his history as delineated in the Acts of the Apostles, and say if the fear of death once blanched his cheek. He knew that he must die, but no terrors seemed to seize his soul as he contemplated her gory visage. He comes at last before death with the exclamation: O Death, thou terrible destroyer of the young and fair, where is thy sting? I have met you before; I have encountered your terrible form on the ocean wave; I have seen you coming beneath a shower of stones; I have viewed you under the guise of the serpent bright, but no terror seized my soul. And if now thou hast a sting, if there is a fang concealed beneath thy deadly robe, let me, I beseech of thee, see it! Let me behold thy form as others see it! Let me understand why it is that men dread and shrink from thee with horror!

---

56   Iconium was the furthest east of the fortified cities of Galatia in the Roman Empire. Lystra was about 20 miles south of Iconium. Twenty miles was a normal day's travel in the Roman Empire at this time. Lystra served as a market town of Lycaonia in south central modern-day Turkey.

Could we, my hearers, understand that problem, we would attain a truer wealth, and we may have it. There is a sting in death, but Christ has seized the dread monster and extracted the sting. The word of Paul attests that there is no sting in death now to the good man. The dying declarations of Christian men and women tell me that they have met death, but the sting had been removed. And beyond they saw, as Stephen of old, the son of Man, the great conqueror of death, at the throne of God. And this is the fate that admits us over this gate. I see Death, but beyond I see Life. And Life has grappled with Death. Life has thrown down the monster Death and extracted her sting, and Death now comes shorn of all her power before this battle of Life with Death. Death reigned supreme. The gate of death disclosed on the other side a dark and dismal night. I could behold the weird spirits of the dead walking over and dropping down, down in eternal darkness. Death stood at the door and struck down her victims pitilessly and remorselessly into eternal night, but thanks be to God, there is a brighter view now. This monster Death has encountered the Prince of Life. He has entered that dark and dismal gate of death, but he has not conquered. For three long days the battle raged and the great Prince of our salvation has rolled back the dark and dismal cloud overhead and ascended to the mansion of light, and has led [taken] captivity captive. And now, my brethren, while darkness shrouds the depths below, a brighter cloud looms above. The healing beams of the sun of righteousness are shining around that gate of death. The weary traveler may cry as he passes through the gate of death: O Death, thou terrible monster of despair, where is thy sting? Tis true tis dark below, but there is life above. There is victory over death. Our great Prince of Life had rolled back that dark black cloud. And we may, my hearers, see the Son of Righteousness standing at the right hand of God.

We may hear his voice saying: "Come, come unto me, all ye that are weary and heavy laden, and I will give you rest. Whosoever will, may come and have everlasting life."[57] The angel of God has written above the gates of death these glorious promises. And as we view them coming in, we may see some of [the] pilgrims with the balm of life in their hand. They are crowding through that gate of death, my hearers, at the rate of two every moment of time. Over 7500 thousand enter her dark and dismal portals every day. And it remains for you to say, my unconverted brother, whether you will [enter] eternal night or eternal darkness — whether Christ will take you by the hand on the other side of this dreadful gate, or whether Satan shall claim you as his own.

57   Matthew 11:28

You are in the procession that is entering that gate, and you cannot leave, like a tremendous procession that viewed in one of our large cities the lifeless form of Abraham Lincoln as he lay in state. So there is, my hearers, a procession that numbers the teeming millions of earth, that is in this grand procession of death to the gates of death. China has over three hundred million in that grand and terrible procession; Europe has over 75 million; Africa has her unknown millions; and America is swelling the procession to unnumbered millions. Like the stars of heaven and the sands of the sea shore, so they are tramping on to the gate of death. They are coming in decrepit age and in innocent youth. They are coming from the marble palace and from the wretched hovel. They are crowding over this worn way of death whose steps have been marked by the swarming myriads of earth for three thousand years, and they are dropping at the rate of two every moment of time over this portal of this gate into an eternity of happiness or misery. You are in that procession, my unconverted brother! Your little boy or girl is traveling by your side! And you may be, for aught I know, on the very threshold of the gate. Even now, you may be entering its portals. And is there a sting in its fang? Is death filled with terrors? Is the grave a terrible thought to you? Does eternity open up a place of eternal night? If it does, become, like Paul, a follower of Christ! Enlist under the Prince of Light. And then you will feel no more its terrible sting.

In conclusion, my brethren, hear some of the dying words of this grand Christian army. In death Alfred Cookman, one of our most eminent, exclaimed with his dying breath, "Sweeping through the gates of the city to the new Jerusalem!" Another eminent Christian man exclaimed in death, "Hark, don't you hear them coming? Oh, bear me away on your snowy wings to my immortal home!" Perhaps your old father or mother may have been a Christian man or woman. If so, what were their last words to you? Do they never ring in your ears and tell you there is another life to come? Perhaps a little one may have died with song of joy on her lips. Does that sound ever come ringing in your ears? Perhaps a loving wife may have gone on before. Do her dying words ever come back to you again? If they do, my brother, hear them for her good and your own.

Religion is the only power that will extract this deadly sting. By its power you can pluck out the deadly fang and come at last before its door like Paul of old, with the language of my text upon your lips! You can, through the religion of Christ, find victory in death. You can welcome her [as] a sweet messenger of peace. She will come in royal robes and garland flowers if you will only accept Christ. The grave will lose its terrors then, and heaven may be yours forever and ever.

ASSURANCE, COMFORT, REST

Blessed Assurance, Jesus Is Mine 446

But thanks be to God, who gives us the victory through our Lord Jesus Christ! 1 Corinthians 15:57

1. Bless-ed as-sur-ance, Je-sus is mine! Oh, what a fore-taste of
2. Per-fect sub-mis-sion, per-fect de-light, Vi-sions of rap-ture now
3. Per-fect sub-mis-sion, all is at rest, I in my Sav-ior am

glo-ry di-vine! Heir of sal-va-tion, pur-chase of God,
burst on my sight; An-gels de-scend-ing bring from a-bove
hap-py and blest; Watch-ing and wait-ing, look-ing a-bove,

Born of His Spir-it, washed in His blood.
Ech-oes of mer-cy, whis-pers of love.
Filled with His good-ness, lost in His love.

This is my sto-ry, this is my song, Prais-ing my Sav-ior all the day long; This is my sto-ry, this is my song, Prais-ing my Sav-ior all the day long.

WORDS: Fanny J. Crosby
MUSIC: Phoebe Palmer Knapp

ASSURANCE
Irregular meter

"Blessed Assurance," by Fanny J. Crosby and Mrs. Joseph F. Knapp. 1873. Benziger and Dickinson, *That Old-Time Religion*. New York, Harper and Row, 1975; *Baptist Hymnal* 2008.

FATHER, I HAVE SINNED

> Luke 15:18. I will arise and go to my father, and will say unto him, Father, I have sinned against heaven and before thee, And am no more worthy to be called thy son: make me as one of thy hired servants.

This verse forms a part of the ever to be remembered prodigal son whose story is known wherever the name of Christ [is] preached. Our Saviour, in this beautiful parable, seeks to impress upon his hearers the willingness of God to receive back again into his family those who have rebelled against his laws, and to carry home with all its force the willingness of our heavenly father to forgive. [He] paints to their minds the misfortunes of this young man until we hear his final resolve which is that he will arise and go to his father and make a full confession of his faults and claim his forgiveness. What more beautiful story can we find than this?

In imagination I can almost see that young man surrounded by all the comforts and blessings of life. Every wish and taste gratified, he becomes tired of home. He has read somewhere of the exhaustless treasures of gold and silver to be obtained in some far distant land, and he imagines to himself boundless wealth in that distant land. His condition then is something like the weak-hearted Christian who is blown hither and thither by every wind and tide, who cannot bear the restraints of the Church, but casts his longing eyes back again to the beggarly elements of the world. And at last he cuts loose once more from the temple of God and plunges into sin more deeply than ever before.

So with this young man. He finally makes up his mind to leave his loved home and he makes the announcement to his father. And oh! As that father views his darling son, what must have been his emotions as he thought that perhaps this might be his last fond look at his loved son?

But we do not read that he painted to him the folly of his course, we do not see that he pled with him not to leave his house. No, no, God will not force you to remain within the pale of the Church. You are free as the air you breathe. But let not a false sense of what is liberty deceive you. The Church imposes no oppressive rules. The law that governs our heavenly father's house is embraced in these words: "Love the Lord thy God with all thy heart, soul, mind, and strength, and thy neighbor as thyself. On these two commandments hang all the law and the prophets."[58] This is the law of our heavenly Father's house. And I venture the assertion that none can be found who cannot obey them.

The day was at last set when he should leave his home, his father's house. Oh, my dear hearers, would that I could paint before your minds that parting, as he takes one more last final look at the home of his childhood, where so many happy days have been spent! His father hangs upon his arm. He has just given him his earthly blessing and fortune. He stands before him, dressed in the finest clothes. No pains have been spared by that loving parent to make his son happy. But when at last the carriage is driven before the door and the announcement is made that the time is up, how tightly does that father draw him once more to his bosom! The parental kiss is given while the silent tear is trickling down his face. And as he is lost in sight, a feeling of sadness comes over him that no tongue can tell. So, my dear hearers, God's holy spirit is ever drawing you toward the mansions of the blest. His voice may be heard as he stands before Jerusalem's walls and views the children of Israel in these words: "Oh, Jerusalem, Jerusalem, how I would have gathered you under my wing as a hen gathereth her young, but ye would not."[59]

So with this young man. He starts out from his home, casts a deaf ear to all his father's loving words, and pushes on. But as he views perhaps for the last time some loved spot of his childhood the silent tear comes to his eye in spite of his most desperate efforts to suppress it. But hardening his heart against all such emotions, he soon forgets his home in the wild maze of his new surroundings. As he travels on, day after day, going farther from home, he commences to realize that he is indeed in a far country. Not only are all the faces strange to him, but the very air seems to be unlike the balmy breeze of home. No more can he look out and see his father's hills and valleys, but instead he views as far as his eye can read the unbroken prairie without one tree or brook to cheer his wandering look.

This then, he says to himself, is the land that has been painted in song and story to me as abounding in untold wealth. Tis indeed far different to me than represented. I had fondly hoped for some of my native hills and valleys, but instead I am presented with an unbroken waste. I cannot endure to live here. And thus communing with himself,

---

58   Matthew 22:37-40, quoting Deuteronomy 6:5 and Leviticus 19:18.

59   Psalm 36:7; Psalm 57:1; Psalm 63:7; Psalm 91:4; Matthew 23:37; Luke 13:34; Ruth 2:12

he resolves to go to the city and live in ease and comfort on his wealth. But alas, like that man who clothes himself in a garment of self-righteousness and expects to overcome every temptation and sin of the world in his own strength, so this young man expected to enjoy all the pleasures of sin in this city and spend his life in an endless round of joys. But soon he becomes lost in its maze. He goes to the wildest excesses, spends his money like water, and wakes up at last penniless. One of his first thoughts, when sober thought takes possession, is his far-off [home]. Oh then how he curses the day that ever saw him leave his home! He recalls that spot now as he sits in wretchedness and woe. He thinks of his dear father sitting by his lonely fire thinking of his far-off boy. He now would long to go home but pride stays his step. He thinks to himself that he will wait and get a good position and earn his own living. But alas there arose a mighty famine in that land. There was no work to be obtained. Driven at last to desperation, he is forced to pawn his clothes to obtain goods. But at last they are all gone, and still he can get no place. He is indeed now on the verge of despair.

But there is one lower step to go in sin, and his cup is full. He has drained the bitter dregs of humiliation. He hires himself to a citizen of that country and he sends him out to feed the swine. What more humiliating thing for this young man to do, who all his life was taught to abhor all such animals! But at last, as he sits there bewailing his miserable condition, he comes to himself. Calm reason is enthroned once more, and he makes the noble resolve of my text: "I will arise and go to my father and will say unto him: Father, I have sinned against heaven and before thee." He does not say that I will wait and send word of my condition to my father. Oh no, my dear hearers, God is sensible already of your miserable situation! As you violate his laws every day he calls you to come back to his arms. His voice may be heard saying "Spare him another year!" This young man did not stop to look at his clothes. He did not say as he viewed his rags and tatters that I am ashamed to go to my father's house as I am. No, no! but he starts out just as he is. His cry is like that of the poet:

Just as I am without one plea …
But that thy blood was shed for me
Oh, Lamb of God, I come, I come[60]

Oh, my dear hearers, you that are mourning the love of God, know you that would have that loving father's forgiveness. Take a lesson from this young man. As he came, so must you. When you start out for your father's house, start just as you are. Do not stop and array yourself

60   Methodist Hymnal, # 119.

in the garment of self. Come to him covered all over with the wounds of sin and he will cleanse thee from all unrighteousness.

And he said to himself, I will arise. These words show a determination on his part to come back to his father's house. It required a great effort on his part to get up and say that. He would go home. And so, my dear hearers, it requires a great effort for you that have spent your whole life in the pleasures of sin to finally make this resolve and stand up on the Lord's side. As you rise up you think of your companions in sin who are ready to jeer and scoff at you. But remember that God's approval is resting upon you and if God is on your side, who can be against you?

How hard it is when once sin has become rooted and grounded in a person to break away. Tis a difficult thing for him then to say, I will arise and leave my wicked companions. Think of the drunkard as he rolls the intoxicating drink beneath his lips as a sweet morsel, and say if it is an easy matter for him to say: I will arise and leave forever this cursed drink that makes my home miserable, that sends my dear wife out on the cold charity of the world, that robes my children in rags and tatters, and that makes me despised and detested by all men. Think you as he recounts to himself his miserable condition he would not arise and join himself to the people of God? But ah, my dear hearers, he cannot. Whiskey, like some huge serpent, holds him in bonds of iron. It drives him before like the sheep is driven to the slaughter. And nothing but the all-conquering arm of Jehovah can arrest him in his downward course. That power and that alone can make him stand up and assert his manhood and say, I will arise from this fearful condition and be a man once more!

How insidious is the approach of sin! Its charm is only felt when we are fully within its power. The boy who commences to pitch pennies is but taking the first lessons of a vice that will finally plunge him into the fearful vortex of a gambler's hell. The young man of today imagines tis a manly art to be able to smoke the longest and tell to his wondering companions how soon he can leave a box of cigars empty. But when at last age with her decaying finger has crept upon him he commences to think of the thousands of dollars he has spent, foolishly thrown away — for what? The clouds of smoke that have clouded his brain for so many years echo back the answer: Smoke. Only this, and nothing more.

The young man imagines tis a fine thing to stand before the dazzling bar and call for drinks for him and his companions. In other words, "to treat" as the phrase goes. But when at last whiskey has marked him as his victim, when his bloated face and trembling step tell of the blight and curse it has left upon him, tis then he recalls that first glass and asks himself the sober question, for what have I spent my money and cursed my soul and body? And the Echo comes back: Whiskey.

Oh, young men, you that have yet time to make a name and fame for good in this world, you that are halting between two opinions whether to be the Lord's or not, you that are feeding your souls upon the husks of this life, come to your Father's house! Resolve to be the Lord's! Lead a life of virtue and honor and you will find that true happiness that the world cannot give and cannot take away. Say tonight in the language of this young man, I will arise and leave the sin I abhor! And God is faithful and just to forgive you.

But to my text. This young man not only arose but he starts for his father's. He bends his steps towards home. And oh, as he comes near his home, what think you must have been his feelings dressed in the garb he was! But he nears home once more. He recalls that house over there, and he remembers this stream that he is crossing now. Yonder is the old mill pond where he so often went to swim, and over there are George and Harry, his old playmates. But they do not know him. He is altered so much they think perhaps tis some traveler going that way. And he passes on.

But at last he sees his aged father. He is even now looking down the road, waiting to catch another look at his long lost boy. And he remembers him immediately. And down the road he starts to welcome him back to his home once more. I can see him in imagination coming to his lost boy. The son stands with streaming eyes before his father and downcast look. He does not feel that he is worthy to look up but, like the poor publican, cries: God be merciful to me, a sinner. Mourner, can you realize that young man's condition? Can you feel your load of sin as he did? As that young man was, so are you. He was fully conscious of his sin. He bore about his body the stain of its deep pollution and he had no merits to bring in his behalf. And as he comes home once more, his soul was filled with joy to get within the music of its breeze. He did not want to assume again the position of a son, but his prayer is to be made a hired servant so that he might be at home.

My dear hearers, have any of you been far away from home for a long time? Not only hundreds, but thousands of miles in a strange land and among a strange people? If not, let me tell you the experience of one that has, as he nears his native place once more from that far distant shore. It has been my fortune to travel far away from my loved home to the western prairies almost three thousand miles from my native place. And when at last I started for home once more I cannot tell you the joy I felt. Weary days had been spent in travel when the joyful announcement was made that we were once more in sight of old Pennsylvania. As I viewed her hills, I thought to myself: within her bosom and by the side of one of her lofty mountains, perhaps lifting up her soul in prayer to God for the safe return of her far-distant son, was my devoted mother. Around her side gathered my sister and brothers. And the silent prayer of my heart was that the rich blessing of heaven might be hers.

Who can describe home? Who can tell the throbbing of a mother's heart as she prays for her children? And the anxiety of a loving father for the success of his son? Poets and statesmen have written and sung of the charms of home. But pen cannot depict the emotion of the heart as he nears once more the home of his childhood, as the kiss of the sister and the welcome of the brother are extended to him. He feels there are hearts that beat within those sacred walls in unison with his. But when he clasps the hand of his father and mother and receives their embrace, he feels that while they extend their hand they also extend their sympathy and are ever ready to [hear] his story, whether it be of fortune or misfortune. And as the parent and children are gathered around the bountiful board, he can feel that he is indeed home.

I cannot close these thoughts on home without telling you the experience of one of the world's most celebrated poets after having wandered over almost all the continent of Europe and satisfied to his heart's content his craving after travel and adventure. He exclaims in these words:

In all my wanderings round this world of care
And so on

But not only does this young man go home, but he makes a full confession of sin. His language is: Father I have sinned against heaven and before thee. How hard must that have been to him! He not only comes home in the worst possible garment, but he acknowledges that he was wrong in leaving his father's house. Have you ever done wrong to a dear friend whose love you prize above all things else? If so, how miserable do you feel when you meet him, perhaps like that one who feels himself too proud to ask his forgiveness? You pass him day after day and week after week until you feel at last that you will sink into the ground without his love for the heart cannot live without a kindred spirit beating in unison with it. At last, as you wish — oh how eagerly! — to take him by the hand once more and acknowledge your fault, some messenger of peace takes you by the arm and leading you before your loved friend bids you embrace and be friends once more. It does not take a second telling, but clasping hands you once more feel that you have his love. And oh! as you leave his side and find yourself once more in your secret chamber you feel like a new man. You can look every man in the face with a calm and steadfast eye as you walk the streets and meet that friend once more. You can grasp him by the hand with all the warmth of true affection. Like poor Pilgrim, as he views the cross and feels his load of sin removed, so you can feel your guilt removed.

Confession means an acknowledgment of sin and a desire for pardon. But ah, like the fearful tornado, tis better viewed from [afar]. It requires true manliness to say to that one who has felt the cruel insult, I have sinned and I ask your forgiveness. Tis that that stamps upon man the impress of the divine. Tis a noble act to plunge into the burning flames and rescue the innocent babe from a fiery death. But tis a nobler one to say I have done wrong. That must be done in calm reason. No burning glare and crackling crumbling walls urge him on. He sees before him one who has felt down to his heart's depths the cruel word, and it remains for him to step up and claim his pardon.

Oh, my dear hearers, religion is noble. It lifts a man up. It places him by the side of his father in heaven. Tis a rare thing to see the people of the world, those outside the pale of the church ask forgiveness for their faults. But let a man have the all-conquering love of God in his heart, and as he bows before a throne of grace his prayers may be heard in this language: Oh father, forgive mine enemies! Hear the dying words of our blessed lord as he expires amid a blazing sun covered with his gore and writhing in the agonies of death and you will hear no threatenings and curses but his language is: Father forgive them for they know not what they do.

Not only does this young man ask his father's forgiveness, but he asks the forgiveness of heaven. And if you will take notice, he first asks pardon from on high. His language is: t have sinned against heaven and in thy sight. Tis not enough when you start out to reform to say. I will try and treat every person right. I will, in other words, stop at the moral point in life. No, no! This young man first seeks pardon from God. The language of God's holy word is first seek the kingdom of heaven. First seek God's forgiveness and when you come before him and before your injured friend and look for a blessing from on high, while you are asking forgiveness from your earthly friend, thrice blessed will you be. Like that man who has succored some needy one and receives his blessing while the rich blessing of God is descending on his heart, so you will be enabled while you hear your friend saying I forgive you, to hear also from on high that still small voice saying, Thy sins which were many are all forgiven thee. Arise and go in peace.

And now, my dear unconverted friend, you that are standing on the brink of the grave, you that are separated from an eternity that shall live forever by the brittle thread of life. You are that prodigal son. You have wandered far from your father's house. And Oh, as you sit in the bonds of iniquity and the gall of bitterness, as you feed your soul on the husks of this world, have you never said to yourself like that young man, I will arise and go to my father. Oh make this noble resolve tonight. Leave the sin you abhor and become a Christian man and woman. Put off the garments of sin that have polluted thy soul for so long. Come back to that father who has been knocking at the door of thy heart for so long and receive his kiss of forgiveness and put on the robe of righteousness and the wedding ring that joins you to the people of God. Lend a helping hand to push forward the glorious banner of the cross. Christianity will make you happy in this life and fit you to enjoy that mansion which your heavenly father has gone to prepare for you. There will be joy in heaven over your return. The heavenly host will be your companions and will sing the song of rejoicing over a son that was lost in the far-off country of sin but is found once more under the standard of the cross. Oh resolve tonight in the language of the poet:

I'll go to Jesus though my sin
Like mountains round me roll[61]

---

61   Lines from verse 2 of "Come, humble sinner," which follows. Hymns for the Use of the Methodist Episcopal Church, 1870, # 359.

Come, humble sinner, in whose breast
    A thousand thoughts revolve,
Come, with your guilt and fear oppess'd,
    And make this last resolve: --
2 I'll go to Jesus, though my sin
    Like mountains round me close;
I know his courts, I'll enter in,
    Whatever may oppose.
3 Prostrate I'll lie before his throne,
    And there my guilt confess;
I'll tell him, I'm a wretch undone
    Without his sov'reign grace.

"Come, humble sinner." *Hymns for the Use of the Methodist Episcopal Church*, 1870, hymn # 359.

Conversion

GOD WILL DELIVER US

> **Daniel 6:20.** And when he came to the den, he
> cried with a lamentable voice unto Daniel: and the
> king spake and said to Daniel, O Daniel, servant of the
> living God, is thy God, whom thou servest continually,
> able to deliver thee from the lions?

Jealousy has ever, it seems, been one of the predominating
characteristics of man, especially among men of the same class. Men are
ever ready to strike a blow at that man above them and if possible to pull
him down so that they may walk over him to place [position] and power.
Daniel was no exception to the rule. A captive in a strange land—a
slave, as it were—he had worked himself up from bondage and chains
to power and place among the great men of that nation. The history of
Daniel, my hearers, is filled with instruction for every Christian man
and woman. Led captive into the land of the Chaldeans when a mere
stripling of a boy, we find him devoted to the religion of his fathers. He
would not defile himself with the king's meat;[62] and God rewards him
and his companions with a fairer complexion than all those that ate the
king's meat. God seemed to watch over his servant Daniel with especial
favor from that hour, and we next see this man of God unfolding to
Nebuchadnezzar a dream that all the magicians and astrologers and
sorcerers of that land were unable to fathom. He is now elevated to the
highest position in the land. But yet he shrinks not from his duty to his
God, but tells the king fearlessly and with undaunted courage that his
kingdom will pass from him and he will be driven from men, and his
dwelling will be with the beasts of the field "till thou know that the Most
High ruleth in the kingdoms of men." And then, like an earnest Christian
man that loves his immortal soul, he urges him to forsake his sins by
righteousness "and thine iniquities by showing mercy to the poor."

After this we find him as dauntlessly declaring the truth to
Belshazzar and interpreting the handwriting of God on the wall. And
coming down still later we read that Cyrus made three presidents to be
over all the princes, of which Daniel was the first. This naturally incensed
the rest. Here, no doubt, they said, Is a Jew, a captive and a slave, next
in power to the King? There mighty men were left in the background

---

62   As a Jew, Daniel would not have eaten pork.

by this Jew. They had endured a long and hard campaign and were rewarded at last in this way. Jealousy deep and unrelenting commenced to concoct some scheme to rid them of this, to them, miserable Jew. They watched him, my hearers, as the Christian is ever watched. They were ready now to strain at a gnat and swallow a camel. From every corner their spies were at work. Hell, as it were, let loose a legion of devils to encompass, if possible, this man's destruction. But all to no purpose. His honesty was inflexible, his truthfulness was unswerving, his character was unblemished by one blot or blur for a long number of years.

And they retreated like condemned criminals before this man of God to put their heads together and see if some charge could not be trumped up against him. But all to no purpose. Hell was baffled for once, but not defeated. And soon a wiser seer than all the rest appears. He tells them that there is only one means left yet to effect this man's destruction. We cannot question his honesty, we cannot question his truthfulness. We can bring no charge against his character. But he loves God, his God that will effect his destruction. This man will not cease for Cyrus, for flames, for dens of lions — for nothing that we can mention — this man will not cease to pray to his God before all the powers of earth. And here is our plan for his destruction.

This plan was no sooner devised than it was executed. A petition was drawn up that would, as these men supposed, rid them of this Daniel, and was to the effect that whosoever shall ask a petition of any God or of any man for thirty days, save of thee, O King, he shall be cast into the den of lions. And with cringing mien and hearts that were blacker than the demons of hell, they came to the King with a lie on their lips and said: All the presidents and princes, the governors, the counselors and the captains have consulted together to establish a royal decree. All had, my brethren, I suppose, but one, and that was Daniel. His name, I venture to say, was not on that petition. There had been a grand gathering of the hosts [of] hell, from what I can read in this chapter. The governors and captains, the counselors and princes and presidents had assembled. And Satan came also to help on the good word, to stir up this boiling cauldron of hate and malice, and heat it, if possible, to seven times its original heat. And one universal cry went up for Daniel's destruction at any cost or by any means that could be used. The plan, as far as men were concerned, was successful. The king was flattered, and signed the writing according to the law of the Medes and Persians, which altereth not. Death was to be the punishment for a violation of the writing. Nothing else would satisfy these blood-thirsty villains. Blood was their cry, and blood they received. Like Haman,[63] they built a gallows and were hanged thereon themselves.

Now we read in this chapter that Daniel knew that the writing was signed. There could be a charge brought against me now. One week ago it was not wrong to pray to my father God, but now a royal decree is in force, forbidding it on pain of death. Now a legion of devils is on my track, watching my every action like so many blood hounds. Now it is death for me to pray. These no doubt, my hearers, were the thoughts of Daniel as he viewed from every corner a spy watching his every motion. But he shrank not. Like Marshall Ney[64] when led to execution, they asked him if they should bandage his eyes before being shot, and he exclaims in these words, "Think you that after facing death on a hundred fields of battle [I] will shrink now?"

And so, my brethren, with Daniel. After warning Nebuchadnezzar of his sins, after fearlessly declaring the truth to Belshazzar, think you that now this man of God will shrink? Think you that now he will close his window and cover it with a blind so dark that it is impenetrable? Think you he will bolt and bar his door and then, like a condemned fellow, pray to his God in heaven? Think you after facing danger so long he will shrink now? No, no, my hearers, the brave man that has a conscience void of offence toward God and man is as brave as a lion. Tis the wicked that flee when no man pursueth. Daniel knew the writing had been signed. He knew that there were spies watching his every motion. He knew that there were men thirsting for his blood. But he knew also that his heart was right with God. He had done nothing against his king nor his God, and he goes fearlessly on, praying and giving thanks unto God every day. Three times, we read, this man of God knelt in prayer every day. His window was open and his face was pointed in the way of Jerusalem. And from a heart filled with the love of God went up an earnest petition to his father three times a day.

His enemies, my hearers, were just as jealous for his destruction. And I can see in thought a legion of them beneath his window. They no doubt were on the housetops and in the branches of every surrounding tree. His window now was the center of attraction, and a hundred

---

63   Haman is the villain in the Book of Esther.

64   Michel Ney (1769-1815), Marshal of the French Republic, was a military commander who fought in the French Revolution and the Napoleonic Wars. When Napoleon was exiled in 1815, Ney was arrested and tried for treason by the restored Bourbon monarchy. He was found guilty and condemned to die. At his execution he said, "Soldiers, when I give the command to fire, fire straight at my heart. Wait for the order. It will be my last to you. I protest against my condemnation. I have fought a hundred battles for France, and not one against her ... Soldiers, fire!" Tsouras, P.G. (2005). *The book of Military Quotations*, page 245.

gleaming eyes of demons damned were peering into this devoted man's room. They did not wait long. Soon, my brethren, this man of God is in his old place lifting up his heart to God while from a hundred gleaming eyes the news is being confirmed that the man prayed. What a terrible crime! How hard these men must have been pushed when they had to go so far to obtain a charge against one man. A royal decree must be published. The whole machinery of the empire must be stopped in a manner for thirty days. Spies must be set on his track that if by any means we can effect his ruin. At last their object is effected. A charge clear and conclusive is brought against him. He has at last violated a royal decree. He has done wrong at last. He has, my hearers, committed the fearful and horrible crime of praying. For this he must be torn from his high position. For this he must be bound and hurled into a den of lions.

Have you ever, my hearers, thought of this punishment? Some of you no doubt have seen a den of these ferocious beasts if so you can recall their majestic mien. You can hear their roar and see in imagination their blood-shot eyes and shaggy mane. Well have they been called the King of Beasts. Among such animals was this good man to be cast for the fearful crime of praying. The king was informed that Daniel prayed not to gods of wood and stone but to his God in heaven. And according to the law of the Medes and Persians he must die.

Now, my hearers, Darius commences to see his mistake. Now he sees through the whole plot. And we read that his heart was grieved. He was sore displeased with himself and the law was examined all that day till the going down of the sun to deliver Daniel. But all to no purpose. The law according to the rules of the Medes and Persians was irrevocable, and Daniel must be cast into the den of lions. The king, however, had not lost all hope. Yet he remembered what Daniel had done in the past. He knew that his God was above all other gods, and he tells him as he is being led away that thy God whom thou servest continually, He will deliver thee.

God, my brethren, is able and willing to deliver his children at all times and in all places. Though Daniel was cast into the den of lions, he was not hurt. His Father went down also with him. Angels accompanied him and while Daniel was falling apparently into the jaws of lions, while these men were expecting to see him torn limb from limb before he reached the ground, another was falling also. An invisible guardian was accompanying him. An angel of God came down from the courts of high heaven with the speed of winds and shut by almighty power every lion's mouth. The powers of heaven were called to battle against the hosts of hell. War was declared by God himself against these wicked men, and hell for once was defeated.

Daniel slept soundly that night, though in a den of lions. A royal sentinel of the eternal King of Kings and Lord of Lords walked up and down that prison house of despair on that eventful night. Daniel held communion with God[65] on that terrible night. The lions' four mouths were locked and barred by almighty hands. And like the Roman Guard around our Saviour's tomb, they lay as dead men before the majesty of high heaven. Morning dawns at last and we find the terror-stricken king at the mouth of the den and with a lamentable voice he cries in the language of my text: "O Daniel, servant of the living God, is thy God continually able to deliver thee from the lions?" He was, my brethren, and who may I ask of you, my unconverted brethren—who, may I ask, do you expect to have for your master? Daniel was the servant of the living God.

And then I read in another place that "ye cannot serve two masters, for either ye will hate the one and love the other or ye will cling to the one and despise the other. Ye cannot serve God and Mammon."[66] God, my unconverted brother, is always ready to deliver us and Satan is always ready to drag us down deeper into the depths of hell. Two leaders are presented for your consideration in this passage—the Living God and the living Satan. One promises to lead you off more than conquer, and the other promises you misery in this life and eternal death in the life to come.

Let us consider the first master, God our father. For, my hearers, we may all be servants of the living God unless we sell ourselves to the devil. If, my hearers, you were engaging under a leader, you would naturally desire to engage under one that promised you victory. Men love to be on the winning side. There is power in the very name of some leaders. The Indians under their great leader Tecumseh fought with marvelous valor. But when he was slain they retreated in dismay. Sheridan,[67] by the magic of his presence, reorganized a flying and disorganized army and led them on as invincible legions against a victorious army, snatched a victory from defeat.

So Daniel knew that he had a victorious leader who was able and willing to deliver him from his enemies. So, my hearers, the good

---

65   Communicated with God
66   Matthew 6:24, Luke 16:13.
67   Philip Henry Sheridan (1831-1888) was a Irish-American career United States Army officer and a Union general in the American Civil War.

man marches through this world of sorrow and care armed with all the power of his father. Job, the old servant of God, when all seemed to be against him, still leaned on his God when his possessions had been swept away, when all he loved had fallen beneath the hand of death, when his body had been rendered loathsome and disgusting by a horrible mass of corruption, still is heard exclaiming, "Deliver thee in six troubles and in the seventh, there shall no evil touch thee."[68] Though all seemed to be against him, though his God seemingly had forsaken him, still he exclaims he shall deliver thee. He is able to deliver me.

The Prophet Jeremiah, after hurling the anathemas[69] of God upon the rebellious Jews, is cast into a dungeon where his enemies supposed that inevitable death awaited him. Then the God of Abraham and of Isaac and of Jacob was found to be continually able to deliver him. Shadrac, Meshac, and Abednigo, as they stood before the fiery furnace that was heated seven times hotter than it was before, exclaim to Nebuchadrezzar, who is boiling over with rage because they would not bow down to his golden calf, "Our God whom we serve is able to deliver us from the burning fire and He will deliver us out of thy hand, O King."

Because of this fact, my brethren, because we have a leader who has fought the legions of hell through all the rolling ages and has come off more than conquerer, because of this fact men are ready to declare the truth dauntlessly before the world. Shadrac, Meshac and Abednigo were ready because of this to defy the king with all his mighty men of valor. Daniel was ready to defy Darius with all his power. John Knox[70] was ready because of this fact to stand in his prison cell with shackles and manacles binding him to stone walls and defy the Pope and all his power — because we have a leader who is strong to deliver and mighty to save. Because of this Archbishop Cranmer[71] was nerved to hold forth his right hand till it was burnt to the socket, in shame exclaiming, "Thou are unworthy, right hand." Because we have a leader who is strong to deliver, men are willing to bid goodbye to father and mother, to sister

---

68   Job 5:19.

69   In the 19th century, "anathemas" were formal ecclesiastical curses. In the book of Jeremiah, the prophet calls the people of the city of Anathoth to repent or be lost—a "fire and brimstone" speech of its day. See the Book of *Jeremiah* in the *Bible*.

70   John Knox (1513-1572) was a Scottish minister, theologian, and writer who was a leader of the country's Reformation. He was the founder of the Presbyterian Church of Scotland.

71   Thomas Cranmer (1489-1556) was a leader of the English Reformation and Archbishop of Canterbury during the reigns of Henry VIII, Edward VI and, for a short time, Mary I. He was executed by Mary as a heretic to the Roman Catholic church. See Foxe's Book of Martyrs (1563).

and brother, and cross tempestuous oceans where sickness and death await them, to tell the heathen in all his blindness and darkness of Jesus the mighty to save.

There is power in this name. Men love to enlist under leaders who have braved death more than once and come off more than conquerer. His scars and wounds are so many proofs of his courage and valor. This is related of Washington that in the celebrated defeat of Braddock[72] he rode up and down that bloody field of carnage like some celestial being. One horse was shot from under him, but he immediately mounts another. That one is shot, and still this wonderful man is seen by unseen foes mounted again. The bullets fly like pelting hail, but Washington remains untouched. His clothes are riddled with bullets, but the man escapes without a scar to tell that he had viewed such deadly scenes. There is power, my hearers, in such a leader. His name is a tower of strength.

One of Napoleon's favorite marshals always wore a white plume on his hat and amid death and carnage his troops ever followed that plume. They knew that where their leader dared go his soldiers dared follow. And when that invincible army of veterans were seen coming over the hills with their victorious leader in advance, the stoutest hearts quailed. And with the watchword "victory or death" the flying squadrons of the enemy retreated in dismay. He knew no such word as defeat. "Victory or death" was the battle cry.

And, my brethren, we have a leader who has been crowned King of Kings and Lord of Lords. And he has enlisted under his banner every humble and devoted Christian man and woman under the blue canopy of heaven. His army numbers millions of devoted men and women. And when he comes over these hills of difficulties with gleaming banners, when you behold his soldiers armed with this sword of the spirit, when you hear such grand old gospel hymns swelling out from their ranks as:

---

72   Major General Edward Braddock (1695-1755), British commanding officer. "Braddock's Defeat was easily the most consequential battle in North America before 1775. British contemporaries were utterly shocked by this unprecedented defeat of a conventional British army by an irregular army largely composed of American Indian warriors. The battle's horrific slaughter was also a compelling if macabre story to tell: two out of every three British soldiers who crossed the Monongahela River on July 9, 1755 would be killed or wounded in the space of three to four hours. The Battle of the Monongahela also changed how and where war was fought in America. It prompted British and American military adaptations to campaigning in the wilderness against formidable Canadian and Indian opponents. Braddock's Road also helped to shift the center of gravity in American warfare from the Atlantic seaboard to the continent's interior. Finally, no other battle before Lexington and Concord did more to forge a sense of Americanness among the British colonists than Braddock's Defeat." See *Braddock's Defeat* by David Preston (2015).

Rescue the perishing
Care for the dying
Weep o'er the erring ones, Lift up the fallen,
Tell them of Jesus the mighty to save.[73]

Know that not victory or death but victory over death is the battle cry. Our leader, my hearers, has gone down in the darkened places of the earth. He has raised up the fallen. He has sighed over the fallen. He has contended with the hosts of Satan on a thousand battlefields. The shafts of sin have filled the air on every side and his scars and his wounds, his pierced hands and lacerated feet, his bleeding side and mangled forehead, are so many proofs of his power and of his matchless might and will.

We, my hearers, shrink from following such a leader. If he has defied earth and hell, will we falter? Will we, like Peter, when temptation and danger stare us in the face, swear by all the powers of heaven and earth we never knew the man? If Christ could eat with publicans and sinners, will we be content to sit and sing ourselves to everlasting bliss when the perishing ones are going down to eternal death on every hand? If Christ could declare with a voice that wakes the dead and bids the sleeper rise, "I came to seek and to save that which was lost,"[74] will we as Christian men and women see the sinner covered all over perhaps with the wounds and bruises of sin sunk to the very depths of hell? Will we see such an one and not try to save him? Will we pass by on the other side like the priest and the Levite[75] and leave him to die?

Let us be more noble than that, my hearers! Let us be noble Christians like the Christians of Berea. Let us have true manliness and courage about us. Christ did not stand afar off and pity us and then pass by. But he came among fallen humanity on the devil's ground, as it were, and challenged Satan to deadly combat. The Chinese wrestlers will strip themselves for the conflict and before haughty kings and courtiers will contend for hours. Who shall be the victor? So Christ by the command of his father God left the courts of high heaven, came among men, and grappled with Satan on his own ground. He drives him from his presence on the mountain top like the slave is driven before his master. "Get thee behind me, Satan!" There is power there. The master is speaking there. That, my hearers, was a victory for you and me. He cast out devils from those whom the devil had captured and bound hand and foot, as it were. He has come off more than conqueror in every encounter—a leader, a

---

73   Hymn by Fannie J. Crosby, 1870.
74   Luke 19:10.
75   A reference to the parable of the Good Samaritan, Luke 10:25-37.

champion, a captain who has victory written all over his banner. He is able to deliver us in six troubles, and in the seventh he will not forsake us.

Are you, my hearers, enlisted under his flag, or under the flag of Satan? Have you chosen the living God as your master or the Living Satan? Have you, like one of old, after viewing all the victories of the cross, said "as for me and my house we will serve the Lord,"[76] or have you decided that as for me and my house we will serve the devil?

A certain king of Persia by the name of Xerxes was notorious, not for victories but defeats. He will live in history because of his defeats. This king left his kingdom with an army of over 2,600,000 fighting men to invade Greece. He commanded his soldiers to dig down a mountain in his way. And because the sea was violent and tempestuous his ire was raised to the highest pitch, and he commands that chains be thrown into its waters to prove his power over it. But with all his vaunting glory he had no power. With his immense army, he was powerless, as it were.

He, my hearers, was a coward at heart. Three hundred brave and determined men stopped his onward progress at Thermopylae and slew 20,000 of his best soldiers before they succumbed to overwhelming numbers. And as Xerxes walked over that bloody field of carnage and beheld the Spartans victorious in death, as it were, as he viewed them with their javelins and breastplates, with their spears and helmets piled over the dead body of Leonidas making a monument to his memory by their bleeding bodies; he exclaims in dismay, "How many such soldiers are there yet in Sparta?" and receives for his answer that there were 8 thousand more soldiers like these he saw before him. He was defeated at Salamis and fled in dismay before such invincible troops. He with all his army was vanquished by a mere handful of men.

Tis not, my hearers, numbers but valor that wins the conflict. The race is not always to the swift. Satan with all his teeming millions is being vanquished every day. Christ has captured the world not by swarming myriads of men, but by twelve followers. He has sent them forth two by two. Paul, armed with the whole armor of God, tells the Atheneans that Christ is able and willing to save them. One man is able to capture.

So with all the Apostles. They go in strange lands, among strange people, among idolaters and turn their feet into the testimonies of God. Well has holy writ exclaimed, "One shall chase a thousand, and two put

---

76   Joshua 24:15b.

ten thousand to flight."[77] What, my hearers, would you think of a man who would attack an army with nothing but a jawbone and put them to flight? You would say that man was more than mortal man. You would view him as some being of celestial worlds. They would come from near and from far to see such a man.

And yet, my brethren, Christ has captured this world with twelve men. His name is a tower of strength for every earnest Christian man and woman. His victories are written on the banners of heaven. He has triumphed over Satan in every encounter Satan has been defeated more than once. His name is only great in defeats. There was war in heaven. We read the armies of Emmanuel encountered Satan on the plains of Paradise, and Satan was thrust out, and all through this blessed Book Satan has been defeated in every encounter. He is powerless, my hearers, to deliver you. Defeat, Defeat, Defeat is written all over his banners.

Let me then urge you in conclusion to choose God as your master. He, my unconverted brother, will deliver you in this life from sin in every form, from the intoxicating bowl that has dragged down thousands and thousands of the brightest and best in our land to an untimely death. He will deliver you from the gambler's coil, from the allurements of the dance hall. He will, if you put your trust in him, deliver you in this life from every sin and he will deliver [you] in the hour of death and crown you in heaven victorious at last. Let us, my brethren, like Daniel of old, be servants of the Living God. Let us, like Enoch of old, walk with God.

And if the way leads down in affliction and sorrow, let us never falter but cling to his hand. He is able to deliver us. If the way is beset with temptation, if we are derided and mocked, if the powers of hell seem to be ready to swallow us up, never waver! Sing like Daniel of old, "My God whom I serve is able to deliver me."[78] And when death, my Christian friends, shall claim us at last; when this vile body, like the old clock, has run down; when the machinery of life shall stop and death and the grave shall open up, let us sing with weeping friends that grand old strain:

> Though friends should all fail and foes all unite
> Yet one thing assures us whatever betides
> The promise assures us the Lord will provide
> When life sinks apace and death heaves in view
> The word of his grace shall comfort us through
> Not fearing or doubting with Christ on our side
> We hope to die shouting: "The Lord will provide!"[79]

---

77   Deuteronomy 32:30a
78   Daniel 3:17.
79   Poem by C. Augustus Price. Price, *American Poetry,* 1850

Jesus, Savior, Pilot Me   601

When you pass through the waters, I will be with you. Is. 43:2

1. Je - sus, Sav - ior, pi - lot me o - ver life's tem - pes - tuous sea;
2. As a moth - er stills her child, thou canst hush the o - cean wild;
3. When at last I near the shore, and the fear - ful break - ers roar

un - known waves be - fore me roll, hid - ing rock and treach-'rous shoal;
bois - t'rous waves o - bey thy will when thou say'st to them, "Be still."
'twixt me and the peace- ful rest, then, while lean - ing on thy breast,

chart and com - pass come from thee: Je - sus, Sav - ior, pi - lot me.
Won- drous Sov - ereign of the sea, Je - sus, Sav - ior, pi - lot me.
may I hear thee say to me, "Fear not, I will pi - lot thee."

Edward Hopper 1871

PILOT 7 7 7 7 7 7
John E. Gould 1871

Jesus, Savior, pilot me, by Edward Hopper, 1871. "Pilot," as in navigating a ship.

CONVERSION

WHERE ARE YOUR FATHERS?

> Zechariah 1:5.Your fathers, where are they? and the
> prophets, do they live forever?

The prophet Zechariah had just been receiving a divine commission to warn the children of Israel to turn from their evil way. They have been following the way of their ungodly fathers, bowing down to wood, and they have no doubt worshipped these idols from their infancy. Their fathers have no doubt taught them that there was no God and have instructed them in these words, "These be thy gods."[80] And God in his infinite goodness and mercy looks down upon them in their ignorance and misery, and with that tender love which is God's attribute he desires once more to own them as his children. And he sends the prophet to warn them of how their fathers fell and to exhort them to turn from their evil way.

I should love to have seen this man of God on that eventful day as he comes robed in the garments of holiness [to] this people! I should love to have viewed him as — perhaps on some hill or eminence, surrounded by this idolatrous people — he sounded these words in their ears! o with what eloquence he must {have] sent this truth home to their hearts! "Your fathers, where are they?" It did not take them long to answer that question, I predict. Their minds ran back to that one here, and circle their camp with living steel. No, no! God's presence was mightier than all the armies of the world. But where, oh where, is all that mighty host? The fierce wrath of God has long since consumed them. They have long since passed away.

How many millions of people have lived since that day? How many nations have risen and shined out like some bright meteor and then vanished away? Where will the living mass of humanity that lives

---

80   This was during the time following the destruction of the First Temple, when Zechariah was calling the people to repent of their evil ways, much as William Freed calls to his hearers to do the same. Zechariah reminds the people that when their forefathers heard similar calls from other prophets and ignored the call, terrible things happened to them. Thus, he says, don't be as stubborn as they were—repent now, and be saved. The people joined with Zechariah and worked for the next four and one-half years to rebuild the temple, which was dedicated in 516 B.C. The book of Zechariah proves God's love and His steadfast desire to forgive His children if they are willing to return to Him.

today be in 1976? Oh ask yourself that question. Today, my unconverted friend, we are passing away down the stream of life with lightning speed. Soon the place that now knows us will know us no more forever. Soon these farms all around your beautiful town will have other owners.

Perhaps one may be in this house today who is laying out great projects for the future. Perhaps he is preparing to build a new house, to put a beautiful fence all around his farm, to adorn his garden with bright flowers and his yard with lovely trees. But oh, as [you] prepare for this world's ease and comfort, prepare also to meet your God! You cannot enjoy life long at the farthest. Soon you will sink beneath the stroke of death. Soon this mortal body that we inhabit will decay and perish. Soon this beautiful town that is trodden by your feet will have other faces walking up and down its streets, this church that you fondly call yours, that you come to so often, will have other faces in its seats. Soon its bright and cheerful look will assume the hue of age, and the place that knows us now will know us no more.

Ask these old veterans of the cross that are sprinkled around so thinly: Where are all the friends and neighbors, your boon companions in youth? Where are they? You will find their names on some lonely tombstone, and their bodies have long since passed into its mother dust. I love, my dear hearers, to view these old veterans of the cross dotted here and there so thinly all over this land of ours. They seem to be left as living monuments of God's good[ness]. Oh what thronging scenes cluster around their memory? Perhaps some of them are 100 years old. They remember the War of 1812. They remember our late war. They remember when the town was all a forest. Where shops and streets are now, was the wild beast 100 years ago.

Some 20 years since, a call was made in Philadelphia for the old soldiers of the Revolution to parade on Washington's birthday. And when the time came, the people as were the custom turned out to see the old Revolutionary heroes. But they awaited in vain. It was announced by the mayor that they had all sunk into the grave. Oh what stillness pervaded that assembly when that announcement was made! The minds of [those] more than hardened and careless were turned to the subject of death when that solemn announcement was made. The tear came into more than one eye as the mayor told that vast assembly that the last soldier of the Revolution in Philadelphia was dead. Oh, my dear hearers, we are passing away!

Twelve years ago my father lived in Bridgeville,[81] and last fall

---

81   Bridgeville is a borough in Allegheny County in the U.S. state of Pennsylvania. The population was 5,148 at the 2010 census.

I stopped there on a a visit. And oh, how many changes were there in those twelve short years! Those that were my schoolmates then are the men and women of the town now. Those that were old then are in the silent tomb now. Those that were getting along then are the old people now. I was a stranger in my own land. I did not know my old home now. Many had died, some had left, others had come. I could look out then and see the old depot from my father's house, but now there are a row of buildings there.

Twelve years ago this town of yours was not known and today you see a splendid village. Twelve years hence these little boys and girls that are going to school now will be the young men and women of the town. Twelve years from today the old soldiers of the cross will sleep the sleep of death. You that are middle age now will be old then. You who are young and in the bloom of youth will then be middle aged.

And O! how many of this audience that I address now will be living then? It would be a hard matter even to collect all that were living. Some will [be] far away from this place, scattered here and there and everywhere. Some of you may be far out on the western prairies. Some may be in the depths of misery and wretchedness. Some may have acquired great wealth and some of you may sing in the realms of bliss around God's great throne. And some of you, alas that it is true! some of you may be eternally lost.

You are passing away. Death is in the land. Men are dying every day. If you would live in the city, you might see the funeral train carrying its victims almost every hour of the day. There are two immortal souls that must live forever falling every moment of our existence. Were it possible to assemble the host of earth in one place and view the sickle of death going round and round that vast army, what think you would be your feeling as he drives on, reaping his harvest? Every moment he would cut down two. In one minute 60 human souls would have fallen beneath his stroke, in one hour 3600, and in 24 hours 86,400. Think of that, my unconverted friends! Think that today 86,400 human souls have died! 0 what a terrible calamity we would think [it] was if that many people were killed in one day. In this land of ours every paper would appear in mourning for those unfortunate men and women. How many mourning ones would be seen!

Could you see that great army of the dead laying out here, what would be your thought? In that host are young men and women, old men and women, and there is the little innocent babe. There is the strong man who bid fair to live many years. There are the rich and the poor, the bond and the free, the heathen in his blindness and the unconverted man in this land of Gospel light. Of all nations and nationalities, there they all are. They have all passed away—86,000 souls in one day. O think, think where you stand, my unconverted friend!

Could you take a balloon and go up and view that living mass of earth's inhabitants, you might get a better view of death-doing than it were possible for you to see on earth. As you looked down upon them, you might see this one dropping and there is another, and you could not count them fast enough! Battles are a terrible sight, but as you looked at that sight you would say that was more awful. Man is falling by every conceivable way. Earth opens and swallows him up. The waves of the sea sink him beneath its depth. Oh how many have found a watery grave!

Some years ago I remember a bridal party that started for Europe on the ill-fated *Shiller*. She was wrecked on the Irish coast, and that young lady was sent back a corpse, bloated and disfigured. She had been washed ashore near some rocks and dashed upon them. Within that vessel a father went down clasping his two daughters. How many have fallen beneath the lightning bolts of heaven! How many have dropped beneath the leaden hail of his opposing foe! How many hearts are sorrowing in this land for sons and husbands and fathers slain in battle!

Man is weak and helpless against the enemy of death. But thanks be to God, we have one who has died and burst the bars of death! He has loosed the power of the law! He has rolled back the tide of death that threatened eternal death! And we may have life. We may live again, though after worms destroy this body. "Yet in my flesh shall I see God."[82]

Oh, my dear hearers, that is a great comfort—to know that we shall not always sleep, to know that Christ has burst the bars of death, and that we may follow on! That by the power of his blood we will be enabled to burst through these bricks and mortar to unbolt that old coffin that holds your mortal remains, to throw back that dirt that has sunk down upon you, and to come forth robed in spotless white! We read that the caterpillar becomes a butterfly, but before that takes place she lays like one dead for one whole winter in her grave and then she comes forth in beauty and glory when all nature is covered with verdure.

And so, my dear Christian friends, we must die and pass through a long, long winter. But when at last we come forth we shall be changed.

---

82   Job 19:26.

These vile bodies of ours that walk this earth, that grovel here below, fond of these earthly joys, shall put on the robe of immortality. We shall come out in the garment of heaven. This halting, trembling step that I see some of you with will walk firm and erect. The sunken eyes and wrinkled faces will be robed in youth and beauty. You won't want your spectacles then. No, no! You can see ten thousand miles. And o, I believe you will have the wings of heaven. You can fly away, away far on and and on, till you lose sight of earth and catch a glimpse of the golden City, and there you can bask in the sunlight of God forever and ever.

Where are your fathers? Ask yourself that question, my unconverted friend, who viewed your dying father or mother in their death struggles who told you with their dying breath to meet them in heaven. They have gone before you. They are beckoning you on. Their dying words have sounded in your ears more than once when you engaged in the pleasures of sin. Perhaps you have seen them in midnight visions. Perhaps they have come back in dreams to you more than once and told you the beauty of that country, told you of the shining companions in that glorious land, pled with you to turn from your evil way and be saved. Stop and think, my unconverted friends, where are your fathers? They have gone to glory. They are shouting around God's great white throne today.

Now O the dying saint of God can catch the music of the golden shore as he passes over Jordan. His face lightens up as he commences to hear that grand choir of God's martyrs and prophets and apostles joining in with the angels of heaven, singing his glory forever and forever. Oh, could you see that father now, young man, you would repent in sackcloth and ashes and turn from your evil way! You may be a father yourself. If so, you don't intend to leave it to be told when you are dead and gone that he died without hope. You don't intend that your children who gather around your bed in that dread hour shall hear these words, "I am lost." that will be a fearful thing to think about in after years for their young minds. O, prepare to meet your father in heaven before it is forever too late! Where are your fathers, you that are almost persuaded to turn back to the beggarly elements of the world, you that are sighing once more for the pleasures of sin, that are wishing I could enjoy this sin and that, that are wanting to carry the world in one hand and heaven in the other. Stop and turn your eyes toward heaven! Throw away every weight that doth so easily beset you, and press forward to the end of the race. Heaven is worth more than all this earth besides to you and me and everyone.

Where is your father, trembling one? Who feels you are there? You may have an earthly father there, but God is your Father. He will lead you in the straight and narrow path. Oh, if you want to meet your earthly father who has gone on before you, keep very near to God. Try and be so near him that you can feel His love kindling fire on the altar of your heart every hour of your life, and you will be enabled like poor Pilgrim, to say, "I will fear no evil, for thy rod and thy staff do comfort me."83 God is a Sun and a shield to them that put their trust in them.

Where is your father, you that are old in this heavenly way? You know better than I can tell you. You are nearing the banks of Jordan's stream. Some of you, perhaps, have one foot in its water. Now you will soon meet your fathers and mothers who have gone on before. They are waiting on the other side to strike hands with you. You have fought long in God's army, but you are almost home now. you will have a happy meeting when you meet that good old father and mother of yours! You can talk over your struggles and trials here. You can tell them how many times you were almost persuaded to turn back. You can tell them of how good God has been to you, and you can sing your sufferings o'er forever and ever.

Oh, that will be a happy meeting, my Christian friends, when parents and children, friends and neighbors will meet to part no more! Oh think of the heavenly host waiting to receive us crowding down to the banks of the river to see their long lost boys and girls. Oh, when we get over there they won't pass us by and say: I don't know who that is. No, no they will welcome us home with songs of rejoicing and we [will] sing our suffering o'er forever and ever.

> Where are your fathers? Once again
> Let every heart and mind ascend
> And trace again these sacred words,
> And think of those dear friends of theirs
> Who sleep the long, long sleep of death;
> Died, and with their gasping breath
> They spake these words so faint and clear
> That all within that room could hear:
> "We'll meet above, I trust, my child.
> We'll meet around the Saviour's side."
> And thus beneath the stroke of death,
> That good old father sank to rest.
> But still forevermore I hear
> An echo sound: Your fathers where?84

---

83   *Pilgrim's Progress*, quoting Psalm 23:4.

84   Judging from the editing which he did of this poem, it seems to have been an original composition. The remaining text in this booklet may have been intended as the beginning of another sermon. Since it was not his usual practice to include fragments of two sermons in the same booklet, it is included here. However, it does not come to his normal conclusion. It would be more customary for him to have ended with this poem.

Seek ye first the kingdom of heaven and his righteousness. Our Saviour is never done giving us good advice, and this is one of the lessons of instruction that he ever gave us. He wants us to make sure of heaven first. And oh, my hearers, it is very important that we stir ourselves in this glorious search! He commended us to seek and in thinking over this the thought occurs of how God has sought us. He sent his dear son into the world to seek us in the first place, and he went about seeking us continually. He was never done looking for us. He found some of us sunk very low, almost lost. But he saved all that came unto him. And we find him saving the thieves as he was almost expiring on the cross. And his last words are in our behalf.

And now he has left his good spirit to seek after us. And that good spirit has sought and found a great many of you, but ye would not come. God is seeking you every hour of the day, but you must also seek him. He is willing to come more than half way after you, but he won't force [you] to come to him. You are your own master in that respect. God wants you to join hands with these good people and save your soul. He wants you to be a follower of Christ. He wants you to seek that country not made with hands, eternal in the heaven. And he wants you to do it right away. He doesn't want you to wait till you are on a dying bed. He doesn't want you to wait till your heart becomes as adamant, and you won't care to seek him. No, no, he wants you to start out just now while your heart is tender, while you can feel for others' woes and seek this glorious kingdom of heaven.

Now, my Christian friends, you know what that kingdom of heaven is. You have felt its power more than once in that old classroom. You have felt its melting influence there, as some old sister or brother has told of how Christ eased his burden and made him to rejoice in his love. And then, as that good brother sat down and told them all to pray for him, you might have got a faint idea of the kingdom of heaven. The kingdom of heaven means childlike simplicity in God. It means a taking away of that that is evil in the heart and making you love your God, your neighbor, and become as a little child.

Not long since I remember a little boy who was just going to bed and before he went his father made him say his prayers. And among the rest he quoted these words: "Give me a clean heart." Oh, how that struck me.

Education

Church Music:
How shall it be improved?

I feel, my hearers, in discussing this subject, that I am out on an unknown ocean of that I am on a ship that has lost her compass and rudder, with a great probability of being lost. Feeling thus, I come before you this morning with fear and trembling. I am no singer, yet in common with all men and women I love to hear the inspiring strain of human voices blending together and rising to a heaven of song, to a heaven where angels and saints unite in singing "hallelujah, hallelujah for the lord God omnipotent reigneth!"

Music, my brethren, seems to be part of human nature, and the arch enemy of the soul has debased this attribute in our nature in common with all other attributes. I care [not] where you find the man, you will find him indulging in song. Go with me to the house of vice and you will hear this heavenly attribute debased to the lowest depths of shame. Pick up some of the lewd song books that have been published and you will see that in music as in all things else there is a bad as well as a good article. And some of these vendors of music have piled upon their shelves books that seem to be full of wounds and bruises and putrifying sores that are only fit to be cast out and trodden under foot of men. But there are dogs and jackals and hyenas in human shape that are following in the wake of the army of the world and eating up—or in other words, singing up—this refuse matter. There are thousands of vendors and thousands of buyers in wholesale stores of perdition.

Then there is another class of music that is not bad. There is no harm in it. But there is no good in it. While it does not make men worse, it does not make them better. Unlike the fog, it rolls like the dark black cloud between the clear sky and the darkening fog. This class of music does not make men demons in human shape, it does not drag them down to the depth of perdition, and it does not lift them up to heaven. It makes them skeptics and doubters, and they are always in a region of despair.

But there is a purer music than either of the two I have been dwelling on and, and that is heavenly music or church music. For church music is the swelling of men and women that are filled with the

Holy Ghost. This music does not make men bad, it does not make them doubters, but it seeks to impress upon them the grand fact that

"There is a God that rules on high,
And all the earth surveys,
That rides upon the stormy sky
And calms the troubled wave."

It seeks to impress upon them the thought that sin's dark wave has swept over them, and that Jesus is able to save them from its contaminating influence.

God is speaking to man from a thousand different voices. He is speaking to him through the voices. He is speaking to him through the misery that sin entails on men and women. As the sinner writhes beneath the terrible punishment his sin has brought upon him, he hears a still small voice whispering in his ear "the way of the transgressor is hard" and he instinctfully seeks the remedy for his sin through Christ. Some men are saved only through the misery their sin brings upon them.

Another class of men are saved through   the   foolishness of preaching. They are attentive listeners, and the words spoken fall into [a] good and honest heart. There was a man that I knew once, that always [paid] attention while the minister spoke. It was a pleasure to preach to that man because he seemed to enjoy it. He seemed to love to hear the word of God. He would come through rain or shine, through mud and slush, and always be found in his place listening intently to the words the minister spoke. If we had a congregation of men like that, my hearers, I believe the divine fire would descend on preacher and people.

But there are a good many men that are not saved by the foolishness of preaching. Preaching, in other words, seems to be absurd nonsense to them. And when the minister takes his text they commence to fix themselves for a nap. Oh how sleepy they are apparently! You would imagine they toiled all the week and served God on Sunday in dreamland. I do not believe, my brethren, that God will hear a prayer made up of snoring. Christ taught his followers a prayer somewhat different from that. And we read that he reproved his disciples for sleeping while he was watching. There would be more power in the ministry today were men more fully alive to the interest of their salvation. We cannot, my hearers, we cannot serve God in this lukewarm manner. We cannot sleep ourselves away to the paradise of the best. But with eager heart and hands we must run with patience the race set before us.

Another class of men are saved by the holy influence of song, and that alone. The swelling anthems of God's people are the only weapons God employs in that man's salvation. The minister may present

salvation to them under the form of an eloquent appeal, he may carry
them to the throne of grace on the wings of prayer, but all to no avail.
He still remains stubborn and unsubdued. But when the little boy or girl
who sits by his side catches up the strain of sacred song and rings out
the anthem

>"Oh come angel band,
>Come and around me stand,
>Oh bear me away on your snowy wings
>To my immortal home"

The tear forces itself to his eye, and Johnny or Mary are dearer
than ever before, the cross of Christ is dearer than ever before, and a
lasting impression is produced. Thousands of men have been saved for
God and heaven by the sacred and hallowed influence of sacred music,
that never would have been saved in any other way. The music of song
comes like the gentle zephyr [breeze] and penetrates every part of the
maze.

God has his preachers out in this world in the form of sweet
singers that fill and thrill the soul with joy unutterable and full of glory. I
remember one of these heavenly preachers. I shall never forget him, my
brethren. His name was Willie Dean. He sang before an audience of five
thousand people in a large city, and that sermon did more good than
hundreds of eloquent appeals. It was not a long sermon, my brethren.
There were only four or five verses of that delightful [hymn]:

>"We're going home no more to roam
>No more to sin and sorrow
>No more to wear the brow of care
>We're going home tomorrow"[85]

But as he sang, my brethren, the tear commenced to flow and
the stoutest hearts melted before its holy and heavenly influence. It
went down into the stubborn heart and broke down the embankment
that sin had reared on every side. And for once the river overflowed its
banks, for once the better part of his nature overflowed the bank of sin,
and the pentecostal shower descended in every heart. I venture to say,
my hearers, that in the last great day there will [be] some bright and
sparking jewels in the crown of that little one's rejoicing.

God, my brethren, is working at the stubborn heart from every
direction like the beseiging army. He is struggling to dig his way in
through the power of preaching, he is striving to undermine the fort
of sin and blow it by the power of song into a purer atmosphere. He is
striking him down sometimes like Saul of old by the hand of affliction.

---

85   Hymn by Griswold. Mennonite.

And in every possible way he is struggling to save fallen humanity. Song is one of those weapons. For we read that the immortal ones in heaven sing of the strain of "Hallelujah, hallelujah for the Lord God omnipotent reigneth."86 We read that angel bands sang at the birth of our lord, the strain of peace and good will to men. We read that the ransomed of the lord shall come up with songs of joy on their lips.

And God, my brother, has given that power of song to you and me. He has entrusted that weapon   to our keeping. And it remains for us to use it. We have, tis true — some of us — a limited amount of this power of song. Some men are running off with the music of the soul, and some have such a small quantity that they have long ere this buried it in [the] fathomless pit of this world.

But some men are all song. When you meet them on the street they are singing. When you see them at work they are humming or whistling, and forever song comes like the bubbling spring up from the depths of their souls. The colored people are great singers. And I remember once a little babe of a good old colored sister who was always humming something about the gospel ship. This boy, my hearers, was only a year old, and somehow it leaked out that our good sister had an infant prodigy in this little babe. The little fellow did love to hear singing, and he wasn't very particular whether it breathed of heaven or hell, so that it was a good big noise. Well as I remarked before, the ladies got to hear it, and our fair young ladies would capture our little black boy, dirt and all, on the street and commence singing, and the little fellow would commence swaying his body with the music. And it did seem that music was all that boy possessed. He had all his talents in one. I believe there are a great many more just like that boy that God intended to sing the songs of Zion. And if the good singers were all united, this question of how church music can be improved would be more than half answered.

God never intended that all men should be singers. Some men have been apostles specially adapted for that work. Some have been prophets specially adapted for that work by the divine will of God, and some have been singers filled with the music of heaven. That music is a power for good, all will admit. That all men are adapted to the special work of song, none can believe.

Now to come to the first part of my subject in detail. How various it is! Like everything else that is varied, so music is varied. Church music: what is it? How does it stand in this land today? And what are the opinions of men in regard to it?

---

86   Handel's *Messiah.*

Some men of the older and more staid of our Christian fellowship are unutterably opposed to the organ in connection with singing. "Why," said a good old brother back in Pennsylvania, "our fathers did not have organs and they were good Christian men." This brother reminds me of the story of one of our missionaries in India. He stood by a bank where the natives were carrying away the earth on their heads and in the integrity of his heart he pitied them and contrived to have a wheelbarrow made. He brought it to one of them and showed him by the actual process how much easier it was to wheel the dirt than to carry it on their heads. They all admitted it, and our good native commenced to wheel the dirt instead of carrying it on his head. All went along smoothly for a time. Our missionary left congratulating himself that he had effected a great work among [them] and that it would lighten their labor and be a blessing to them. But shortly after this he returned, and what a sight he beheld! Our native filled his wheelbarrow as before, and instead of wheeling it back to its place he deliberately took it up and placed it on his head. "Why," said the missionary, "that is not the way. That is just as hard as it was before!" "But, replied our native, "our fathers carried dirt in this way and we are no better than they." And he walked off in disgust for all improvements.

And thus it was with our good brother in Pennsylvania. This organ that the good people had bought without any help from him, he styled it a wooden devil. And for some time after it was introduced he would shuffle his feet while the organist was playing, and do all that he could to worry the congretation. This good brother was no singer, but that did not prevent him from singing as best he could. He would take his place in the Amen corner and hem and haw out "Oh! for a thousand tongues to sing" until you would imaging a screeching mob was on your track. Now, brethren, I do not believe church music is going to be built up by any such music as that, but the church will be filled with empty seats if such a course were pursued. If some men have no soul for music, let them stand still and see the salvation of the Lord.

The church music of today in a great many instances is too much like an Italian hand organ[87] ground out to fill in time. The church must, my brethren, recognize the great fact that God is preaching to dying men and women through the hallowed influence of song. And as the church feels and recognizes the great fact that her ministry must be composed of men that are not only willing but able to present the gospel of Christ with power and the unction of the Holy Ghost, so individual churches must recognize the great fact that they, as part of the body of Christ's

---

87   Accordion.

visible church, must have men and women who are not only willing but able to sing with the spirit and with the understanding. This is an age of progress. Men are becoming more intelligent on every hand. And this rotary motion singing that is drawled and hemmed and hawed out will not do good. On the contrary, it will be like a wet blanket thrown over the sermon of the preacher. The man may be eloquent and effective in preaching, but if his discourse is followed with a long spiritless and see-saw hymn the congregation will feel that this has been a weariness of the flesh.

Now how is the church going to improve her singing? And what is good singing? The most effective singing is that that has the elements of sweetness. I am no singer, but as far as I have been able to see and hear, this is the general verdict. The heart of man is touched by the sweet voice of the sweet singer and the words that come forth sink deep in the soul. Mr. Moody recognized this fact when he selected for his companion in his grand work the sweet and soul-stirring singer Mr. Sankey.[88] And I venture that there are thousands that have been saved to the church through his soul-inspiring songs. Now here are two men. One is working on the hearts of his hearers by the power of preaching, and the other by the power of song. And which has gathered in the greatest harvest, the judgment day alone will reveal.

Where, my brethren, is the church to find the sweet singer that will touch the hearts of men and women? And I would answer, among the children. The voice of the child is far more eloquent than the voice of the parent in song. And if the Christian men and women of our land would fully recognize this fact there would be less empty houses of worship. There was a large church in the city of Philadelphia that [had] for her singers a choir of thirty boys and girls about twelve years of age, and that church is filled every time. My brethren, there are hundreds that come to hear the little ones singing the songs of Zion. Their sweet voices ring in at the end of the sermon as the clinching iron to drive home the words of the minister of God. The surrounding churches felt that there was power there in that like the hunter of gold, so these hunters of souls had unearthed a tremendous weapon for good and they adopted the plan. They filled their side galleries with the Sunday School children and helped on the words of the pastor by their sweet and innocent voices.

---

88   Dwight L. Moody and Ira D. Sankey began in the Midwestern revival circuits, and rose to a modest international prominence. Moody preached the gospel; Sankey sang it. Sankey was a powerful tenor and a great favorite with the crowds. He accompanied himself on the melodeon. In 1875 the New York Times declared that "In England everybody is mad with the Moody and Sankey fever." Sandra S. Sizer, *Gospel Hymns and Social Religion* (Phildelphia, 1978), pp. 3-4. The Moody Bible Institute still exists. See moody.edu.

And these are crowded houses now.

Another power in singing is to sing with the spirit. This is cultivated more in the large cities than in the country. This man's fearing spirit seems to have full possession of some men and women. And when they sing they seem to be afraid that some one will hear them. This is especially the case if the leader starts the hymn in a low tone. The church should select for her leader in singing a man that is not only capable, but that is not afraid to sing. Here especially in the country should this be the case. They are entirely dependent on congregational singing. And in order to be a power for good, it should breathe out the power of the spirit.

The most effectual singing is congregational singing if conducted in the right way. Mr. Talmage's church in Brooklyn[89] has this form of song. And I tell you, my brethren, it is grandly effectual. They have a man that knows how and is not ashamed of the gospel of Christ. And when he leads off a congregation of five thousand people in a song of praise, it is a power for good. It fills all the house and every heart. Let me then, my hearers, urge upon you the importance of singing with the spirit.

Another power is unity. There is an old saying that in union there is power, and it is doubly powerful in song. Some singers are of the spirit. No lack of spirit, but a sad lack of unity with the other singers, and sometimes you would imagine you were in a church that had four or five congregations in it. This man is sitting here with eyes shut, singing away as if he were unconscious any other person were in the house, and drawling out the last line of every verse to a terrible length. Here is a good sister that is just a little behind him. And the congregation is singing away, trying if possible to drown these two old members, but all to no effect. For every now and then you will hear their twang above all the rest, and it creates discord. And the singing, instead of being a power for good, is only a laughing stock. Not only must the congregation sing with the spirit, but they must, in order to be effectual, sing in unity.

Another power in song is to enlist the sympathy of all in the singing. There is today in the church too much self-importance displayed. A select number of singers will take some selected spot and do all the singing themselves. I believe, my hearers, this is not godlike. It does not display the true Christian spirit. I, for instance, am a stranger. I enter your church and take a seat among strangers. Is it not your place to make me feel welcome? How are you going to do it by leaving me to sit and sing

---

89   T. DeWitt Talmage (1832-1902) was one of the most prominent religious leaders in the United States in the mid to late 18th century, and was renowned for his talent in preaching.

as best I can? Christ said that whosoever presented a cup of cold water in my name should have his reward; and whosoever will present a hymn book to a stranger in a strange church will have his reward. Besides all that, my brethren, this should be the rule among all Christian churches and it will add to the power of song. Effectually all should have a voice in the hymn of praise, and it can only be done by distributing a book to every man and woman and child in the house. And then when the pastor gives out the hymn

> "O for a thousand tongues to sing
> My great redeemer's praise ..."[90]

he will not look around to find one or two singing the hymn in a crowded house. Besides all that, my hearers, there may be, for aught you know, an angel of song in the house whose sweet voice you have not heard because of your own indiscretion. Let a man — no matter how depraved he may be — let him feel that there are men and women in the house of God by giving him a hymn book, and you may be sowing seed that shall spring up for everlasting life.

Church singing can be rendered effectual also by music, and we as Christian men and women should adopt all the means that God and nature has put in our power to draw men to God. If you believe the time has come when the church should have an organ, give it to her. Do not stand at enmity with your brother because he believes the church's interest would be advanced by an organ or piano. Paul was willing to be all things to all men so that he might save some. And the Christian man or woman should join hands and work unitedly in this grand cause of the salvation of men and women. If you do not like music, I venture to say your children do. And if it will do you no good, it will them. And if you are a Christian man, it cannot harm you.

These, my hearers, are a few of the thoughts that have suggested themselves to me on the subject of church music and the manner of its improvement. I love the church, and I believe that the gospel hymn is a power for good. And we as Christian men and women should join hands and unitedly to rear a pillar of song that shall live to bless dying men and women. Almost every man and woman loves to sing. I care not how wicked he is, he wants to raise his voice in song. And it remains for the Christian church to seize that power in his nature and turn it towards heaven. It remains for the church to teach him to praise God. And if the church will do that, she will go forward with gigantic strides in this grand work of the salvation of men and women.

---

90   Hymn by John Wesley. *Methodist Hymnal* # 1.

FAITH

Just as I Am, without One Plea

453

1. Just as I am, with-out one plea, but that thy
2. Just as I am, and wait-ing not to rid my
3. Just as I am, though tossed a-bout with man-y a
4. Just as I am, poor, wretch-ed, blind; sight, rich-es,

blood was shed for me, and that thou bidd'st me
soul of one dark blot, to thee, whose blood can
con-flict, man-y a doubt, fight-ings and fears with-
heal-ing of the mind, yea, all I need, in

come to thee, O Lamb of God, I come, I come.
cleanse each spot, O Lamb of God, I come, I come.
in, with-out, O Lamb of God, I come, I come.
thee to find, O Lamb of God, I come, I come.

5. Just as I am, thou wilt receive,
   wilt welcome, pardon, cleanse, relieve;
   because thy promise I believe,
   O Lamb of God, I come, I come.

6. Just as I am, thy love unknown
   has broken ev'ry barrier down;
   now, to be thine, yea, thine alone,
   O Lamb of God, I come, I come.

Charlotte Elliott, 1836

WOODWORTH L.M.
William B. Bradbury, 1849

"Just as I am." "The authoress of this poem, Miss Charlotte Elliott of Brighton, England, was born in 1789, and was an invalid almost all her life till her death in 1871. This is one of several hymns she wrote for a little book in 1836, intended to help and comfort other sick people. She never dreamed that it would come to be loved by everybody." Benson, *The Best Church Hymns*, Philadelphia, 1898, Hymn # 26. Text from *The Camp-Meeting Chorister*, 1852, image from *Trinity Psalter*.

THE

CAMP-MEETING

CHORISTER;

OR, A

COLLECTION OF HYMNS

AND

SPIRITUAL SONGS,

FOR THE PIOUS OF ALL DENOMINATIONS.

TO BE SUNG AT CAMP MEETINGS, DURING REVIVALS
OF RELIGION, AND ON OTHER OCCASIONS.

" O Lord, I will praise thee."—*Isaiah.*
" Is any merry? let him sing Psalms."—*James*
" I will sing with the spirit, and with the under-
standing also."—*Paul.*

Philadelphia:
PUBLISHED BY W. A. LEARY & CO.
108 NORTH SECOND STREET, TEN DOORS BELOW NEW
AND FOR SALE BY ALL THE METHODIST BOOK-
SELLERS IN THE UNITED STATES.

1852.

The Spirit and Truth of Singing[91]

¶55. To guard against formality in singing: --

§ 1. Choose such hymns as are appropriate for the occasion, and do not sing too much at once; seldom more than four or five verses.

§ 2. Let the tune be suited to the sentiment, and do not suffer the people to sing too slowly.

§ 3. In every Society let due attention be given to the cultivation of sacred music.

§ 4. Should the Preacher In Charge desire it, let the Quarterly Conference appoint annually a committee of three or more, who, cooperating with him, shall regulate all matters relating to this part of divine worship.

§ 5. As singing is a part of divine worshipin which all ought to unite, therefore exhort every person in the congregation to sing, not one in ten only.

---

91   *Doctrine and Discipline*, pp. 42-43.

EDUCATION

TOBACCO

The subject of this lecture is entitled "Tobacco," and as all have a foundation stone to found or lay the burden of their arguments upon I suppose I shall have to choose a stone of some kind. This, my hearers, is essential, and before going any farther let me impress upon your mind the grand foundation stones of all arguments and the importance of having a strong stone of some kind. This, my hearers, is essential, and before going any farther let me impress upon your mind the grand foundation stones of all arguments and the importance of having a strong stone of some kind. You all remember the time you entered some church and saw the old parson in the pulpit unfold his spectacles, wipe them with his handkerchief and then carefully putting them on, look out his text and say, "We will take for the foundation of a few remarks this evening the words found in such or such a place." And then he would commence the foundation here. And his building was blown to the four winds of heaven, his foundation stone and his building or argument—if any man can be so cruel as to call it an argument—were as far from each other as the north pole is from the south. Hoping that this foundation stone that I have chosen tonight will bear all that I shall endeavor to put upon it, I beg leave to inform you that my foundation stone consists of that old saying running in this wise:

> Tobacco is an evil weed,
> And from the devil doth proceed.
> It spoils your breath and scents your clothes
> And makes a chimney of your nose."

Tobacco is an American production. But that [whether] America is the original stamping ground of the devil I cannot say, and shall leave you to judge. Nearly four centuries ago when Columbus discovered the West Indies, his sailors that were sent ashore upon the Island of Cuba were astonished to find the uncivilized inhabitants puffing smoke from their mouths and nostrils, which they afterwards learned was derived from the combustion of the dried leaves of a plant unknown in Europe. When he landed on the Island of Hispaniola his scouts reported that in their explorations they saw the natives smoking a plant the perfume of which was fragrant and grateful. They subsequently learned that from

260 WILLIAM WALTON FREED

the earliest ages it had been the custom of those savages to offer it in their sacrifices, believing that their divinity would be more pleased with its aroma than with any other incense. As other portions of America were discovered, this same plant was generally met as a favorite of the natives. The degraded savages of the American wilds from the northwest coast to Patagonia, were slaves to the use of this new and strange plant.

Those who were first discovered inhaled the smoke through a hollow cane, one end of which was introduced into the mouth and the other was applied to the burning leaves. The Aztecs of Mexico used wooden pipes made of some of the most beautiful wood susceptible of the finest polish for which Mexico is so famous. They also rolled the leaves into cigars which they ignited and smoked in tubes of tortoise shells or silver. Columbus on his second voyage found some who pulverized the dried leaves and snuffed the dust up into the nostrils through hollow canes. We have failed to find any evidence that the untutored savage as he was found in this country with all his degradation had ever become so filthy as to indulge in chewing the Quid.[92] It is evident, however, that for ages he had been fondly attached to his pipe, as it is found everywhere in association with Indian relics and served as a symbol of peace at their council fires. The Mound Builders whose history is without beginning or end and who are known only by the monumental testimony were worshippers of the God of this narcotic plant as is indicated by the finding of the pipe in the mounds of the Mississippi Valley with other relics of that unknown race.

This plant whose use is of heathen origin has been classed by botanists in the genus of poisonous plants. The most deadly poison it is possible to conceive of being extracted from it. The common name "tobacco" was probably derived from "tobacos", the name given by the Caribs to the pipe in which they smoked the plant. This narcotic poisonous plant used by the barbarous natives of the American wilds was carried to Europe and presented to the devotees of fashion and luxury as a sweet smelling savor. Its use was popularized by the dissemination of false notions concerning its properties and strengthened by the slavery of appetite, which it fastened upon its victims. The cultivation of tobacco has become an important factor in American industry and the commerce of the world is today largely affected by it.

This is a short outline of the history of this wonderful plant that, like the Colorado potato bug, has left the shores of America and went from hovel to palace and permeated every heathen tribe almost on the

92   Cut, as of chewing tobacco. From the Middle English *cud* (a cow chews its cud). American Heritage Dictionary.

face of the earth in the course of four centuries. Never was victorious army more successful in achieving her victories! The production of tobacco today in the United States sums up the grand total of 434 million 209 thousand 461 pounds that is gulped and snuffed and smoked by some party or parties unknown to your humble servant. Tobacco I have often thought as I have looked at men chawing away with the regularity of the cow at her cud and gazing into thin air serves about the same purpose as the cow's cud does to her. You and I have often heard the expression "I can't do without it now." Tobacco has bound them with iron bands and riveted them with a thousand rivets — or chawes, I should have said. "Oh," said a young man once in my hearing, "the comfort there is in it!" I have seen men taking comfort from books, I have seen them taking comfort in rum and in almost everything we can think of, and last of all I have seen them taking comfort in a good chaw of "terbacker". As I heard an old fellow say, "Give us a chaw of terbacker, Bob!"

It has been my fortune to capture one of these comforters known as a tobacco Quid. This Comforter has, as you may all see by its chawed appearance, done duty in its time. It has been rolled from side to side as a sweet morsel. It has stood on the ramparts of tobacco land. And when the chawing legions of this army advanced to take another chaw, it has filled a pretty big chasm in the breach and comforted some poor fellow's heart for a short time. It wears a comfortable look now and sings it suffering o'er henceforth. It will for a great many of its neighbors in our large cities be captured by some hunter of cigar stumps and quids and pressed into service again as fine cut tobacco. And I venture to say it will answer truthfully to its name.

Tobacco chewers are the most liberal and yet the stingiest men I have ever met. There seems to be a supply brigade whose purse strings are pretty heavy and a regular army of tramps following after them and yelling: Give us a chaw, Bob — or Jim or Harry as the case may be. I have heard of such a thing as cheek. Hard cheek, some call it, and I tell you that their cheeks have been hammered as hard as they make them. Let us follow one of these gentry and view his proceedings. He will walk up to a man whom he knows and sometimes one whom he does not know and commence to talk about weather. "Fine day," perhaps he will say, and the next question is "Got any more tobacco, Bob?" Bob hauls out a new plug. "The very best navy[93]," he says. Our cheeky friend will take

---

93   Navy Flake, Navy cut, Navy tobacco is a Burley tobacco. In colonial times sailors twisted tobacco into a roll and "tied it tightly, often moistening the leaves with rum, molasses, or spice solutions." Stored in this way the flavors melded. To smoke it a slice was cut, known as a "twist" or "curly". Eventually all twisted tobacco, and then pressed tobacco, became known

it, look at it, smell it, and gulp down about half of it at one chaw, and thus he goes on. Having devoured that, another victim crosses his track, and another chaw of tobacco fills his mouth. He will go from store to store, from corner to corner, and chaw and slobber gratis week in and week out. In our large cities they have what is called wharf rats—not four legged rats, but two footed urchins. And they will crawl out of their barrels and bins, take one look at you, and say "Mister, give us a chaw of tobacco." That is their first and only query. They don't know anything about cheek, but it is all brass with them. And their older brothers are scattered all over this land of ours.

I am afraid I am soaring away from my foundation, however, and in order to get back on the old rock again let me invite your attention to the manufacture of tobacco in the United States. There are in the United States 5204 establishments for manufacturing tobacco employing 32,000 males and 8,000 females in its production. These manufacturers employ on their business a capital of over $25,000,000; use material costing over $35,000,000; and produce for market manufactured tobacco worth $72,000,000 of dollars. These, my hearers, are a few of the figures showing the amount of money that is chawed and smoked away in a year in these United States. I have not mentioned the millions spent for this weed in other countries, but confining myself simply to the United States might I not ask of an intelligent public, are they not enormous? The records show that there are over 5,000 establishments in this country for the manufacture of tobacco in this country.

But there is an unwritten record that I shall endeavor to bring before your mind. You ask where are they? and I would answer right in the mouth of men. For you must know that all this slobber and juice, all these quids and stumps, have a fountainhead or manufacturing establishment and in connection with this I have often thought of the poor dentist that must bore and pry right over the terrible smoke or breath of this volcano. A friend of mine back in the East is a dentist and one day I was in his office talking away when a man about 60 years of age, a German by the way, came in and, said he, "Me gotten a tooth that pains. Me want it out." The doctor told him to take a seat, and he showed him where it was. Curiosity impelled me forward to see this destroyer of his peace. I approached with trembling steps to look into the yawning chasm, when horror of horrors to relate, a stench exhumed from that mouth that I cannot describe, and leave you to imagine if the

---

as "Navy" "because of the convenience for sailors and outdoorsmen who favored its compact size "and long-lasting, slow-burning qualities." Navy Flake tobacco is pressed into bricks and sliced into broad flakes. Quote from tobacconistuniversity.org as quoted in Wikipedia.

crater of Vesuvius has a more terrible smell than that I am constrained to exclaim in the language of a good Episcopalian brother, "From all such, Good Lord deliver us!"

Having escaped in safety without being overcome by foul air, I stood by to see how the doctor would make out. He stood his ground like a martyr, and finally dragged the offending molar from his den of vice and showed it to me. I looked at it and looked, and still the wonder grew that any mortal man could carry such an awful tooth. You have seen horse teeth all covered over with a dead substance, and I tell you when you have converted that tooth to all kinds of nasty uses you will not have it to look like this man's tooth. This tooth looked as if it might have lain in an old swill barrel filled with tobacco juice for ages. Tobacco had not only entered the outward part, but like the piece of meat laying in salt brine till it is thoroughly soaked, so this tooth had lain in tobacco juice so long that I venture the assertion you could have extracted a poison from it that would have killed about as quick as the bite of the rattlesnake. There are any amount of these establishments in this country that seem to have for their sole pleasure the ceaseless grinding of this weed till their teeth are ground down to stumps and almost ready to drop out.

Now what are the properties of tobacco? And I would answer on the highest medical authority that it is deadly poison. There is a poison extracted from tobacco known as nicotine that is as deadly as any poison in existence. And while druggists label strychnine with a skeleton figure to denote its deadly character, they might well engrave the same motto on tobacco. One drop of nicotine of tobacco placed on the tongue of a cat will enter into the circulation of the blood and do its deadly work in about two minutes. Three drops will kill a large dog and ten drops thus administered will kill an ox in ten minutes. There is enough poison in one old pipe to kill twenty infants if extracted and so administered as to enter the circulation of the blood. These, my hearers, are some of the deadly effects of tobacco.

Almost every boy or girl that smoked was first sickened by its deadly effects. And when I make that assertion, I speak that I know! I remember my own sad experience. And while I shall not shed any tears over it now, I shall endeavor to tell you just how it was. Well, I went to school with a lot of other boys in the Eastern shore of Maryland where everybody chews enough and smokes. The boys, of course, chewed, and I as a greenhorn, as it were, stood in wonder and amazement and looked on. They treated me as an inferior because I could not chew, so I thought, and one day a great big burly fellow asked me if I didn't want a chaw of "terbacker". Of course I did. I took a great big chaw, stuck my hands in my pocket, and started off with the boys, slobbering and spitting as big as the next fellow.

But alas for my bright dreams of manhood, my knees commenced to quiver. I commenced to feel sick all over, and concluded that the best place for me was home. I wanted to go home. I struck a bee line for that delightful place, hung my coat on a willow, and crawled under the house near a big hole, and there I laid and disgorged and disgorged till I thought my very heart was in my throat. They talk sometimes about their dear Johnny or Willy that is sick because he has emptied a sugar bowl, but I believe you will believe my statement when I told my good mother I was taken suddenly ill and could not tell the cause.

She put me to bed, gave me a catnip tea to take inwardly, put warm bricks to my feet and cold cloths to my head, and sent out to gather in all the good mothers to hold a pow-wow over me and devise ways and means for my speedy restoration to health once more. Of course I was doctored and physicked to death almost, but to make a long story short I got well, thanks be to a good providence. I recovered again, and there and then resolved that as for me and my house, we would abstain from the use of tobacco forever after. And if the sick boys that have been sickened by its use would follow the advice of nature, they would save their ruddy cheeks and their depleted pocket book.

I must say I do not know how tobacco effects the fairer sex when first they dabble in its waters, but I know that away down in Maryland in good old days of yore they used to have tremendous fireplaces. And instead of coal oil lights they used what they call fat pine to light the room. The colored boy would bring in a couple of good arm fulls of this wood. The women would start a good fire in their big hearths, and then every one of them would bring a low stool and hold a council over that fire, silent and grim like weird spirits of the dead. They would sit around while the flickering light threw a lurid glare over them. With snuff box in one hand and brush in the other, they say and ever and anon you might see a good old sister or a young one as the case might be take her brush and gouge in that box, capturing a pretty big haul of the delicious stuff. She would carefully convey it to her mouth, and then the rubbing process would commence. Some people scour their teeth to make them look bright and clear. But down there they scrub them to make them look dark and repulsive. And that process is continued till tobacco has ruined the teeth.

Not only poisonous and deadly in its effects, but it is expensive in the highest degree. There is spent today in the United States over two hundred millions of dollars annually for tobacco, one billions of dollars every five years, and twenty billions in a century. Why we cannot realize the amount of money we spend for this useless weed! And if that money were turned into a proper channel instead of vanishing away in this drain of slobber and smoke, what blessings would be conferred on the human race! There are 44,000 clergymen in the United States including Catholic priests whose average salary amounts to $600 a year, showing that our entire religious instruction including Catholic and Protestant cost only $26,400,000. If we add fifty percent for incidental expenses and collections for benevolent enterprises, we have a total of $39,600,000. This great Christian nation boasting of its religion and devotion to a crucified redeemer pays annually $40,000,000 for its religion and $200,000,000 for its tobacco!

There are in the United States 141,629 schools including seminaries, colleges, universities, academies and public and private schools employing 221,042 teachers at an average salary of $400. The entire cost of all the schools in this country is $95,402,726, less than one-half the amount wasted — yea, worse than wasted — in the use of tobacco. If we add to our education and religion the cost of all the printing done in our country including books, pamphlets, magazines, newspapers, maps, and job work we have an additional bill of $66,862,447. Our whole bill for intellectual and moral culture foots up as follows

Religion	$39,600,000
Education	95,402,726
B M and news	66,862,447
Total	$201,865,173

It is a sad yet stern reality, my hearers, that we [spend] as much money for tobacco as we do for mental and moral culture. Noisy populations may clamor for reform, but reform must commence in the hearts of the people in a personal victory over the vices. Men will talk of hard times and spend the last copper [penny] they have to satisfy not their wants but their sordid passions. Not long since I read of a tramp bewailing his hard condition to another tramp. They talked sometime about wages and the war between capital and labor, and wound up by asking his friend to come and take a drink. And there are thousands just like that tramp that will spend their last copper for the gratification of their passions.

Arnerica has been a fruitful field, not only for luxuries but for vices. Starting from the mountain wilds of America, Liberty first struck off the shackles of despotism and planted her standard on the plains of Italy, crossed over the Alps and asserted her power in the fertile valley of France, and made the lot of all Europe more tolerable. This has been the achievement of Liberty. But where, might I ask, is the birth place of this savior of down trodden humanity? And I would answer with my finger toward old Independence Hall in the city of Philadelphia, There and there! Is there any in my audience that have seen that venerable hall with her worn steps and shattered bell that can tell you that they have seen the birth place of that glorious liberty? That was more sacred to Patrick Henry than life itself. America has also produced tobacco, a weed that the untutored savages of America used centuries and centuries before this country was discovered. I cannot tell how long it has been since this weed has been used. Its history lies buried in the mounds of the Mississippi. And we can only conjecture. But it remains as a fact that this weed has left the shores of America in company with liberty, and permeated every tribe on the face of the globe in the short space of four centuries. While liberty is striking off the bands of a galling despotism, tobacco has forged a new weapon of tyranny and holds the struggling ones of earth in a vice-like grip.

The Cafra[94] of Africa is in the same chain of despotism that binds the peasantry of Europe. And while he lays at one end of his improvised pipe consisting of a hole dug in the ground and leading to the fumes of tobacco, while he lays at the mouth of this hole sucking its smoke till tired and exhausted, nature succumbs to its effects. He is doing no more than his white brother on the shores of America. There is a beautiful residence on the shores of Long Island that was built—how do you suppose it was built? By the savings of a man that resolves that he would save every cent that he would spend on tobacco. And every day he put by the amount he would have spent for the use of the weed. In the course of years this sum swelled to the amount of fifteen thousand dollars. That, had he taken an opposite course, would have robbed him of his beautiful residence.

Tobacco is a robber. It robs the poor man of many comforts and some of the comfortable homes that they could not have in any other way. Suppose all the men and women engaged in the business were in

94   Kaffir. This word derives from the Arab word *kaffir* which means "unbeliever" (in Allah). The word was originally applied to non-Muslim people in the south and east of the continent by coastal Arab and Somalitraders. It is likely that Portuguese explorers, encountering these traders, interpreted the word as the ethnicity of the native African people they had encountered. The Portuguese national poet Camões used the plural form of the term (cafres) in the fifth canto of his 1572 poem Os Lusíadas. Today this word is considered to be an ethnic slur.. Article from Originalpeople.org, November 15, 2012.

some useful pursuit. Would the world not be happier? Suppose all the land employed in raising tobacco was sown in wheat or corn. Would the world not be happier? Suppose all the capital invested in this business was invested in some other more profitable pursuit. Would the world not be better? I venture to say all candid men would say yes, the tobacco users of the world are supporting an army of drones that are producing nothing but poverty in their track. These are facts that cannot be denied

Not only has America produced liberty and tobacco, but there is another destroyer that starting from the wild of Colorado has steadily advance at the rate of 50 miles a year till it reached the shores of the Atlantic. You all know what that pest is — the Colorado potato bug. It has crossed over the briny waters of the Atlantic and penetrated the fields of Europe. I venture to say that it will follow its cousin tobacco to the jungles of India and the forests of Africa and while tobacco is robbing the man of his hard earned labor, while tobacco will be rolling out his dollars on the the counter of the store keeper to gratify his passions, the potato bug will be spreading desolation in his fields. Both are robbers. One robs the man in the guise of a friend, whispers in his ears something about comfort, and then robs him of his money; and the other comes to him as an open robber of his fields and puts on no disguise. I should rather meet the known enemy that pleads only malice than a wolf in sheep's clothing that whispers "comfort, comfort" while she is robbing you of houses and lands by this same comfort.

I shall close this lecture by a parable not found in scripture and entitled "A Lately Discovered Parable." Then shall the kingdom of Satan be likened to a grain of tobacco seed which though being exceedingly small, being cast into the ground grew and became a great plant and spread its leaves lank and broad so that huge and vile worms found a habitation thereon. And it came to pass in the course of time that the sons of men looked upon it and thought it beautiful to look upon and much to be desired, to make lads look big and manly. So they put forth their hands and did chew thereof and some it made sick and others to vomit it most filthily. And it further came to pass that those who chewed it became weak and unmanly and said "We are enslaved and cannot cease from chewing it." And the mouth of all that were enslaved became foul and they were seized with violent spittings and they did even in ladies' parlors and the house of the Lord of Hosts. And the saints of the Most High were greatly plagued thereby.

And in the course of time it came to pass that others snuffed it. And they were taken suddenly with fits and they did sneeze so that their eyes were filled with tears. And yet others did cunningly make leaves thereof into rolls and did set fire to one end thereof and did look very grave and cat-like. And the smoke thereof ascended up forever and ever. And the cultivation thereof became a great and mighty business in the earth. Merchantmen. waxed rich by the commerce thereof. And it came to pass that the saints of the most high defiled themselves with it, even the poor who could not buy shoes nor bread nor books for their little ones spent their money for it. And the Lord was greatly displeased therewith and said, "Wherefore this waste and why do these little ones lack bread and shoes and books? Turn new your fields into corn and wheat and put this evil thing from you." But they all with one accord exclaimed, "We cannot cease from chewing, snuffing, and puffing. We are slaves and cannot cease."

First page of the original manuscript of the lecture on "Tobacco"
by William Walton Freed, in his handwriting.

The subject of this lecture is entitled Tobacco

I beg leave to inform you that my foundation stone consists of that old saying

Tobacco is an american product

Those who were first discovered inhaled the smoke through a hollow cane

This plant whose use is of heathen orgin has been classed in the genus of Poisonous plants

This is a short history of this wonderful plant

it has been my fortune to capture one of these comforters

Tobacco chewers are the most liberal

I am afraid however I am soaring away from

Now what are the properties of tobacco and I would answer

almost every boy or girl that ever smoked

I must say I do not know how Tobacco effects the fairer sex

Not only is Tobacco noxious and deadly in its effects but it is Expensive

america has been a fruitful field not only for luxeries but for rices

The Cape of Africa is in the same Curse of Despotism that lived

Not only has america produced Liberty and Tobacco

I shall close this lecture by a parable not found in scripture

Speaking notes for his talk on Tobacco.

EDUCATION

CORPORAL PUNISHMENT

All teachers are expected to govern their schools. And as we find in all schools bad children, we must find means to control and keep them to their studies. Most children can be controlled by private reproof; others require harsher means.

Children under twelve years can and should be governed by the teacher. And if they can not be controlled by mild or severe reproof then the rod should be used. And it never needs to be used very severe[ly] on children of this age, and the majority of scholars over this age know what they are going to school for. And when reproof fails to secure order amongst them, then I think the best way to bring them to submission is to suspend them and have them to acknowledge their wrongs before the Board of Directors before they are permitted to come back to the school. This will do more good than if you use the rod every day.

This rule, when established by the Board of Directors, has the effect of improving the order of the school and making it much easier for the teacher to govern his pupils.

One of the worst boys I ever saw was conquered in this way, and when this rule is carried out, a teacher will have very few cases that he will be compelled to enforce the rule for. When scholars know that it will be enforced, there will be very few who will give the teacher the chance to carry it into execution, and the worst scholar would rather take many thrashings than to have the shame of being suspended from the school.

If suspension from school will not bring a scholar to submission, the rod will also fail. And when a scholar is so far gone as to disregard the shame of being suspended, then they are unfit to be in the school and should be expelled.

There are people in every town that will object to this rule. They would rather leave the teacher use the rod, and they are always anxiously looking for the chance to have the teacher arrested for cruelty to their children. We find this rule in all our institutions of learning and I see no reason should not be found in our common schools.

I do not believe in corporal punishment as a general rule but sometimes we come across pupils that it is necessary to use the rod. But [for] large scholars I believe in suspension and expulsion.

16 EVENTIDE. 10 10. 10 10.   W. H. MONK, 1861.

A - men.

Alternative tune, CONGLETON, Nos. 144 and 309.

Rev. H. F. Lyte, 1847.

ABIDE with me; fast falls the eventide;
The darkness deepens; LORD, with me abide;
When other helpers fail, and comforts flee,
Help of the helpless, O abide with me.

2 Swift to its close ebbs out life's little day;
Earth's joys grow dim, its glories pass away;
Change and decay in all around I see;
O thou, who changest not, abide with me.

3 I need thy presence every passing hour;
What but thy grace can foil the tempter's power?
Who like thyself my guide and stay can be?
Through cloud and sunshine, LORD, abide with me.

4 I fear no foe with thee at hand to bless;
Ills have no weight, and tears no bitterness;
Where is death's sting? Where, grave, thy victory?
I triumph still, if thou abide with me.

5 Hold thou thy Cross before my closing eyes;
Shine through the gloom, and point me to the skies;
Heaven's morning breaks, and earth's vain shadows flee;
In life, in death, O LORD, abide with me.

EDUCATION

WISDOM

> James 1: 5. If any of you lack wisdom, let him ask of God, that giveth to all men liberally, and upbraideth not; and it shall be given him.

This, my hearers, is the advice of James the servant of God to the churches all over the world — a general advice, suited to every case. If any man in Asia or Jerusalem, in Egypt or in Spain, in prison or in palace — no matter where he is — if he lacks wisdom, let him ask not of some wise man, not in some book of learned lore, but let him ask of God who giveth liberally and upbraideth not. Wisdom is recommended here, and everywhere, throughout this inspired word, as a priceless jewel to be obtained at any cost or any sacrifice. Solomon the son of David, when told to ask what he would, was not long in deciding. His decision, my hearers, was somewhat different from some young men whom you and I have heard wishing, when standing as it were on the very threshold of life, when the world was before them, when fortune and fame or disgrace or shame loomed up far away in this grand struggle of life. They did not wish for wisdom and religion to stem the torrent of sin around, but their cry was for some man's land or house. "If only I had that man's property, I would be happy!" is their song. They only look at the outward man. They never wish for wisdom. But the outward garnish, the outward gloss, seems to be their whole struggle. They are satisfied with the mere daub of the picture instead of the reality.

There are thousands of fathers and mothers in this land that have toiled and struggled till they have amassed a competency, that are leaving their children run wild, as it were. If I should ask that man or woman what is the secret of your success, he would tell me it was by the hard knocks and cuffs of the world in his boyhood days that infused a manly reliance into his nature and that never yielded to the word surrender.

Starting away from his home in Boston, Benjamin Franklin carried nothing comparatively but the clothes on his back. A good old Quaker lady, beholding his noble mien, gave him some good advice about his intercourse [interactions] with bad men and women. And he arrives at last in the city of Brotherly Love almost penniless. He stands on one of the streets eating his humble crust of bread among strangers, with his fortune to make and a manly reliance on himself. As he stands there, my hearers, he has a fortune that any young man or woman might have felt proud of. You cannot see it with the outward eye. Tis not in his tall form and rugged aspect. Tis not in his humble garb. Tis not in the outward man. You must look deeper. You must look within the veil of the temple, within a clear brain that runs like the mountain brook, untarnished by a single bad element, and the invincible determination to do right. This with strong arms and a rugged constitution was all he possessed. And yet in the race for fortune and fame, he outstripped all his competitors and stands today at the head of American statesmen.

Wisdom, my hearers, is more to be desired than gold or precious jewels. And it would be well for fathers and mothers, while they are sending their children to school to learn writing and reading, to learn grammar and arithmetic, to send them to the fountain where wisdom bubbles up and let them drink of its waters, to find strength and comfort for coming conflicts. Said a father once in my hearing, as he thought over his wayward boy who seemed to have but one song "Come easy and go easy" — said he, "I wish I could put my boy out once on the same footing that I stood on. I wish he could be placed in such a position that I could watch and see that no harm befell him and there let him learn as I had to learn. I wish," said he, "that I could see him stripped of the last cent, hundreds of miles from home and thrown on his own resources. And then he would value some of the advice I now give him. But I am afraid he will never make a man here. The words that I speak fall on deadened ears and he takes his own course. In spite of all that, I can say if trouble comes upon him 'Here is home' and he comes home." But the time will come, my hearers, that father and mother will pass away and he must contend then for his own life, as it were.

What fathers and mothers want to [teach] their children today are the stern realities of life instead of varnishing them over with a mere gloss and sending them forth like some skeleton ship to battle with the storms of life. Germany has some wise laws in this regard. The law there is seven years for play, seven for study, and seven for work. And by the time they acquire all these accomplishments they are ready to stand up like men and fight their own battles with a manly self-reliance instead of sitting down like children and yielding up the conflict when trouble assails them. Wisdom, my hearers, is a costly jewel and no wonder that Solomon wisely conjectured that if he had wisdom he had the whole. Well has the poet exclaimed, "Wisdom Divine!" Who tells the price of wisdom?

> Wisdom to silver we prefer
> And gold is dross compared to her.[95]

The child in the cradle is void of all knowledge. He is ignorant of everything and he must learn all. How well do some of us remember our schoolboy days? With what reluctance we took up our books and dragged off to school! Here is spelling. How long will it take me to master that? A whole dictionary of words to learn! Here is arithmetic a whole shelf full apparently [of] mental, common and higher arithmetic. Algebra, geometry, trigonometry are all before me. Here is writing. What wonderful dimensions for improvement when I compare my poor scrawl to that man's penmanship! And my reading. I can hardly spell out the words, and here is a man that can read till you would imagine the person was unconscious. He had a book in his hand. Here is all this vast ocean of knowledge before me and I am just on the edge, just commencing. This, my hearers, is enough to appall any boy or girl as they calmly contemplate it. Yet we must all commence at the beginning. We must all start at the letter A and study hard and long before we sail over the mere outside of this wondrous ocean.

And thus it is with wisdom. It has been said that experience is a dear teacher, and all who have traveled over the road will confirm that statement. Ask the aged man whose locks are whitening for the grave, and he will tell you that that statement is true. Ask the wise philosopher who has spent his life in the study of nature around and he will tell you that statement is true. Ask the learned man that has mastered the hardest study and he will tell you the same old story, that experience, or in other words wisdom—for experience is wisdom—wisdom is a dear teacher.

Where, then, might I ask, do we learn wisdom? And I would answer that home is the first school where the child receives instruction in this respect, for we were all once children, my hearers. The love of parent, no matter how debased he may be, prompts him to give good advice to his or her child. Home, my hearers, is where the child first learns. And how important is this, then, for that father whose boy is looking up to him for instruction, for wisdom and knowledge! How important, I remark again! It is for him to shed forth a pure and true light. No flickering and flaring blaze will do. It must be the same today, tomorrow, and forever. How important it is for you that are parents to draw your instruction from a fountain whose every element is pure, to

95   Lines from "Happy the man that finds the grace" by Charles Wesley, See page 282. Dross is the residue (waste product) left after smelting metal.

shed forth to your child not only by word but by deed the proper course in life. That old saying so oft repeated—"Do as I say and not as I do"—will not prove sufficient around our homes and firesides. The child is not governed so much by the words as by the deeds of his parents. And home, above all things else, should be a pure fountain.

The love of the parent should prompt him to make every sacrifice for his boy or girl if he desires to leave behind him a son or daughter upon whose brow true nobility is stamped. If he desires to leave behind him a worthy successor, let him set him a good example. Let him show the nobility of his nature. Let him prove himself worthy of a worthy son. That is a poor cry of some men whose boys have grown up to be a curse instead of a blessing. Tis a poor cry that they utter about the disgrace their son or daughter has brought upon them, when they perhaps have been a disgrace to themselves. The son has been cast from the mold that stamps the father. And if a besotted look and a terrible oath issue from his lips, think you the son will not be a fit representative of such a sire? Love, my hearers, and every man and woman loves to see a home of love where the child is learning from a fountain unsullied and pure, where the father and mother are stamping on every alignment of their little ones' true nobility and wisdom. And here, my hearers, is the first step in this race for wisdom.

I remark that the second place where we may receive this priceless jewel is the world—actual contact with men and women. Children may go to school forever, but they will never graduate in the true sense of the term until they put their knowledge into actual practice. Theory is all very fine—how to do this or that—but what we want is actual experience. I might stand and look at a painter tracing a beautiful painting: "How easily it is done, I might say." It is done easily with him. His hand moves as easily and gracefully as the waving tree, But when I attempt to do the same thing I find it entirely different. I find that I am out of my element. I have the theory, however. I know how it is done. But that will not suffice. I must seize the brush and daub and paint as best I can for long months and years, perhaps, before I am able to produce a like result.

And thus it is with the child. The father may instruct and tell him how he must do. He may dread and shudder to think of the contaminating world that is all around and that he would love to save his boy from. He may show him how to live at home. But the son may go farther than home. The theory of good actions around the hearth will not suffice. But like the eagle that shows her young how to fly in the blue of ether, so he must at last launch out on the troubled waters of life. And by the hard knocks and kicks and cuffs of unsympathetic men and women who would strip him of the last cent and leave him penniless in the street, he must learn wisdom. Wisdom has no bounds. She is not marked out by the mockery of lines, but it is picked up in the home circle and on the ocean wave, among honest men and among thieves. Among all classes you can find this priceless jewel.

Parents, I imagine, often make a mistake here in their over-cautiousness of their child coming in actual contact with the world. They kill him by not [putting him] in noble honorable struggle with the world around. Like the fond mother they kill him by kindness — smother him to death, in other words by the pernicious idea that they will make a noble man of him without ever giving him a chance to see what true nobility is. If home is pure, if the fountain is unsullied, the son will grow stronger by co-mingling with the world around, with all classes of men and all conditions. And it is only the boy or girl that has this experience that will prove worthy of a worthy sire. Your son or daughter, my hearers, must meet temptation, must meet vice in every form. And it is not for you to learn [teach] them to shun temptation and sin, but to overcome through Christ our living head.

One of the first lessons the mother of the Sandwich Islander gives her babe is a bath in the briny waters of the deep, and the result is that the Sandwich Islanders are the most expert swimmers in the world. And thus it will be with you, my hearers, if you not only show your boy how but make him resist temptation. Tis thus he will learn wisdom by actual contact with the world around.

Let me remark before I leave this point of the knowledge we learn from the world, of the marvelous ignorance of some men. Wisdom or experience is a dear teacher. No matter in what light you turn it, it costs some men a thousand dollars, some two thousand, and some it ruins entirely. They in other words never learn. The man who is hunting for knowledge can cull out the precious jewel amid misfortune dire.[96] He always pours out the dregs and finds the reason why beneath all his misfortunes. But other men rush on, regardless of every reason. Theirs seems to be not to reason why, not to make reply, but to do and die.

Remember, my hearers, that wisdom is holding out the precious fruit in the guise of friendship and in the guise [of] hatred, in the guise of brotherly love and in the guise of the deadly cup. She is crying from the sacred desk and from the gilded bar. She is crying from the wise

---

96   Dire misfortune.

man who is giving good advice and from the man whose mouth is filled with oaths and curses. She is crying from the honest man who would [take] any advantage, and from the man who would strip you of the last copper. And her language is: learn to do good, and scorn to do wrong.

These, my hearers, might be said to be the two books of the world: worldly wisdom (in other words, home) where our fathers teach us; and the world where all classes and conditions of men are our teachers. These two books do not finish the series. There is a higher Book. Yet after learning all that, it is possible to learn here still. You find on close examination that you lack. There is an unutterable void that cannot be filled. And the eager hands and hearts of men are reaching out farther and farther. We are not satisfied. Still there is a lack of wisdom to fight successfully the battles of life. Where shall we find this higher wisdom? And I would answer, In the secret chamber, lifting up your heart like Daniel of old to the great giver of wisdom who giveth liberally and upbraideth not! If any man, after having learned all the wisdom of this world, lacks yet; if he is still in ignorance; let him ask of God who giveth liberally.

This, my hearers, is essential, as God teaches us the wisdom that cometh from above. The young man just starting out in the world needs something more than worldly wisdom. For you must remember that that has self trust. All self, and the world sometimes \carries away our best resolutions. He is fighting alone. If I were going into a lonely forest where robbers and thieves were ready to murder and kill me for my property, I believe I should feel stronger had I a true and tried friend by my side. And you, my unconverted brother, are going out into the world where thieves and robbers of your character abound on every hand, where men are willing to sell your soul — not like Judas for twenty pieces of silver, but some of them for 20 cents in silver! You are standing alone in this great forest of iniquity. You have, as you supposed, acquired wisdom, but it is the wisdom of the world. It will not do for your boys and girls. It will not carry you through the troubled waters of life. Why not, then, my hearers, partake of a fountain whose element is pure? Why not take a friend along the troubled waves of life that will give you that true wisdom? That shall not be taken away from you.

True wisdom, my hearers, consists in adopting a right course, in adopting a course that has been tried and proved. And the wisdom of heaven, the wisdom that God giveth, has been tried and proved. Worldly wisdom costs us something. No matter where we look for it, college and schools cost not only the humble student dollars and cents, but hard and persistent study. The wisdom of this world costs us something. It costs some men their fortunes. But here is a wisdom that shall cost you nothing, and promises inestimable blessings—the wisdom of heaven which, if any man will ask for, God will give liberally and upbraideth not. Besides all this, my hearers, wisdom will enable you to apply the other instruction of the world. No matter how noble and good and pure father and mother have been, this will lift you higher. No matter how hard unfeeling men have been, this wisdom will enable you to overcome, and it [will] robe you in the true dignity of men and women. We talk sometimes about the noble man whose every action seems to be a lesson for his fellow men, but the noblest and best man is that man that has this inestimable wisdom that God giveth liberally to every man and woman. I love, my hearers, to see such wisdom as that. The world loves it. No matter how bad the man may be, he loves to see the good man who has this heavenly wisdom. And this is the leaven that leavens the whole.

Another thought in relation to wisdom is that it is power. Knowledge or wisdom is power, and it is an advantage to have wisdom. For this reason ignorance or brute force never accomplished much in this life. I do not remember that her achievements have been emblazoned in living letters that the whole cannot fail but discern. I cannot find in history that ignorance made any people happy, but on the contrary miserable. I remember one thing in reference to ignorance, and I imagine that you will remember that a certain wise man wrote: Where Ignorance is bliss, tis folly to be wise. Her achievements, my hearers, will be summed up in blunders, disgrace, shame, and misery. Napoleon tells about a certain emperor that he never learned anything and never forgot anything. But we may alter the phrase somewhat in regard to Ignorance—that she never learns anything and forgets everything. We will to a man assert that knowledge is the jewel, while ignorance is the dross.

Having therefore, my hearers, obtained wisdom, how, might I ask, do men use it? Some men—a good many men in our day—work hard to obtain the scanty pittance they get and then throw it away. For when they come home they are minus their money, and they are minus of an equivalent. You would imagine they worked for nothing all their lives for the love they bore to their fellow men, for they never seem to be any richer. On the contrary some of them, it seems, the longer they work the poorer they get. So with these men in reference to knowledge: Having obtained this priceless jewel, as far as colleges and schools can give them this wisdom, [they] expect the world will now fall down and worship them like the king that sits on his throne. So these wise men sit enthroned in their little kingdom and worship themselves [rather] than God, like the Sadducees. See that they are not as other men. Knowledge is power only as we develop it, like the steam engine.

Another class, having obtained this wisdom through the hard knocks of the world, resolve to adopt the Jewish standard of belief: an eye for an eye and a tooth for a tooth. They use their wisdom not to make men happy, but miserable. A poor man in one of our adjoining countries had by untiring effort acquired a little store of wealth—a little over three hundred dollars—and resolved to come west. He went to a land agent and told him his wishes and he [the agent] showed him the piece of land that would, so he said, just suit him. But as the old prophet said in a certain place in this book, he lied. Our poor neighbor believed him and paid for his claim, packing up his goods. He started west to find not a land flowing with milk and honey but a miserable sand hill that would not produce prairie grass hardly. This man, my hearers, was deliberately robbed of his hard-earned labor. Tis true, the thief did not come like some strong man with burglarous tools and rob him by main force, but he came like the wolf in sheep's clothing. He came like Judas with a holy kiss. While he was ready and eager to strip him of the last cent, this man, my hearers, robbed him by his superior knowledge and cast a deaf ear to the prayer of his wife and family. The world or worldly men term this sharpness—a shrewd man, in other words—and this is one of the greatest curses that is cursing this land today. This is worldly wisdom. Well has it been named. It is of the earth, earthy. Such wisdom as that, my hearers, is despicable. Such wisdom does not become the noble man but only the thief. Robbing a man under the guise of a friend is the basest of robberies.

There is a certain island in the Pacific where the natives are great thieves, and of course the child is an apt scholar. The little one is taught to believe that it is smart to steal from his neighbor and escape detection. But if he should be so unfortunate as to be caught, an unmerciful thrashing is in store for him. And thus it is in this land today. The young man is taught to believe by his older and more experienced friend that it is a smart thing to drive a sharp bargain—in other words to get the best of his neighbor. But if he is so unfortunate as to be cheated himself, his friends will only laugh at him and encourage him to try again. Resolve, my hearers, whatever comes, to do right, to love your neighbor as yourself. This is true and heavenly wisdom. Had men a nobler manhood than base and sordid self, there would be less suffering, less woe and sorrow. We are walking, it does seem to me sometimes, over a volcano. Men have taken the advantage in every possible way so long till the honest man cannot decide to trust any man. Law and jail are the natural outcrop of this worldly wisdom that has no tear of sympathy for others' woes.

But there is a nobler wisdom than worldly wisdom, and that, my hearers, is heavenly wisdom. Tis that wisdom, my brethren, that turns the wisdom of the world into a proper channel. Worldly wisdom and heavenly wisdom must be combined in order to make the perfect man. We love to see the wise man in this life. Men instinctively homage them and pay reverence to their shrine. But if he is not only wise but good, doubly precious he seems to the world. His every action seems to be not to take advantage of his neighbor, but to treat every man as a brother. And as he stands before the people to tell them the proper course to pursue, they are ready to receive his gospel because it comes from a pure fountain. A certain philosopher says that the orator should not only be eloquent but good, and the man who attempts to tell others their duty should be a perfect pattern. And if, my hearers, heavenly wisdom combines with earthly wisdom, a light will shine around his every action. Let me, my brethren, urge upon you the importance of not only acquiring earthly knowledge but heavenly knowledge, a knowledge that will lift you above the base and sordid passions of this life and implant within you a heavenly halo of life.

And finally, my hearers, heavenly wisdom will enable us to solve the dark problem of God. Let me ask, did you ever study any of these mysterious dispensations? How mysterious and utterly past finding out they are to finite men! We can look back over the history of the world and view the first bud as it was of some tremendous design. We can see it unfolding, hour by hour and day by day, until it looks all plain enough to us. I can understand why a wise God permitted Joseph in his boyhood day to be taken away from his old father whose hairs were whitening for the grave, and [be] sold to Egyptian traders. It is all plain enough now. But the old father could not understand it. His brethren could not see why it was they could not sit down and trace along the map of history till they came to the place where grim and ghastly famine stalked like some weird spirit up and down that land. They could not see the earth parched and dry for seven long years. They could [not] view in imagination the barns of old Egypt filled with food, with faithful Joseph at their head. It was all mysterious to them. But God saw it. And long years before Joseph is carried away to engraft [ingratiate] himself in the affections of the Egyptian king, here is the person that will carry the whole civilized world over this deadly famine in safety—a mere boy, the hope of an aged father. He is destined to be the hope of the world.

And thus it is today, my brethren, with you and me. Mysterious providences are occurring all around. And if we possess this heavenly wisdom, we shall not be at loss to find out the mysterious dispensations of providence in our own history. How remarkable they have been! With what awe we read of the time our revolutionary fathers retreated before the victorious troops of England, almost ready to despair of escape. They cross a running stream that swells on the approach of the British troops to a roaring torrent. Not only once but twice [were] our revolutionary fathers saved in this way. Will you not admit, my unconverted brother, that an all-wise God was watching over our struggling sires in those dark days? View him raising up France when she was almost overcome, and ask yourself if an almighty wisdom was not displayed?

That wisdom is still watching over the earth. It has rescued the suffering followers of Turkish power from falling yoke. It has carried this nation through the throes of civil war. And it is for you and me. If any of you lack wisdom, let him ask of God. Do you not, my unconverted brother, feel that you need this divine wisdom? A wisdom that will clothe your knowledge of books in a heavenly garb? A wisdom that will clothe your knowledge of men with a heavenly love? A wisdom that will make you worthy of such a father as Our Father? Let us, my hearers, resolve to have the wisdom that cometh from above, and may God add his blessing. Amen.

Happy the man that finds the grace,
    The blessing of God's chosen race,
The wisdom coming from above,
The faith that sweetly works by love.

2   Happy, beyond description, he
Who knows, "the Saviour died for me!"
The gift unspeakable obtains,
And heavenly understanding gains.

3   Wisdom divine! who tells the price
Of wisdom's costly merchandise?
Wisdom to silver we prefer.
And gold is dross compared to her.

4.   Her hands are filled with length of days,
True riches and immortal praise --
Riches of Christ on all bestowed,
And honor that descends from God.

5   To purest joys she all invites,
Chaste, holy, spiritual delights;
Her ways are ways of pleasantness,
And all her flowery paths are peace.

6   Happy the man who wisdom gains;
Thrice happy who his guest retains;
He owns, and shall for ever own,
Wisdom, and Christ, and heaven, are one.

"Happy the man that finds the grace," by Charles Wesley, one of his *Redemption Hymns*, 1747. It is based on Proverbs 3:13-18: "Happy is the man that findeth wisdom, and the man that giveth understanding..." Wilbur Fisk Tillett, *Our Hymns and their Authors, an Annotated Edition of the Hymn Book of the Methodist Episcopal Church South*, 1892, hymn # 396.

AMERICA

TRAVELS IN THE SOUTH

No man that ever saw his country's Capitol can forget it. It stands at the head of Washington's grandest street. It looms high up above all the other buildings. Built of the purest marble, it defies competition and seems to say to the admiring thousands: Rejoice and be glad, for the Lord reigneth. There are a great many very, very fine buildings in Washington, but none that can compare to the Capitol with the first dawn of light.

I started for the sacred soil of the Southern Confederacy. Crossing the long bridge, we soon lost sight of Washington and found ourselves safely landed in Alexandria. I thought of Col. Ellsworth[97] here, and made up my mind I would see the Marshall house. Asking an old darling where it was, I was informed it was burnt. But still curiosity urged me on. I stood upon its ashes. I viewed the pavement that caught his young life's blood, and saw in imagination the lifeless remains of young Ellsworth again.

Alexandria is about as large as Sunbury, seemingly finished like the Alexandria of Egypt, about as dead. There is a beautiful cemetery here, and that is all I saw that bore any resemblance to beauty in this place. Leaving here, I traveled in about 5 miles where who should I meet but a good old colored man and his wife with their little bundle. I inquired which way they were bound, and says the old darkey, "We are going norf. Massay has got so hard since election that he done drove all the collered folks off the place." I sat and talked with him awhile, had a few of my bright visions of the South dispelled, and left him with a sadder and wiser heart.

The country between Alexandria and Fredericksburg is rolling and poor. Poor, in the language of John B. Gough,[98] is a feeble word. If ever the curse of God rested on a country, it rests on that. Nature is exhausted and lifts up her voice in dumb appeal for rest. You have heard that the [people] of the South never put back what they took from their

97   Elmer Ephraim Ellsworth was a law clerk and United States Army soldier and a friend of President Lincoln. He was the first casualty and the first Union officer to die in the American Civil War. He was killed while removing a Confederate flag from the roof of the Marshall House inn in Alexandria, Virginia. *Wikipedia*.
98   John Bartholomew Gough (1817-1886) was a temperance speaker.

land, but I can say of a truth tonight they have left it desolated.

Picked it and picked it till it is as bare the rocks. On Peter's Mountain the poor whites farm the land for two thirds [of the yield], supplying their own teams, and then can scarcely manage to keep soul and body together.

The land through this part of Virginia — and in fact all the way to Norfolk — most, with varying spots, is a yellow sandy soil having about enough stamina in it to raise brush wood. There is no limestone through this part of the country, and the people raise their own fertilizers through the ordinary methods. Land, as you may suppose, is cheap. You can get a farm down in Virginia of about three hundred acres for a couple thousand dolllars, and brush wood and all. A great part of the land down in Virginia has been standing since the war without cultivation and will stand there forever I suppose if some more industrious race does not get a hold of it. The people of Virginia are wondering when the northern capitalist will buy him out, and it is nothing but land agencies from one end to the other. If there is a man in this house tonight that is thinking of trying his fortune down south, I would say to you, there is no better place — that is if you have money enough to buy a place. Don't go there if you haven't. You might as well be in the jungles of India. But if you have, there is no better place.

Plantation slaves loading rice to a barge on the Savannah River on the Georgia South Carolina border 1800s. North Wind Picture Archives/Alamy stock photo.

Labor is cheap. No white man can compete with the negro on his own ground. You can hire a negro for 8 dollars a month and board. This does not include a bed nor wheat bread. None of these extras are allowed. One bushel of corn meal, 20 lb. of bacon, and 2 quarts of black molasses sets out a colored gentleman for one month. His sleeping arrangements are simple: an old log cabin—just enough to turn around in and stretch out—is all he wants. Building himself a huge fire and fixing his feet near enough to toast, as he calls it, he stretches out on the soft side of the floor and dreams of home and friends. Thus he lives, day after day, week after week, corn bread and flitch,[99] corn bread and flitch, until I can imagine I see a huge side and a bushel of meal stare at him in ghastly horror and appeal for mercy. Is there a poor man in this audience would live in that way? I venture to say no. Sooner let my right arm be paralyzed than that ever I should be willing to grovel as the brute! The Southern people have raised the darkey, and think that he only is fit for work. They seem to consider it a disgrace to work. And in all my travels through the south, from Virginia to Texas, I never found a southern born man but what was ready to do anything by work. And they never seem to imagine that a white man ought to work. If he has work to do, he will give it to a black man; and if perchance he does give a poor white man a job, he has to bunk out with his negro man and fare as he does. He is not good enough to be with the F. F. V.'s.[100] Oh, no, that would disgrace the family forever! I was talking to a Southern planter one day near Richmond, and he told me the Southern people did not want white men. "For," says he, "they are too much trouble. We can't be bothered with them. We," says he, "want men that can rough it like our darkeys. They are used to it, and don't know the difference."

And according to their logic they didn't mean to let them know any difference. Not only does the Southern aristocrat look with contempt on the poor white man, but among the negro he encounters the greatest enmity. [Having] raised [him] to do everything in the labor line, he [the aristocrat] shuns with disgust the poor man who has to work for his living and has put them all in one class and labeled them poor white trash. Sad indeed is the condition of the poor white man in the South. He is forced to labor for the same pay. He is treated as was the Southern slave of yore, cringing and crouching in the depth of ignorance. He submits to everything. And as I viewed him in his wretchedness, I fain would have exclaimed in the language of Byron "Arise thou cringing

99   The side of a hog or other animal, salted and cured.
100   First Families of Virginia.

crouching slave or be forever fallen!"[101]

Afroamerican slaves picking cotton in the South.
North Wind Picture Archives/Alamy Stock Photo.

This is but a faint picture of Virginia. I found as I traveled South and entered North Carolina the reign of the colored race linked with ignorance complete. Here his sable majesty swarms in every avenue of trade. I did not see a white brakeman in North or South Carolina. Almost every store has their negro porter to carry home the wares purchased. And so I might go on enumerating the different things he does, but time would fail [to] tell of all his employments. North Carolina is where you commence to see the cotton plantations in all their glory, stretching out either side of the railroad and looming up far in the distance. I saw a cotton plantation for the first time with wonder, and astonishment, and as I looked at it I thought of that familiar hymn:

"Fields are white and harvest waving.
Who will go and work today?"[102]

The cotton stalk of North Carolina grows about two feet and a half high, and looks very much like a flower bush. The cotton itself is enclosed in a round pod, very much resembling a walnut before it is hulled. The pod is divided in four equal parts and, as it ripens, bursts open, and the sun soon finishes the work. Cotton commences to ripen

101   From *Fallen Greece* by Lord Byron (1788-1824)
102   From "Hark the voice of Jesus calling" by Joseph Barnby, 1869.

about the first of November, and from that time till New Year's a constant stream of cotton comes pouring in to all the seaboard towns for shipment.

As you travel south, the cotton stalk rises high and higher. The cotton stalk of South Carolina is about four foot high, in Georgia five feet, and in Louisiana and Texas it waves above your head. It is a beautiful sight to look on a cotton plantation when it has ripened. Each pod as it reveals its snow white harvest reminds you of comfort and contentment. As you stand perhaps on some little hill and look out on some large plantation, every pod appears like some little star bending to the breeze. All over that vast field you will see these little white specks like so many snow flakes glittering in the sun light of heaven. And ever and anon as the breeze sweeps over, it bends and rises in majestic grandeur to its touch.

The darkeys, as you may suppose, do the picking. From the little black urchin hardly able to walk, to the old man of the household, all turn out to gather in King Cotton. Invariably you will see a whole family together in the cotton field, for Sambo[103] generally has a large family and a small revenue. And as a natural consequence, he presses all hands into the service to increase his financial income. Every picker is supplied with a bag which he ties on his back with the mouth opening under his arm. 100 lb. of cotton is considered a good day's work, for which he gets 60 cents. This does not include board. A not very large salary, you will say. The farther South you go, the less they give. In South Carolina and Georgia, 50 cents a hundred is the standard pay for cotton picking, rising however in Texas to 75 cents, which is the highest pay I saw given for cotton picking.

---

103   The word "sambo" came into the English language from the Latin American Spanish word zambo, the Spanish word in Latin America for a person of mixed African and Native American descent. This in turn may have come from one of three African language sources. Webster's Third International Dictionary holds that it may have come from the Kongo word nzambu ("monkey") — the z of (Latin American) Spanish being pronounced here like the English s. The Royal Spanish Academy gives the origin from a Latin word, possibly the adjective valgus or another modern Spanish term (patizambo), both of which translate to "bow-legged". The equivalent term in Portuguese-speaking areas, such as Brazil, is cafuzo. Examples of "Sambo" as a common name can be found as far back as the 19th century. In Thackeray's novel *Vanity Fair* (serialised from 1847), the black-skinned Indian servant of the Sedley family from Chapter One, is called Sambo. Similarly, in Harriet Beecher Stowe's novel, *Uncle Tom's Cabin* (1852), one of Simon Legree's overseers is named Sambo. Instances of it being used as a stereotypical name for African Americans can be found as early as the Civil War. It is now considered to be a derogatory term for a person with Indian heritage and/or mixed African American heritage. *Wikipedia*.

Gordonsville in North Carolina is a great cotton center for all the surrounding country. Here you will [see] the poor white trash and his darkey neighbor come rolling in on every imaginable vehicle from the surrounding plantation and selling their cotton for what they can get. The whites generally have their cotton in bales ready for shipment. Not so, however, with Sambo. He hauls it in town on some tumble down cart that looks like as if it might have been washed up there by the flood. And for fear perhaps that he might lose time in baling it, he seizes his good wife's wash tubs, buckets, and all — if there are any bags on the place he presses them in also — and filling all with cotton, he tumbles them in one promiscuous [huge] mass. He starts for town. It is a laughable sight to see him coming in town. He fills the air with his "Hotha! Woege!" and when a spare moment occurs, rejoices his heart in such familiar hymns as:

> "Oh you can see the mote in the other people's eyes
> But you can't see the beam in your own
> You'd better go home and sweep out you own house
> And let God's children alone."

Saturday during the cotton season is payday. This is indeed "a high day in Israel" [a holiday]. Poor white trash, Southern aristocrats, and darkeys all don their Sunday go-to-meeting clothes and start for town. Here they guzzle whiskey and talk politics all the day long. The darkeys cluster around some wise man of their color and listen with bated breath as he enlarges on the political situation, while the whites congregate around their political oracles to hear the glad tidings of their deliverance from negro reign.

And just here let me for a moment leave the beaten track and talk of the political situation in the South. I went down there, rooted and grounded in Republican principles. I believed they were the party of the right and honor. But standing before you tonight, I declare that I don't blame the Southern people for wanting to rid themselves of negro political supremacy. Republican Pennsylvania is not Republican South Carolina. The negro in Philadelphia with a population of 75 or 100 thousand have no political rights farther than voting. They hold [no] offices of trust and profit except forsooth the high and lofty position of locking up prisoners in their cells, commonly called turnkeys. Pittsburgh is the same way. Williamsport, I understand, has a colored policeman. Generous Williamsport! Let all the people exclaim! No [negro] Senator or Representatives grace the halls of Congress from the Republican north. No, no! Careful that the colored man votes and they get the offices, they calmly view the situation in the South with indifference.

What, my hearers is the condition of the South today politically? The darkeys are in the majority and having been raised in slavery they naturally look upon the white man as their oppressor. They associate only with each other. And not being able to read, they receive as Gospel truths all that is said against [the white men]. Naturally suspicious, they trust [the speaker], not believing his every motion is some new scheme to rivet slavery on them. They fawn and cling to him in the store, and on the street, and meet at night in their cabins and swear eternal enmity to the white man.

The negro, I found occupying every political position in the calendar. But it is as a policeman that you see him in all his glory in Charlestown. I saw a negro policeman beating without mercy a drunken white man who was not able to walk as fast as he was walking. Swaggering along the street, insolent and defiant, they bid defiance to the white man and gloat in triumph over him. In Florence, South Carolina, they have a full darkey force of policemen, not one white man being on the force. In Charlestown, about one half the letter carriers are negroes. And so through all the avenues of life, both in the social and political world, occupying a prominent place.

And, my hearers, not only is there a vast difference between Republicanism in the North and Republicanism in the South, but there is a vast difference in the negro of the North and that of the South. The negro of the North is educated to a certain extent and though he is proverbially saucy, we can to a certain degree get along with him. How is he in the south? Not only is he steeped in the depth of ignorance, but he is steeped in the depths of insolence. You are ready, my hearers, to bear with that man who is willing to listen to reason. But you are not ready to bear with ignorance and insolence. And that is the reason that the people of the South, goaded on at last to madness, seize their rifles to root out with fire and sword the negro population.

I will close on this subject. There is an old saying in the Methodist Discipline that says it is only those who are planted in the house of the Lord that shall flourish in the courts of our God. And so I would say to you tonight, my hearers, that it is only those who have seen the suffering South that can imagine the condition of things in that country today.

I shall in conclusion speak of the rice plantation and of a few of the cities of the South. The first rice plantation I saw was in Wilmington, North Carolina. There was a very fine mansion standing out apparently in the swamp. And It was a mystery to me why the owner should choose to me such an outlandish place to build his house. A darkey was near, and on my inquiring why that man built his house on such a muddy foundation he says that was a rice plantation. The prospect looked poor to me of raising anything but sea weed, but his sable majesty gave me a full description in a short time. Do you see, says he, that bank running all around there? On my closely looking I did see the bank, although almost covered up with weed and very low. That, said he, is the first operation that is performed in rescuing this vast field from a marsh and bringing it under cultivation. The planter, he continued, first selects some marshy land that lays in close proximity to fresh water and also tide water, and having built a bank all around it just high enough to keep out the tide, he constructs sluices at certain distance just like our grist mills, and then you have a rice plantation, just cut out but no rice on it yet. It was my good fortune to see some rice that had been left standing over from last year, and let me this evening see if I can't cover over our plantation with rice now. Our planter having finished his preliminary operation, now waits till the tide falls and then shuts down his sluices. Everything is very wet inside our rice field now, but Old Sol[104] soon dries it as dry as a chip.

In about four days it is dry enough to burn the grass. He waits until the wind blows from the land and toward the river. The he sends his darkey to set the grass on fire.

This is soon consumed. Now he sets his negroes to work. One colored man is supposed to farm five acres. Furnishing each one with a hoe, they sally forth. No plowing is required. Each man, hoe in hand, commences diligently to dig little rows about as deep as your little finger, all along his five acres the rows are about a foot apart, having laid out his field in rows. He sows his rice along about as thick as you would plant peas. Each man having finished sowing, the rice sluices are opened, and the tide left in till it stands about one foot deep all over the plantation. In about two weeks the rice is peeping out of its watery bed, the sluices are opened again, and all the water is left off. When they are shut down the field soon dries again and now commences the hoeing. This simply consists in cutting down the grass in between each row. Having cut down all the grass, the water is left in again till it stands about tree feet all over the field. It is kept at this depth now till the rice grows above it and ripens.

Rice resembles wheat when ripe. Before harvesting it is cut down with an old time sickle and stored away till thrashed. Each darkey receives one half of the product of his five ancres. The bete wages I saw

---

104   Old Sol = the sun

given to darkeys. No white man can stand it on the rice plantations as they get what is called the swamp fever, which soon carries them off. It is very unhealthy. These, my hearers, are a few of the incidents that attend rice growing. And when you eat your nice rice pudding, just think of poor Sambo way down South in Dixie, hoeing rice.

I linger yet in North Carolina. It has been appropriately called the land of tar. Here, my friends, in the dense forests are the smoke and tar begrimed sons of North Carolina, making that that floats our ships, that sends through every seaman's soul a thrill of joy, as he views the precious material for with his ships tarred in every seam[105] he can bid defiance to old ocean and ride upon its watery surface in perfect security. North Carolina is emphatically a land of forests. You have perhaps read that every pine tree pays tribute to raise tar, but there is one place that has bid defiance to man's efforts, and that place is the Great Dismal Swamp.

You picture to yourself as I say something that makes man stand back in horror and dismay. And as I passed through it, my hearers, I must confess I looked at it in silent awe and terror. And well might have exclaimed in the language of holy writ, "What is man that thou art mindful of him, O Thou great and awful ruler of the universe?" Imagine to yourself my hearers, a dense forest as far as your eye can reach almost 100 miles broad and about 50 miles through, laying so low that the water stands from a foot to a fathom deep all over it and then cover that all over with tall marshy grass about five feet high. And you have some faint conception of the Great Dismal Swamp. No man can describe that swamp, my hearers. It has been appropriately called Great, but the namer did not stop here. He calls it Dismal. And it is dismal, my friends — terribly so. As you stand in its depths you feel an unearthly silence come over you. Ever and anon a flying bird passes lazily by, or from some log of wood, turtle or snake rolls in the water with a dull splash. Here is the paradise of all animal nature. It would seem that God had made this place for them and had set the bounds for man with these words: "Thus far shalt thou come and no farther."

---

105 Tar was used to seal the joints between the wooden planks of a ship to make it water-tight.

Slavery

¶ 36. We declare that we are as much as ever convinced of the great evil of Slavery. We believe that the buying, selling, or holding of human beings, to be used as chattels, is contrary to the laws of God and nature, and inconsistent with the Golden Rule, and with that rule in our Discipline which requires all who desire to continue among us to "do no harm," and to "avoid evil of every kind." We therefore affectionately admonish all our preachers and people to keep themselves pure from this great evil, and to seek its extirpation by all lawful and Christian means.

Doctrines and Discipline of the Methodist Episcopal Church, New York, 1876.

Jesus Calls Us O'er the Tumult   486

1. Je-sus calls us   o'er the tu-mult   of our life's wild   rest-less sea;
2. Je-sus calls us   from the wor-ship   of the vain world's gold-en store,
3. In our joys and   in our sor-rows, days of toil and   hours of ease,
4. Je-sus calls us: by Your mer-cies, Sav-ior, may we   hear Your call,

day   by day His sweet voice sound-eth,   say-ing "Chris-tian, fol-low me!"
from each i - dol that would keep   us,   say-ing "Chris-tian, love me more."
still   He calls in cares and plea-sures, "Chris-tian, love Me more than these."
give   our hearts to full   o - be - dience, serve and love You best of   all.

WORDS: Cecil F. Alexander, 1852   RESTORATION
MUSIC: William Walker's *Southern Harmony*, 1835   8.7.8.7
                                        Alternate tune, GALILEE

"Jesus Calls Us O'er the Tumult," *Celebrating Grace Hymnal* #486

AMERICA

HELP IN TIME OF TROUBLE

II Kings, chapter 11.

There were men and women, my hearers, during the terrible day and night in the city of New York known as Black Friday,[106] that turned gray in one night. All their fondest hopes were swept away, all their bright dreams were banished. They retired to bed in ease and comfort and woke up to find themselves penniless and destitute. I have never known wealth, my hearers, but I imagine that one of the greatest curses this world was ever cursed with is the inordinate desire for wealth. A certain ruler of Sparta banished all wealth from the land because of its evil consequences. Wealth in itself is not wrong, but the use that it is put to in a great many instances is the death blow of thousands of our best men and women.

And just here let me pause and enumerate a few of these baleful results. The wealthy man will naturally desire to have a residence a little finer than his neighbor, and neighbor not to be undone will strain every nerve to keep on a par. What is the result? Ruin and despair, wretchedness and woe. The wealthy man must have two span of fine horses which none should deny his right to, but his neighbor will try and keep on a part. What is the result? Mortgaged property, debt and ruin. I knew a gentleman in Pennsylvania who was ruined ... he could not bear to have ... it was that when panic ... he went down in the crash and reduced his family that were in good circumstances to poverty and despair while his more fortunate neighbor continued on in property. I do not deny and no man or woman can deny that man's right to a fine house and horse and everything. This desire for dress, my hearers, has been the cause of ruin to thousands of the women of our land. Men, as a general rule, are not so ambitious in this respect as women and as a result there are fewer saddened hearts among the men in this respect than women.

Another great cause of trouble in this world of ours is the discontented dispositions of men never satisfied they are doing well. Here is peace and prosperity crowning their labors; there is more in their

---

106   September 24, 1869. The New York Stock Exchange reported numerous failures. This was the beginning of what became known as the Gold Panic of 1869.

imagination some other place. Instead of being satisfied with what God has given them, they sigh in thought for the flesh pots of another clime. And, my brethren, there are mountains of trouble surrounding that man all the time! The climate is too cold; he shrinks in terror from it. The country that perhaps is a garden of Eden is in that man's imagination a desert of Sahara. The climate is too wet, and nothing suits him. While he is planting his crop he is thinking of another place, and he is ready to give his place away for a mere song so that he may be traveling to better lands. The old adage "a rolling stone never gathers any moss" applies here.

Men bring a great many troubles on themselves. They may sit like the prodigal son and bewail in a great many instances buried hopes and blasted prospects that they have cast away, but there is another cause of

The Scene at Broad Street in New York City on Black Friday,
The Gold Panic of September 24 1869. Contemporary American Engraving.

trouble that seems to be sent from God upon the children of men, and that, my brethren, is affliction. Perhaps success is crowning the man's labors, perhaps he is now in such a position that he can keep his wife and family in ease and comfort by his labor, when suddenly affliction lays her heavy hand upon him. And day after day and week after week he languishes on a bed of sickness, while he beholds his hard earned savings swept away. And when he at last recovers, he finds himself a poor man again. Nothing daunted, however, he goes to work again, and by patient struggles he again achieves a little store for a time of need, when perhaps wife or child is prostrated again, and again he sees his little store swept away. And thus he goes on. Affliction, like a terrible demon, is struggling to keep him down, while hope is lifting him up; and he seems to be between two fires all the time. There are, my hearers, thousands of industrious, hard-working men that might have been well off had it not been for the heavy hand of affliction and sickness. Their whole life with all their industry seems to be a constant struggle to keep the wolf of want from the door, and the patience that some men display under their heavy load of affliction is a miracle to behold.

Trouble, under whatever guise it comes, is not natural to our feelings, and we immediately seek relief. Like the sick man that sends for the doctor, so we send trouble away as soon as possible. How, might I ask, do men rid themselves of their troubles? Some men believe that the only way is wine. Let a man drink wine and forget. His misery seems to be their consolation in the hour of trouble, and they drown their sorrows in drink, only to increase their trouble. No brave man will meet his enemy under a mask, but like David of old he will come out to meet his foe face to face. No brave man will meet his trouble under the mask of intemperance, to stumble unconscious against his foe and meet a greater danger, to steep his brain in drink and then resign himself to his foe. That is brute force, not intelligent battle. Tis written [that] in the battle of Gettysburg the Southern troops drank whiskey and gunpowder before their final charge on the Union position. My hearers, I venture to say there is not a man here that would be willing to face death in such a condition. Why then, may I ask, will thousands of brave men in every other sense of the word meet trouble with their brain clouded with drink instead of standing up like men and fighting their battles with reason enthroned?

Another remedy with some—and, my hearers, that some is increasing to fearful proportions—is suicide. When trouble comes upon them, they resolve to take to themselves greater trouble by taking their own life. I cannot imagine what terrible demon of despair urges them on to such a step instead of battling manfully for their rights. They shrink in terror from trouble, and resolve to end their trouble and their life together. Men have said that the suicide is a coward, but, my hearers, I cannot but think that it takes a terrible effort for them to take their own life. I cannot believe that he can do it in his own strength, but that the devil is his helpmeet to such a deed. Men will sit down in all the calmness of despair and pen their last lines to wife and family and then blow out their brain. I cannot, my hearers, but believe that they do it by the power of Beelzebub.

Some years ago it was my fortune to see a man that had committed suicide. I shall never forget the scene, my hearers! Strong and healthy apparently, he lay before me weltering in his own blood. Here, said I, is a man that has gone before his Maker unbidden. Here is a man that was afraid to live. Trouble loomed up on this side. He knew what it was. He could find a remedy for his affliction, but he shrank from it. "I will not meet my trouble like a brave man," and in terror he fled to the darkness of eternity that stood on the other side of death—jumped from a trouble that he could see into the darkness of eternity that he could not see. Let me, my hearers, urge you as a minister of God to resolve that whatever your remedy for trouble, never take such a remedy as that! Pilgrim and faithful were tried like that by the giant despair again and again. They were on the point of yielding, but hope led them out. And so, my brethren, with you. When trouble and despair seem to be on the verge of driving you to such a fearful step, take the advice of hope and resolve to try again.

Here, my hearers, is where religion stands out like a rock, a strong tower of defense, to present her healing wave to the suffering sons of men. And did religion do nothing more for men than what it does in this life, it would repay its voteries, [devotees, adherents] said a celebrated infidel. Infidelity has nothing to present to her followers in the hour of trouble. The wicked man is driven hither and thither seeking a place where he may find rest, but finding none, wine may alleviate your sorrows. For a moment, my brother, but only for a moment. You may cloud your brain in smoke, you may contemplate suicide, but if you want a sure remedy, take the religion of Christ with all its imperfections and find the only relief that it is possible for you to obtain.

And finally, my hearers, we have the religion of Christ as the remedy of the good man in time of trouble, the grandest remedy yet provided for the suffering ones of earth. Said a sick lady to me not long since, "I have traveled over the earth with my husband. I have enjoyed wealth and I have suffered poverty. But I find the religion of Christ able to deliver me in the hour of trouble." That woman, my hearers, was on the verge of the grave. Religion was her only stay. And because of that fact, she was willing and ready to die. What, think you, would have been her condition had she not had the consolations of religion in such an hour? Religion, like the ferry boat, stood by her side, ready to carry her over the stream of death. Take away the ferry boat of religion, let her look out over the dark waters of death and see no hope, see nothing but a blank and void before her, and what a wretched being she will be! Religion, my hearers, stands out as a tower of defense to every Christian man and woman. Does trouble come upon him, he has an inward comforter. And though the waves of trouble seem to be ready to engulf him, still we may hear him exclaiming "Though I walk through the valley of death, I will fear no evil, for thy rod and staff do comfort me."[107]

Said a certain unbeliever in the religion of Jesus once after a long discourse before a crowded house: If there is one here that wishes to ask me any question, let them come forward and ask them now! And rising far back in the house, an old woman came tottering up the aisle and stood before the young man as the champion of Christianity. Said she, this religion of Christ is my only hope now. It has stood by me for over 60 years. It has enabled me to raise a large family of little children to be young men and women and I rejoice to know that I feel its previous influence with me now. What, may I ask, has your religion done for you? The young man was speechless.

And now, my unconverted brother, let me recount some of the grand achievements of this religion. This religion has filled the world with happiness and peace. This religion has saved the victims of idolatry from cruel death. This religion has been the only consolation of the poor woman when husband has died and poverty has assailed her, and has enabled her to shout victory over death and die with songs of joy on her lips. This religion has been the only stay of thousands of good men and women, when all things else have failed. What might I ask, my unconverted brother, has your religion done for you? Has it lightened your sorrows in time of trouble?   Has it ministered to your fevered brow in the hour of sickness? Does it lift up the pall of gloom that hangs over eternity and whisper in your ears that there is a better country beyond these scenes of trouble? Or does it drown your sorrows in the intoxicating bowl? Does it present nothing but an impenetrable gloom in the future? If it does, my hearers, accept the grand offers of the cross

---

107   Psalm 23:4

and take a religion that will alleviate your troubles in the hour of danger and fill you with joy unspeakable.

Another thought that assails men and women is why does trouble assail them? Everything in this life seems to have some purpose in view and I have thought more than once as I have seen some insignificant animal for what purpose was this created and that? They all have their purposes in view. Have you, my hearers, ever walked out in a grove and sat down by a running brook on a beautiful summer day and watched the teeming life all around you? If you have not, take the advice of Holy Writ and go to the ant to find instruction. Here you will see the brook covered over with little water spiders. And as you view them in happiness skimming over its surface, you ask for what was this created? The study of its use will perhaps occupy your life. Here you will see the ant busily engaged in its labors, laying up store against the cold winter. Every power of their nature seems to be busily employed. A moment seems to be precious to them. We can learn there of industry. Here you will behold the brook teeming with fish in happiness and apparently enjoyment, and the trees filled with birds building their nests and filling the air with songs. The bee is seen busily engaged, and even the leaves of the trees seem to be vying with animated life to outstrip them in the race for wealth.

And as you view them, my brother, cannot you learn the lesson of industry which nature teaches from the teeming life around? Some men can make the inanimate marble speak. Such a man as Agassiz[108] can find a volume of instruction from such an insignificant animal as a spider, while others will learn nothing, though it should speak with the tongue of men and angels. Shortly before Professor Agassiz' death a young man came to his school and wanted to learn from him natural philosophy. The teacher took a piece of coral rock and handed it to him with the exclamation, "Study that!"

And, my unconverted brother, let me present to you your trouble in a new form today. Let me present it to you as the philosopher presented the piece of marble. Do not sit down and brood and worry over it. Do not shrink in terror from it and rush out of life by your own hand. Do not drown your better nature in drink and then meet your trouble, but face it like a man. Sit down and solve the problem. Behind

---

108   Jean Louis Rodolphe Agassiz (1807-1873) was a Swiss-born American biologist and geologist recognized as an innovative and prodigious scholar of Earth's natural history. He immigrated to the United States in 1847 after visiting Harvard University. He went on to become professor of zoology and geology at Harvard, to head its Lawrence Scientific School, and to found its Museum of Comparative Zoology. *Wikipedia*

its frowning walls there is a clear sky.

Trouble is often a blessing in disguise. Prosperity, after elevating the Roman Empire to the highest pitch of power, commenced like the canker worm to eat out its vital powers and it fell not in battle, contending against its foes, but by the deceitfulness of prosperity. When the Goths and Vandals overran that mighty empire they found that prosperity and wealth had enervated every power of that people. Instead of meeting noble men that bore the scars and wounds of noble honorable battle, they found a nation of children, as it were. Debauch had conquered what the powers of the world had been unable to subdue. Prosperity, after carrying Alexander the Great from his little kingdom in Macedonia all over the known world as a victorious leader, proved his overthrow at last. Prosperity, my hearers, and not adversity, was the downfall of Napoleon. Men must have trouble and the only question with you and me is that we solve the problem correctly.

Trouble in the first place teaches men what they are. This word exclaims "Man, know thyself!" and never did nobler work engage the thoughts of men than their own imperfections. Here is a life study for us, my hearers. Does trouble assail us, let us find out the reason why we have in a great many instances brought it on ourselves. Is it because of our ungovernable passion? Here is the remedy. Christ the righteous is able to deliver us from that.

Our loved Washington's greatest trouble was his temper. He could conquer invincible armies, he could endure the suffering of Valley Forge, he could sacrifice his all on the altar of his country. But he could not conquer his own temper. And it was only by a life of faith and prayer that he was enabled to keep it under. Ah, my brethren, these tempers of ours gleam out from every [element] of the man and turn him into a demon instead of a son of God. This temper, my hearers, has brought more than one gray-headed father and mother hairs in sorrow to the grave. The boy is a good boy in every other instance. His mother could not want a more loving son. He is brace and generous, but his passion urges him on like some huge wave over all his better nature and the man seems to be helpless beneath its power. And when that passion in his nature is aroused he will imbrue [stain] his hands in innocent blood before he is aware of wrong. More than one half the murders committed in our land have been caused through the ungovernable tempers of men and women. The religion of Jesus is the only remedy, my hearers, for our tempers. And let me present this religion as a sovereign balm against your tempers. That power and that alone can carry you over your passion and land you in a purer realm where all is love.

Is it because of your pride? Christ is the remedy. Pride has brought down more than it has lifted up. Pride, my hearers, does not prove that you are either great or good. The intelligent man does not prove his greatness by his fine house or clothes but by his abundant store of knowledge. As men grow more intelligent they grow more ignorant in their own eyes. They sink to mere ciphers as they see the wealth of knowledge before them. Does he graduate at Yale or Harvard College, he desires to go to Germany and learn there more than he could learn here. And when he has exhausted the store of knowledge there, he weeps like Alexander because he cannot grasp the ocean beyond. And so, my brethren, with this religion of Christ. As the man knows more of this religion he becomes more humble. He is willing to be a servant if he cannot be a son. This religion, my brethren, banishes pride and robes the nobleman and the peasant into heavenly beings.

Does trouble assail you, my brother, because of drink? Christ is the only remedy. Men may sign the pledge, but how many break it almost as soon as it is signed. They did not intend to break it. He signed it in good faith. But his passion was his master. Men will promise by all the powers of heaven and earth to their wife and children that they will come home sober tonight and, my hearers, he means it. He intends to come home sober. But when the clock strikes twelve the wife greets her husband in beastly intoxication. Passion has conquered him. Passion, my hearers, leads men blind-folded into trouble. I knew a man that was addicted to the use of opium. Opium had captured him soul and body. He could [not] break off and Oh! my hearers, how hard was that man's condition! He resolved and resolved to break off, but his passion led him like a sheep to the slaughter till he died a miserable death.

Does trouble assail you because of affliction? Christ, my brother, is the only remedy. Men want above all things a strong support in time of affliction. When father is prostrated and Child, when affliction is rending your very soul, where, may I ask, will you flee for refuge? The world cannot help you. It will laugh at your suffering and like the priest and Levite pass by on the other side. Satan has no consolation to give you. Infidelity presents nothing but an unbroken waste of despair. But Christ lifts the veil of death and cheers the fainting soul by the joyful promise of eternal life beyond the vale of tears.[109]

This religion, my brethren, is a balm for every wound. This religion has been the only consolation of the wounded veteran on the field of battle. He can view his life blood ebbing away, he can pen his last

---

109   Vale = valley, See Psalm 84:7

words to some old father or mother and cry victory over death. At last the cannons roar, and [the] rattling hail of death cannot drown the still small voice within that cries above it all. Beyond these scenes of care and woe there is a life above unnumbered by the flight of years and all that life is. Love. This religion, my brethren, has nerved the wasting form of that man or woman who is coughing away his lungs day by day to look beyond. There are no haggard faces there. Consumption cannot enter there and religion is his only hope. Take away religion, my hearer, and you strike down the last tower of defense for the suffering ones of earth. Then you turn the world over, to the armies of trouble and give the poor man and woman nothing to hope for in the future.

The rich man may enjoy this life here. He may roll his train of long-drawn pomp before his poor neighbor here. He may cry, "Soul, take thine ease! Eat, drink, and be merry!" And life to him may be a heaven below. But what has the poor man to enjoy life? Here is a struggle to keep soul and body together. Life here is nothing but suffering, and if you rob him of his religion you leave him a wretched being. Like David you take away his lamb and leave him penniless. Let me then, my brethren, in conclusion present to you the Lamb of God as a sovereign balm for every woe. Religion will arm you with a flaming sword that like the sword around the tree of life will enable you to beat down your temper and rise above the troubled waves of passion. Religion will enable you to overcome your besetting sins of every kind. Religion will robe your pillow in death with angel guards and fill the room with such grand old songs as

> O come, angel bands,
> Come and around me stand!
> Oh bear me away on your snowy wings
> To my immortal home![110]

Religion, my brother, is able to save you from every woe and trouble in this life and open up an eternal life of happiness beyond the tomb. Oh then let me urge you to accept this grand old religion of Christ as a sovereign balm for every woe. And may God help you and shower his richest blessing upon you.

---

110   "My latest sun is sinking fast," by Jefferson Hascall, 1860. Published in 160 hymnals.

AMERICA

THE PROMISED LAND

> **Genesis 13:14-15.** And the Lord said until Abram, after that Lot ·was separated from him, Lift up now thine eyes, and look from the place where thou art northward, and southward, and eastward, and westward: For all the land which thou seest, to thee will I give it, and to thy seed forever.

Abraham the chosen servant of God has just been viewing the country of his posterity. God commands him to look northward first—I suppose he stood on some high mountain with no companion but his God – and as he looks northward, and southward, and eastward, and westward, I can imagine the grandeur of the view presented. He sees, as far as his eye can reach, nothing but green fields and forests, nothing but waving corn and bending wheat. And as he hears the words of God, I have no doubt he worshipped and adored him. His language no doubt was, What shall I render to Thee for all Thy mercies, O Lord?[111] as he viewed all this lovely land and then thought of the words of God: "All this land will I give thee." That was a great gift, my hearers! He need not worry now over this son's portion and that one's. He need not toil long and weary years to obtain a place for each one of his boys. No, no! God gave him and his children the whole land and declared that his blessing should rest ...

[page missing]

... was blest in that gift. No doubt Abraham as he looked on that splendid present cried out, "Lord, what shall I render to Thee for all thy goodness to me?" And God's answer is, "Only do thou love and serve me."[112]

Oh how much did God give to Abraham to have his love! He must have thought a great deal of Abraham. If some wealthy man gave you such a present as that, think you you would not love him? I have no doubt you would revere his name forever and [erect] statues and monuments to commemorate his name. And yet God has given you a land fairer than that promised land to Abraham, a land smiling with beauty and verdure all over its wide extent, a land that can produce

---

111   Genesis 12:7, Psalm 116:12.
112   Joshua 22:5, Deuteronomy 10:12b.

everything that heart can wish and desire, a land where you can worship God in your own [way] and manner.

Oh when we read of how the martyrs suffered in old times, how we should love this land of ours! We read of how they were burnt at the flaming stake. What a death that must have been! You know how the pain strikes through your limbs when you burn your hand and yet those men were burnt to death in those cruel lands.

Have you ever seen a person burnt very badly, burnt so badly that it seemed impossible for them to live? Oh what a heartrending sight that is! I remember once a woman I saw burnt almost to death. I shall never forget that sight as long as I live. As they brought her out of the carriage her sobs and moans were piteous to hear. Her blacked and larcered [charred] limbs were a terrible sight. And as I recall that sight, the thought comes of the suffering martyrs who were called on to die in that terrible manner for their religion.

Oh, my Christian friends, we should erect in each of our hearts a monument to God for his love in giving us such a land as this to live in! We don't have to go to the stake here for our religion. We don't have to go way off in the caves of the earth to worship God as some do in North American and no farther than Mexico. Bishop Simpson says he found Christian men and women worshipping God in the caves of the earth. Oh think of that, my Christian friends, you who walked out publicly today to come to this house of worship! Think of those men and women in Mexico slinking and crouching along as though some wild beast were after them to that wild cave to worship God in their own way and manner! Think of them as they take that old path and follow along in this stream to cover up their track! See them in that wild cave, you that are sitting here in this gospel land of liberty! As that sentinel stands at the mouth of the cave covered with thick foliage, peering out to see if he can catch a glimpse of their persecutors coming to drive them away! See that man of God as he unfolds that precious Book that contains the words of eternal life while one of his companions stands by his side with the candle and lights up its pages!

Oh that must be a sad sight as that little company of men and women worship God in that old cave and under the gospel light of the 19th Century! And yet, my hearers, while you are sitting here this day in peace and quiet there are men and women worshipping in the caves of the earth. Think of all that, and bless God that you have such a glorious heritage as this gospel land of liberty!

But there are lands that are in greater misery than Mexico. Turn your thought to the heathen lands. There are men and women bowing down today to idols, calling with as great a devotion as ever you called upon God, for the blessing of that piece of brass. They don't even know that there is a God that rides upon the stormy sky. They never heard of Christ. They never heard how he came into the world, how he suffered and died that they might live.

Some of them perhaps are throwing themselves under the wheels of Judgment now to save their souls. Some of them perhaps are throwing their little innocent babes into the Ganges to propitiate for their sins. Oh think of that, Christian mothers! You that are sitting beneath this Gospel of Christ, think of those poor heathen mothers in their darkness and misery! Their affections are as strong as ours, their love centers around their little ones as tightly as ours. And how it must wring their hearts to see their little babes sink to rise no more! Oh how they would gladly give this thing or that or any thing that they have in the world if they might only keep their little babe! But the heathen priest is inexorable and it must be sacrificed. That and only that will suffice. But not only do they sacrifice their babes, but the priest demands that they also shall swell the flames of their husband's funeral pyre!

Think of all that, my hearers, and let your prayer arise again that God has given you such a land as this for your inheritance! As you see in thought that heathen mother lying alongside her dead husband with the flames rising all around! And hear the wild shouts of the multitude! Know that there is a darkness hanging over that land deeper and more dense than ever was around the Egyptian homes. And let your prayer rise up again in prayer and praise to God for this unspeakable gift.

But not only has God provided us such a goodly land to live in in this life, a land separated from the everlasting snows and blasts of polar climes and the burning rays of torrid suns, a land flowing with milk and [honey] in this life — but he has provided an eternal home for us. He has obtained for us a land where we shall never get sick any more.

Oh what a healthy country that must be! We sometimes see people that have struggled a long time with disease. Their wasting forms tell us that they cannot live here long any more. But when they get over there in that better land they never suffer any more. They won't want the doctor to come today and stop in tomorrow. They won't want to take a long trip to Europe to see if that won't help them. No, no! No chilling winds nor poisonous breath can reach that healthful shore.

We have, my Christian friends, a glorious Heritage. This word declares that the streets of that country are paved with gold. Oh what a beautiful country that must be! There are some grand views to be had in this country of ours. I remember once of going to the top of a mountain to get a view of the country where I was stopping and I thought I [had] never seen any sight so lovely as that. Yonder were the roads winding and turning round in every different [way], and there were waving fields of corn. Over there was a town, and yonder was another, and they were dotted all over the plains. And I stood in silence and awe as I viewed all these sights. And then I turned and saw the Susquehanna breaking through mountains and hills and sweeping on, and I said, This is a beautiful sight! And it was a grand sight. But could you climb to the top of some of those mountains in that heavenly sight, you would see a far better sight! You might see — as far as your eye could reach — the golden streets of the new Jerusalem going out this way and that way and following the river of Jordan. And if you looked way over yonder you might see — skirting along this grand highway — the Tree of Life. And there is that noble river sweeping on that we may bathe our wearied limbs in forever and forever. Oh that will be a grand sight better than we can imagine or think of here!

And then in that land there will be no night. You need not fear of the cold night air there. And there is a grand City there, the new Jerusalem, the Capital of heaven. If you get up on one of her towers you will see a sight worth all the toil and trials of this earth. We talk sometimes of the beauty of Niagara, but that will far exceed that.

And we may possess that land. We may obtain a mansion there in that grand country. It has been bought with the blood of Christ. Oh my hearers there was a great price paid for the land, and it took a long time to buy it. Our Saviour had to go up and down this earth of ours three years in order to tell us about it and to urge us to come up and possess it, and then he sealed the deed with his own precious blood. Oh think of that, my unconverted friend! Christ paid a great price for your redemption. He paid a great price that you might have a part in that land.

And not only that, but we came very near losing the land. We came very near being cast out into outer darkness. For this word tells us that the son of man came to seek and save the lost sheep of the house of Israel. And the Jews in their madness and blindness refused to have it. They said, We will not have this man to rule over us. And then Christ sent out to the gentiles the glorious news that they might come up and be a partaker of the land.

Oh, my unconverted friends, let me urge you today to accept this great gift. If some man gave you a great present it would be madness and foolishness not to accept it. You would accept it with joy. There is [not] one in this house that would not accept, especially if we were poor. And we are very poor, my hearers, [with]in ourselves. Our inheritance by nature is eternal death. We have, an inheritance by nature where the worm dieth not and the fire is not quenched, where eternal darkness clouds the sky. It is very different from the land that has been bought for us. And then, my unconverted friend, you that are going down to that land in spite of all the prayers and tears of your fathers and mothers, in spite of all the warnings of God's servants, there will be eternal misery there. Oh that must be an awful place! Darkness so dense that it would be impossible to see your hand while the glare of the suffering ones in that dense fire that will burn forever must wring the heart with anguish unspeakable!

How sorry would God be to see you choose that land! This word declares that He delights not in the death of any one. And God in his infinite mercy doesn't want to see you go down to that. He offers you this good land without money and without price. He is pleading with you every day and every hour to come and be a partaker in this good land. He has sent his holy word to tell you of the beauty of the place, and he has sent his ministering servants to urge you to accept it. And Oh let me urge you to accept it today and give your love! It won't be very hard to do that when he has done so much for you.

Some of you love the world very much. You can't see how it were possible for you to give it up. But there is a time coming when you must give it up. You must part with all your loved ones some time, and that perhaps not very far off. This world that you fondly cling to will soon pass away. Your health that you think so much about will soon commence to give way. You can't go out and defy all kinds of weather. No, No! Sickness will warn you that you must get ready for another state of existence soon. These elastic limbs will commence to hang heavy by your side and ere long you must give up your earthly habitation for a home in heaven or in hell.

Oh stop, my unconverted friend, and ask yourself the question: whither am I tending? What country am I going to? Stop and listen to the pleading voice of God's dear son as he urges you to be a partaker in that glorious land! Don't listen to the words of sin and the world. Heed the pleading voice of God's dear son. No doubt he has pled with you more than once in this church as you heard his children sounding his praises, as you sat in your seat. Perhaps your brother has come to you and wept over your obstinacy. Perhaps the tear has come to your eye as that dear brother or sister has urged you to accept Christ. No doubt you have thought more than once of coming into that glorious possession. But then you would say to yourself, there is John and Harry. They have been good friends to me and I can't leave them. I don't like to be laughed at. And what is the reason I can't be as good a Christian out of the church as in it? Oh stop and think if your friend was ever as good to you as God has been. What has your friend done for you; and what has God done for you? Your friend can't save you in a dying hour. Your friend never gave you a beautiful house. And God has promised you a house not made with hands, eternal in the heavens.

And now God wants you to come out and join the Church. You want a home in heaven and God wants you to have your name on the church record on earth. You can't live as well out in the forest as you can in your own home, and you must have a spiritual haven to repose in. You must have some place where you can go and feel that you are at home; some place where God's people can gather around you and give you the right hand of fellowship; some place where you can come and renew your strength and take a day's march toward that heavenly land; some place where you will be rooted and grounded in the faith. There is power within the ranks; there is weakness outside. Come into this army. Come out and let the world know that, "As for me and my house, we will serve the Lord."[113]

And now, my Christian friends, you that are old in the way, let me encourage you to press forward to the end of the race. You have a good land in view. You won't have to toil and struggle in that land. You won't want ploughs and harrows there, and wonder what this will bring and that. No, no! We shall live on the fruit of the Tree of Life. Our sufferings and toilings will be over when we get over in that land. We shall be kings and priests forever! We shall have crowns of gold upon our heads and palms in our hand!

Oh, my Christian friends, struggle on through the short journey of life. Run with patience the race that is set before you,[114] though some of you may have bitter trials and temptations in this life, though some of you may be almost ready to faint down by the wayside. Struggle on a little longer! When you are almost ready to faint down, cast your eyes to the end of the race, and see the great possessor of that good land putting the crown of life on this old soldier of the cross that has sunk down at Jesus' feet, and hear his glad words:

113   Joshua 24:15b.
114   Hebrews 12:1b.

Come into the mansions prepared for you from the foundation of the world!"[115] And as you see all that, you will be strengthened to press forward to that eternal home of yours where suffering and sighing shall flee away forever! Oh that God may strengthen you to press forward to that good land above!

270 I Am Coming to the Cross

If we confess our sins, He is faithful and just to forgive . . . 1 John 1:9

William McDonald, 1870

TRUSTING 7 7 7 7 Ref.
William G. Fischer, 1870

1. I am com - ing to the cross; I am poor and weak and blind;
2. Long my heart has sighed for Thee; Long has e - vil dwelt with - in;
3. Here I give my all to Thee; Friends and time and earth - ly store,
4. In the prom - is - es I trust; Now I feel the blood ap - plied;
Ref. I am trust - ing, Lord, in Thee, Dear Lamb of Cal - va - ry.

D.C. Refrain

I am count - ing all but dross; I shall full sal - va - tion find.
Je - sus sweet - ly speaks to me, "I will cleanse you from all sin."
Soul and bod - y Thine to be, Whol - ly Thine for - ev - er - more.
I am pros - trate in the dust; I with Christ am cru - ci - fied.
Hum - bly at the cross I bow; Save me, Je - sus, save me now.

"I am Coming to the Cross," by William McDonald (1820-1901), music by William G. Fischer (1835-1912). *Hymns for the Living Church.*

---

115   Matthew 25:34.

338   When I Survey the Wondrous Cross

1. When   I   sur - vey   the   won - drous   cross   on   which the
2. For - bid   it,   Lord,   that   I   should   boast,   save   in   the
3. See,   from his   head,   his   hands,   his   feet,   sor - row   and
4. Were   the whole realm   of   na - ture   mine,   that   were   a

Prince   of   glo - ry   died,   my   rich - est   gain   I
death   of   Christ   my   God: all   the   vain   things   that
love   flow   min - gled   down: did   e'er   such   love   and
pres - ent   far   too   small;   love   so   a - maz - ing,

count   but   loss,   and   pour con - tempt   on   all   my   pride.
charm   me   most,   I   sac - ri - fice   them   to   his   blood.
sor - row   meet,   or   thorns com - pose   so   rich   a   crown?
so   di - vine,   de - mands my   soul,   my   life,   my   all.

Isaac Watts, 1707, 1709

HAMBURG L.M.
Gregorian chant
Arr. Lowell Mason, 1824

"When I Survey the Wondrous Cross," by Isaac Watts,
music by Lowell Mason. *Trinity Psalter.*

Barque.

Vintage engraving of a barque, a sailing ship, typically with three masts, in which the foremast and mainmast are square-rigged and the mizzenmast is rigged fore and aft. 19th Century. Getty Images.

Editor's note:

William traveled across the continent by rail, visiting every state and the two territories which would become the 47th and 48th states.

At age 28 he found himself in San Francisco with no money for the journey home. He signed aboard a merchant vessel as an unlicensed seaman. Working aboard ship he would earn his passage to London. Once there, he would have enough money to pay his way back to New York. It seemed rather roundabout, but in addition to being a way home it was also an opportunity to see more of the world.

The British barque *Iron Crag*, build in 1877, was listed in Lloyd's Register of shipping for 1878/9 as being out of Liverpool. Captain Jones assembled a crew in San Francisco to carry a load of American grain to Britain. William Freed signed on for adventure as much as for pay. Later in his life, he frequently lectured on his experiences on this trip. Tickets to his lecture were sold for five cents.[116]

116   The identity of the vessel was determined by a check of the ALTA CALIFORNIA newspaper records of the time by Ms. Barbara Bernhart, Assistant Librarian, National Maritime Museum, San Francisco. Bernhart to Graff, 29 January 1981. A transcript of this talk is on file in the library collection.

AMERICA AND BEYOND

BEFORE THE MAST

Ladies and Gentlemen, the subject of my lecture this evening is entitled, "Before the Mast,"[117] which means in sailor parlance a man that will take all the kicks and cuffs, all the hard knocks and abuse, which a cruel captain and a surly mate choose to inflict. It means a man that will climb to the Main Royal [mast] in all kinds of weather — that will stand on the Gallant forecastle holding on to the life line amid old ocean's wildest fury and keep a sharp lookout for icebergs, land, or ships in the dark and silent watches of the night. It means also a man that will stand by the helm of the ship when ocean waves are rolling mountain-high and steer her safely on her course. This, my hearers, is what in common conversation among sailors is meant by the expression, "before the mast." And another expression in use is "shipping" which means that you walk up before the British or American counsel as the case may be and sign your name to a paper containing many conditions for your government during the long voyage before you.

Let me then lead your thoughts away for a short time from the quiet scenes that here surround you to the far-away City of San Francisco, and there in imagination see your humble servant, hat in hand, standing before the British Counsel and appending his name to the ship's articles. In that I promised to be faithful, prompt, and obedient to my superior officers, in that I promised to live on one quart of water a day, one lb. of salt pork or beef every day, and also a pound of bread of which this is a specimen. There were many other conditions that we were to observe which I fully learned before the voyage was over — and some of them to my sorrow.

Having signed the ship's articles, we were the Captain's prisoners, for once a man has affixed his signature to that paper, he is bound by the law of nations to remain on board until the captain lands his ship in the port of her destination.

I can remember well the day we left San Francisco. It was on the 19th day of September 1878. The noble ship lay far out in the bay safely anchored. The men that had shipped stood by the wharf ready to be rowed off in the yawl [a ship's small boat, manned by four to six oarsmen]. Most of them were so drunk that they could hardly stand, but

---

117   To serve "before the mast" is to serve as an unlicensed seaman aboard ship.

all of them by a little help were embarked, and the shores soon receded far away.

Having arrived alongside the ship, another difficulty was experienced in getting our noble tars [seamen] on board ship. Some were so drunk that ropes were fastened around their waists and they were hoisted on board like so many cattle and stowed away in their bunks to sleep off their debauch.

We were two days in the harbor before leaving; for although our captain was all ready to put to sea, the law says he must remain two days in port after his crew is aboard to see if he had any men aboard who have been Shanghaied. San Francisco, in the good old days long since gone by, was a hard place to obtain crews, and the sailors tell of a man that the Boardinghouse Keepers shipped as a good man who was drunk—dead drunk—so drunk that he could lay in an August sun with face turned to all [its] intense rays and never feel any evil effects. Well, this was the condition of this man. He would, however, be all right after the whiskey was out and the wit in. The Captain paid fifty dollars in advance for this good man and took him aboard. Soon after he left the port, and two days after he discovered that his "good man," like all the good Indians and good little Boys, died early in the voyage. He was dead—and amid curses long and deep, Jack was consigned to his last sleep from the end of a plank over the ship's side.

At other times these boarding house runners would accost an unsuspecting man and after a pleasant chat, take him into some of their haunts, there to be drugged in drinking some of their vile whiskey. And when he woke up, nothing but sea and sky greeted his eye—bound away perhaps to China or some other distant land.

There were none of our men, however, either dead or drugged, but some of them after having spent a fifty-dollar advance were eager to get ashore again. And in order to prevent this, two policemen walked our decks to keep these same boarding house runners from stealing them away again.

On Sunday, the 22nd day of September, we hoisted our anchor. Amid the songs of our Sailors we were bound away this very day from Frisco Bay and spread our sails to the breeze. Golden Gate[118] was soon passed, and before night the Coast was bouncing dimly in the distance. Darkness spread her mantle o'er the sea and by its glimmering rays I saw the last vestige of civilization for four months—the streaming lights

118   Golden Gate is the strait between San Francisco Bay and the Pacific. It is 2 miles wide. The Golden Gate Bridge was not built until 1937.

of Golden Gate, 20 miles away. About 12 o'clock it faded from view, and the stars above and the water beneath told me that we were indeed at sea.

The watches were divided shortly after leaving San Francisco, for at sea there must always be enough men on deck to man the ship. A watch has four hours on deck and four hours below. And in that four hours below they must wash and mend their own clothes, for poor Jack has no loving hands to bear away these necessary duties. He must eat and sleep in that four hours, and at 8 bells [8:00 A.M.] he must be on deck, rain or shine, calm or blow, to do anything his superior officer demands at his hands. And for 115 days I never got more than four hours sleep at any one time.

After leaving San Francisco we had nothing to mar our enjoyment for some time. Occasionally a school of porpoises crossed our bow or perhaps far away we might see a whale spouting up water in the air. Birds hovered o'er our ship and told us we were still on God's footstool, and all went merry as a marriage ball.

Every two hours we would hear from the Quarter deck the ominous sound, "Heave the log!" and just here I will try and explain what the log is. I can assure you we do not heave any logs over at that time, but in my ignorance when I first heard that expression, I looked around for something to throw overboard. I soon, however, found out my mistake.

The log consists of a line sometimes a hundred and sometimes a hundred and fifty feet long. On the end of this line there is a small canvas bag about as large as a large glass formed in the shape of a funnel, and all along the line, after the first five feet are over, there are knots generally 14 feet apart. And then in connection with this line they use one of the old time hour glasses with sand in it, generally one that runs out in about a minute. One man holds this glass in his hand while the other has the line, generally the mate. He throws the line overboard, and after the first 25 feet is out he calls to the man with the glass to turn it over. And while the line is running out and the sand is running from one side to the other, he tells the distance the ship is traveling in one hour. As soon as the sand is out, he calls, "Up!" The line is stopped. If now the ship travels 80 ft. in one minute, she is traveling so many miles in the hour.

'Tis in this manner, my hearers, that the Captain can tell with unerring certainty how far he had traveled in 24 hours. And while there are no apparent mile posts to mark the watery waste of the deep, man by his divine genius has planted mile posts all over the wide extent of old Ocean.

After being ten days out, on October 2, just after I had finished my last piece of salt pork, I heard the steward call out, "Lime juice!" Everyone turned out to obtain his cupful, which is put up in the form of lemonade and is given on all long voyages on English Ships to prevent scurvy. Sailors must necessarily eat at sea large quantities of salt provisions, and it produces scurvy, one of the most loathsome and terrible of diseases. I saw a sailor that had had the scurvy and he was a complete wreck of his former self. Lime juice is one of the greatest remedies yet discovered for this disease, and every British ship must supply their crew with a good tea cup full every day.

The first 25 days passed with nothing of special moment to occur. Our week days were employed in scrubbing decks or washing paint work. Sunday was a general holiday, and while some were gambling for tobacco, others were washing clothes, and God's day passed on board ship as Thanksgiving Day passes among us on the land.

But at last, as we neared the Line [the Equator], ominous sounds commenced to be heard of old Neptune. Santa Claus was never painted to childish mind as was Neptune to your humble speaker. I was told what he had done—that he had caught the defenseless sailor who first appeared in his waters—that he hath shaved his head as clean as a billiard ball—that he had bedecked him with tar and feathers—and that he had sent him aloft to dance to His Highness—until I was ready to believe almost anything! And it was indeed with fear and trembling that I expected at last, like Pilgrims of old, to wake up in the clutches of this Giant. Despair! I knew not what would be my fate, but I was not long in suspense. My mustache that had cost me the labor of years, that I had nursed with a fatherly care and bedewed with many and various kinds of hair restorers—the pride and joy of every young man—must come off with my hair. I pled and begged, but in vain. My prayers and tears availed not. And the next morning I woke up minus my mustache, and hair as short as a Sing Sing convict. However, time, the great restorer as well as destroyer of all our woes, has healed the wounds there inflicted; and Neptune, I trust, has buried the hatchet forever in my favor.

We crossed the line going south on October 15, and gradually, as we neared Cape Horn, the waves of old Ocean commenced to roll themselves up in grander power.

The ship commenced to rock beneath its power as the cradle rocks to the touch of Mother's love. And though we were yet 1000 miles from Cape Horn, we could commence to feel the swellings as we traveled south. We also observed that every day grew longer and yet it was cold. In that far-away land, the sun's rays seemed powerless to dispel the frosty winds of Antarctic seas.

On November 2, just at dawn of day, we saw running along the line of Heaven's canopy flashes of lightning. No storm, however, seemed to be apparent. All hands were called on deck to take in sail, and in one hour from that time it was blowing a perfect hurricane of wind. This was my first storm, and though the sea was tossing our good ship as a feather on its bosom, I thought surely it cannot come over its side. Thinking thus, what was my surprise to see the ship lurch to one side and take in enough water to lift me from my feet and wash me from side to side! After this I was more careful how I put myself in its grasp. This storm, however, was of short duration, and the next day we were scudding along before the wind with a clear sky and a fair wind.

This, however, did not last long. We were nearing Cape Horn now. Every day our spurs were lashed down to the decks tighter than ever. New and stronger sails were hoisted in the place of the old ones. The fore and mizzen royal [sails] were unbent and, if possible, our ship was made doubly strong. This was on November 15. It was cold and dreary. Then we were off the coast of Patagonia, and our good ship was surrounded by flocks of huge birds called Albatrosses, denizens of that land of Giants, who seemed like weird spirits from some accursed land, to hover o'er our ship and sing our funeral dirge. The skies were dark. The sea was blue in its intense depth. The winds were cold, and all nature seemed to portend some terrible disaster. That night the winds of Heaven seemed to let loose all their batteries on our devoted ship. Ever and anon some dark blue wave would come like a charging legion upon us, leaping over our sides and sweeping over the decks in matchless power and grandeur.

Albatross.

About 8 o'clock that night I and one of my shipmates by the name of Wilson were ordered aloft to take in the main royal [sail]. I shall never forget that terrible night—terrible to me because my friend never returned on deck again. We ascended that gray height together, but I could see that he was very cold his hands especially and it was with great difficulty that he managed to hang on. But at last he stood on the foot rope of the yard when by some means the clew [lower corner] of the sail which is on the extreme end, hit him on the head in the fierce wind that prevailed, and poor Harry dropped forever out of sight. The roar of the sea hushed his voice if he called and we never saw him again. Tis amid such scenes as this that sailors live. I at last furled the sail and returned on deck with a heavy heart to report the sad occurrence. He was a noble fellow and a general favorite among the whole crew. An American by birth, he leaves a widowed mother in the state of Connecticut to mourn his loss.

All that night the sea seemed to conspire for our destruction. About 11 o'clock a tremendous wave burst over the stern of the ship washing away the grating on which the man at the wheel stood, carrying away the compass and a lot of chickens that had been the joy and pride of our captain. Twelve o'clock at last came when our watch was relieved and I congratulated to myself at least four hours rest. But scarcely had I lain down tired and weary with the labors of four hours when a tremendous sea struck the forecastle sending, I confess, a shudder through my frame and breaking in our door, which was two inches thick of solid oak, like so much paper. The forecastle was filled at once. I, as misfortune would have it, had a lower bunk and had the full benefit of all the water. Our beds and clothes were wringing wet, and we were indeed most miserable beings. This was one of the nights which I shall long remember. I could indeed say "Amen" to the good Episcopalian's prayer when he cries, "Lord, bless us most miserable offenders." This night, however, like all the long roads, had an end, and the next morning the sea was calmer although very rough yet and we saw our first land, named the Diago Rameree Island[119], after being 64 days out. This was a dreary, desolate-looking island around which immense flocks of birds were flying.

We were now south of Cape Horn and steered in an easterly direction. This was November 16. That night about 11 o'clock the joyful announcement was made that we had passed the dreaded Cape, and our Captain ordered the lead to be hove, and at 600 feet we struck bottom in deep sea sounding.[120]

The lead is covered on the bottom with tallow in order to take hold of anything it touches. When the lead was brought up, it was covered with a very small shell that had been crumbled to pieces. After this time our course was North.

---

119   The Diego Ramirez islands, Chile, are in the Drake passage, 100 km southwest of Cape Horn, at the tip of South America.

120   The lead (pronounced "led") is a large iron weight tied to the end of a rope which is cast overboard to test the depth of the channel.

On November 19 I saw my first iceberg. About 3 o'clock the cry was heard, "Sail ho!" It looked indeed like a big ship, but soon we could see by its irregular shape that it was an iceberg. To describe it would be impossible. No man can paint a picture that will represent reality. Some of you have stood by Niagara and heard its roar and seen its dark and seething mass, hurried on by the unseen power of God, tumbling over that immense height and dashing all its force beneath. And where yet has been the artist that [could] depict that awfully grand sight on canvas? Where yet is the painter who has painted Gettysburg in all its grandeur on the memorable three days of July, when the host of Rebellion swept over the plain, to the tune of 200 cannons' roar, to meet death on Cemetery Hill?

And so [it is], my hearers, with a silent statue-like Mountain of Ice as it floats on old ocean's breast with hills and valleys, with towers and turrets jumbled up in a thousand different fancies. But there they all are silent, yet speaking as no orator ever yet spoke. I stood in silent awe before the power of omnipotent God far away in Antarctic seas where this huge monster was formed. Who can, among my audience, conceive of the cold which froze into being this mass? Years may have elapsed, but at last the work is complete. The last prop is knocked from under, the mountain mass drops from her mooring, and stately and grandly she takes her course toward northern seas. This iceberg was over 1 mile long and 100 feet above the sea level. Our captain supposed it was 600 feet high in the dusk of the evening.

On another day we passed an immense piece of this ice that would perhaps fill this room, floating very near our ship, but thanks to the man on the lookout, we escaped its power. These small pieces, hidden away as it were from sight, are the greatest dread of sailors at sea. Many a noble ship has gone down from such pieces, with all on board. We were among icebergs about one week, and during that time we passed one almost every day. During that time the air was colder also, as the atmosphere is sensibly affected by these huge monsters. Having left these ugly neighbors, we slept in more peace.

The next curiosity I saw was a school of strangelooking fish called penwinks [penguins]. There is an old and doubtless a true saying that there is nothing on land that has not its counterpart in the ocean. If this is so, these fish represented a flock of ducks, minus feathers. This fish is seldom seen and only far at sea. They swim with their wings and are indeed a great curiosity.[121]

121   Penguins are, of course, not fish but birds - flightless aquatic birds of the family Speniscidae of the Southern Hemisphere, having webbed feet and wings reduced to flippers.

Flying fish were also numerous at this time. Doubtless you have all heard of this fish. Their wings seem to be nothing more than enlarged fins on the side which they have the power of extending into wings. They rise with a sudden bound, generally to escape the dolphin, their greatest enemy, and fly a hundred yards or so. Whenever flying fish were seen, the spears were got out for dolphin is a delicious fish that is only seen far at sea. The dolphin is

Penguin

a very greedy fish and in pursuit of his game will frequently jump out of the water. They are sometimes speared, but the most common way of catching them is to tie a white rag on the end of a hook and then dance it along on the surface of the water. The dolphin will frequently jump out of the water to grasp it, when he is easily secured. This fish has the power of changing its color. Sometimes as he swims alongside the ship he resembles sparkling diamonds in the rays of the sun; and again he assumes a purple color; and in death he turns almost dark.[122]

On the 3rd day of December I witnessed the sight of a fish called the thresher [shark] killing a whale.[123] The thresher is a long eel, only much heavier and longer. The whale, like the seal, must come to the surface to breathe and just as he rises to the top of the water, you will see the thresher leap high in the air and come down with terrific force on the whale's back and thus he follows him up until the whale rolls over in death, literally beaten to a jelly when the thresher — like the tiger [shark] sucks his blood and leaves the balance for smaller game.

There was a very large whale that kept our company for over 1/2 a day. He came so near the ship that you could touch him with a pole, and I got a good view of him. Right on the top of his back there was an immense hole that seemed big enough for a man to get inside of. This is his blower. When he sinks, this hole naturally fills with water. When he desires to breathe, he rises to the surface and blows out this water and takes in a fresh supply of air. Whales are fond of company and frequently they imagine the bottom of the ship is another whale and

---

122   This is a visual phenomenon caused by water and light rather than any real changing done by the porpoise.

123   Thresher shark. A large shark of the genus Alopias, which threshes the water with its long tail to drive together the small fish on which it feeds. Under normal circumstances a thresher shark would not be interested in a whale. However, there are a number of accounts on record of thresher sharks and also swordfish attacking and sometimes killing whales. Judy Perkins, paper presented at the Kendal1 Whaling Museum, Sharon, Massachusetts, 1979. The tiger shark is a large shark found in warm water which is known for its voracious habits.

will follow them for a long distance.

On Sunday, December 8, we passed the Island of Trinidad, another desolate-looking island rising like a mountain right up from the sea. This island we saw after being 77 days out.

Our next adventure came very near being our last. There was a great amount of work to do now the ship was got ready for the home port, and a ship is a captain's baby in an enlarged form. An engineer loves his engine and takes good care of her. A mother loves her infant and all her soul is wrapped up in her child. A farmer loves his horse because his horse, next to himself, is the most valuable thing he has. And a sea Captain as he walks the deck of his ship notes her every movement with eagle eye. More particularly is this the case as he draws near his home. Then it is his greatest ambition to sail into the home port with his ship looking as neat as a new pin. And about this time poor Jack[124] earns all his wages. The rigging must be tarred down and these hands of mine have dipped, you may believe, more than once into the depths of a tar bucket. The decks must be corked and holloystoned.[125] The sides of the ship must be painted, and in fact everything about her must have the artistic touch of a sailor's paint brush for I think Jack represents quite a number of building trades in his makeup.

Well to commence with was the decks—they must be corked and pitched—and for a week nothing but boiling pitch and ringing corking hammers resounded on our ship. The pitch was melted on deck by means of a hand forge. And somehow or other tar coal and fire were pitched down the fore hatch and in an instant a tremendous blaze shot up from beneath, and consternation seized every face. The ship was hove to [brought to a halt]. The hand pumps were quickly manned, and our bold tars became bold firemen. After about an hour's work, we succeeded in getting out the fire, ruining about 200 bags of wheat.[126] We breathed the air of freedom again. There is an excitement about a fire at sea that you cannot feel on land when you feel that the ship beneath your feet is burning up. When this plank on which I stand is gone and the dark blue waters of death are before me, 'tis then that every arm is stirred and every heart fired to do and to dare and to die for the salvation of the ship.

---

124   Jack. Refers to all the lowly seamen like himself.
125   Holloystoned. Rubbed with a pumice-like stone in order to polish them to a high gloss.
126   This was a merchant vessel carrying grain from the west to England. There was a flourishing grain trade between the two countries at that time. Barbara Bernhart, San Francisco Maritime Association.

After the fire was put out, the cleaning process continued with redoubled vigor. The masts were scraped down and oiled, the paint washed with soap and repainted, the decks were holloystoned and oiled, and lastly the rigging was tarred down. Everything looked as snug as could be and we were ready for the home port.

After this our captain rested easy for some time until one morning we were all summoned aft to give information in regard to his cats. Our captain's loves were in two things: his cats and his brown jug. Puss would fawn over him and burr in his arms when whiskey drove all else away. This cat stole something belonging to one of our sailors, and that night it went over the side. Of course no one knew its whereabouts, and the captain after that centered all his love in his bottles. Thus it has ever been—when we are robbed of one treasure, our hearts center more closely around the other.

On December 24 we crossed the line coming north and the next day was Christmas when all hearts are reunited by thoughts of a diviner love—the birth of him who died on Calvary's Cross. And while merry hearts were made glad on the land, there was a merry company far away on old ocean's breast, eating a good Christmas dinner. We had two sheep and two hogs aboard. One of the sheep was killed and a fresh mess prepared for the ship's crew with regular sea duff[127] for a dessert, and after so long a seige of salt hog, you may imagine how sweet to the taste was a piece of fresh meat. Anything, they say, tastes good to a hungry man, and after living on salt provisions any length of time, I think a man could eat a piece of fresh elephant, or like the old apostle would call nothing under God's heaven common or unclean.

We saw on Christmas Day a curious fish whose name I forget who have the power of erecting a small sail and scudding along before the wind. This sail looked like a blood red sheet about as large as a human hand.[128]

On the 28th day of December a thunder storm came upon us so all sails were taken in and for about 1/2 hour the sea was calm—no sound but the muttering thunder; and flashing gleam of lightning as it coursed along the sky greeted the eye. Every man was standing by, as the sailors say, when suddenly a ball of fire, as it were, hung over the Main Royal Mast, creating a solemn feeling in every mind. For a couple of seconds it hung there when, gliding along across the braces,

---

127   Duff. A stiff flour pudding, boiled or steamed and often flavored with currants, citron, spices, etc.
128   Sailfish. The red color must have been an optical illusion created by the sunlight.

it lighted on the fore Royal Mast. There it hung for a moment, and then we saw it far out on the jib boom. It soon faded away, leaving behind the remembrance of a visitor from spirit lands. The rain shortly after descended in torrents, and in about 1/2 hour after the sun was shining again as bright as ever.

Nothing of moment occurred after this till January 9 when we encountered a furious gale of wind lasting two days, four hundred miles from Cape Clear, the southernmost point in Ireland. About 3 o'clock at night one of our sails was carried away by its power. I never saw the wind blow harder, nor have I ever seen its force more fully tested. It has been my privilege to stand on some naked prairie and view the fire as it swept o'er its plain with lightning speed. The thunder storm that sweeps up· your valley will not tell the tale. No eye but he that sees can imagine how tremendous is the power of that zephyr-like wind that has often lulled you to sleep. At the height of this gale I was standing in the forward part of the ship when a new sail blew completely away, snapping new "inch" rope [an inch in diameter] like so much paper. The masts of our ship strained and bent beneath its force so much that we were afraid they would have to be cut away. Sometimes it blows so hard at sea that nothing but the sacrifice of the masts will save the ship. We were, however, saved this disaster.

The next morning opened with the seas rolling mountain high. The wind still blew a gale. The whole atmosphere was filled with spray. Now our good ship was high in the air on the crest of some huge wave and now deep in the trough of the sea with walls of surging billows on every side. And thus it raged for two days and two nights. During that time many noble ships went down forever as we saw afterwards in the papers, but we escaped.

I wish, my hearers, I could describe to you a storm at sea. When the forces of Heaven and Earth are arrayed for man's destruction, standing upon the deck of the noble ship, holding on to some life line or perhaps up in the rigging, now rolled on this side and now on that, you look up at a sky dark and portentous [threatening]. The winds are blowing with all their power, singing, as it were, your funeral knell through the rigging of the ship. Never has wind sounded around the eaves of your house like that wind through every part of the ship. The ship is rolling and creaking amid a terrible sea. Ever and anon a tremendous wave washes over the deck, carrying death and destruction in its track. The whole surface of the ocean is covered with foam while breaking waves and furious wind combine to make a noise as if a thousand cannons roared around. This, my hearers, is a faint picture of a storm at sea. I think one of the most grandly beautiful pictures I ever saw was when high up on the yard, I looked down on our noble ship, now tossed on this side, now on that—that ship that you would imagine nothing could harm. How its greatness and strength faded into weakness and nothingness before the matchless power of the ocean!

Many persons cannot imagine how the sea can produce so much destruction—how a wave that breaks over its side can wrench and twist an iron bar as we would break a stick. Let me then endeavor to explain it. The sea always travels with the wind, and sometimes in a hurricane it runs at the rate of 12 to 15 miles an hour. And when an immense wave breaks over the side of the ship, it strikes anything it comes in contact with at just that rate of speed. See what power is manifested on our rivers in the spring when the ice breaks up.

Imagine five or six tons of salt water—and you will remember that salt water is much more powerful than fresh—breaking over the side of the ship and traveling at the rate of 12 or 15 miles an hour over its decks, and then, my friend, you may form some idea of the power of Old Ocean! Then you can understand why some ships look like rolling bogs[129] after being out in such a storm with masts all gone and sides or bulwarks gone and paint all washed off.

On the 12th day of January the sun was bright again and we commenced to think of "home, sweet home." We were nearing the port of our destination. The first sign of land is seen on the water. Two days before we saw the land, the water changed from a dark blue to a lighter color; and on the 14th day of January 1879 I first saw the dim outlines of the Green Isle written, as it were, on the sky. And the next day our good ship dropped her anchor in the harbour of Queenstown [now Cobh, the seaport for Cork in The Republic of Ireland], 115 [days] out from San Francisco.

Soon after that our ship was surrounded by small boats called Bum Boats by the sailors because, I suppose, they bum all his wages or all they can get, for you must know that Jack rises in importance when he arrives in the home port. Clothiers were anxious to obtain our orders for clothing. Shoemakers wanted to take our measure then and there, and among the rest came a poor woman with fresh bread and butter and eggs and a bottle of whiskey under her coat. The last of the cake [of these], like the fairie wand, this was the touch that melted every Irishman's heart—and some of the rest, too—and boots and clothing were forgotten among all her things. However, the one that touched

---

129   Bog. British slang for a privy or outhouse.

Queenstown, Cobh Harbor, 1870. Alamy Images.

those rough sailors' hearts was the woman herself. We hadn't seen a woman now for almost four months. We had bedecked our bunks with her fair face and form. 'Tis true we had talked of her beauty, we had sung of her charms, but we hadn't seen the reality. And when at last this poor woman with her "God bless you" came among us, we thought of Mother and sister and home again. Her stock in trade was soon bought, and with many a "God bless you" she left us with more money than she had had for some time.

Queenstown is a small but very pretty place. The country all around looked like a garden, and while we were here we enjoyed fresh provisions and country air. Leaving here after 10 days we started for Dublin, but on the way we were becalmed two days. Our captain at this time was constantly walking the deck and stamping his feet with suppressed rage. But on the third day we got a fair wind again and soon arrived in Kingston, 6 miles from Dublin, where we layed 8 days waiting for a high tide to take us over the bar.[130] When we arrived at last in Dublin the next day, we were discharged, and here my lecture properly ends.

I will, however, pause a moment to tell some of the things I took notice to in Dublin. The first thing that took my eye was intemperance among the women. Here I saw respectable-looking women entering

---

130   They needed a high tide to give them enough clearance to make it over the sand bar.

grocery stores with a bar on the back [in the rear] and ordering drinks for themselves and giving it to their little ones. Here also I first became acquainted with the habit of feeing [tipping], a practice in which the well-dressed man pays to every person who does the slightest turn for him.

Dublin is a beautiful city adorned with many works of art. Sackwell Street is its greatest business street, and opposite the Post Office is a beautiful statue of Lord Wellington. This impressed me more than anything I saw in the city. I crossed over from Dublin to Liverpool and saw something of that city of ships.

Before I left, I went to see the Court of Assizes in St. James Hall [in London] and saw His Lordship Chief Justice Lindsay as he came to court. Democratic America has still something to learn of the dignity of the Court from old England. His Lordship came in a coach driven by four horses with a footman, a coachman, and two butlers on the outside of the coach. One held the horse (the coachman), the footman opened the coach door, the butler left down the steps, and I forgot what the other man did; but his most Royal Lordship came at last in flowing wig and stately mein. He came with sound of music accompanying him to open court. When he entered court, every head was uncovered and every lawyer rose and bowed to His Honour when court was opened. This is a little different from American usage.

I came [back to America] from Liverpool on the "White Star Steamship *Marathon*". We had a crazy man aboard who wanted to go ashore in mid-ocean, and he was tied down like a wild beast till we got to New York.

Certificate of Discharge from the Sailing ship *Iron Crag* of W. W. Freed, age 27, born in Pennsylvania, who signed on in San Francisco as an unlicensed seaman 19 September 1878 and was discharged 3 February 1879 in Dublin. Character for Ability in whatever capacity engaged: Very Good. Character for Conduct: Very Good. His trip around Cape Horn is chronicled in his lecture "Before the Mast." He subsequently returned to America from Liverpool on the White Star Steamship *Marathon*.

And the story continues…

Summer 1919, William Walton Freed with his family in the garden behind his house at 1507 Scott Street, Williamsport, Pennsylvania.
Left to right: Walter C. Freed Sr, Amelia Doebler Freed with grandson Walter C. Freed Jr, Ella Freed, and William with his granddaughter June Freed.

Children and Grandchildren of Abraham and Mary Singer Freed

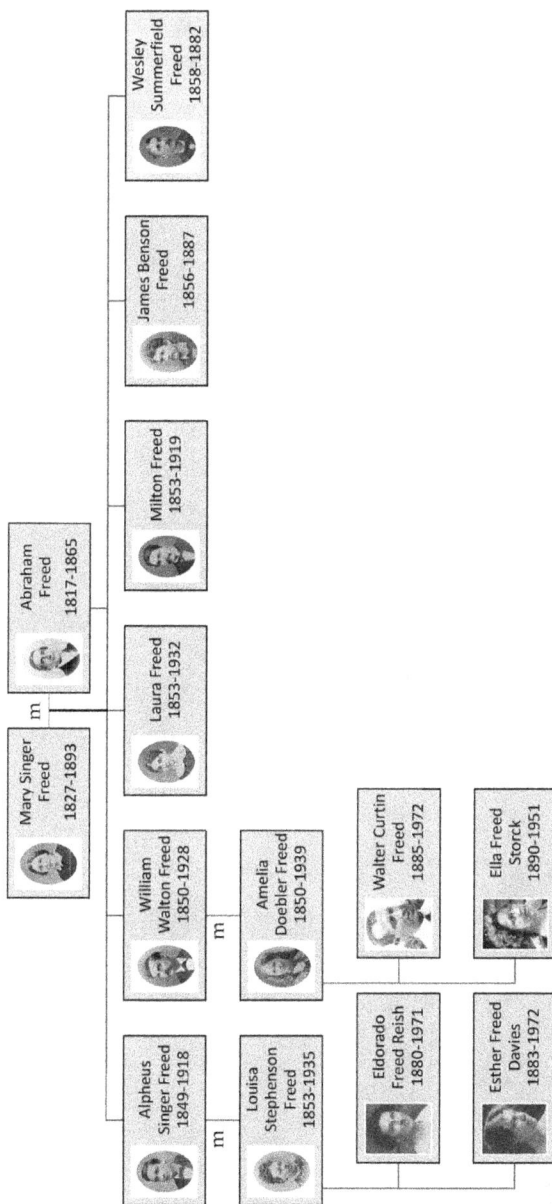

Mary Singer Freed 1827-1893 — m — Abraham Freed 1817-1865

Alpheus Singer Freed 1849-1918 — m — Louisa Stephenson Freed 1853-1935

William Walton Freed 1850-1928 — m — Amelia Doebler Freed 1850-1939

Laura Freed 1853-1932

Milton Freed 1853-1919

James Benson Freed 1856-1887

Wesley Summerfield Freed 1858-1882

Eldorado Freed Reish 1880-1971

Esther Freed Davies 1883-1972

Walter Curtin Freed 1885-1972

Ella Freed Storck 1890-1951

BIBLIOGRAPHY

Many of the following works, especially those on early Methodism and music, are to be found in the library of the School of Theology, Boston University, where there are significant collections pertaining to Methodism in America. Works published before 1900 are in their Nutter, Metcalf, and New England Methodist Historical collections of rare books. Many have now been digitized and are available on the internet. In updating this manuscript, hymnary.org has made it much easier to find older hymns! Our thanks to Harry Plantinga and the consortium for this invaluable resource.

Bangs, Jeremy Dupertuis, *Letters on Toleration: Dutch Aid to Persecuted Swiss and Palatine Mennonites, 1615-1699.* Picton Press, Rockport, Maine, 2004

Beardsley, Frank Grenville. *Religious Progress through Religious Revivals.* New York, American Tract Society, 1943.

Bell, Marion L. *Crusade in the City: Revivalism in Nineteenth-century.* Philadelphia. Lewisburg, Bucknell University Press, 1977.

Benson, Rev. Louis F. *The Best Church Hymns.* Philadelphia, The Westminster Press, 1898.

Benziger, Barbara, and Eleanor Dickinson. *That Old-Time Religion: 100 Hymns, Songs, and Stories.* New York, Harper and Row, 1975.

The Book of Common Praise, Being the Hymn Book of the Church of England in Canada. Oxford, University Press, 1938.

Bunyan, John. *The Pilgrim's Progress from This World, to That Which Is to Come,* W.R. Owens, ed., Oxford World's Classics (Oxford: Oxford University Press, 2003)

Camp-Meeting Chorister; or, a Collection of Hymns and Spiritual Songs for the Pious of all Denominations. Philadelphia, W. A. Leary & Co., 1852.

Chiles, Robert E. *Theological Transition in American Methodism: 1790-1935.* New York, Abingdon Press, 1965.

Clow, Rev. W. M., *The Bible Reader's Encyclopaedia and Concordance.* London, Collins, 1934.

Davis, Richard W. *The Stauffer families of Switzerland, Germany, and America (inclduding Stouffer and Stover),* self-published, 1992.

Dickinson, H. T. "The Poor Palatines and the Parties," *The English Historical Review,* Vol. 82, No. 324 (July 1967), pp. 464-485.

Diehl, Katharine Smith. *Hymns and Tunes -- An Index.* New York, Scarecrow Press, 1966.

Dimond, Sydney G. *The Psychology of the Methodist Revival: An Empirical and Descriptive Study.* London, Oxford University Press, 1926.

Doctrines and Discipline of the Methodist Episcopal Church, 1876. New York,

Nelson & Phillips, 1876.

Fosnocht, Bruce, Ed., "Swiss Surname Finding Aid." published via LMHS.org.

Freed, Isaac G. *History of the Freed Family, self-published,* 1919, Allentown, Pennsylvania. Available at archive.org.

Fretz, A. J., and Eli Wismer. *A Brief History of Jacob Wismer and a Complete Genealogical Family Register With Biographies of His Descendants from the Earliest Available Records to the Present Time.* Facsimile reprint of the 1893 original by Kessinger Publishing, 2009.

Futhey, J. Smith, and Gilbert Cope, *History of Chester County, Pennsylvania, with genealogical and biographical sketches.* Louis H. Everts, 1881, Philadelphia.

Graff, Joyce Wilcox, and June Freed Wilcox. *A Freed Family History.* Baltimore, Gateway Press, 1981. A.k.a. "the Red Book" because of its red leather binding. Some hard copies still available through Garnet Star Publishing, Boston. Text also available at archive.org

Haldeman, Milton S. *Descendants of Christopher Haldeman: son of immigrant Nicholas Haldeman.* Masthof Press, Morgantown, Pennsylvania, 2008.

Heiberger, Charles A. *Descendents of Johannes Friedt/Freed (1682-1744).* Princeton, New Jersey, 1984.

Hymn Book of the Methodist Protestant Church, 19th edition, Baltimore, 1856.

Hymns for the Use of the Methodist Episcopal Church, revised edition, New York, Lane & Scott, 1851.

Jones, Henry Z Jr, and Lewis Bunker Rohrback. *Even More Palatine Families: 18th Century Immigrants to the American Colonies and their German, Swiss and Austrian Origins.* Picton Press, Rockport, Maine, 2002.

Knittle, Walter Allen, Ph.D, *Early Eighteenth Century Palatine Emigration.* Philadelphia, 1937

Lowry, James W., *Documents of Brotherly Love: Dutch Mennonite Aid to Swiss Anabaptists, Vol. 1, 1635-1709.* Edited by David J. Rempel Smucker and John L. Ruth. Ohio Amish Library, Millersburg, Ohio, 2007.

Martin, Ruth. *International Distionary of Food and Cooking.* New York, Hastings House, 1973.

McDormand, Thomas B. and Frederic S. Crossman. *Judson Concordance to Hymns.* Valley Forge, Pennsylvania, 1965.

A New Book of Hymns for the Use of the Methodist Episcopal and other Churches. New York, Edward Jones, publisher, 1879.

Otterness, Philip. *Becoming German: The 1709 Palatine Migration to New York.* Cornell University Press, 2006.

Pennypacker, Samuel Whitaker, "Bebber's Township and the Dutch Patroons of Pennsylvannia", *Pennsylvania Magazine of History and Biography,* 1907.

Pennsylvania Mennonite Heritage, the journal of the Lancaster Mennonite Historical Society, Lancaster, Pennsylvania.

Preston, David. *Braddock's Defeat: The Battle of the Monongahela and the Road to Revolution.* Oxford University Press, 2015.

Priestly, Joseph. *An History of the Corruptions of Christianity,* 1793, (reprinted 1871), vol. 2, p. 166.

Random House Dictionary of the English Language, unabridged edition. New York, Random House, 1967.

Rice, Timothy. *Deep Run Mennonite Church East: A 250-Year Pilgrimage, 1746-1996.* Perkasie, Pennsylvania, 1996.

Sizer, Sandra S. *Gospel Hymns and Social Religion: The Rhetoric of Nineteenth-century Revivalism.* Philadelphia, Temple University Press, 1978.

Smith, Gene. *American Gothic: the story of America›s legendary theatrical family, Junius, Edwin, and John Wilkes Booth.* New York: Simon & Schuster, 1992. pp. 23, 210-213.

Stevenson, George John. *The Methodist Hymn-Book and its Associations.* London, Hamilton, Adams & Co., 1870.

Torrey, R. A., ed. *How to Promote and Conduct and Successful Revival.* Chicago, Flemind H. Revell Co., 1901.

U.S. Congress Committee on Finance, *Coinage Laws of the United States 1792-1894.* 53rd Congress, report number 235, 1894, pp 668-670.

Vincent, Rev. H., A.M. *History of the Camp-Meeting and Grounds at Wesleyan Grove, Martha's Vineyard, for the Eleven Years ending with the Meeting of 1869.* Boston, Lee and Shepard, 1870.

HYMNS & ILLUSTRATIONS

INDEX

www.ingramcontent.com/pod-product-compliance
Lightning Source LLC
Chambersburg PA
CBHW071637270326
41928CB00010B/1957